THE KHOTYN CAMPAIGN OF 1621

Polish, Lithuanian and Cossack armies against the Ottoman Empire

Michał Paradowski

'This is the Century of the Soldier', Fulvio Testi, Poet, 1641

HELION &
COMPANY

Helion & Company Limited
Unit 8 Amherst Business Centre
Budbrooke Road
Warwick
CV34 5WE
England
Tel. 01926 499 619
Email: info@helion.co.uk
Website: www.helion.co.uk
Twitter: @helionbooks
Visit our blog http://blog.helion.co.uk/

Published by Helion & Company 2023
Designed and typeset by Mary Woolley, Battlefield Design (www.battlefield-design.co.uk)
Cover designed by Paul Hewitt, Battlefield Design (www.battlefield-design.co.uk)

ISBN 978-1-804513-50-7

British Library Cataloguing-in-Publication Data.
A catalogue record for this book is available from the British Library.

For details of other military history titles published by Helion & Company Limited
contact the above address or visit our website: http://www.helion.co.uk.

We always welcome receiving book proposals from prospective authors.

Contents

Acknowledgements

Massive thanks to Helion & Company for constant support and for yet again allowing me to present a piece of the Polish-Lithuanian Commonwealth's military history. My sincere gratitude to series' editor Charles Singleton for his patience and encouragement during the writing process. Special recognition and thanks to Sergey Shamenkov, who supported my new book with his well-researched illustrations. It was especially vital for me that Sergey, Ukrainian patriot and historian, could contribute to the history of Poles, Lithuanians and Cossacks jointly facing overwhelming enemy force. 400 years after the Battle of Khotyn, words of Hetman Jan Karol Chodkiewicz still rung true: 'For the brave knights, here is the way of the immortal fame! I do not think nor do I suspect, that any of you here is scared; let the necessity become bravery.'

I would like to thank Zbigniew Hundert, Przemysław Gawron, Łukasz Wrona, Maciej Okołowicz, Taras Kovalets, Kevin Mulley, Jerzy Czajewski and Tomasz Ratyński for their help with gathering materials for this book. Special thanks to Paweł Duda for kindly providing many letters from Biblioteca Apostolica Vaticana and to Bruno Mugnai for his insight into Italian terminology. I'm very grateful to Paul Arblaster for permission to use his splendid translation of the issues of *Nieuwe Tijdinghen*.

To my wife Patrycja and son Ezra: as with every previous book, thanks for all your love, understanding and patience ('Look at my football trading cards Dad, I do not want to hear about hussars again…')

Introduction

War waged between the Polish-Lithuanian Commonwealth and the Ottoman Empire in 1620–1621 played an important role in the history and relations between those two countries. The Polish expedition to Moldavia in 1620 ended in disaster and the loss of the vast majority of the Polish army. In 1621 the Commonwealth had to face the might of the Ottoman army led by Sultan Osman II himself and it took the joint effort of Polish, Lithuanian and Cossack armies to stop this huge threat. Lack of success in the campaign of 1621 led to the attempted reform of the Ottoman military, which in turn culminated in the janissaries' rebellion and the death of Osman II. Post war, the Commonwealth had to face a mutiny of unpaid troops, while at the same time dealing with renewed Swedish pressure in Livonia.

While initially I planned to focus only on the campaign of 1621, especially the Battle of Khotyn, during the writing process I decided to extend the work and cover the whole war. That's why, despite the title, readers will be able to find here a relatively detailed (and hopefully interesting) description of Żółkiewski's last campaign in 1620 and his defeat during this expedition. I think that it provides good and in-depth historical background, helping to better understand the situation in which the Commonwealth found itself in 1621.

Something probably already familiar to readers of my previous books: a few additional notes regarding terminology used in the book. Where possible, current geographical names provided in the English version are used, usually with its Polish name from the period as an additional reference. While it may lead to some controversy, the name Constantinople is used instead of Istanbul, to keep up with the spirit of the Polish documents from the period. Polish, German and Latin terms (except people's and geographical names) are written in italics. Names of Polish and Lithuanian officers and soldiers are written in their Polish version, while with Cossacks, Ottomans and Tatars an attempt has been made to use the most accurate English version. Certain Eastern European and German words that already are established in English language nomenclature are not marked in italics, i.e. hetman, haiduks, reiters. For many Polish military words, that do not have an English equivalent, the original form will be used, i.e. *rusznica* or *rotmistrz*.[1]

---

[1] While *rotmistrz* is the equivalent of a Western European cavalry captain, I decided to keep the original form, especially since in the Polish and Lithuanian military 'captain' was normally used

On its first appearance it will be accompanied by a footnote explaining its meaning. The same approach has been taken with terms used to describe measurements or any other Polish words. In the seventeenth century Poles tended to use the word *Wołoszczyna* (Wallachia) to describe Moldavia, while term *Multany* was used to describe Wallachia. To avoid such confusion, I have used Moldavia and Wallachia for the respective countries and if the seventeenth century Polish form has been used in quotes, it will be explained in a footnote. Currency mentioned in the text is the Polish *złoty* (abbreviated to zl), which was divided into 30 *groszy* (abbreviated to gr). During the early seventeenth century one *grosz* equalled 0.27 grams of silver, so one *złoty* was approx. 8.1 grams of silver. If a different currency is mentioned, its equivalent in Polish currency will be given as well. In the primary sources, Polish and Lithuanian commanders, even on the banner level, tend to be called by their official title, e.g. Voivode of Ruthenia, Castellan of Cracow, etc, without their name being mentioned. For the purpose of this book, even when quoting original documents, the name of the official has been used instead and the title, except a military one (e.g. hetman), tending to be ignored. I decided on such an approach to simplify a bit, what is already a confusing way of the official documents and diaries written in the seventeenth century. German surnames of officers are often written in many different ways, i.e. Denhof, Denhoff, Dönhoff or Weyher, Wejher, Weiher. Again, in order to simplify it, just one version has been used, even when quoting sources already translated into English. All dates are given according to the Gregorian calendar that was already in use at that time in the Commonwealth.

Notes on sources

Both campaigns of 1620 and (especially) that of 1621 have, over the years, been researched by many authors, especially in Poland and Ukraine. We are lucky to have fairly large number of surviving primary sources, including army related documents, letters and diaries – although most of these were written by the Polish-Lithuanian side. During the writing of this book I made an attempt to gather as many of those as possible, as I believe that it is always crucial for the historical researcher to work primarily from them. At the same time it was also important to rely on already well established works of previous authors, in order to present to the non-Polish readers with a wide picture of the war. Amongst them were works by Józef Tretiak, Jan Wimmer, Leszek Podhorodecki, Ryszard Majewski, Wiesław Majewski, Przemysław Gawron, Noj Raszba and Petro Sas, to name just a few of the most important ones. Using such publications also helped me with utilising those sources that, for many different reasons, I did not have direct access to.

I would like to use this space to describe a few main primary sources used in this book, with special emphasis on those that were based on the description of the events in 1621, during the fights in Moldavia between

---

only in regards to foreign troops.

the joint Polish-Lithuanian-Cossack army and the Ottomans and their allies. It should help to provide some background on the authors, their involvement in the events and their point of view. I think it is also useful to have their description gathered in the initial part of the book, to make it easier for readers to look for information about them during following chapters describing the events. As for campaign of 1620, all main references are described within Chapter 2.

Polish and Lithuanian officers and soldiers left a few diaries that, interestingly enough, often contradict each other in certain details, clearly showing they have different levels of involvement in and knowledge of the situation. Probably most crucial is one written by Jakub Sobieski, father of future Polish King, Jan III. Jakub was one of the commissioners appointed by the *Sejm* to support Hetman Chodkiewicz in commanding the army, thus as a part of the 'inner circle' he was privy to important information and negotiations. We have a few surviving copies of his diary, with some differences in detail, so on occasion more than one will be used and quoted.[2] The diary, attributed mistakenly to Hetman Lubomirski (often called by Polish authors pseudo-Lubomirski, so that form will be used when quoting as well), is also a very detailed source, indicating that it was written by someone from Lubomirski's entourage.[3] Prokop Zbigniewski took direct part in the campaign and he seems to have been fighting in the ranks of Royal Prince[4] Władysław's regiment so his diary is another example of an eyewitness. As with Sobieski's, this source also exists in a few versions that differ in details, so they could be quoted in different parts of the book.[5] While Jan Ostroróg was not taking part in the fight, he had very good sources of information, thus in his diary of the war can be found many interesting details.[6] Lithuanian volunteer Jan Czapliński described his military adventure at Khotyn in a diary-like letter written near the end of the fighting, providing a good insight from the perspective of the noble companion serving in the ranks.[7] There

---

2   Jakub Sobieski, *Commentariorum Chotinensis bellii libri tres* (Gdańsk: Georgii Forsteri, 1646), 'Jakóba Sobieskiego Dziennik wyprawy chocimskiej' in: Żegota Pauli (ed.) *Pamiętniki o wyprawie chocimskiej r. 1621* (Kraków: Nakład i druk Józefa Czecha, 1853), pp.105-184; Jakub Sobieski, *Pamiętnik wojny chocimskiej xiąg troje* (Petersburg: Nakładem Bolesława Maurycego Wolffa, 1854); Jakub Sobieski, *Dyariusz expedycyi tureckiey pod Chocimiem Roku Pańskiego 1621*, Biblioteka Kórnica (BK) 335.

3   'Stanisława Lubomirskiego Dziennik wyprawy chocimskiej' in: Żegota Pauli (ed.) *Pamiętniki o wyprawie chocimskiej r. 1621* (Kraków: Nakład i druk Józefa Czecha, 1853), pp.65-103.

4   I have used the term 'Royal Prince' to describe Władysław Vasa for two reasons. Firstly is that the Polish term *królewicz*, which means 'Prince, son of the King', does not have a direct English equivalent. Secondly is that it will allow me to differentiate him from princes of non-royal families, such as Zbaraski or Korycki.

5   'Prokopa Zbigniewskiego Dziennik wyprawy chocimskiej' in: Żegota Pauli (ed.) *Pamiętniki o wyprawie chocimskiej r. 1621* (Kraków: Nakład i druk Józefa Czecha, 1853), pp.41-64; *Diarius expeditiey królewicza polskiego Władysława przeciwko Osmanowi II, cesarzowi tureckiemu y chanowi tatarskiemu w osobach swych na woynie będących w Wołoszech pod Chociniem roku 1621*, Biblioteka Kórnicka (BK) 342, ff.50r-59v.

6   'Jana hrabi z Ostroroga Dziennik wyprawy chocimskiej' in: Żegota Pauli (ed.) *Pamiętniki o wyprawie chocimskiej r. 1621* (Kraków: Nakład i druk Józefa Czecha, 1853), pp.15-39.

7   'Kopia listu od pana [Jana] Czaplińskiego do Jerzego Radzimińskiego 1 Octobris z obozu pisanego', in: Hanna Malewska, *Listy staropolskie z epoki Wazów* (Warszawa: Państwowy Instytut Wydawniczy, 1977), pp.206–214.

are also anonymous diaries, providing plenty of information and most likely written by soldiers taking part in the campaign and which describe the overall campaign.[8] In a fairly unusual form, as it was written as a poem, is a diary under the name of Fridrich Warzuchtig, 'poor soldier from Bavaria', published in Polish in 1640. It seems that actually Fridrich Warzuchtig was the *nom de plume* of Jan Rudomina, who in 1621 was *rotmistrz* of one of the hussar banners.[9]

Front cover of Jakub Sobieski's *Commentariorum Chotinensis Belli Libri Tres*, published in 1646. Sobieski was one of the commissioners in the Polish-Lithuanian army and took part in the Khotyn war and the peace negotiations with Ottomans (National Library, Warsaw)

A very interesting source is one titled *Zeitung aus der Walachei* (*News from Wallachia*), published in 1622.[10] It is a relation written by an anonymous German officer, possibly from Denhoff's regiment. He provides a great insight into the campaign, praising his German fellows and the Zaporozhian Cossacks but being fairly critical of the Poles. It is definitely a very interesting contrast to the diaries authored by Polish and Lithuanian soldiers. Large numbers of letters, including prisoners' confessions and reports, were included in volume VIII of the printed *Sources to the history of Ukraine-Rus*, published in 1908 in Lviv.[11] Another important point of view is provided by an Armenian chronicle written by Auxent, the so-called *An Armeno-Kipchak Chronicle of the Polish-Turkish Wars in 1620–1621*. It was translated from Kipchak to English and published in 1968 by Ödön (Edmund) Schütz, making this unique source more easily accessible.[12] Another Armenian chronicle, this time authored by Joannis (Owanis) from Kamianets-Podilskyi also known as Hovhan Kamenaci, is available thanks to the Russian translation published in 1958.[13] When quoted, I will use the form Joannis as the

8 'Opisanie wyprawy chocimskiej' in: Józef Tretiak, *Historya wojny chocimskiej 1621 r.* (Lwów: Nakładem Księgarni Seyfartha i Czajkowskiego, 1889), pp.209-218; 'Relacya prawdziwa o expediciey przeciwko Turkom, na którey sam cesarz turecki był Ao 1621, Woyska koronnego y W. X. Litte pod regimentem Pana Karola Chodkiewicza W. X. Litte które pod Chocimiem leżało' in Józef Tretiak, *Historya wojny chocimskiej 1621 r.* (Lwów: Nakładem Księgarni Seyfartha i Czajkowskiego, 1889), pp.219-229; 'Diaryusz wojny tureckiej, która się toczyła R. 1621. Dostatecznie wypisany' in: Ambroży Grabowski (ed.) *Starożytności historyczne polskie, czyli pisma i pamiętniki do dziejów dawnej Polski, listy królów i znakomitych mężów, przypowieści, przysłowia i.t.p.*, volume I (Kraków: Józef Czech, 1840), pp.134-146.

9 Fridrich Warzuchtig (Jan Rudomina), *Diariusz prawdziwy expediciey Korony Polskiey, y Wielkiego Xięstwa Litewskiego przeciw Osmanowi Cesarzowi Tureckiemu w roku 1621 pod Chocimiem w Wołoszech Fortunnie odprawioney. Fridrych Warzuchtig Bawarczyk Zoldath ubogi będąc przytomny opisał* (place of publishing unknown, 1640), Biblioteka Jagiellońska (BJ) 311062.

10 Biblioteka Uniwersytetu Wrocławskiego (BUWr.), 536284, *Zeitung aus der Walachei* (no place of publishing, 1622).

11 *Zherela do istoriï Ukraïny-Rusy*, volume VIII (Lviv: Archeographic Commission of the Shevchenko Scientific Society, 1908).

12 Ödön (Edmund) Schütz(ed.), *An Armeno-Kipchak Chronicle of the Polish-Turkish Wars in 1620–1621*, (Budapest: Akadémiai Kiadó, 1968).

13 'Istoriya Khotinksoy voyny Ioannesa Kamenetskogo', *Istoriko-filologicheskiy Zhurnal,* year 1958, volume 2 (Erevan: Akademiya Nauk Armyanskoi SSR, 1958), pp.258-286. I would like to thank Przemysław Gawron for pointing out and sharing this source with me.

name of its author. While written between 1675 and 1677, Miron Costin's chronicle of Moldavia, *Letopiseţul Ţării Moldovei de la Aaron Vodă încoace*, is full of interesting comments relating to both 1620 and 1621. For the purpose of this work, I used the Polish translation by Ilona Czamańska, published in 1998.[14] Unfortunately access to Ottoman sources is very limited and I was only able to obtain a Polish translation of the chronicle of Mustafa Naima (Naima Efendi). On a positive note, he described in detail the campaigns of both 1620[15] and 1621.[16] Helpful in providing a Turkish perspective was the article by Kadir Kazalak and Tufan Gündüz, published in 2003. The authors described in it Osman II's campaign of 1621, using a number of primary sources, which added to better understanding of the Ottoman point of view.[17]

The biography of Tomasz Zamoyski (1594–1638), written by his servant Stanisław Żurkowski in 1643, is a treasury of interesting information regarding the campaign of 1620 and its aftermath, especially the preparation of the new army in 1621. Żurkowski also provided copies of many important letters written by and to Zamoyski during that time.[18] Stanisław Kobierzycki in 1655 published *History of Władysław, Polish and Swedish Royal Prince*, where there are many well-researched descriptions of Władysław's involvement in the Khotyn war and the composition of his regiment that accompanied him on the campaign.[19] From the other Polish chronicles describing the event, I mostly used the one written by Paweł Piasecki.[20] Another interesting point of view is provided by politician and historian Albrycht Stanisław Radziwiłł in his *Notes on the reign of Sigismund III*. Radziwiłł was very close to the Royal Court and in 1621 was a Lithuanian Vice-Chancellor, so had access to information available to the royal 'inner circle'.[21] Decrees of the *Sejm* from 1620, 1621 and 1623 are provided from volume III of *Volumina Legum*.[22] Various correspondences of Papal Nuncios, with their important observations and comments on the situation in Poland are provided thanks to original documents from Biblioteca Apostolica Vaticana[23] and partially

---

14 Miron Costin, *Latopis ziemi mołdawskiej i inne utwory historyczne* (Poznań: Wydawnictwo Naukowe, 1998).

15 Mustafa Naima (Naima Efendi), *Zatargi z Otomanami z powodu Kozaków*, in: Józef Sękowski, *Collectanea z dziejów tureckich*, volume I (Warszawa: Zawadzki i Wędzki, 1824), pp.123-144.

16 Mustafa Naima (Naima Efendi), *Dziennik wyprawy chocimskiey*, in: Józef Sękowski, *Collectanea z dziejów tureckich*, volume I (Warszawa: Zawadzki i Wędzki, 1824), pp.145-182.

17 Kadir *Kazalak*, Tufan *Gündüz,*, 'Osman'in Hotin Seferi (1621)', *OTAM: Ankara Üniversitesi Osmanlı Tarihi Araştırma ve Uygulama Merkezi Dergisi*, issue 14 (Ankara: Ankara University, 2003), pp.129-144.

18 Stanisław Żurkowski, *Żywot Tomasza Zamoyskiego* (Lwów: Drukarnia Zakładu Narodowego im. Ossolińskich, 1860).

19 Stanisław Kobierzycki, *Historia Władysława, królewicza polskiego i szwedzkiego* (Wrocław: Wydawnictwo Uniwersytetu Wrocławskiego, 2005).

20 *Kronika Pawła Piaseckiego biskupa przemyślskiego*, (Kraków: Drukarnia Uniwersytetu Jagiellońskiego, 1870).

21 Albrycht Stanisław Radziwiłł, *Rys panowania Zygmunta III* (Opole: Wydawnictwo Uniwersytetu Opolskiego, 2011).

22 *Volumina Legum*, volume III (Petersburg: Nakładem i Drukiem Jozafata Okryzki, 1859).

23 Courtesy of Paweł Duda, to whom I'm grateful for his generous help with this.

thanks to already published Polish editions.[24] Very interesting and, to the best of my knowledge, not previously used by Polish researchers is *Nieuwe Tijdinghen*, a newspaper published in Antwerp by Abraham Verhoeven in the 1620s. Based on reports received from Poland, it presents a unique view on the conflict and shows how the conflict echoed in Western Europe.[25] Of course many more primary sources, regarding both the campaigns of 1620 and 1621, were utilised during the writing of this volume; information about all of them is provided in the relevant footnotes.

Apotheosis of King Sigismund III, presented as a triumphator in the war against Turks. Karl Audran, *c.*1629 (National Library, Warsaw)

As with all my previous books in Helion's 'Century of the Soldier 1618–1721 series', I have made my best efforts to find and use the most appropriate iconography, based on paintings, drawings and engravings from the period. Avid readers of the series will, no doubt, recognise some of them from my first book, *Despite Destruction, Misery and Privations…The Polish army in Prussia during war against Sweden 1626–1629.*[26] Unfortunately there is a limited range of available iconography presenting Polish and Lithuanian troops in the 1620s, so I had to operate with a rather narrow group of available pictorial references. Luckily the Ottoman side presents us with many more options, representing different aspects of its military and showing good representation of troops under the command of Sultan Osman II. As for original battle-plans

---

24 Erazm Rykaczewski (ed.), *Relacye nuncyuszów apostolskich i innych osób o Polsce od roku 1548 do 1690*, volume I (Poznań-Berlin: Księgarnia B. Behra, 1864).

25 *Nieuwe Tijdinghen*, Antwerp, Erfgoedbiblioth. English translation by Paul Alblaster available on https://www.facebook.com/NieuweTijdinghen (last entry 01/06/2023). Translation used with permission (all rights reserved).

26 Michał Paradowski, *Despite Destruction, Misery and Privations… The Polish army in Prussia during war against Sweden 1626-1629* (Warwick: Helion & Company, 2020).

or paintings presenting the battle, I relied on Giacomo Lauro's engraving, created between 1621 and 1624. There is also a recently identified painting of the battle, attributed to Pieter Snayers, that is usually mistaken as a depiction of the siege of Vienna in 1529 or as a siege of Esztergom in 1543, in which case it is attributed to Sebastiaen Vrancx. Unfortunately, as it is currently in a private collection in England, I was not able to use it in this book. It is a very interesting representation of the battle though, depicting it from the point of view of the Ottoman army. Hopefully in future we will see a more detailed study of this painting, perhaps discussing it as a fairly newly discovered pictorial source for the battle.

As many primary sources, especially diaries, tend to contradict each other, providing different dates or even completely different descriptions of the outcome of the fights, it may lead to errors in their interpretation. Written Polish from the era is often rather ambiguous, as authors tend not to explain in much detail things that were pretty common or easy to understand for them and their contemporaries. It also makes it fairly difficult to translate them into English, although I have tried my best to retain both the essence and 'the feel' of the original texts. As such, any inaccuracies and errors in both interpretation and translation of the primary sources are mine and mine alone.

1

Relations between the Commonwealth and the Ottomans in the Early Seventeenth century

There were two main points of conflict between the Polish-Lithuanian Commonwealth (or rather specifically the Kingdom of Poland) and the Ottoman Empire. A first point, and very direct one, was linked with the actions of their vassals – Tatars for the Ottoman Empire – and subjects – Zaporozhian Cossacks for the Commonwealth. Tatar raids, made not only by Crimean Horde but also Nogay ones (especially from Budjak), were almost annual events, bringing destruction and misery to the border regions. It forced small, standing Polish troops, the so-called 'quarter army', to be stationed in the Ukraine and Podolia and to cooperate with the private troops of the local magnates and the Zaporozhian Cossacks, although even despite the fact that the border was closely monitored, Tatars often managed to sneak past the Polish troops and return home with captives and loot. At the same time the Zaporozhian Cossacks were often raiding Tatar lands and even on occasions attacking Turkish towns, especially those ports linked to the Dnieper River. It led to a circle of retaliation, with Tatars attempting to avenge the Cossack raids and vice versa. While both Poles and Ottomans were supposed to control those raiding activities and punish those guilty of breaking the treaties, in reality not much was done, leading to the diplomatic clashes.

The second most important point of conflict was connected with the attempts to control the Principality of Moldavia. Here, especially from the end of the sixteenth century, Poles and Ottomans clashed over and over again, often waging a sort of 'proxy war', utilising private troops, Cossacks and Tatars; without either State engaging their main armies. Both sides attempted to set up their own candidate for the throne of the Principality, which would shift the country to their sphere of influence. Between 1595 and 1600, Hetman Jan Zamoyski intervened in Moldavia, fighting against Michael the Brave and establishing the pro-Polish Movilă (Mohyła) family on the throne. Newly installed voivode Ieremia Movilă had good links with Poland, as his daughters were married to Polish magnates: Maria to Stefan Potocki, Raina (Regina) to Michał Wiśniowiecki and Catherina (Katarzyna) to Samuel Korecki. This connection would play an important role between 1607 and 1616, during the Magnate Wars, known in Poland under the modern name of the Moldavian Ventures (*Awantury Mołdawskie*). It was a series of campaigns waged mostly by Polish magnates, who attempted to use their military forces to support their own candidates from the Movilă family against pro-Ottoman candidates. Stefan Potocki (1568–1631) led a military force into Moldavia on two occasions. He was successful in 1607 but was then defeated in 1612 and for a few years was kept in Turkish captivity. Between 1615 and 1616 another Polish noble and experienced soldier, Samuel Korecki (1586–1622), attempted to control Moldavia. While initially successful in late 1615, he was, in February 1616, forced to retreat by the joint Turkish-Tatar army. He returned to Moldavia in March 1616, this time reinforced by Transylvanians but again, despite some initial success, he was defeated and captured by Turks.[1] While those military interventions were officially private affairs organised by magnates, King Sigismund III allowed for them to happen, as a way of extending Polish influence and control over the regions of Moldavia and Wallachia.

In the autumn of 1615 and of 1616 Tatar raiders struck against Poland, pillaging without mercy and taking many prisoners. Crown Field Hetman Stanisław Żółkiewski (1547–1620), in charge of a small 'quarter army' was unable to stop these attacks. His proposal of a reform of the military system, presented during the *Sejm* in 1616, went without response. He then suggested peaceful contacts with the Tatar Khanate and the Ottomans, paying them annual 'gifts' and taking Zaporozhian Cossacks under stricter control, to prevent them from raiding across the border. The Country was not yet ready to deal with such issues, especially as King Sigismund III was preparing an army to accompany Royal Prince Władysław to Moscow, in yet another attempt to capture the city. Unsurprisingly Hetman Żółkiewski was unable to prevent the Cossacks from even more attacks against the Ottoman ports, which led to another Turkish intervention. In autumn 1617, Iskender Pasha, beylerbey of Ochakiv, with a strong Turkish, Tatar, Wallachian and Transylvanian army opened a campaign against Poland. Żółkiewski opposed him with the 'quarter army', supported by a fairly strong contingent of magnates' troops. Neither side

Crown Grand Hetman Stanisław Żółkiewski (1547–1620). Portrait by unknown artist from the second half of the seventeenth century (National Museum, Cracow)

---

1   He fled captivity in 1617. In 1620, during the battle of Cecora, he was once again taken prisoner. In 1622 he was strangled in Yedikule Castle but his body was ransomed by Poles and smuggled back to the country.

was eager for a fight in the open field though and they decided to negotiate instead, and on 23 September 1617, they signed the Treaty of Busza (Busha), also known as the Treaty of Jaruga (from the name of the river). On one side the Commonwealth agreed to stop its interventions in Moldavia, Wallachia and Transylvania, and also ceded the important Moldavian fortress of Khotyn back to the control of the Moldavian Voivode. The Poles were also to stop further Cossack raids. It allowed for the protection of the Polish border while Royal Prince Władysław and a large part of the army were engaged in Muscovy. On their side, the Ottomans promised to prevent Tatar raids and accepted that Moldavia, Wallachia and Transylvania were now in their sphere of influence. The Treaty was seen as a clear example of the Commonwealth's weakness, especially when the Tatars decided to ignore it and immediately after its signing attacked Podolia, with the Polish army unable to stop them. Month later, on 28 October 1617, Żółkiewski signed an agreement in Olszanica with Cossacks, in which he managed to convince them to decrease the register, stop their raids and send a strong contingent to the Muscovy to support Royal Prince Władysław. It was another point of discord between the hetman and the border magnates, with the latter supporting armed pacification of Cossacks and continuation of the pro-Polish politics in both Moldavia and Wallachia. It is no surprise though, that during the *Sejm* of 1618 the magnate faction, led by wealthy brothers Jerzy and Krzysztof Zbaraski, openly attacked Żółkiewski and his policy of defence of the border. King Sigismund showed his support to his army commander however, promoting him to Crown Grand Hetman and Crown Grand Chancellor. Based on Żółkiewski's recommendation, his former son-in-law Stanisław Koniecpolski (1591–1646) became Crown Field Hetman.

King Sigismund III (1566–1632). Detail from the sarcophagus of King Sigismund III at Wawel Castle in Cracow (Author's archive)

In spring 1618 Khan Temir and his Budjak Horde attacked again, and during a few raids avoided the scattered small number of Polish troops and captured a large amount of booty and many prisoners. Żółkiewski was helpless and, of course, once more faced strong criticism of what was seen as total inaction on his part. In early autumn 1618 the Poles managed to gather a much stronger force, with a large concentration of the 'quarter army', private troops and Zaporozhian Cossacks. Between 14,000 and 20,000 men arrived in camp at Orynin to face the new Tatar raid. The magnates did not want to serve under command of Żółkiewski though, so each placed their own troops in a separate camp. When Kalga-Sultan Dewlet Giray and Khan Temir arrived on 28 September with their army, they attacked the magnates' camps and in the ensuing fight the Poles took heavy losses. It forced the private troops to rejoin the Hetman's camp but the Tatars avoided further fights and, under cover of darkness, outmanoeuvred the Polish troops, spreading raiding parties through Volhynia. This debacle yet again encouraged the anti-Żółkiewski opposition to accuse him of idleness, lack of control over his troops or even, and an accusation which was completely baseless, plans to ally with Turks and Tatars and fight for the Polish Crown. The 'Quarter army' was demoralised, especially after a long period of war in the Muscovy, where soldiers were used to looting and not following officers' commands. No surprise then that Żółkiewski had problems with keeping discipline in unpaid troops, a situation which was made worse by the magnates being unwilling to cooperate with him against Tatar raids. Bitter and tired, during proceedings of the *Sejm* in 1619, the Hetman offered to resign from his office. King Sigismund III yet again showed him his support though and was strongly against such dismissal. Therefore Żółkiewski remained in command of the Polish army, with which he soon was to face the Ottomans and Tatars again. In 1618 and 1619 Polish-Ottoman relations deteriorated slightly, as the Porte was allowing the Transylvanian Prince, Gabriel Bethlen, to take part, on the side of the Protestant forces, in the early stages of the Thirty Years' War, while Sigismund III supported the Catholic cause, sending mercenary *lisowczycy* cavalry to fight in the ranks of the Imperial army. They even raided Transylvania, looting and destroying everything in their path, which according to some researchers had an impact on Bethlen's decision to lift the siege of Vienna in 1619. The Ottomans were unwilling to enter into open conflict with the Commonwealth, hoping that the Poles would be able to stop Cossack raids, as agreed to in the Treaty of May 1619. A diplomatic mission, led by Hieronim Otwinowski, was sent to Constantinople in the autumn 1619 to further discuss the relations between both countries; it was not successful though, while another Cossack raid attacked the suburbs of the Ottoman capital in the spring of 1620. It seems that Otwinowski was under the influence of the Imperial Ambassador in Constantinople, Mollart, who was feeding him with fictional information about Turkish plans to start a war against the Commonwealth. The Austrian even suggested that the life of the Polish envoy was in danger – all in the hope that the Pole would leave the Ottoman capital without coming to any sort of agreement. Imperial politics in this were pretty clear – any conflict between the Commonwealth and the Ottoman Empire would mean that Turks would be unable to attack the Austrian Habsburgs while they were fighting their Protestant subjects. Otwinowski, afraid for his life, decided to flee Constantinople but before he left, in his letter to King Sigismund III, he highlighted that the Ottomans were preparing for war and that it would be a good idea for the Polish army to launch a pre-emptive strike.[2]

---

2   Leszek Podhorodecki, *Jan Karol Chodkiewicz 1560–1621* (Warszawa: Wydawnictwo Ministerstwa Obrony Narodowej, 1982), pp.289–290.

2

The Campaign of 1620

Reasons behind the Hetman Żółkiewski's expedition to Moldavia in 1620 and the outbreak of the war between the Polish-Lithuanian Commonwealth and the Ottoman Empire were for many years the topic of discussions between researchers. Some blamed the 'war party' in the Ottoman court – represented especially by aggressive Iskander Pasha, beylerbey of Silistria and Ochakiv – that was looking for military success after the end of the war against Persia and deciding to shift their interest towards increasing their influence in the European borders of the empire. There are also many suggestions that Żółkiewski's decision was influenced by the court politics of Sigismund III. It was hoped that the Hetman could easily win a fairly simple campaign, leading to the establishment of Polish control over Moldavia and also, at the same time, deal a blow to the private ambitions of the anti-Royal Polish magnates. Some researchers pointed to the wider aspects of the conflict, with both sides indirectly taking part in Thirty Years' War: the Ottomans supporting Gabriel Bethlen's Transylvania allied with the Protestant side and the Commonwealth helping Habsburgs by providing *lisowczycy* mercenary cavalry and allowing for recruitment on Polish soil. One cannot even rule out the personal ambition of Hetman Żółkiewski, who by helping Moldavian Voivode Gaspar Graziani to take back his throne, was hoping to achieve military success that would have to have silenced his opponents in Poland. There were even theories that tried to present the whole expedition as some sort of suicide charge of an ill and elderly Hetman, who wanted to sacrifice his life to shake up the elite of the Commonwealth; it seems though, that such explanation of the whole venture can be dismissed. Apparently Żółkiewski was fairly certain of the success of his planned operation, although, as we will see, he seemed to have miscalculated in a few ways, which led to his defeat. Another factor leading to the outbreak of the armed conflict was connected with the Zaporozhian Cossacks. Despite treaties with the Ottomans and mutual assurances, the Poles were unable to stop these warlike raiders from further attacks against the Sultan's lands. Even primary sources from the period give a variety of reasons for the war, often based on the incorrect

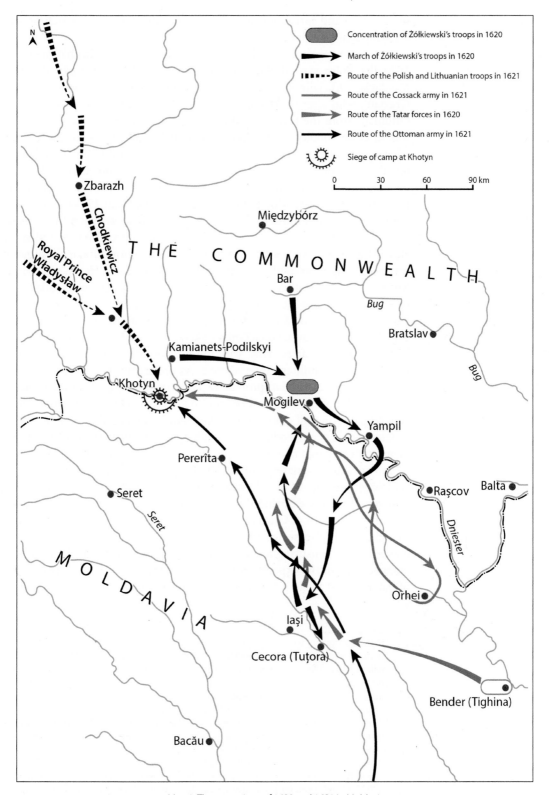

Map 1. The campaigns of 1620 and 1621 in Moldavia
[Source: Zdzisław Spieralski, Jan Wimmer (ed.), *Wypisy źródłowe do historii polskiej sztuki wojennej. Zeszyt piąty. Polska sztuka wojenna w latach 1563-1647*]

information and spreading rumours about Sultan Osman II marching with his army against Poland.[1]

Whatever reasons were the most important, it is certain that in August 1620 the Poles started their preparation for the military expedition to Moldavia. Officially they were to enter the country to support Gaspar Graziani, who after short reign (since 1619) was about to be removed by Ottomans from the throne of Moldavia for his pro-Polish stance. Graziani was in close contact with Żółkiewski though, and in the string of letters advising the Hetman of the situation, encouraged him to enter Moldavian territory and provided him with rather exaggerated information about his own military force. He mentioned that his troops would be ready and willing to support the Poles, with estimated figures of between 15,000 and 25,000 men[2] that he could muster. The Moldavian Voivode was soon to be visited by an Ottoman envoy, who was to 'invite' him to Constantinople, which was clearly meant as a way of dethroning him, and therefore Graziani's situation was becoming more and more precarious. While Field Hetman Stanisław Koniecpolski was gathering troops in the camp in Śledziówka (today Slidy in Ukraine), Grand Hetman Żółkiewski was waiting for the confirmation from King Sigismund III that the monarch would allow him to organise the expedition to Moldavia. Once Żółkiewski received *carte blanche* from Warsaw, he rejoined the 'quarter army' with the mission of convincing his troops to take part in the military intervention. As ordinarily they were part of the defence force organised to protect the country, the soldiers could, in theory, reject the idea of crossing the border into Moldavia. During his talks with the general gathering[3] of companions, the Hetman managed to convince them to take part in the expedition – probably by presenting them with a vision of an easy campaign taking place in a friendly country. Further forces would be provided by magnates, with some of them personally taking part in the campaign; a regiment of volunteer mercenary cavalry, known as *lisowczycy* also joined the force during the march. Żółkiewski was counting on strong military support from Graziani as well. Private troops were gathering slowly though, and it also seems that Żółkiewski and Koniecpolski did not take enough care in ensuring a sufficient supply of provisions for the army. The planned start of the expedition had to be further delayed, as a strong force of Tatars (most likely Nogays) appeared near Koniecpolski's estate and the

---

1   For the summary of the different points of view on those topics, see Ryszard Majewski, *Cecora rok 1620* (Warszawa: Wydawnictwo Ministerstwa Obrony Narodowej, 1970), pp.13–83; Leszek Podhorodecki, *Sławni hetmani Rzeczypospolitej* (Warszawa: Wydawnictwo MADA, 1994), pp.224–225.

2   Ksawery Liske, 'Stanisława Żółkiewskiego hetmana i kanclerza w. kor. klęska i zgon na Polach Czoczorskich', *Dziennik Literacki*, Year 18, no.15, 13 April 1869 (Lwów: Drukarnia Zakładu Narodowego imienia Ossolińskich, 1869), List P. Szemberka do Ksdza Andrzeja Opalińskiego, biskupa Poznańskiego, w którym opisuje porażkę wojska Polskiego w Wołoszech przez Skinder Baszę a die 18. Septemb. ad 6 Octobris. Anno 1620, p.239.

3   As mentioned in Michał Paradowski, *Despite Destruction, Misery and Privations...The Polish army in Prussia during war against Sweden 1626–1629* (Warwick: Helion & Company, 2020), p.140, the Polish word for it was *koło* (plural: *koła*), which meant 'circle', as in 'gathering of a circle of equals'. I prefer to use the term 'gathering' in English, as it represents the essence of the original without the confusion coming from the direct translation.

Field Hetman, with strong cavalry force, rushed to chase them out. Finally on 1 September 1620 around 7,000 soldiers under Żółkiewski's command started their slow march towards the Moldavian border. (The Hetman divided them into five regiments, details of which can be found in Appendix I.) Less than half of the initial strength of the army was composed of 'quarter' troops, and these were supplemented by private units of both Żółkiewski and Koniecpolski and some Hungarian infantry from the Household Guard, provided by King Sigismund III. The remainder was composed of the private magnates' troops and volunteer nobles, with even more joining the army during the march through Moldavian. Considering that some of those magnates were previously in political opposition to Żółkiewski and rather unwilling to follow all his commands, it had to lead to the issues with army hierarchy and the proper chain of command.

Crown Field Hetman Stanisław Koniecpolski (1591–1646). Portrait by unknown author from the mid-seventeenth century (National Museum, Cracow)

On 3 September the army crossed the Dniester River and entered Moldavia. The Poles rested for one day, while Żółkiewski sent units of cavalry on reconnaissance and left some infantry in a few Moldavian castles, including the strategic fortress of Khotyn. Graziani, after receiving a message about the incoming Polish army, decided to take action against the Turks. He captured the envoy of Iskander Pasha, and 300 Turks from their entourage were also captured, and later executed.[4] According to Miron Costin, the envoy was in fact sent directly by the Sultan, his name was Skirmini Aga and he was killed by Moldavians.[5] At the same time a mob in the Moldavian capital of Iaşi rioted intending to massacre the Turks present in the city, killing between 1,000 and 2,300 of them. '[Graziani] ordered the townsmen to put to the sword all Turks that stayed in the town, the merchants, as well as the any others. As soon as the people in the town heard the order of

4   Ksawery Liske, 'Stanisława Żółkiewskiego hetmana i kanclerza w. kor. klęska i zgon na Polach Czoczorskich', *Dziennik Literacki*, Year 18, no.14, 6 April 1869 (Lwów: Drukarnia Zakładu Narodowego imienia Ossolińskich, 1869), List p. Stanisława Żółkiewskiego K . i H. K. do króla Jego Mci. d. d. z obozu w Łozowej 6. Septembr. 1620, p.224.

5   Miron Costin, *Latopis ziemi mołdawskiej i inne utwory historyczne* (Poznań: Wydawnictwo Naukowe, 1998), p.130.

the Prince, they immediately killed the Turks wherever they found them, whether indoors, in the caravan-serails or at the inns; whomever they found, they did not spare his life.'[6] The Moldavian Voivode had to rely on Żółkiewski now; there was no other way for him to keep the throne in the face of a soon-to-arrive Ottoman retaliation. After receiving despatches from Graziani, the Poles moved again, setting up a new camp near the village of Łozowa, on the north bank of the river Krajany. It was a good strategic position, one day's march from the Dniester, allowing for a quick retreat route to Poland if needed. The Poles stayed there until 9 September awaiting the further reinforcements. On 7 September magnate Janusz Tyszkiewicz arrived with four banner of cavalry and two banners of infantry. On 9 September Stefan Chmielecki joined the army with 800 men, who were either Zaporozhian Cossacks or cossack cavalry raised from the Ukrainian estates of Polish magnates.

Moldavian Voivode Gaspar Graziani (1575/1580–1620). Seventeenth century portrait by an unknown artist (author's collection)

It seems that Hetman Żółkiewski was severely disappointed with Graziani and his actions. The massacre of Turks in Iaşi was a rather unpleasant surprise, and what is worse the Voivode lost his nerve, decided to abandon Moldavia and fled to Khotyn, from where he was probably hoping to flee to Germany. Most likely he realised he did not have such strong support in his own country and that he would not be able to provide the Poles with the thousands of soldiers, as in his earlier promises. Żółkiewski, probably thanks to the Polish garrison in Khotyn, was aware of the Voivode's arrival and he 'encouraged' Graziani by some strongly written letters to join him in the army camp.

On 7 September, Graziani arrived at Łazowa with some of his court officials and with between 500 and 600 soldiers. Despite the big show of dashing outfits and well-presented troops, led by 100 Household infantry, it was clear that he had arrived with just a token force. The Hetman, trying to make sure that his army was not aware of any issues between him and the Voivode, met the Moldavians with the proper ceremony and celebrated them during an evening feast. The next day, during a council between Polish commanders and Graziani, they discussed the next steps of the campaign. The Moldavians wanted quick military action, with a strike against the still fairly weak forces of Iskander Pasha, not yet reinforced by the arrival of stronger contingents of Crimean and Nogay Tatars. Żółkiewski was more focused on the political goals, as he wanted to ensure that Graziani could return to the throne in Iaşi; he also was still awaiting further units, both Polish and Moldavian, that could strengthen his army. In his letter to King Sigismund III, written on 6 September, thus before the arrival of Graziani, the Hetman mentioned his hopes that a strong Polish presence in Moldavia could lead to building of a strong anti-Ottoman front. Once the Moldavians rose to support the Poles, a similar movement would start amongst Wallachians and even Transylvanians. Żółkiewski asked for

---

6   Ödön (Edmund) Schütz (ed.), *An Armeno-Kipchak Chronicle of the Polish-Turkish Wars in 1620–1621*, p.43.

further reinforcements from Poland, including the remaining troops of 'quarter army'.

After some talks, considering that Hetman's voice was the most important on the council, it was decided that the army would march to Iași to ensure Graziani's return. From there, the Poles were to move to set up the camp at Cecora (Țuțora), in the same place that, in October 1595, Crown Grand Hetman Jan Zamoyski successfully defended against joint Tatar-Ottoman armies. Apparently at an earlier stage of the expedition, the Hetman was not so keen to move to Cecora, writing to Crown Vice-treasurer Mikołaj Daniłowicz that 'they advise me to set up my troops at Cecora but I would have to be a madman to do it.'[7] It is not clear why he had sudden change of heart but, according to his orders, the army marched to the old Polish camp. It seems that he was not keen on taking any offensive steps against the Ottoman troops of Iskander Pasha, hoping that the whole conflict could be dealt with through negotiation. Thus he did not march towards Bender (Tehinia) where he could have prevented the Ottomans from joining with Tatar reinforcements. Not only had the Poles lost the initiative, but they quickly started to antagonise the Moldavians, with Polish troops and their servants, especially those of private troops, looting the local population. Despite orders from the Hetman, decrees issued via letters by King Sigismund III himself, and Graziani's offers to provide provisions for troops, the unruly behaviour of the Poles did not stop. It was probably one of the main reasons why in total no more than 1,000 Moldavian soldiers, including Graziani's initial contingent, joined the Poles. The army started to march towards Cecora on 9 September, and on 11 September was reinforced by a regiment of *lisowczycy* under Walenty Rogawski (12 banners, a total of up to 1700 men) and some further private troops (see Appendix I). In total the army had now just over 10,000 men, including more than 2,000 hussars. The position at Cecora was set up in the strategic location, protecting the route to Iași and utilising old field fortifications from the Polish campaign of 1595 – although the latter only started to be reinforced on 14 September, when the enemy was already approaching Cecora.

While good to be used as a defensive position, with enough infantry to defend the main lines and strong cavalry to be used for counter-attacks, the Cecora location did not have a proper escape route in the case of a change in the military situation or a decision to retreat. The Poles did not build the bridge over the Prut River nor did they leave any force on its right bank, to ensure an open road for the evacuation from the camp. Polish camp servants continued to be sent out into neighbouring areas, in order to gather food, although fresh water and grass for the horses was available in suitable quantities in the camp itself. There were no attempts to send out reconnaissance forces in order to find if the enemy was approaching, and what was worse Graziani decided not to return to the capital and remained with Żółkiewski's army.

---

7   Albrycht Stanisław Radziwiłł, *Rys panowania Zygmunta*, p.67.

In a rather surprising turn of events, the Polish Hetman remained almost completely passive, focusing on just despatching letters to Wallachia, Transylvania and Crimea, hoping to build some sort of pro-Polish coalition and to ensure that Graziani could remain in Moldavia as its Voivode. Sigismund III, in his later dated 17 September, encouraged quick actions against Iskander Pasha, hoping that the Polish army could attack and defeat the Turks before the arrival of Tatar reinforcements. The King also reminded the Hetman to keep his soldiers in order, to impose strong discipline and to not discourage allied Moldavians by looting. He even highlighted that the Hetman should warn soldiers that for any ill-disciplined actions they could be punished by death. Sigismund hoped that the '[hetman] will raise the hearts of his soldiers, so they with all their might strike the enemy and with God's blessing will win a great victory.'[8] Unfortunately, due to delay in receiving and despatching post, the King did not know that this was all pointless and that the Hetman had already surrendered the initiative at this stage of the campaign.

Such inactivity allowed Turks and Tatars to gather their forces and prepare to march towards Cecora. In late August, Iskander Pasha only had 1,000 soldiers from his *sanjak* stationed at Bender, with a mix of *timarot sipahi* and the Pasha's own troops (mostly cavalry). He was waiting for the reinforcements from neighbouring *sanjaks* and, especially, on the contingents of Tatars from Budjak and Crimea. Iskander Pasha was an experienced warrior, who had previously fought with great success against the Polish armies at Sasowy Róg in 1612, and during the campaign of 1616 in Moldavia. The description by the Ottoman chronicler Mustafa Naima says 'this commander was a terrifying figure and really heroic one; with piercing gaze and of great and splendid height. His huge moustache was very distinguished; he shaved his beard [though] in the Bulgarian style, [and] in bravery and courage none of the ancient heroes, even Rustam[9] himself, could match him.'[10] In a fairly short period of time he managed to gather further Ottoman troops, again most likely a mix of provincial troops and hastily raised *timarot sipahi*. Yusuf Pasha led men from Rumelia, Teryaki Mohammed Pasha, known as *Sarimsak* (garlic, from his favourite snack) had with him troops from Nikopol (in today's Bulgaria), Khizir Pasha[11] was in command of soldiers from Vidin (also in today's Bulgaria). Other commanders: Circassian Hussein Pasha, Kior Hussein Pasha and Ash Mohmmander Pasha led men from unidentified *sanjaks*.[12] We can estimate the overall strength of all Ottoman troops, as between 2,000 (which seems to be too low) and 5,000 men (slightly on the high end), perhaps realistically with up to 3,000 available at Cecora. If Polish sources are to be believed, there

8   BK 330, *Akta Zygmunta III od roku 1618 do 1621*, no 256, pp.373–376.
9   Legendary hero from the Persian mythology, whose life and deeds were described in the epic poem *Shahnameh* from the tenth century.
10   Mustafa Naima (Naima Efendi), *Zatargi z Otomanami z powodu Kozaków*, p.136.
11   Son of the former Wallachian Voivode, Mihnea Turcitul (1564–1601), they both converted to Islam after 1591.
12   Mustafa Naima (Naima Efendi), *Zatargi z Otomanami z powodu Kozaków*, pp.134-136.

were more than 1,000 janissaries and two cannon.[13] While the presence of the infantry seems to be certain, most of them would probably have been local provincial infantry like *segbans*, supported by janissaries from the local garrisons. Due to fairly small number of his own troops, Iskander Pasha had to rely on the Tatar reinforcements. From Crimea arrived Kalga-Sultan Dewlet Giray, with a contingent that numbered between 4,000 and 8,000 horsemen, while Khan Temir had under his command 3,000–5,000 Nogay Tatars from Budjak. It seems that in total, the joint army was between 10,000 and 15,000 men, mostly cavalry with an especially strong presence of Tatar horsemen. Although most of the main commanders disliked each other, Iskander Pasha managed to smooth out any personal conflicts and cooperation during the campaign went pretty smoothly. Once Crimean reinforcements arrived in mid-September, the Ottomans and Tatars were ready to move against the Polish army.

Some Polish sources estimated the enemy's force in realistic ways, for example Teofil Szembergin, in his letter to Tomasz Zamoyski, stated that there were 11,500 Ottomans and Tatars, with the figure being provided by a prisoner.[14] Interestingly enough, Mustafa Naima gives a very similar number of 10,000, in his chronicle.[15] At the same time we also can find highly exaggerated figures, no doubt to highlight the power of the enemy. Hetman Żółkiewski,

A well equipped unit of Polish cavalry, possibly indicating *petyhorcy* that were sometimes present in the army in the first few decades of the seventeenth century. The horsemen have bows, sabres and spears with pennants, all also have helmets with feathers. From the portrait of King Sigismund III by Wolfgang Kilian, based on the composition by Tomasz Dolabella, 1609–1611. (Print Room of the University of Warsaw Library. Photo by Tomasz Ratyński)

reporting to King Sigismund III about the lack of success during the battle at Cecora, clearly exaggerated the size of the joint Turkish-Tatars army, writing in his letter of 24 September that there are more than 60,000 Ottomans and Tatars. He even tried to indicate that this force was marching towards the borders of the Commonwealth and only thanks to brave and selfless actions of his soldiers that the Poles managed to stop them for now.[16] Bishop Piasecki, in his chronicle, wrote about 20,000 Nogay Tatars, 30,000 Crimean Tatars alone, not to mention Turks, and supported by Transylvanians and Moldavians.[17] Szemberg in one of his relations estimated the allied army as 30,000–40,000 soldiers, including 7000–8,000 Turks.[18] Such changes when

13 'Opisanie wejścia do Wołoch p. Stanisława Żółkiewskiego, kanclerza y hetmana wielkiego Korony polskiej, anno domini 1620', in: Eudoxiou de Hurmuzaki (ed.), *Documente privitoare la istoria românilor, supplement 2, volume 2, 1601-1640* (Bucureşti: Academia Română, 1895), p.492.

14 Stanisław Żurkowski, *Żywot Tomasza* Zamoyskiego, p.59.

15 Mustafa Naima (Naima Efendi), *Zatargi z Otomanami z powodu Kozaków*, p.133.

16 Stanisław Żurkowski, *Żywot Tomasza* Zamoyskiego, pp.43–44.

17 *Kronika Pawła Piaseckiego biskupa przemyślskiego*, p.281.

18 'Relacya prawdziwa o wejściu wojska polskiego do Wołoch i o potrzebie jego z pogaństwem w roku 1620…' in: *Pisma Stanisława Żółkiewskiego kanclerza koronnego i hetmana* (Lwow:

compared to the letter sent to Zamoyski are not surprising. Szemberg's official relation, published three times in 1621 alone, was after all an attempt to defend himself, so increasing the number of the enemies that defeated him was clearly a means to an end. Mustafa Naima also vastly exaggerated the Polish forces, writing that there were 60,000 Poles and that 10,000 of them died during the battle of Cecora.[19]

The vanguard of the Ottoman-Tatar force – Nogays under Khan Temir – arrived near Cecora on 17 September. A few hundred Tatars completely surprised the Poles, capturing large numbers of camp servants foraging outside of the camp, and it was reported 'we lost 1,000 servants or maybe more.'[20] Polish Military Guard[21] Jan Odrzywolski was later despatched with some cavalry to capture prisoners that could provide information about the strength and disposition of the enemy force, he was unsuccessful though. Costin says that the Poles only managed to bring in a few severed Tartar heads but not a single prisoner.[22] On 18 September, once the main force of Turks and Tatars had arrived, the two sides engaged in open battle. It seems that Iskander Pasha wanted to survey the battlefield, to see if the terrain was suitable for his masses of cavalry. At the same time the Poles were eager to capture some prisoners, to get proper information about the strength and disposition of the enemy army. Żółkiewski deployed four of his regiments next to each camp gate, with hussars at the front of every regiment. Iskander Pasha's men ignored the main camp and instead focused their attack on *lisowczycy*'s camp, which had been set up separate from the main army. Khizir Pasha with 500 light cavalry (probably a mix of Turks and Tatars) attacked first but he seems to have been hard-pressed by Polish cavalry. He was reinforced with another 500 horsemen under the command of Teryaki Mohammed Pasha and this time it was the *lisowczycy* that started to waver. Żółkiewski despatched some cavalry reinforcements, including Denhoff's reiters, who managed to force the Turks and Tatars back. The Hetman then proceeded to move all his regiments outside the camp, trying to lure Iskander Pasha into a pitched battle but without success. Skirmishers from both sides clashed through the rest of the day. The *Lisowczycy* joined the main Polish army in the camp, while both sides started to prepare to engage in the battle next day.

For the main action on 19 September, facing large number of fast Tatars cavalry Żółkiewski, probably with some helpful input from Koniecpolski and some experienced officers, decided to come up with an unusual battle plan. He wanted to utilise the much stronger firepower of the Polish army, at the same time opening the way for, hopefully decisive, charges of lance-armed hussars. On each Polish flank he deployed a tabor, which was to act

---

Drukarnia Zakładu Narodowego im. Ossolińskiego, 1861), pp.571-572.

19   Mustafa Naima (Naima Efendi), *Zatargi z Otomanami z powodu Kozaków*,pp. 134, 139, 144.

20   Relacya prawdziwa o wejściu wojska Polskiego do Wołoch i o potrzebie jego z pogaństwem w roku 1620...', p.571.

21   Military Guard (*strażnik wojskowy*) was one of the few permanent military offices in Poland. His task was to deal with reconnaissance, protecting army during both march and camping. It was the role well established during the border wars against Tatars.

22   Miron Costin, *Latopis ziemi mołdawskiej i inne utwory historyczne*, p.131.

as a mobile fortress. The left tabor was under the command of Wolmar Farensbach and manned by 300 German infantry and 200 Hungarian haiduks, supported by eight cannon and some hook-guns. Four cannon were at the front, other four at the back of the tabor. In the right-hand tabor, under the command of Teofil Szemberg, were two banners of *wybraniecka* infantry (200 men each) under Rybiński and Damięcki, supported by 300 Hungarian haiduks from the Household Guard, six or eight small cannon (set up in the same way as in the left-hand tabor) and a few hook-guns. The wagons were set up in four rows, with between 50 and 60 wagons in each row. As a link between tabors and the Polish camp, and also to protect the former from being outflanked, were deployed some strong support forces. On the left flank it was Stefan Chmielecki with 1,300 men, a mix of cavalry and infantry, mostly drawn from Ukrainian subjects of the Polish magnates. On the right flank there was a force of at least 2,000 men under the command of Colonel Walenty Rogawski. It was composed of his *lisowczycy* regiment, supported by volunteer cavalry and Moldavian forces. The main cavalry force, grouped into five regiments, was deployed between tabors, with hussars in the first line and cossack cavalry in the second. From left to right these were the regiments of; Samuel Korecki (who was in command of the left flank), Walenty Kalinowski, Hetman Żółkiewski (leading the centre), Hetman Koniecpolski and Mikołaj Struś (in charge of the right flank). The remaining Polish infantry was deployed in the field fortification of the camp, with the rest of the guns, while the camp servants stayed within the camp itself.[23] Graziani was not leading his Moldavians, as Hetman Żółkiewski decided to keep him close, so the Voivode was stationed with him in the centre. The Polish commander hoped that well supported tabors would be able to resist the attacks from the Tatars and prevent any outflanking actions. Once Polish firepower had taken its toll amongst the Turks and Tatars, the Polish cavalry would be able to charge and break through the enemy ranks. While interestingly innovative, the Hetman's plan relied a lot on the discipline and coordination of his force. As already mentioned, the Polish army was a conglomerate of the regular 'quarter army' troops, private units and volunteers, with some of the magnate commanders rather unwilling to obey Żółkiewski's orders. While before the battle morale was high and it seems that the soldiers were looking forward to fighting the enemy, during the battle all weaknesses of the Polish army were to be quickly revealed and affected the performance of the troops.

Both the Ottomans and Tatars also wanted to engage in battle, although initially Iskander Pasha had to calm down the tense situation between his allies. He tried to convince Dewlet Giray to stay with part of his troops in reserve, while Kalga-Sultan was arguing that he should take part in the fight. The argument became more heated, up to the point where Dewlet Giray

---

23 'Dziennik wyprawy wołoskiej w roku 1620', *Pamiętnik Warszawski Czyli Dziennik Nauk i Umiejętności*, volume 14, May 1819 (Warszawa: Zawadzki i Węcki, 1819), p.100–101; 'Dyariusz expedycy ejcecorskiej Stanisława Żółkiewskiego kancl. i hetm. w. kor. Przeciw Skinderbaszy tureckiemu e. 1620' in: Stanisław Żurkowski, *Żywot Tomasza Zamoyskiego*, p.381; Relacya Prawdziwa o Wejściu wojska Polskiego do Wołoch i o potrzebie jego z pogaństwem w roku 1620...', pp.572–573.

THE KHOTYN CAMPAIGN OF 1621

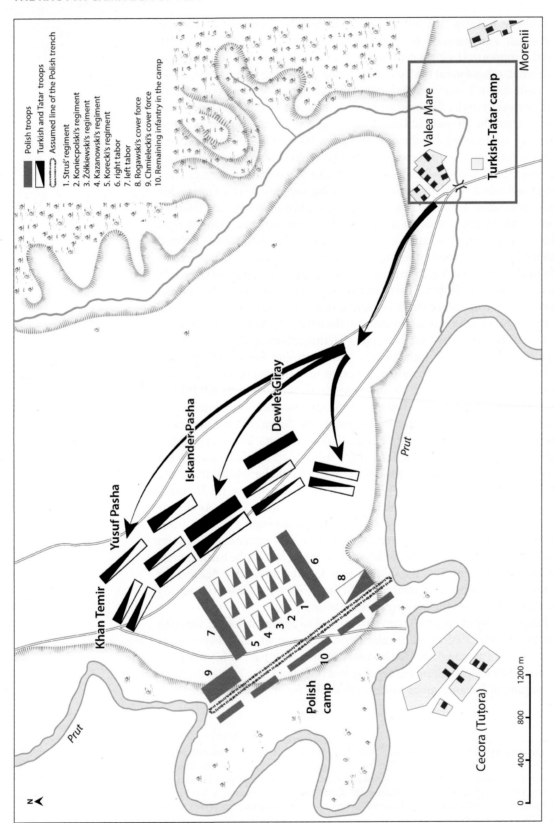

Polish troops

Turkish and Tatar troops

Assumed line of the Polish trench

1. Struś' regiment
2. Koniecpolski's regiment
3. Żółkiewski's regiment
4. Kazanowski's regiment
5. Korecki's regiment
6. right tabor
7. left tabor
8. Rogawski's cover force
9. Chmielecki's cover force
10. Remaining infantry in the camp

Morenii

Valea Mare

Turkish-Tatar camp

Prut

Iskander-Pasha

Dewlet-Giray

Yusuf Pasha

Khan Temir

Prut

Polish camp

Cecora (Ţuţora)

0   400   800   1200 m

N

Map 2. Initial deployment during the battle of Cecora, 19 September 1620 (Source: Ryszard Majewski, *Cecora rok 1620*)

threatened to take his warriors and leave for the Crimea. The Ottoman general had to concede and allow the Crimean Tatars' commander to lead the left flank. On the right wing he deployed Khan Temir with the Nogay Tatars. All Turkish forces were in the centre, under the direct commander of Iskander Pasha himself. They seem to have prepared some sort of a trench or used a natural ravine to deploy their infantry, with two cannon, behind, to act as a defensive position in the centre of the line. With the Polish army leaving the camp through four gates and setting up its fairly complicated battle line with tabors on wings, Iskander Pasha decided to attack, most likely attempting to lure the Polish cavalry out from the support zone of both tabors.

Around noon, part of the Ottoman cavalry charged against the Polish right flank of the Polish centre, facing Struś' regiment. Iskander Pasha chose the terrain well, as Polish accounts mention that the hussars were unable to use their lances, indicating that the cavalry did not have enough space for a proper charge. Koniecpolski's regiment was also quickly involved in the fight but what was worse, the tabors were not able to properly catch up with the main Polish battle line. It seems that the complicated task of setting up and moving the defensive tabor became too difficult for both Ferensbach and Szemberg, despite the presence of experienced soldiers such as Drogoń, Lewikowski and Ochyj, 'knowledgeable in the way of Cossack tabors.' Szemberg's tabor moved too forward, leading to the opening of a gap between it and the Polish centre. Rogawski with his cavalry was trying to cover it but the crack in the Polish battle line became obvious to both the Ottoman and Tatar commanders. At the same time Ferensbach's tabor seems to have stopped soon after leaving the camp and consequently was pushed more to the right by the cavalry banners of regiments leaving the camp, especially by the regiment under the command of Struś. As such this tabor was not able to adequately support the Polish cavalry engaged now against Ottoman *sipahi*. Worse was to come however, as suddenly Tatars moved to attack the gaps in the Polish lines. Dewlet Giray led the Crimean Tatars on the left wing of Żółkiewski's army, clashing with Rogawski's covering force. It seems that the ragtag formation of the Polish colonel did not resist for long. The volunteers broke first, followed by Moldavians, and to make matters worse, it appears that part of the latter changed sides and started to fight against the Poles. The *Lisowczycy* continued to fight but were pushed towards the already hard-pressed regiment of Maciej Struś. Struś's own troops started to waver; some hussars, unable to use their lances, dropped them and retreated towards the camp. This widened the gap in the Polish line and allowed Tatar horsemen to attack the rear units of the Polish army, including regiments of both Hetman Żółkiewski and Hetman Koniecpolski. Cossack cavalry banners, that were deployed in the second line of the regiments, clashed fiercely with Tatars. The Polish horsemen resisted three charges, then they were supported by hussars who also had to abandon their lances and fight 'with sabre and pistol'. The melee was extremely bloody, with both sides taking heavy losses. The hussar banner of Hetman Żółkiewski had almost half of its companions killed, Tatars or Turks also captured its standard. The hussar banner of Hetman Koniecpolski also took heavy losses: amongst the killed were Lieutenant Stan and Standard-bearer Boczkowski, the unit's standard was also taken.

Koniecpolski himself led charges of his men and single-handed killed two of the enemy. The reiter banner of Denhoff was practically annihilated, with just 15 or 16 survivors and its *rotmistrz* wounded twice.[24] Also among the dead were *rotmistrz* Krzysztof Kostocki and *rotmistrz* Owakowski, both from cossack cavalry banners. There were also many wounded, including Jan Żółkiewski (the Hetman's son), Łukasz Żółkiewski, Aleksander Bałłaban (both shot in the leg), Denhoff (wounded in the neck and the leg)[25] and Małyński (lieutenant of Żółkiewski's hussar banner).

Hard-pressed and severely bloodied banners retreated towards the camp, while only the regiment of Samuel Korecki managed to hold its position. Supported by Chmielecki's covering force and the left tabor, that part of the Polish army that did not break, resisted all attacks of the Nogay Tatars and by evening managed an orderly return to the camp. They paid a heavy price though, with *rotmistrz* Wrzeszcz killed leading a charge of his hussar banner, while his unit lost 20 companions killed. All that was left on the battlefield from the Polish army was the right wing tabor, surrounded by Ottoman and Tatar cavalry. With no available reserves and Polish cavalry retreating to the camp, the fate of the defenders of the tabor was sealed. They fought until evening but at the end their defence was broken and they were put to the sword or captured. Only a handful managed to survive and break through

Fight between Polish and Turkish horsemen. Johan Wilhelm Bauer, 1635 (Rijksmuseum, Amsterdam)

the enemy force, amongst them was Teofil Szemberg and Captain Almady, the officer in charge of the Household Guard haiduks. A Hungarian officer managed to lead around 20 men to safety; it seems that survivors also managed to save a few wagons with three hook-guns. Szemberg in his relation was fairly scant in the details of the defeat of his tabor, most likely due to the fact that he was partially to blame for its loss. Although he did record that 'most of the infantry [in the tabor], with seven cannon and several hook-guns, perished.'[26]

24 Relacya prawdziwa o wejściu wojska Polskiego do Wołoch i o potrzebie jego z pogaństwem w roku 1620…', pp.573–574.

25 Ksawery Liske, 'Stanisława Żółkiewskiego hetmana i kanclerza w. kor. klęska i zgon na Polach Czoczorskich', *Dziennik Literacki*, Year 18, no 15, 13 April 1869 (Lwów: Drukarnia Zakładu Narodowego imienia Ossolińskich, 1869), List P. Szemberka do Ksdza Andrzeja Opalińskiego, biskupa Poznańskiego, w którym opisuje porażkę wojska Polskiego w Wołoszech przez Skinder Baszę a die 18. Septemb. Ad 6. Octobris. Anno 1620, p.240.

26 Ksawery Liske, 'Stanisława Żółkiewskiego hetmana i kanclerza w. kor. klęska i zgon na Polach Czoczorskich', *Dziennik Literacki*, Year 18, no 15, 13 April 1869 (Lwów: Drukarnia Zakładu Narodowego imienia Ossolińskich, 1869), List P. Szemberka do Ksdza Andrzeja Opalińskiego, biskupa Poznańskiego, w którym opisuje porażkę wojska Polskiego w Wołoszech przez Skinder Baszę a die 18. Septemb. Ad 6. Octobris. Anno 1620, p.240.

After five or six hours of heavy fighting, the battlefield was in the hands of the Ottoman and Tatar forces. Both sides took heavy losses but the Poles were clearly defeated and forced to retreat to their camp.

As always with such events, estimates of losses vary, depending on the side. The Turkish account of Mustafa Naima mentioned 10,000 killed Poles, which is obviously a clear exaggeration.[27] Polish estimates of their own losses range between as low as 100 killed, which is far too low, to as high as 2,500 killed. Szemberg in his letter to Tomasz Zamoyski mentioned that he thought there were no more than 800 and that it includes a 'larger number of servants who were driving tabor wagons.'[28] Considering that one tabor was destroyed with practically all the men in it being killed, and adding the high losses of Polish cavalry in the centre, estimates of at least 1,000 killed and another 1,000 wounded seems to be the minimum number that should be considered, with a maximum of 3,000 men killed, wounded and leaving the ranks (either deserting or switching sides). It is even more difficult to estimate the losses of Iskander Pasha's troops as the Poles often mentioned that enemy losses were 'high' or 'higher than ours'. One relation has a very specific numbers of 250 killed and 700 wounded,[29] which seems fairly plausible but cannot be verified. Szemberg gives a rather high figure of 3,500 killed, taken from two days of fighting and based on relations of captives[30]. It seems that the worst losses were taken by the Ottoman cavalry that engaged the Polish centre, where the melee was the most fierce. Probably the lowest were the losses from Nogays that fought against the Polish left wing. Overall the losses could be estimated as close to 1,500 killed and wounded, with the majority of them amongst Turkish cavalry fighting in the centre.

While Polish losses were severe, even worse was the psychological effect of the defeat. Morale hit the bottom low and antagonisms between Żółkiewski and the magnates flared up again. During the war council that took place on 20 September, the Hetman presented a plan of retreating to Poland under the cover of a defensive tabor, with a route towards Mohyliv-Podilskyi (Mohylew). Many magnates and officers were not happy with such an idea, seeing it as very risky and preferring to try their luck in a quick break out from the camp. Discontent spread between soldiers as well. 'Some [were saying] that commanders want to get us killed; others that officers wanted to flee; others that it is wrong idea, as it is impossible to flee from Tatars and it would be better to cross Prut and move through Bukovina.'[31] Voivode Graziani feared for his life, probably being afraid that Żółkiewski might use him as a bargaining chip during the negotiations with Iskander Pasha, and then hand him over to Turks. The Moldavian decided to flee from the Polish camp but he did not want to do it alone. He convinced, and probably bribed, Walenty Kalinowski to take his soldiers and leave the camp with him.

27   Mustafa Naima (Naima Efendi), *Zatargi z Otomanami z powodu Kozaków*, p.133.
28   Stanisław Żurkowski, *Żywot Tomasza Zamoyskiego*, p.56.
29   'Dyariusz expedycyej cecorskiej Stanisława Żółkiewskiego kancl. i hetm. w. kor. Przeciw Skinderbaszy tureckiemu e. 1620' in: Stanisław Żurkowski, *Żywot Tomasza Zamoyskiego*, p.381.
30   Stanisław Żurkowski, *Żywot Tomasza Zamoyskiego*, p.56.
31   'Relacya prawdziwa o wejściu wojska polskiego do Wołoch i o potrzebie jego z pogaństwem w roku 1620…', p.575.

Many other magnates and nobles decided to join them, hoping to save their lives by escaping. In the evening, rumours were spread through the Polish army that Żółkiewski and Koniecpolski were abandoning the army and in the ensuing panic and riots, the magnates put their escape plan in motion. Graziani and Kalinowski, with his men, left camp and rode towards the Prut River, followed by Samuel Korecki, Janusz Tyszkiewicz and many others. Large numbers of soldiers and camp servants started to flee as well. Stefan Chmielecki with 400 men and Jan Odrzywolski with a further 500 men initially tried to stop the escaping soldiery but at some point they also joined them and fled.[32] Both officers managed to escape and return to Poland safely, Odrzywolski was punished for his cowardliness by being demoted from the office of Military Guard.

In the meantime both Żółkiewski and Koniecpolski also attempted to stop the panic and force their men to return to camp but to no avail. One of their officers, Marcin Kazanowski, was ordered by Żółkiewski to stay at the river bank and try to rally fleeing men, while both commanders returned to camp. They found it pillaged by individual soldiers, volunteers and servants; even Hetman Żółkiewski's tents were not spared. There were also multiple fires set by looters, adding to the overall chaos. It seems that only the German infantry managed to keep their discipline and prevent many others from fleeing.[33] Gradually groups of soldiers returned to the camp, so by the morning some semblance of order was restored and units were back in their assigned part of the fortifications. During the night, fleeing through Prut River, several hundred escapees drowned, amongst them Kalinowski. Many others were captured by Tatars, picking them up on the other side of the river. Graziani managed to avoid capture but soon after was murdered by his grand Boyars, Dvornik Nicorica and Hetman Szaptelicz. His head was cut off and, depending on the source, delivered either to Iskander Pasha or to the new pro-Ottoman Voivode, Alexandru Iliaş. The latter did not forgive the killers of Graziani though, as at the beginning of January 1621 both of them were tortured and executed either by drowning[34] or by beheading. and their bodies were thrown into a latrine.[35]

As for the Polish army, probably at least 2,000 men, mostly from private units and volunteers, had gone – fled, drowned or captured during the escape. Amongst those that tried to escape and did not succeed but managed to survive and return to camp was Samuel Korecki. Szemberg estimates even higher losses, 'up to 3,000 men, of whom all either drown, were killed by Wallachians [Moldavians] or captured by Tatars, not many managed to escape to their homeland.'[36] After long discussions with angry soldiers

32 *Kronika Pawła Piaseckiego biskupa przemyślskiego*, p.283.

33 'Dyariusz expedycyej cecorskiej Stanisława Żółkiewskiego kancl. i hetm. w. kor. Przeciw Skinderbaszy tureckiemu e. 1620' in: Stanisław Żurkowski, *Żywot Tomasza Zamoyskiego*, p.382.

34 Ödön (Edmund) Schütz (ed.), *An Armeno-Kipchak chronicle of the Polish-Turkish Wars in 1620–1621*, p.49.

35 Miron Costin, *Latopis ziemi mołdawskiej i inne utwory historyczne*, p.133.

36 Ksawery Liske, 'Stanisława Żółkiewskiego Hetmana i Kanclerza w. kor. klęska i zgon na Polach Czoczorskich', *Dziennik Literacki*, Year 18, no 15, 13 April 1869 (Lwów: Drukarnia Zakładu Narodowego imienia Ossolińskich, 1869), List P. Szemberka do Ksdza Andrzeja Opalińskiego,

Żółkiewski managed to calm down the situation and restore order. He even found the way to check which of the soldiers in the camp were amongst those trying to escape, and failing. 'To find out whose heart was brave, he ordered a fire to be set up and, starting with himself, to dry the clothing if it was wet. In this way many [men] were ashamed, as [drying] water betrayed every one of those that had tried fleeing.'[37] What's more important though, in order to not antagonise his soldiers, the Hetman decided to not punish anyone for the riots and the chaos. While, for the time being, it helped to pacify the army, this action later returned to haunt the Polish commander in the worse possible moment at the end of the campaign. Żółkiewski, in his post-battle letter to King Sigismund III, mentioned the cowardly escape of a part of his army, although he did not name any of them, 'soon they will show themselves [in Poland] those that left us in such a dishonourable fashion.' He did comment that probably not many of them would survive, as while escaping across the River Prut overnight, 'many drown and a large part was killed [or] captured by the enemy.' The Hetman admitted that this escape badly affected the rest of the army and only his intervention, supported by Koniecpolski and a few other officers, managed to keep the army together.[38]

For the next few days, under the initiative of Iskander Pasha, the two sides took part in negotiations. The Ottoman commander probably realised that he had no chances of capturing the fortified Polish camp but at the same time Żółkiewski seemed to be rather inclined to march with a defensive tabor to Poland, to show some military success and protect his reputation. Iskander Pasha initially requested a ransom of 100,000zl, although after long discussions the Polish envoys managed to convince him to lower this fairly outrageous demand to 20,000zl. The problem was that the Poles did not have such a large amount of cash with them, so the only way that they could pay it would be once they safely returned to Poland. Another issue was the proposed exchange of the hostages that were to be guarantees of truce. The Poles requested that one of them be their sworn enemy, Khan Temir. Hearing about this suggestion, Nogay shouted at Iskander Pasha: 'My word, for the love of unbelievers' gold you became unbeliever yourself! Me, that for thirty years killed with iron their fathers and sons, are to be handed over to them, so they can roast me alive. These are pagans and we shall not have a truce with them.'[39] Another Tatar noble, hearing that the Poles were dictating some of the conditions of truce, was to bare his blade and said that all that they can expect was the sabre.[40] Seeing such opposition from his allies, Iskander Pasha broke off negotiations on 28 September.

The situation turned the way that Żółkiewski wanted, so he could now, with the full support of the remaining soldiers, order the evacuation. A tabor was set up under the supervision of Samuel Korecki, possibly with the help of

biskupa Poznańskiego, w którym opisuje porażkę wojska Polskiego w Wołoszech przez Skinder Baszę a die 18. Septemb. Ad 6. Octobris. Anno 1620, p.240; Stanisław Żurkowski, *Żywot Tomasza Zamoyskiego*, p.56.

37 Albrycht Stanisław Radziwiłł, *Rys panowania Zygmunta,* p.68.

38 Stanisław Żurkowski, *Żywot Tomasza Zamoyskiego*, pp.43–44.

39 Mustafa Naima (Naima Efendi), *Zatargi z Otomanami z powodu Kozaków*, pp.141–142.

40 Miron Costin, *Latopis ziemi mołdawskiej i inne utwory historyczne*, p.134.

Marcin Kazanowski. Marching troops were deployed in a way so as to protect the tabor and provide the best defence against Tatars. The army was to march on foot, travelling during the night:[41]

> First there were all our horses, then tabor on six wagons wide and 100 wagons long; if the good terrain allowed [we] marched wide but where terrain was bad or when we were crossing [river] we even march 200 wagons long; on those wagons some put [hussars'] lances and sticks with some cloth on it, so it looked like tabor is much bigger; we marched next to those wagons in following order: first, there were five cannon and few hook guns, with them 200 Polish infantry and 100 German infantry of [Wolmar] Farensbach, on the end [of the column] also five cannon and some hook guns, with them 500 Polish infantry, 50 German infantry and *lisowczycy* cavalry; while on the sides of the wagons were marching hussars and cossack cavalrymen in three rows; all of us dismounted, with carbines or musket in hands or [carried] on arms. Before we left the camp, we make oath that we will defend [the tabor] on foot, and if someone will dare to get on horse [except ill, wounded, shot] then we were ordered to kill him.

During the first night of this retreat, the Turks and Tatars did not even pursue the Poles and were too busy with looting and destroying the abandoned camp. It is also possible that Iskander Pasha and other commanders were not expecting that Żółkiewski's army would be travelling during the night and

An engraving described as 'A Fight between Poles and Turks', with Polish infantry (haiduks?) fighting Turkish horsemen. Johan Wilhelm Bauer, 1636 (Herzog Anton Ulrich-Museum, J W Baur AB 3.16)

---

41 'Opisanie wejścia do Wołoch p. Stanisława Żółkiewskiego, kanclerza y hetmana wielkiego Korony polskiej, anno domini 1620', in Eudoxiou de Hurmuzaki (ed.), *Documente privitoare la istoria românilor*, supplement 2, volume 2, 1601-1640, p.496.

their soldiers were not ready (or eager) to attack a defensive tabor on the move. Despite the lack of pursuit, the Poles lost some wagons and horses during the crossing of the small River Deli and only energetic action by Żółkiewski and Koniecpolski restored order.

On 30 September and 1 October the Tatars did attempt some attacks during the mornings, when the Poles had stopped for the day to rest. All these attacks were repulsed, primarily thanks to the heavy firepower of the Polish and German infantry. The Tatars, under the command of Dewlet Giray who at that stage was leading the pursuit, tried to convince Poles to negotiate. It appears that Żółkiewski, hoping to gain some respite for his already tired troops, agreed but the Polish envoy, Krzysztof Drużbic, was captured by Tatars and negotiations were broken off once some Ottoman infantry, supported by two ex-Polish cannon (captured at Cecora) arrived with support. As the Poles did not march on the night of 1/2 October but stayed in place, on the morning of 2 October Dewlet Giray led the Ottoman and Tatars forces to an all-out attack on the Polish tabor. Not only was the attack repulsed but a unit of German infantry counter-attacked and recaptured the two cannon.[42] Facing mortal danger, even previously unruly elements of the army like the remaining private troops, fought bravely to beat off their attackers. One of the diarists praised 'this rabble, Ukrainians[43] with scythes and bows [who] were very tough for [the enemy]'.[44]

Between 2 and 4 October the Polish army continued their march, harassed by Tatars. Iskander Pasha and the Tatar commanders were ordered to implement a scorched earth policy, with groups of Tatars burning villages, crops and dry grass along the route of the Polish army.[45] Żółkiewski's army started to lose horses due to thirst; and at the same time the men were suffering from hunger, thirst and exhaustion. They were forced to resort to drinking muddy water found in fields, to eating horseflesh, and also cabbages found in large gardens near to the road. The mental factor also played a role here, as the soldiers were constantly on edge because of the enemy's hit-and-run attacks, and thus also not sleeping enough during the rests. Szemberg said '[we lost] many men over those two days, so tired from marching, from hunger, from lack of sleep, some of them lost consciousness, others fell on the ground sleeping like the dead, so we could not wake them up.'[46] Ottoman sources mentioned similar situations, 'some of those wagons were under cover of darkness captured by Tatars, who found [Poles] exhausted and sleeping, taking them to vizier's [Iskander Pasha] camp [by] putting one end

42 'Opisanie wejścia do Wołoch p. Stanisława Żółkiewskiego, kanclerza y hetmana wielkiego Korony polskiej, anno domini 1620', p.497.

43 Most likely units composed of the Ukrainian subjects of Polish magnates, or even those serving as camp followers.

44 Stanisław Żurkowski, *Żywot Tomasza Zamoyskiego*, p.382.

45 Ksawery Liske, 'Stanisława Żółkiewskiego hetmana i kanclerza w. kor. klęska i zgon na Polach Czoczorskich', *Dziennik Literacki*, Year 18, no 15, 13 April 1869 (Lwów: Drukarnia Zakładu Narodowego imienia Ossolińskich, 1869), List P. Szemberka do Ksdza Andrzeja Opalińskiego, biskupa Poznańskiego, w którym opisuje porażkę wojska Polskiego w Wołoszech przez Skinder Baszę a die 18. Septemb. Ad 6. Octobris. Anno 1620, p.240.

46 'Opisanie wejścia do Wołoch p. Stanisława Żółkiewskiego, kanclerza y hetmana wielkiego Korony polskiej, anno domini 1620', p.498.

of rope on their necks and the other to the tails of their horses; but during this journey, so strongly pulled by the ropes, many of those unbelievers fell down from their wagons and being hurt on the stones and ground, half-strangled and beaten were dragged to the camp of the faithful. In this way many of the captured pagans were turned into [our] slaves.'[47] Despite such difficult conditions, the tabor kept a good pace, from 2 to 3 October marching 24km, and next night 30km. It seems that on 4 October the tabor marched even further as by noon it arrived near the River Reut. It is probable that Żółkiewski was forcing his soldiers to an extra effort so as to be able to camp near the ford on the river.

Iskander Pasha, whose troops finally caught up with Tatars, decided to try another attack. Ottoman soldiers struck against the Polish rearguard, where they faced *lisowczycy* and Polish and German infantry. At the same time the Tatars attacked the sides of tabor, to engage the remaining Polish troops. Again the defenders of the tabor succeeded in repulsing all attacks and the Polish army continued with their march towards Reut. The Poles even managed to capture two enemy flags and take some Tatar prisoners.[48] It seems that the attackers took serious losses and therefore started to act in a more cautious way, 'they followed us but no longer screaming but whining, not bothering us over the night.'[49] Żółkiewski's men managed to cross the river, although even more wagons were lost, stuck on the muddy embankments. From 4 to 5 October the army marched another 30km but from 5 to 6 October the Poles managed only half of this distance. The exhausted army stopped near the village of Serwini (Sauka), some 10–15km from Dniester River. Half-hearted attacks by marauding Tatars were easily brushed off. Żółkiewski wanted to press onward, eager to arrive at the Polish border. The Army was too tired though, and forced him to stop for a rest. Some Nogay Tatars were nearby but the main force of Iskander Pasha, including Crimean Tatars, was a long way behind, probably at that stage believing that the Polish army was out of reach.

Until then, in the face of constant danger, the Polish army managed to keep up their discipline and largely follow the orders of Żółkiewski and Koniecpolski. Paradoxically, being so close to the Polish border led to bickering and growing discontent. Many officers and soldiers that had lost their belongings during the camp riots on the night from 20 to 21 September petitioned Żółkiewski to order the search of camp servants

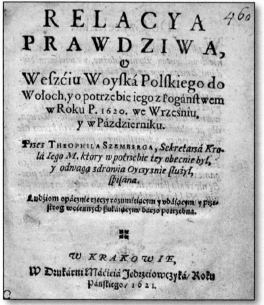

Front cover of an edition of Teofil Szemberg's relation of Hetman Żółkiewski's expedition to Moldavia in 1620, published in 1621 (National Library, Warsaw)

---

47 Mustafa Naima (Naima Efendi), *Zatargi z Otomanami z powodu Kozaków*, p.142.

48 Miron Costin, *Latopis ziemi mołdawskiej i inne utwory historyczne*, p.134.

49 Ksawery Liske, 'Stanisława Żółkiewskiego hetmana i kanclerza w. kor. klęska i zgon na Polach Czoczorskich', *Dziennik Literacki*, Year 18, no 15, 13 April 1869 (Lwów: Drukarnia Zakładu Narodowego imienia Ossolińskich, 1869), List P. Szemberka do Ksdza Andrzeja Opalińskiego, biskupa Poznańskiego, w którym opisuje porażkę wojska Polskiego w Wołoszech przez Skinder Baszę a die 18. Septemb. Ad 6. Octobris. Anno 1620, p.240.

and other 'loose men' in order to look for the stolen goods. The Hetman agreed to it but only once the army was safely on Polish soil. As Żółkiewski was known as a harsh disciplinarian, not shy of using capital punishment, such an announcement spread out through the army like wildfire, seriously terrifying those that had taken part in the riots. On the evening of 6 October the tabor moved again, travelling towards Dniester. Nogays tried one more time to attack the rearguard but *lisowczycy* and infantry forced them to retreat. During the evening, the discipline of the army broke, with servants and other previous 'September rioters' deciding it was time to try to save their lives and flee from both the Tatars and Żółkiewski's vengeance. Some stole horses that were pulling the wagons, trying to escape on them. Others were looting soldiers' belongings. In the ensuing chaos, discipline collapsed and the tabor was broken. Officers tried to stop the new riot and restore the orderly retreat but it was too late. 'Servants were fleeing with their masters' horses, [Zaporozhian] Cossacks were throwing nobles from their mounts.'[50] Worse, the Nogay Tatars following the Polish army used the opportunity and attacked again, slaughtering the defenceless men as they were fleeing. Many of those wounded during earlier fights and bring transported on wagons, were now abandoned and captured – amongst them Jan Żółkiewski and Łukasz Żółkiewski.[51] Nobody was listening to Hetman Żółkiewski, who was trying to keep his soldiers under the cover of wagons. Finally even he had to abandon the tabor and fled with a few hundred men towards the Dniester. To show the soldiers the scale of his own determination, Żółkiewski dismounted and killed his own horse, as a sign that he would be retreating among them.

According to Szemberg, Koniecpolski's stance was exemplary, with the young Field Hetman bravely facing Tatars, 'as long as he had arrows in his quiver and none of them was loosed in vain, as he killed as many pagans as he released arrows.'[52] The Hetman's group managed to march about 1.5km but then it was attacked by Tatars. Some Poles mounted their horses and fled, others were killed or captured. Żółkiewski was fighting next to a few officers and the remaining reiters from Denhoff's banner. Abraham Złotopolski managed to seize a horse from one of the Polish soldiers and forced the Hetman to flee on it. We do not know exactly the circumstances of Żółkiewski's death, but he was found by Tatars on the morning of 7 October, with his right hand severed and a, most likely fatal, wound on his head. The Tatars beheaded him and deliver the grisly trophy to Iskander Pasha. The Ottoman commander despatched the head to Constantinople, as a symbol

---

50 Ksawery Liske, 'Stanisława Żółkiewskiego Hetmana i Kanclerza w. kor. klęska i zgon na Polach Czoczorskich', *Dziennik Literacki*, Year 18, no 15, 13 April 1869 (Lwów: Drukarnia Zakładu Narodowego imienia Ossolińskich, 1869), List P. Szemberka do Ksdza Andrzeja Opalińskiego, biskupa Poznańskiego, w którym opisuje porażkę wojska Polskiego w Wołoszech przez Skinder Baszę a die 18. Septemb. Ad 6. Octobris. Anno 1620, p.240.

51 Miron Costin, *Latopis ziemi mołdawskiej i inne utwory historyczne*, p.135.

52 Ksawery Liske, 'Stanisława Żółkiewskiego hetmana i kanclerza w. kor. klęska i zgon na Polach Czoczorskich', *Dziennik Literacki*, Year 18, no 15, 13 April 1869 (Lwów: Drukarnia Zakładu Narodowego imienia Ossolińskich, 1869), List P. Szemberka do Ksdza Andrzeja Opalińskiego, biskupa Poznańskiego, w którym opisuje porażkę wojska Polskiego w Wołoszech przez Skinder Baszę a die 18. Septemb. Ad 6. Octobris. Anno 1620, p.241.

of his victory. When news of the disaster and the death of Żółkiewski, described in the letters from Prince Krzysztof Zbaraski, reached Warsaw, King Sigismund III took it all very hard. He gathered a few of his closest courtiers and shared the content of the letters. One of the courtiers was Albrycht Stanisław Radziwiłł, who noted that 'it was the first time I have seen the tears in His Majesty's eyes.'[53]

Hetman Żółkiewski (upper panel) and a fight between Polish and Ottoman cavalry (lower panel). Decorations from Hetman Stanisław Żółkiewski's sarcophagus, c.1621 (Sergey Shamenkov's collection)

The Polish army was completely scattered, with many men captured by Tatars and Moldavians. Reiter *Rotmistrz* Denhoff died during Żółkiewski's last stand; amongst the captured officers were Field Hetman Koniecpolski, Żółkiewski's son Jan, Łukasz Żółkiewski, Samuel Korecki,[54] Aleksander Bałłaban, and Wolmar Farensbach. It is estimated that only between 1,200 and 1,800 soldiers from Żółkiewski's army, including those that had fled during earlier stages of retreat, managed to return to Poland. Amongst them were just few officers: artillery commander Teofil Szemberg, Household Guard Haiduks' Captain Almady, *Rotmistrz* Falęcki, Kaliński and Trzebuchowski, Lieutenants Zbigniew and Złotopolski. Szemberg in his letter to Tomasz Zamoyski stated that there were about 200 'quarter army' survivors, although 'without horses, weapons, equipment'; he also added that just under half of *lisowczycy* survived as well, 'although their ranks will quickly fill in.'[55] Based on this and other accounts, Zamoyski wrote that 'our army was crushed, if anyone survived, they are like shipwreck victims, not only without horses and equipment but also without clothes.'[56] The scattered remnants of the regular troops moved to different locations in southern Poland, where they chose three colonels to take charge of the assemblies of soldiers. Stogniew with a few hussar banners was in Kowel, Śliwnicki with a few more banners of hussars in Lubowla while Falęcki with cossack cavalry units was in Dubno. The Polish cavalry was decimated during the campaign, with one account mentioning that 'under each banner, both hussars and cossacks, there were [barely] three companions and up to eight at most.' The same soldier added that the best and the noblest of the Polish army died or were captured during the campaign, including officers and veterans.[57] Due to losses amongst men, equipment and horses, the remaining force was not battle-worthy and the soldiers' morale was very low.

53   Albrycht Stanisław Radziwiłł, *Rys panowania Zygmunta*, p.72.
54   In June 1622 he was strangled in Yedikule Fortress in Constantinople.
55   Stanisław Żurkowski, *Żywot Tomasza Zamoyskiego*, p.59.
56   Stanisław Żurkowski, *Żywot Tomasza Zamoyskiego*, p.51.
57   'Opisanie wejścia do Wołoch p. Stanisława Żółkiewskiego, kanclerza y hetmana wielkiego Korony polskiej, anno domini 1620', p.500.

Ottoman horsemen during archery practice. From *Icones Habitus Monumenta Turcarum,* between 1586 and 1650. (Jagiellonian Library, Cracow)

No surprise that they could not be used to defend the border, that was now open to Tatar raids.

Żółkiewski's expedition to Moldavia ended in disaster, with loss of both Hetmans, and many officers and soldiers. The campaign was poorly planned and it seems that the indecisiveness of the Polish commander played an important role in the final defeat. While he had an opportunity to strike against Iskander Pasha's outnumbered forces in early September, instead he chose to stay idle, allowing the Ottoman and Tatar reinforcements to arrive and take the initiative during the campaign. There were huge problems with discipline within the army's ranks and amongst its camp servants, that left the retreating tabor open for Tatar attack at the last stage of the journey home. Regular units of the Polish army seemed to be in bad shape, fairly demoralised and not used to the serious fighting after the campaigns of 'Time of Trouble' in Muscovy. Private troops, while present in large number to reinforce the expedition, followed the examples of their magnate commanders and were often as disruptive as they were useful. The presence of some of the magnates that were at odds with Żółkiewski also led to conflicts and did not make leading the whole joint army an easier task. Despite the defeat at Cecora, the Hetman managed, up to that final and fatal point, to organise a well defended retreat that, if it had not ended with panic and chaos, could have been counted as one of the great achievements of the Polish army in the seventeenth century. Despite the personal bravery and sacrifice of many officers and soldiers, the army was lost and a new and open conflict with the Ottoman Empire became the new reality. Firstly though, as a direct aftermath of Żółkiewski's defeat, Poland had to face massive raids of Tatars along its border territories.

Due to the lack of a sufficient regular army, defence against the approaching Crimean and Budjak forces had to be borne by the local magnates, supported by some regular troops and the local population. Magnates tended to keep in service some private troops already, they were also able to quickly finance raising more and using their armed subjects and noble clients. Tomasz Zamoyski raised at least 1,000 men including some private hussars, Stanisław Lubomirski 600 and Jan Daniłowicz at least 200. The forces of the former seems to be less active though, focusing on the defence of his own estates, clashing with Tatars next to Żółkiew and forcing them to retreat. Jan Zbaraski was nominated as the overall commander of the defence, although without many troops on his disposal, he seems to have focused on protecting Lviv. Here some of the 'quarter army' banners, Lubomirski's, Zbaraski's and Jan Daniłowicz's private troops, supported by the City Militia and local monks (Benedictines and Dominicans) fought with Tatars between 15 and 19 October, trying to push back the raiders, who were burning and pillaging the outskirts of the city. While initially these actions were successful, the Tatars did not retreat far, destroying small towns and villages. On 18 October, near Stare Sioło, Polish troops, supported by cavalry and volunteers from Lviv (including haiduks from the garrison, acting as ad hoc dragoons riding confiscated cart horses) managed to defeat a large group of raiders.[58] Despite some local success, the Polish defence was too weak and far too outnumbered by the invaders. The levy of nobility from the Polish provinces that were most in danger of the raids was to gather near Lviv, Przemyśl and Sanok but the nobles either quickly dispersed soon after their arrival or did not show up at all.[59] By 21 October the Tatars were back again near Lviv, leading to a semi-blockade of the city. Lubomirski stayed in Lviv but the majority of his men, under the command of Szymon Kopyciński and Jerzy Rzeczycki were active against Tatars. They met with varying levels of success, defeating some raiders and then being badly beaten by a much stronger force. At some point Rzeczycki with a small group of his soldiers was surrounded in the mill where the Poles 'locked themselves in and throwing down the roof were shooting [at the enemy]'.[60] During a few days of hit-and-run actions Lubomirski's force lost up to 200 soldiers. Rumours of the huge Tatar army, that was even said to have 100,000 men, spread out amongst the local population, frightening people and weakening the resolve of the defenders. One of the Tatars captured on 17 October testified that the Horde was to stay in Poland for five weeks, after which they were to take all gathered loot and prisoners and go through Moldavia to march to Białogród (Akkerman) for winter quarters.[61] According to one of the accounts, up to 7,000 people were killed, 'not counting innocent children, of whom some were run over with horses, other left [impaled] on fences while others were

58   Ksawery Liske, 'Stanisława Żółkiewskiego Hetmana i Kanclerza w. kor. klęska i zgon na Polach Czoczorskich', *Dziennik Literacki*, Year 18, no 16, 20 April 1869 (Lwów: Drukarnia Zakładu Narodowego imienia Ossolińskich, 1869), *Dyariusz Wtargnięcia Tatarskiego po Wołoskiej Potrzebie w kraju Podolskie in Anno 1620*, p.256.

59   Ryszard Majewski, 'Polski wysiłek obronny przed wojną chocimską 1621 r.', *Studia i materiały do historii wojskowości*, volume VII, part 1 (Warszawa: Wydawnictwo Ministerstwa Obrony Narodowej, 1961), pp.5-6.

60   Stanisław Żurkowski, *Żywot Tomasza Zamoyskiego*, pp.48–49.

61   Stanisław Żurkowski, *Żywot Tomasza Zamoyskiego*, pp.45–55.

beheaded.'[62] Such cruel behaviour towards children was not unusual during Tatars raids, as they were of no use as captives, with very little chance of surviving the hazardous journey to the Crimea. As Paweł Piasecki later wrote in his chronicle 'The Tatars sent their raiders far and wide into Polish provinces, that is into Ruthenia and Podolia, as there was no troops to stop them, [the Tatars] with fire and sword destroyed everything on their path, taking prisoner uncountable number of [local] people.'[63] Auxent also mentioned devastating raids, during which the Tatars 'obtained a very rich booty and drove off more than 100,000 men' [captured them]. He added that the vast majority of prisoners died en route to Crimea as 'there was a famine and severe cold' and even the Tatars lost many of their own men and horses.[64] Zimorowicz in his chronicle of Lviv wrote that from the hills on the suburbs of the city they could see 'more than 100 burning and dying villages'. Thousands of villagers were marched alongside captured cattle in long columns, with 'Tatars wandering around like they are on their own land, not on the enemy one.'[65] The raids caused such panic in southern Poland that even as far as in Cracow 'anyone that could was running away, hiding in different defensible castles and towns.'[66] Border regions were ravaged by the raids, which ended in late autumn, with the Tatars taking their prisoners and loot back to Crimea and Budjak. The first phase of the war ended with a humiliating defeat for the Polish-Lithuanian Commonwealth but it was just a prelude to the second year of the conflict. Both sides were starting preparations for the open war that was to come in 1621.

---

62 'Dyariusz expedycyej cecorskiej Stanisława Żółkiewskiego kancl. i hetm. w. kor. Przeciw Skinderbaszy tureckiemu e. 1620' in: Stanisław Żurkowski, *Żywot Tomasza Zamoyskiego*, p.384.

63 *Kronika Pawła Piaseckiego biskupa przemyślskiego*, p.288.

64 Ödön (Edmund) Schütz (ed), *An Armeno-Kipchak chronicle of the Polish-Turkish wars in 1620-1621*, pp.48-49.

65 Józef Bartłomiej Zimorowic, *Historya miasta Lwowa, Królestw Galicyi i Lodomeryi stolicy; z opisaniem dokładnem okolic i potróynego oblężenia* (Lwów: Józef Schnayder, 1835), pp.299-300.

66 'Nowiny o niesłychanem zbiciu Polaków pod Cecorą r. 1620' in: Ambroży Grabowski (ed.) *Starożytności historyczne polskie*, vol I (Kraków: Nakładem i drukiem Józefa Czecha, 1840), p.130.

3

The Military Systems of the Warring Nations

Both the Commonwealth's and the Ottoman's military system have already been described in detail in the previous volumes of the *Century of the Soldier* series[1], therefore this is only an overall picture of the two armies, including their organisation and the different formations that they were composed of. This should make it easier to reference such troops and armies in the following chapters describing the campaign of 1621 and the fights at Khotyn. Each of the four armies – Polish-Lithuanian, Zaporozhian Cossack, Ottoman and Tatar – will be described separately, using information from sources from the late sixteenth century and first two decades of the seventeenth century. Where possible, I have tried to utilise those primary sources that are less well known or are not easily available in English.

The Polish-Lithuanian Commonwealth

While the Kingdom of Poland and Grand Duchy of Lithuania were joined by a genuine union and ruled by a single, elected, monarch, each of these countries had its own separate army. Each army would have two hetman: a Grand Hetman in the overall command and a Field Hetman as a second in command. However, only Poland had a regular, standing, army that was focused on defending the country against the Tatar raids. It was known as the 'quarter army' (*wojsko kwarciane*) after the method of financing the troops, a special tax on the income from Crown estates. It was established in 1563, when the tax was set up at a rate of one-fourth of all income. In 1567 it was changed to a rate of one-fifth but the name of the army remained the same. The election of Stephan Báthory in 1576 led to changes in this military

---

1   Bruno Mugnai, *Wars and Soldiers in the Early Reign of Louis XIV. Volume 3 – The Armies of the Ottoman Empire 1645–1718* (Warwick: Helion & Company, 2020); Michał Paradowski, *Despite Destruction, Misery and Privations…The Polish army in Prussia during war against Sweden 1626–1629* (Warwick: Helion & Company, 2020). Some extracts from the latter will be used to describe Polish-Lithuanian military establishment.

formation, as the new monarch was very interested in this 'standing army' and made an effort to expand it. Through the late sixteenth and first two decades of the seventeenth century, the majority of this new force was composed of hussar and cossack cavalry, with some small infantry garrisons deployed in the crucial fortresses of Kamianets-Podilskyi (Kamieniec Podolski) and Lubowla. The 'Quarter army', while serving as standing military force, was far too small to fight on its own during the longer campaigns or against strong enemy armies, e.g. the Turks. Therefore in the case of open war, so-called supplement troops (*wojsko suplementowe*) were raised. The *Sejm* during its proceedings decided size, composition and cost of the newly raised army. These troops were then gathered under the command of the Grand and/or the Field Hetman, only rarely under command of the King himself (the 1609–1611 Siege of Smoleńsk is one of those rare occasions). They could be joined by the 'quarter army' but often, the latter was required to defend the border, while the main campaign was taking place elsewhere (Livonia or Muscovy), it was the supplement troops that constituted the bulk of the army, supported by additional forces such as district troops (enlisted units raised directly by voivodeships and other regions), Zaporozhian Cossacks, volunteer private troops and the levy of nobility. Such *komput*, as the army was normally called, changed its size and organisation during each campaign. Some units were disbanded due to losses or the ending of their agreed period of service; other were newly raised, often including many previously serving soldiers but under a new commander or even reformed into a different formation.

Lithuania normally did not keep the standing army during peacetime, although some garrison units could be in service to protect vital fortresses. When facing the danger of invasion or conflict in neighbouring territories (especially Livonia), the *Sejm* could agree to raise a regular army financed from taxes. As in the case of Poland, additional auxiliary forces could be used to support the 'regular' army; the levy of nobility, private troops and a levy of the Lithuanian Tatars (they were obliged to provide military service as a part of their settlement rights).

An important contingent that became part of the Polish-Lithuanian army at Khotyn was the so-called Lisowski's cossacks (*lisowczycy*). It was a volunteer formation, created by Colonel Aleksander Lisowski in 1614, during the 'Time of Troubles' campaigns in Muscovy. The *Lisowczycy* were known as very good light cavalry, masters of the 'small war' but have somewhat of a bad reputation for being ruthless pillagers and looters, in a similar fashion to the Imperial Croats. Many of the *lisowczycy* units served without pay, living on what they could capture during their operations. After 1618 their banners served as mercenaries, fighting as a part of the Imperial army against Protestant armies in the opening phase of the Thirty Years' War, including a raid into Transylvania in 1619. They also supported Polish armies against the Turks and Tatars in 1620 at Cecora, and in 1621 at Khotyn. A small contingent also fought, without much success, against the Swedes in Livonia in 1622. Finally a few banners of *lisowczycy* took part in the campaign in Prussia in 1626, showing great skill during reconnaissance missions and in skirmishes with the Swedes. Those units were incorporated into the regular army though and became indistinguishable from other banners of cossack cavalry.

The *Lisowczycy* were equipped and organised in the same way as the cossack cavalry in the regular army, with their banners grouped into regiments, led by officers chosen by all companions. While in theory at Khotyn they were under the overall command of Hetman Chodkiewicz, in practice they were a semi-independent force, deployed in their own camp, in the same way as the Zaporozhian Cossacks. This independent status led to some issues and problems in the fights with Ottomans during the campaign.

Cossack cavalryman or *lisowczyk*, armed with sabre and bow. Abraham Booth, *Journael van de Legatie in Jaren 1627 en 1628*, Amsterdam, 1632 (National Archive, Gdańsk)

The cavalry in both Polish and Lithuanian armies could be generally divided into three types: hussars, cossack cavalry and reiters. Amongst the infantry were Polish, Hungarian and German units, the latter often known as 'foreign' (as such both names were used to describe the same units). Dragoons appeared for the first time in 1617 and only one small company of them can be identified as being present during the campaign of 1621 and at Khotyn. This type of soldier became much more popular from 1625 onwards and during the 1626–1629 war in Prussia the Polish army deployed more dragoons than Gustav II Adolf's Swedes. Polish and Lithuanian cavalry units were formed into company-size banners (*chorągwie*), with their 'paper strength' varying from 100 to 200 horses, although reiter units were sometimes known as cornets or companies. Polish and Hungarian infantry units were also known as banners, with their 'paper strength' normally between 100 and 200 portions, although larger units were often divided on the battlefield into two sub-units known as wings. German infantry could be enlisted in different sizes of units, varying from small free companies of 100–150 portions to large regiments in the style of Imperial or Catholic League armies, numbering up to 2,000 to 3,000 portions. While the size of the units was given in horses/portions (*konie/porcje*) it was, as already mentioned, just a 'paper strength'. Between 10 and 15 percent of each unit were in fact 'blind portions' (dead pays), used as an additional pay for the *rotmistrz*, lieutenant (if he was in charge of the cavalry banner during the campaign), colonel or captain.

As we will see from the composition of the Polish-Lithuanian armies during the Khotyn campaign, a mix of different banners were normally grouped into a regiment, known under the Polish word *pułk*. Such a regiment could have just a few banners of cavalry but during 1621 there were very large units, which could be in fact described as divisions: with more than 10 banners of cavalry, some regiments of German infantry and a few banners of Polish/Hungarian infantry. Regimental structure was very flexible, and banners could be moved from one *pułk* to another depending on the circumstances.

Soldiers in the cavalry units would be expected to provide their own horses, weapons, clothing (for both a companion and his retainers) and practically all equipment, including supply wagons, engineering tools, et cetera. There were a few exceptions to this: hussars' lances (*kopie*) were to be provided by *rotmistrz* or from the funds allocated from the national treasury, also a unit's standard was provided in the same way, although such a flag had to be returned when the banner/company was disbanded. In certain situations, for example when raising an expensive unit (hussars, reiters) or when recruitment had to be carried out in a very short period of time, additional advance pay could be provided to the *rotmistrz* to help with equipping the soldiers. Very often the *rotmistrz* himself dug deep into his own pocket and helped companions in purchasing the required items.

In regards to the infantry; soldiers were also expected to join the ranks with their own weapons, although they could also be supplied with one provided by the recruiting officer or from the resources of the main army, and the cost of it was to be deducted from the man's pay. In theory, the national treasury should provide the newly raised unit with uniforms or at least cloth to make them. Similarly troops already serving should receive replacements for their worn-out clothes at least once a year. That requirement was often neglected though and soldiers had to serve in whatever clothes they had or managed to find during a campaign. As with cavalry, infantry companies also received standards paid for by the national treasury and these flags were to be returned to the Hetman or the King when a unit was disbanded.

Hussars and officers of the Polish army. Detail from the copy of the sarcophagus of King Sigismund III at Wawel Castle in Cracow (Author's collection)

Hussars, as the main 'shock' cavalry, were equipped with multiple weapons. In a charge they relied on the use of their *kopia* lances to break both cavalry and infantry. Once the lance was shattered on impact or had to be for some reason abandoned, soldiers would switch to a secondary weapon. Depending on the situation, and the enemy that they were fighting against, this could be an estoc (*koncerz*) or heavy pallasch, kept under the saddle,[2] or the most important weapon for each noble – the sabre. In 1623 during the *Sejm* it was suggested that each hussar should be equipped with two pistols, preferably good quality Dutch ones, although there is enough evidence to prove that hussars had already used them in 1621. Bows and long firearms (*rusznica*, arquebus, even musket) were also part of the armament, although often kept in a tabor wagon and used only during defensive operations or sieges. Frequently used were the horseman's pick (*nadziak*) or the hammer-axe (*czekan*), ideal for both fighting from horseback and for a drunken brawl in the camp. This weapon had a special place in Polish history. On 15 November 1620 it was wielded by Michał Piekarski, during his attempted assassination of King Sigismund III. He managed to wound the monarch but was stopped by the royal retinue.[3] All nobles were thereafter forbidden from carrying such weapon in public, those that were caught with it would be fined an amount of 200zl. When issuing this ban, the *Sejm* made an exception for soldiers, as 'we allow the use of *czekan* and other weapons during the war against enemies of the Crown.'[4]

Well equipped companion of cossack cavalry, with mail, bow and sabre. From the so-called 'Gołuchów table' (*tablica gołuchowska*), c.1620 (National Museum in Poznań)

After the hussars, cossacks were the most common cavalry type in both Polish and Lithuanian armies. They had the dual purpose of serving both as medium cavalry, providing fire support for the hussars, and also as light cavalry, able to skirmish and taking part in reconnaissance and foraging missions. While many banners, especially in the Lithuanian army, could be composed of Tatars, they were not designated specifically as 'light cavalry', all being termed with the generic 'cossack cavalry' name. Only in the mid-seventeenth century was light horse, in the form of Tatar and Wallachian banners, established as separate formations. In the 'quarter army' cossacks were employed to fight against Tatars, perfect for hit-and-run tactics but also for employing the black powder weapons, which tended to affect the Tatars' morale. Recruitment letters issued to *rotmistrz* of cossacks banners usually mentioned that both companions and retainers should have 'good horse and equipment required for [those] serving as cossacks'[5] but sometimes information was added that soldiers should have a 'good gun' (i.e. a harquebus/carbine).[6] One recruitment letter issued for cossack cavalry in 1621, 'to fight against pagans marching against Homeland' specified that companions and retainers alike should

---

2   Sometimes hussars had both, with an estoc on the left side and a pallasch on the right side of the saddle.

3   After short investigation (including torture) he was sentenced to death and then 'drawn by four horses into pieces' in Warsaw on 27 November 1620.

4   *Volumina Legum*, vol.III (Petersburg, 1859), p.185.

5   Archiwum Państwowe w Łodzi; Archiwum rodziny Bartoszewiczów; Dokumenty, uniwersały, przywileje; document 3, List przypowiedni dla Stanisława Kosubudzkiego.

6   Archiwum Państwowe w Łodzi; Archiwum rodziny Bartoszewiczów; Dokumenty, uniwersały, przywileje; document 8, List zapowiedni Zygmunta III króla Polski, etc. dla rotmistrza Hieronima Dembińskiego na zaciąg do roty kozackiej, Warszawa 1627.

be armed with 'three firearms' (*trojga strzelby*),[7] a term which became very common in such documents through the rest of the seventeenth century. Sabres, as the individual weapon of all soldiers, were not mentioned – there was no need for that information, as it was the symbol of status and privilege of each noble. While bows were also not part of 'official' weaponry, they were often employed, especially by companions (again, as a status symbol) and by Tatars serving in cossack banners. While on some iconography from the period there are cossack cavalry armed with both bow and carbine, it was just for ceremonial purposes and such a combination was too cumbersome to be used on the battlefield. Quite often a companion would use a bow while his retainer or retainers had long firearms instead. There is no indication that spears and/or lances were employed by this type of cavalry during the war of 1620 and 1621. 'Quarter army' cossacks in 1623 were to be equipped with two pistols, carbine, light helmet and armour,[8] which would be always included as a requirement in recruitment letters. It is important to mention that both helmet and mail were often absent and such unarmoured units would be termed as serving 'naked' (unarmoured). This issue seems to have been an especially big problem during the preparations for the campaign of 1621, when a large number of new units had to be raised and equipped in a relatively short period of time, leading to problems with availability of both weapons and armour.

The term reiters (*rajtaria*) was used in the Commonwealth to describe all types of Western-style cavalry, from heavily armoured cuirassiers, through demi-cuirassiers to the lighter-style mounted harquebusiers. Some reiters were recruited locally, mostly from German-speaking regions, like Prussia, Livonia and Courland. The units could also include Poles and Lithuanians, although these tended to be in the minority. Recruiters were also often sent to Pomerania, Brandenburg, Saxony and Silesia. Alongside Germans, French and Walloon soldiers were also recruited there and were always sought after as valued cavalry. In the 1620s reiters in both Polish and Lithuanian armies were expected to be equipped with armour, even as late as in 1635 Charles Ogier, who had seen Polish reiters in Prussia, mentioned that they were fully armoured.[9] Hussars that served without *kopia* lances, such as Jan Rudomina's banner which took part in the famous charge at Khotyn on 7 September 1621, were known to be fighting 'in reiter style', indicating that the armour was strongly associated with this formation. As there was no detailed specification of what such armour should comprise, within the units (banners or companies) there was probably a wide mix of different types, from three-quarter cuirassier armour worn by the wealthiest officers and soldiers, to simply a back and breast, or even just helmet for the poorest. A bigger emphasis

Well equipped reiter, armed with 'three firearms', typical for Polish and Lithuanian soldiers of this formation. It is worth noting that he also has a warhammer, an additional close combat weapon very popular in the Commonwealth's armies. *Theatrum Europaeum*, volume II, 1633 (Herzog August Bibliothek Wolfenbüttel)

---

7   BK 330, *Akta Zygmunta III od roku 1618 do 1621*, no 515, pp.827–829.

8   The text indicates that author meant mail.

9   *Karola Ogiera dziennik podróży do Polski 1635-1636*, part I (Gdańsk: Biblioteka Miejska i Towarzystwo Przyjaciół Nauki i Sztuki, 1950), p.271.

was placed on the weapons, recruitment letters stated that reiters should be equipped with 'three firearms' – two pistols and an arquebus or a carbine. On top of that there was of course sword, sabre or pallasch. Reiters serving in the 1620s were normally organised into banners/companies of 100–200 horses, under the command of *rotmistrz*. Units tended to be divided into three corporalships and a small company staff. In some banners many reiters served in two or three horse retinues as in the Polish and Lithuanian national cavalry; in others the structure was more simplified and the rank and file reiters served with just one horse. The primary battlefield role of these units was to provide fire support to the other units of the Polish or Lithuanian cavalry but they would often join the melee, as Denhoff's banner did during the campaign of 1620. Due to the fact that they were well equipped with firearms, in 1621 they were often used as a 'fire bridge', thrown into the fight to support heavily pressed defenders during Ottoman's assaults.

Both Polish and Hungarian infantry would be armed in the same way, with sabres, axes and *rusznica* calivers. Their officers and NCOs (*dziesiętnicy*, so literally '10th man') were equipped with half-pikes known as *dardy*. What is interesting to notice is that despite the large numbers of German/Western-type infantry being employed, all of them seem to be musketeers, with no reference to pikemen being found in the diaries of the soldiers taking part in the campaign. It may have something to do with the fact that the infantry was planned to be used as a defensive force, fighting from behind the field fortifications or a prepared camp. As such it was not seen that it would be vulnerable to charges of the enemy cavalry and the Polish-Lithuanian command preferred to focus on maximising the available firepower. It is worthwhile to add though, that English, Scottish and Irish units recruited during the mission of Jerzy Ossoliński in 1621, were to be equipped with

Polish infantry from the beginning of seventeenth century from the copy of the 'Stockholm Roll', parading at the Royal entry to Cracow in 1605. Artist unknown. The original painting is currently in the collection of the Royal Castle in Warsaw. (Author's collection)

muskets, pikes and armour,[10] so at least some of Western-style troops planned for Khotyn were to be the typical pike and shot regiments of the era. British units never reached the theatre of war, and were sent to Livonia to face the Swedes instead. The small unit of dragoons would be most likely also armed with only muskets and swords, so not really distinguishable from the musketeers of the infantry regiments.

Throughout the reign of King Sigismund III artillery was always the weakest element of both the Polish and the Lithuanian military establishments. Underfunded,

10   *Jerzego Ossolińskiego, kanclerza wielkiego koronnego autobiografia* (Lwów: Zakład Narodowy im. Ossolińskich, 1876), p.140.

lacking a regular standing cadre and without the steady production of new guns, it was spread between different arsenals and fortresses. The 'Quarter army' tended not to field any cannon on a normal day-to-day basis, since they were not really required for protecting the border against Tatar incursion. With each campaign that would require artillery support, e.g. fighting against Cossacks, or where some siege operations were planned, additional funding had to be found to hire skilled gunners, to purchase powder and ball, and to hire horses and wagoners for the artillery train. When available, cannon were usually smaller calibre field pieces, often supported by hook-guns (*hakownice*) and frame guns (*śmigownice*) carried on tabor wagons. The regular army often had to rely on the support from magnates, who brought some artillery with their own private armies. Experienced engineers usually had a double role as an infantry officer and/or artillery master as well, although their numbers was usually very low, with only two to three such specialists available on any given campaign. The logistics of the artillery train were very poor, as in 1621 Jakub Sobieski mentioned that there was not enough powder, and even the supply of it taken with the army to Khotyn was of poor quality. There were not enough cannonballs and barely 28 cannon, 'in total disorder', accompanied Polish and Lithuanian troops.[11]

At both Cecora and Khotyn, a very important role, in both a positive and a negative way, was played in the Polish and Lithuanian army by the camp servants, known as *luźna czeladź*. Each retinue of cavalry had a number of servants, paid from a companion's own pocket. It was their duty to take care of horses and tabor wagons, look after their master's belonging and find provisions and water for both the men and the horses of the whole retinue. All of these servants were armed and in time of need they could, if necessary, engage in combat, i.e. during the defence of the camp and tabor or on foraging missions. When the army was taking part in a battle, they could bring spare horses for companions and retainers, take care of wounded and, of course, they were always on the lookout for chances to loot the battlefield, enemy camp and baggage train. Numbers of servants varied, depending on the personal wealth and needs of each companion. Hussars could have even have as many as a dozen, while poorer nobles serving in cossack cavalry banners probably relied on just two or three. *Czeladź* could, at the same time, play a very disruptive part, often being unruly, undisciplined, and prone to looting. It was most especially seen clearly during the retreat from Cecora to

Musket-armed foreign infantry in the Polish army during the Siege of Smoleńsk in 1609–1611. Detail from the sarcophagus of King Sigismund III at the Wawel Castle in Cracow. (Author's collection)

---

11   'Jakóba Sobieskiego Dziennik wyprawy chocimskiej', p.109.

Poland in 1620, and in the massacre of the Moldavian merchants at Khotyn on 5 September 1621.

Many historians support the theory that the Polish-Lithuanian military at the turn of 1610s and 1620s was in crisis, mostly linked to a problem with internal discipline, that started during long conflicts of the 'Time of Troubles' and which later led to failures at Orynin in 1618 and during Żółkiewski's expedition in 1620. It can be argued that the stubborn defence at Khotyn showed that any such crisis was in fact very short-lived. What is certain is that Polish and Lithuanian armies were often ill-disciplined, usually due to the constant trouble with delays in, or even total lack of, the promised pay. On many occasions it could lead to losing all of the campaign's gains despite victory in pitched battles, as an unpaid army might refuse to continue to fight and to obey any further orders. One of the main reasons for this, which sadly affected the Commonwealth through the whole seventeenth century, was the very ineffective financial system, where taxes agreed by the *Sejm* for army pay tended to be gathered very slowly and often only after many delays. Unpaid soldiers were prone to mutinies, known as confederations (*konfederacje*), often moving to well populated regions of Poland and Lithuania and looting their own population. The army's logistics system was also of a rather poor level, with soldiers often forced to organise their own provisions – a situation for which cavalry (having a number of servants) was well suited for, but which left the infantry at a great disadvantage. The Army also tended to have a very small and inefficient artillery support, even during the siege operations.

On the other hand, it is important to highlight the positive aspects of the Polish and Lithuanian troops fighting at Khotyn. They were under command of an excellent and experienced commander; and Chodkiewicz was able to keep up the morale of the troops and encourage soldiers to fight well, despite the difficult situation they found themselves in. Even after the death of the Lithuanian hetman, his replacement as an overall commander – Stanisław Lubomirski – was able to keep the army together and lead it successfully until the end of the war. While Royal Prince Władysław did not play a direct role in the combats, his presence in the camp was very important symbolically and positively affected Polish, Lithuanian and Cossack troops alike. As the events of the assaults, like the one from 7 September, showed, once Polish and Lithuanian cavalry, especially the famed hussars, had the chance to be used in its designated role, it played a tremendous part on the battlefield. Soldiers showed a stubborn determination and endured many hardships that did not even lead to the conclusion of the war. The Khotyn war was also a good military school for many middle ranking officers, who had the opportunity to experience cooperation between Polish cavalry and Western-style infantry. Such knowledge would later be utilised during the Prussian War of 1626–1629 against the Swedes, and the Smoleńsk War of 1632–1634 against the Muscovites.

Zaporozhian Cossacks

Through the sixteenth and early seventeenth centuries, Zaporozhian Cossacks were known as skilful raiders, honing their profession in almost annual attacks against Tatars and Ottomans. They used boats known as *chaika* (*czajka*) that could carry, depending on size, between 30 and 50 men. During the raiding seasons, of spring and summer, they sailed along the Dniester River to the Black Sea to attack the Ottoman ports, including the outskirts of Constantinople. The most sought after loot was money, weapons and clothing – especially 'Spanish reals, Arabian sequins, carpets, expensive cloths, cotton, silk and other expensive items.'[12] Raiders often attacked at night, completely surprising the local population. A fleet of 80 to 100 boats, with up to 5,000 Cossacks, was even able in the right circumstances to engage the Turkish galleys, especially when just one or two ships had to face the entire Cossack raiding force on the river or near the coast. However, the situation looked completely different when the Cossacks were caught on the open sea – here the situation strongly favoured the Turks. It seems that Cossacks

Cossacks on *chaika* boats fighting against the Ottoman galleys during the raid on Kaffa in 1616. From Kasjan Sakowicz's *Wiersz na Żałosny Pogrzeb Zacnego Rycerza Piotra Konaszewicza Sahajdacznego, hetmana wojsk jego Królewskiej Mości zaporoskich...* A poem read during the Hetman's funeral in Kiev in 1622 and published the same year. (Author's collection)

---

12 *Eryka Lasoty i Wilhelma Beauplana opisy Ukrainy* (Warszawa: Państwowy Instytut Wydawniczy, 1972), p.144.

relied on their firepower, 'not moving from their benches: some are shooting, while others are reloading and passing them guns, so they can continue such fusillade without a break.'[13] Cardinal Ludovico Ludovisi wrote about Cossack raids on the Black Sea, reaching 'up to the gates of Constantinople,' where they arrived in their small ships 'destroying everything with fire and sword with such speed, that the Turks are unable to catch them or cut off their retreat.'[14]

While in the seventeenth century Cossacks did employ cavalry, it was usually of low quality, more like the dragoons of other armies. French engineer Guillaume Le Vasseur de Beauplan (1600–1675), serving between 1630 and 1648 in the Polish army and taking part in the campaigns against Cossacks provided an interesting observation about their military skills:

> [Cossacks] show the best skills and abilities, when fighting in tabor, protected by carts [wagons], because they are excellent shots [while] using *rusznica* calivers, that are their main weapons and they are superb while defending their positions. While at sea, they also can fight with some skill, but they are not great when fighting from the saddle. I recollect, as I have seen it myself, that barely 200 Polish horsemen defeated 2,000 best [mounted] Cossacks. It is an undeniable truth, that while defending tabor, 100 Cossacks are not afraid of 1,000 Poles or even thousands of Tatars and I believe that if they would be as gallant fighting mounted as they are [when] on foot, it would make them invincible.[15]

He also wrote an interesting passage about the way that Cossacks travelled in a defensive tabor, when facing Tatars:

> They march between their wagons, of which they have two ranks, with eight or 12 wagons on the front and same number at the rear. Cossacks themselves, armed with firearms, short pikes and scythes with their blades edgeways, march inside [of the tabor]. Their best horsemen surround the tabor on the outside.[16]

The main armament of the Zaporozhian Cossacks was firearms, usually called *rusznica* or *samopał* which was a generic name used to describe different type of weapons, i.e. both heavier and lighter calivers or, in the case of *samopał*, some lower quality locally produced firearms. They could be obtained from many sources, usually bought or captured from Poles, Muscovites and Turks. As such there could be a variety of guns used even within one *sotnia* (company). While one could think that the sabre would also be a typical part of the Cossacks' armament, it seems not always to have been the case. Probably during raids against Tatars and Turks, when we are dealing with a limited number of better equipped Cossacks, they could all carry such weapons but in a campaign where many thousands of

---

13   *Eryka Lasoty i Wilhelma Beauplana opisy Ukrainy,* p.143.
14   Erazm Rykaczewski (ed.), *Relacye nuncyuszów apostolskich i innych osób o Polsce od roku 1548 do 1690,* volume I, pp.128-129.
15   *Eryka Lasoty i Wilhelma Beauplana opisy Ukrainy,* p.110.
16   *Eryka Lasoty i Wilhelma Beauplana opisy Ukrainy,* p.135.

Zaporozhians were under arms (e.g. Muscovy in 1618 or Khotyn in 1621) not every Cossack could afford to be armed with a sabre. Thus many additional types of weapon were used to supplement the firearms. Sources from 1621 mention axes, *rohatyna* spears, and scythes employed during night sallies against Ottoman positions. Jakub Sobieski, describing Cossacks in 1621, wrote that 'not every one of them is equipped with spear but each one have *rusznica* and if the Polish army would use such firearms in this way, it could be equal to the best infantry in the world.'[17] The firepower of the Cossack infantry was often highlighted in the primary sources, especially by Poles fighting both side-by-side and against Zaporozhians. One of the Polish plans in the preparation for war against Osman II specified, that amongst allied Cossacks there should be at least 'five thousands [men] with *rusznica* firearms with tabor and artillery, that we should not ignore, especially as they are known amongst pagans [Muslims] as rather famous and good.'[18] The Cossack tabor was especially dangerous when Zaporozhians had time for additional preparation, to support it with some trenches and earthworks. When Polish and Lithuanian armies faced rebellious Cossacks in 1596, during the Nalyvaiko Uprising (*powstanie Nalewajki*) Hetman Stanisław Żółkiewski in his letter to King Sigismund III wrote how difficult it would be to fight against the rebels. 'Cossacks set up in well defended and elevated position near River Solonica, from which they have good view of [the area] around them. Their tabor, set up in circle with nine rows of wagon, is defended with earthworks (…) with close to 6,000 armed men, well supported with their chosen terrain, firearms and other military equipment.'[19] It is no surprise that such a well prepared and stubbornly defended position was always a 'hard nut to crack' for the Poles, especially when their armies tended to lack a sufficient number of infantry and cannon. Jakub Sobieski admitted that, 'their camps, known as tabor, made up from wagons set up in certain order, provides them with strong protection against the violent enemy attacks.'[20] As happened in the fighting in 1621 (see below), Cossacks were not idle even in defence, with frequent night sallies and counter-attacks. This also provided them with ample opportunities to loot the enemy camp, taking food, weapons, clothes, money and beasts of burden. At Khotyn it became one of the main methods of supplying the Cossack army, thanks to the numerous raids against Turks and Tatars.

As a society of 'free warriors', known as Zaporozhian Sich (*Sicz Zaporoska*), Cossacks had their own peculiar way of electing their leaders. This was a general gathering of all Cossacks to choose their hetman, or *otaman*, from amongst all colonels and veterans, with each Cossack having one vote and the candidate with the majority of the votes taking over the command. According to Beauplan, such commanders tended to be very strict and could discipline Cossacks, including by the death penalty; they 'could cut their heads off [or] impale those that transgress.' At the same time the hetman had to rely on his

---

17   Jakub Sobieski, *Pamiętnik wojny chocimskiej xiąg troje*, p.45.
18   *Zherela do istoriï Ukraïny-Rusy, volume VIII*, p.221.
19   *Zherela do istoriï Ukraïny-Rusy, volume VIII*, p.90.
20   Jakub Sobieski, *Pamiętnik wojny chocimskiej xiąg troje*, p.45.

Cossack armed with the *rusznica* caliver and sabre, from the coat of arms of the Zaporozhian Sich. From Kasjan Sakowicz's *Wiersz na Żałosny Pogrzeb Zacnego Rycerza Piotra Konaszewicza Sahajdacznego, Hetmana Wojsk Jego Królewskiej Mości Zaporoskich...* A poem read during the Hetman's funeral in Kiev in 1622 and published the same year. (Author's collection)

war council for the decision making during a campaign. The position of such a chosen commander was precarious though, as if a campaign turned bad, or if the 'hetman makes a mistake or appears to be a coward, they kill him like a traitor.'[21] Often personal conflicts and internal politics played an important role, with different officers gathering or losing support depending on the success or failure of their expeditions or their relations with the Polish Crown. Example of such infighting can be clearly seen both prior and during the campaign of 1621 and could be a real hindrance to a Cossack army during longer campaigns.

For the purpose of bigger military operations, Cossacks tended to be formed into a regimental structure, with each regiment (*pułk*) divided into a number of company-size *sotnia*. Such *pułk* would also have a small staff, with a colonel, a few lower rank officers, musicians and a scribe.[22] The structure of Cossack regiments could be flexible, with both overall strength and internal organisation varying from unit to unit. For example, a regiment that took part in the campaign in Livonia in autumn 1601, had 2,039 men, divided as: Hetman Samuel Kokoszka (in command of the regiment), four *atamans* (sub-hetman), eight *yesauls*-rank officers, 20 *sotnik*-rank officers, camp master, clerk, four standard bearers, 12 musicians, 157 NCOs or 10th men rank (*dziesiętnik*), 1,799 rank and file *moloitsy*,[23] 12 artillerymen and 20 cart drivers.[24] The number of atamans and standard bearers indicates that the regiment was divided into four larger sub-units of roughly 500 men each, with two *yesauls*, five *sotniks* and three musicians in each unit. Each *sotnik* would be in charge of the company-level *sotnia*, with *yesuals* and musicians most likely acting as a support staff for *atamans*. It is worthwhile to note that both artillery crew and tabor wagon drivers were mentioned separately.

In Appendix III, are two surviving Cossack army lists from 1621 and, while we do not know their internal structure, we can see that there was large variation in the size of the regiments, with some numbering above 3,000 men. It is likely that, as with the 1601 example mentioned above, such regiments would be divided into some sub-units of a few *sotnia* each. In February 1622, when Lithuanian Field Hetman Krzysztof II Radziwiłł was planning to recruit Zaporozhian Cossacks to fight in Livonia against Swedes, he wrote to Colonel Józef Putywlec, asking him to raise a regiment of 1,000 experienced Cossacks, 'both mounted and on foot' – again indicating a mix of both types of troops within the larger Cossack units.[25] Unfortunately, as the regiment was never recruited and used in the service, we have no further information

---

21   *Eryka Lasoty i Wilhelma Beauplana opisy Ukrainy*, pp.139-140.

22   Petro Sas, Khotyn *War of 1621* (Kiev: National Academy of Sciences of Ukraine. Institute of History of Ukraine, 2011), p.89.

23   Term *mołojec* (plural: *mołojcy*) meant Cossack warrior but was also used in Polish to described someone who was brave and resourceful.

24   Stanisław Herbst, *Wojna inflancka 1600-1602* (Zabrze: Wydanictwo Inforteditions, 2006), p.228.

25   AGAD, Archiwum Warszawskie Radziwiłłów (AR), II, 813.

about its planned internal structure. Of course it is also very difficult to assess how accurate the numbers provided by Cossacks about their regiments actually were. We do not know how many of the men mentioned in the lists were 'dead pays' and existed only on paper, it is also very difficult to estimate the level of losses during the journey through Moldavia to Khotyn, which would further lower the strength of the regiments.

The Cossack army was to play a crucial role in the campaign of 1621, where their support was invaluable for the successful defence against the Ottomans. The Zaporozhians arrived in large numbers, showed a great warrior spirit and eagerness to fight and they were a constant problem for Osman II's army. However, being a volunteer army, always on the lookout for the chances to capture loot, they often lacked proper discipline, and their counter-attacks or sallies ended in the pillaging of the Ottoman camp. Despite stripping part of Moldavia of all the necessary supplies, their army quickly ran out of provisions, which led to quarrels and discord at Khotyn, and it was only the timely intervention of the Polish-Lithuanian command and Cossack elders that stopped the contingent from abandoning the camp and restored morale, keeping the Zaporozhians as a part of the allied army. Overall though, Khotyn 1621 is remembered as an example of the best cooperation between the Commonwealth's regular army and the Cossacks, with the latter playing vital part in the success of the campaign.

Zaporozhian Cossacks from Beauplan's map of Ukraine (Author's collection)

Cebeci armourer. *Rålambska dräktboken*, mid-seventeenth century (National Library of Sweden)

Ottoman Empire

With its vast and often restless borders, combined with often aggressive international politics, the Ottoman Empire had to spend a large part of its annual budget on keeping up a strong military establishment. There were three main components of the army during the sixteenth and seventeenth centuries:

Kapikulu: the Sultan's household troops; divided into three main corps, janissaries, cavalry and artillery
Provincial Cavalry: raised by landowners as a part of their military obligation. They were not part of the standing army and were raised only when needed. Depending on the source, these were known under the names of *askerielayet*, *timarli* or *toprakli*. For simplicity, throughout I have used the term provincial *sipahi* to differentiate them from other types of cavalry
Serhaddkulu: regular or semi-regular troops serving in the provinces. It was corps composed of different types of cavalry and infantry, also additional artillery staff raised for the garrison duties or to support during the campaign

Ottoman armies were also often accompanied by allied troops from vassal states. Most important were Tatars from the Crimean Khanate and from the Budjak Horde, these were especially active during conflicts against the Polish-Lithuanian Commonwealth. Troops from Transylvania, Moldavia and Wallachia could be present as well, although they were usually relegated to less important duties and were not considered as first-line soldiers.

Probably most famous and easily recognisable of all *kapikulu* are the janissaries. Janissaries are an infantry formation created in the fourteenth century, initially recruited from amongst the Christian children of Ottoman subjects, gathered through *devshirme* system and converted to Islam. They were usually used as a core of the Ottoman battle line, and with their fanatical loyalty, stubbornness and eagerness to fight provided elite infantry devoted to Sultan. Throughout the sixteenth century they were present in practically all Ottoman battles, while during the time of peace the main part of the Corps was stationed in Constantinople. They were predominantly firearm-armed infantry, with a few of their units equipped as archers or using halberds, although these latter were mostly for ceremonial purposes. Ottoman firearms, whether of arquebus or musket type, tend to be longer than Western European ones. As well as the most popular matchlock muskets known as *fitilli tüfek*, there were also flintlock muskets known as *çakmaklı tüfek*.[26] In Polish sources they all tend to be described under one generic name, *janczarka* (janissaries' guns), no matter what type of lock they used or whether they were muskets or arquebuses.

---

26 Gábor Ágoston, *Guns for the Sultan. Military Power and the Weapons Industry in the Ottoman Empire (Cambridge: Cambridge University Press, 2005)*, p.89.

The conflicts at the end of the sixteenth and beginning of the seventeenth century brought some important changes in the organisation of this famous formation though. As Tibor Szalontay pointed out, when the Ottoman Empire was facing prolonged campaigns, especially on two fronts, losses among the experienced elite janissaries were very difficult to replace. While he referred to the period of the second half of the sixteenth century, when the Ottomans faced both Habsburgs in Europe and Persians in Asia, it is worth remembering that Osman II's army fighting at Khotyn had ended a prolonged war against Persia (1603–1618) only a few years earlier. The ranks of janissary units might be filled up with recruits to cover all vacancies, but the quality of these new soldiers was lower than their predecessors and standards of training had begun to slip.[27] Another factor that needs to be taken into consideration was the massive enlargement of the Janissary Corps during the so-called 'Long War' against the Habsburgs (1593–1606). In 1602 Grand Vizier Yemişçi Hasan Pasha commented that 'the greater part of the enemy forces are infantry armed with muskets, while the majority of our forces are horsemen, and we have very few specialists skilled in the musket.'[28] It is therefore not a surprise that there were attempts to correct this disparity and one of the ways to do so was to strengthen the Janissary Corps. While during the early stage of the war there were 12,798 janissaries under arms, by 1609 their numbers had almost tripled to 37,627 men, including both troops in Constantinople and those in provinces, plus an additional 9,406 janissary cadets.[29] Despite the fact that many of the units were taking part in the military operations, gaining some experience, the overall level of quality of the soldiers through the ranks decreased.[30] Janissaries in the 1620s did not possess the same skills as those that had fought and died in previous wars. A Polish spy, witnessing the 'games of Turkish Emperor' in the camp near Adrianople (Edirne) in early 1621, mentioned very poor shooting skills, with soldiers not only unable to hit silver plates set up as targets but even missing the hill on which targets were set up. Gunners were also not high quality, missing their targets as well.[31] Another problem was the growing reluctance of janissaries to take part in military campaigns. They were finding excuses such as that they

Janissary (left) and artilleryman (right). Abraham de Bruyn, 1581 (Rijksmuseum, Amsterdam)

---

27 Tibor Szalontay, *The art of war during the Ottoman-Habsburg Long War (1593-1606) according to narrative sources* (Toronto: University of Toronto, 204), pp.206-207.

28 Sam White, *The Climate of Rebellion in the Early Modern Ottoman Empire* (Cambridge: Cambridge University Press, 2011), p.168.

29 Rhoads Murphey, *Ottoman warfare 1500-1700* (London: UCL Press, 2001), p.45.

30 Gábor Ágoston, *Guns for the Sultan. Military Power and the Weapons Industry in the Ottoman Empire, p.26.*

31 BK333, f.1r.

Solak janissary. *Solaks* were left-handed archers, part of the Sultan's bodyguards. Abraham de Bruyn, 1581 (Rijksmuseum, Amsterdam)

were serving in the garrisons that were too important to be left unmanned or they were 'guarding important places' in Constantinople, giving them a perfect pretext not to be part of the field army.[32] While possibly anecdotal, there were also stories of the janissaries based in provinces, who avoided taking part in the wars; they travelled to Constantinople, officially to take part in the campaign but returned home after a few days, claiming that they were exempt from fighting. If proven, men involved in these practices were struck from the janissary rolls.[33] This problem can clearly be seen in the late summer of 1621 as the units of janissaries were severely understrength when they arrived in Moldavia. Mustafa Naima recorded that, when facing rumours that their units were not even at half-strength, Osman II ordered special muster, checking each *orta* (company) individually and, confirming the rumours to be true, their commanders heard some harsh words from their monarch.[34] More interesting perhaps, Auxent records that during the Khotyn campaign losses amongst the janissaries had to be filled in with men drawn from the ranks of *serhaddkulu*, '4,000 Janissaries were recruited from among the *segbans* and *bostanjis*.'[35] It is possible however, that such reinforcements were not only to cover the losses but also to fill up units understrength because of vacancies and the non-combat drain of manpower during the march to Moldavia.

In September 1622, Prince Krzysztof Zbaraski (1579–1627) was sent as a special Polish envoy to Constantinople, where he was to negotiate the ratification of the Treaty of Khotyn. As it often was with any diplomatic mission, Zbaraski recorded a lot of information about the state of the Ottoman Empire and its military. It is interesting to see what he thought about post-Khotyn Ottomans, especially after the janissary mutiny and death of Osman II. It is worth remembering though, that his opinion may well be biased, as he might have wanted to show that the Turkish army was of a poor quality and unable to start the new war against the Commonwealth. He did mention that there were supposed to be 30,000 janissaries in service, spread out mostly through the European part of the empire, and that they served as garrisons in many castles on the Hungarian border. In Constantinople alone there should have been 20,000 janissaries, but Zbaraski wrote that he did not see many there and concluded that it was his belief that there were no more than 10,000 janissaries in total – the same number that, according to him, accompanied Osman II at Khotyn. He said that they were unimpressive, except for their large and long beards, which made them respected by the locals. The soldiers seemed to have been spoiled and poorly trained, with young recruits having no shooting drills. For their weaponry he described only firearms known in Poland as *janczarki*. They were very long 'so you cannot aim from your face, need to [do it] alongside your arm.' Janissaries use very poor quality black

---

32   Tibor Szalontay, *The art of war during the Ottoman-Habsburg Long War (1593-1606) according to narrative sources*, pp.222-223.
33   Kadir Kazalak, Tufan Gündüz, 'Osman'in Hotin Seferi (1621)', pp.133–134.
34   Mustafa Naima (Naima Efendi), *Dziennik wyprawy chocimskiey*, pp.153-154.
35   Ödön (Edmund) Schütz (ed.), *An Armeno-Kipchak chronicle of the Polish-Turkish wars in 1620–1621*, p.59.

powder, not allowing for the proper individual shooting, although 'in mass they are very dangerous.' The envoy also highlighted a lack of experience among the janissaries' officers, with frequent changes in the post of Janissary Agha affecting this part of the army.[36]

Ottoman armies, thanks to their strong artillery corps, known as *topçu*, relied on locally produced guns – from large siege pieces to smaller ones, used to support the infantry. Turkish armies tended to be accompanied by a strong artillery park, which tended to be well supplied with powder and ball. Some more information about the number of cannon in Osman II's campaign is included in Chapters 5 and 7 below.

The *kapikulu* cavalry was divided into six 'regiments' or 'divisions', each with its unique name and role. The oldest were *silahdaran* – silahdars (weapons bearers), fighting under yellow banners, hence their other name of *sari bayrak*. They were heavy cavalry, well armoured (including horse barding), armed with lances, sabres, estoc swords or broadswords. The most numerous and most important unit was *sipaiyan* – sipahi of the guard, from the colour of their red standards known also as *kirmizi bayrak*. They were the core of the *kapikulu* cavalry, some probably armed with lances and other with spears, the rest of their armament was the usual combination of sabres, swords, maces and bows, with some even using pistols or long firearms. Their preferred armour would have been mail, the same as with the Polish cossack style cavalry, supplemented with a helmet and the Eastern-type *kałkan* round shield. The remaining four regiments were lighter cavalry, probably relying more on bows, javelins and sabres. There were two units of 'paid men' (*ulufeciyan*) of which one was named as 'left wing' (*ulufeciyan-iyesar*) and other 'right wing' (*ulufeciyan-iyemin*). Finally there were two regiments of 'foreigners' (*gureba*) composed of non-Turkish soldiers (i.e. Tatars) that were admitted to the Sultan's service after showing feats of bravery during the campaign. As with *ulufeciyan*, also *gureba* were divided into two wings: *gureba-iyesar* and *gureba-iyemin*.

In 1609 the six regiments of *kapikulu* cavalry had 14,869 men, as follows:[37]

sipahiyan – 7,805
silahdaran – 1,683
ulufeciyan-iyemin – 2,055
ulufeciyan-iyesar – 1,423
gureba-iyemin – 928
gureba-iyesar – 975

Kapikulu cavalryman. From *Icones Habitus Monumenta Turcarum*, between 1586 and 1650. (Jagiellonian Library, Cracow)

---

36   Janusz Wojtasik (ed.), 'Uwagi księcia Krzysztofa Zbaraskiego, posła wielkiego do Turcji z 1622 r. – O Państwie Osmańskim i jego siłach zbrojnych', *Studia i Materiały do Historii Wojskowości*, volume VII, part 1 (Warszawa: Wydawnictwo Ministerstwa Obrony Narodowej, 1961), pp.339–340.

37   Rhoads Murphey, *Ottoman warfare 1500–1700*, p.45.

The regiments were to accompany the Sultan during the war, with silahdars designated as guardians of his tent, while chosen groups of cavalry (probably drawn from amongst *silahdards* and *sipahi*) were the close bodyguard of the monarch. Detachments of *kapikulu* could also be deployed with the field army if the Sultan was absent, in such a situation they were there to protect the Grand Vizier and serve as a reserve. As such it is very difficult to find evidence of them taking part in the battle, although we know that a large contingent accompanied Osman II during the Khotyn campaign.

For the provincial cavalry, it is worthwhile to provide a summary of the way it was raised during the campaigns. In each province local cavalrymen known as *sipahi* received a fief of land. They collected taxes from those living on their land but during wartime they had military obligations to meet, serving on their own or accompanied by a retinue. The size of this latter depended on their estate and its revenue. Provincial *sipahi* were required to supply themselves and their retainers with armour, weapons and horses, although retainers were normally paid by the towns and villages within the fief. The two main types of fiefdoms were called *timar* and *ziamet*. The former were smaller, so *sipahi* known as *timarot* would often serve alone or with just one or two retainers. The latter were much larger, so *zaim,* as such *sipahi* was called, could arrive on campaign with a retinue of between 4 and 19 horsemen. However, using just the number of *ziamet* and *timar*is is not an adequate way to estimate the numbers of the Ottoman provincial cavalry. For the period of nine years before the Khotyn campaign, Rhoads Murphey used the formula of an average three retainers per *ziamet* and one-and-half retainers per *timar*, giving a much higher number than just counting the 'main' provincial cavalrymen. He provides the example of the Erivan campaign of Grand Vezier Kara Mehmed Pasha in 1616. There were 16,846 *timarots* mustered, so with two retainers per *timarot* on average it probably amounted to nearly 50,000 provincial cavalry.[38]

Ottoman *sipahi* from the Turkish embassy entering Prague in 1609. They are armed with bows and sabres, and the last two also have axes. The horseman in the middle, probably of a higher status, wears the pelt of an exotic cat. Samuel Suhuduller/Schuduller, *c.*1609 (National Museum, Prague)

38   Rhoads Murphey, *Ottoman warfare 1500–1700*, pp.59–60.

Prince Krzysztof Zbaraskiin's accounts from 1622 described *sipahi* as well, although he seems to include all types of Ottoman cavalry here: *kapikulu* units which he mentioned as elite, provincial *sipahi* and even light cavalry. He wrote that during the reign of Osman II there were no more than 130,000 of cavalry in total. The envoy praised *kapikulu* horsemen, describing them as the best Ottoman cavalry, 'on beautiful horses, wearing expensive turbans and trousers, [with] feathers and wings [on] both men and horses.' As for the provincial horsemen, Zbaraski wrote that European ones were better and more resilient soldiers than Asian ones. The latter, 'in short silk shirts and light weapons' appeared to have suffered terribly during the Khotyn campaign, when 'cold rain and wind fell on them in October.' According to Zbaraski the Turkish cavalry rarely used armour or mail, since because of their chosen weapons they preferred to fight in loose formation and to skirmish. The primary weapon that he attributed to them was the *dzida*, which from his description seems to be a javelin made from rattan (or 'Indian reed'): light, flexible and fitted with an iron head, perfect for throwing. Zbaraski commented that lances seemed not to be very popular amongst the Ottomans, being used mostly by Albanians. Amongst the ranged weapons were bows, 'rarely used and with not much success,' and long firearms (which he called *rusznica*) used 'maybe by one [man] in a thousand, probably only from our renegades.' His observation about the bow seems to be rather odd, as it was the weapon commonly used by all types of the Ottoman cavalry, so most likely he was trying to sound dismissive about this aspect of the former enemy.[39]

As already mentioned, *serhaddkulu* incorporated in their 'corps' many different types of units, both regular and semi-regular. Many of them were used as garrison forces, especially in the frontier provinces, such as the *besli* cavalry serving for small pay. Other were *gonullu* cavalry, often composed of volunteers serving without pay but also those that decided to serve in this formation as regular soldiers receiving pay. Both those formations mostly served as unarmoured light cavalry, although it is probable that shields were often used by these warriors. Amongst their weaponry were sabres, javelins and bows; firearms could also be used by some units serving on the Hungarian border. There were a fairly low number of deli cavalry, famous 'mad men', usually recruited from Balkan (i.e. Bosnian) lands. They served as shock troops and skirmishers, armed with lances and sabres but not utilising any armour except shields. Deli were distinguished by frequent use of wild animal pelts, feathers or even wings attached to shields; on many illustrations from the period they also have self-inflicted wounds, with knives stuck under their skin, and many scars – both from battles and from self-mutilation. While often catching the imagination of the foreign travellers and artists (not to mention the modern wargamers), due to their small numbers they did not play an important role on the battlefield. Another volunteer formation that in the late sixteenth century became more prominent part of the military establishment were the *sekbans*, known also as *semeni*. These

---

39 Janusz Wojtasik (ed.), 'Uwagi Księcia Krzysztofa Zbaraskiego, posła wielkiego do Turcji z 1622 r. – O Państwie Osmańskim i jego siłach zbrojnych', pp.340–341.

were infantry, usually armed with firearms, that were raised to supplement the janissaries but were often – due to their poor discipline and lack of skill – more of a nuisance than help. As many of their units were raised amongst the Anatolian peasants, once disbanded after the campaign on many occasions they pillaged the local population and even started revolts. Older formations of infantry, known as *azabs* or *azaps*, were by the early seventeenth century relegated to garrison duties and serving as support troops on ships of the Ottoman navy. For this latter role they used a wide range of weapons: from firearms, through bows, polearms, axes and sabres. It is unlikely that they took part in the main fighting against the Commonwealth army at Khotyn in 1621 but, as troops serving on galleys, they faced Cossacks during the naval campaign in the summer of that year. Jakub Sobieski, who took part in both the fighting and in the negotiations at Khotyn, provides us with very interesting observations about provincial troops:[40]

> Their cavalry was a splendid sight, with their clothes, beauty of their steeds, [with] pennants topped with the golden knobs. Their horses, coming from milder climate, tired with the long journey, were not as valiant and robust as it was expected. Asians are not a warlike crowd, only making up numbers [of men]; they draw attention not by their deeds but by their long beards; they are scary only by their shouts not by their bravery, always quick to flee, not used to discomforts, accustomed to riches not to fight; not giving any military advantage [over Poles]. Many of them are bothered with old age, with weak bodies, not able to wield arms or stand in the ranks. But European [provincial] Turkish troops can be easily named the core and the pride of this [military] adventure. Well experienced in the Hungarian wars, in their bodies, spirit and even clothes they are different from the other Turks, keeping trace of the old Christian settlers. There were lancers leading their ranks. We have seen typical weapons used by Turks: bows, curved sabres, crooked iron hooks, *rohatyna* spears, and most often short iron javelins, which they throw at the enemy; except janissaries, other [Turks] rarely use firearms, [also] rarely use armour, so Poles, usually better armed, were able to hurt them a lot [in a fight].

Bow-armed *azab* (or *azap*) infantry, during the time of the Khotyn campaign serving on galleys of Ottoman navy. From *Icones Habitus Monumenta Turcarum*, between 1586 and 1650. (Jagiellonian Library, Cracow)

In the early seventeenth century the Ottoman army, despite its multitude of formations and very 'multi-national' structure, was still a formidable opponent on the battlefield. Strong in numbers, with a core of veteran troops, Turkish soldiers were often stubborn and resilient, eager to fight and on many occasions carried the day due to their religious favour. Their armies were usually well supplied, especially with artillery, firearms, and ammunition. While many of its contingents were fighting far from home and in a very unfamiliar part of the world, at Khotyn they showed bravery and stoically

---

40   Jakub Sobieski, *Pamiętnik wojny chocimskiej xiąg troje*, p.23.

faced adversity and the bad weather and problems with provisions. Ottoman military effort was often thwarted by a lack of talented commanders and the constant bickering between those in command. Even the presence of Sultan Osman II during the campaign did not change it; in fact animosities between different leaders of the army played an important role in the outcome of the campaign. Still, it is not surprising that Jakub Sobieski was left very impressed with the display of the military might and the order that he had seen in the Turkish camp in October 1621. Some of his comments are in stark contrast to the less than orderly behaviour of Ottoman troops mentioned by other diarists, and on many occasions the Turks were surprised by Cossacks night sallies. It is very interesting to see what a Polish officer and politician noted about the enemy:[41]

In the crowd of men, horses and all different cattle, there were many decorated tents, numerous cannon, sight that was pleasing to the eyes and dangerous [at the same time]. The most glorious were large house-like tents of the commanders of troops and provinces, shaped like castles and set up on the spears, some decorated with gilded knobs or with flags of many colours or with an eagle's wing, which for them is the symbol of the excellence; there were also horse tails, ornamented with gilded knobs, at the end of the long canes, fluttering on the wind. We did not see the space that would be empty of men and cattle; in fact in day and night, both public and private enclosures were full of herds, either being moved to or returning from the pastures. At dawn and at dusk an uncountable multitude of people and animals are moving towards Dniester to collect water or to drink, raising such dust that it appears that fog is covering everything. It is important to say, that when taking under consideration discipline of this army, it put to shame Christians that lack it. You can see an order, you can see how severely they punish looting, drunkenness; you will not see here conflicts, quarrels or duels. All the screaming during the combat, completely cease once they are in the camp, so one can have impression that he is in the city of the peaceful inhabitants, not in the military camp. Those pagans are so full of superstitious piety that they spend most of the nights on the prayers, full of wild noises. Their guards are set up in the proper order and to avoid any mishaps, during the night there is a lighted lamp in the front of every larger tent. Christians, especially Wallachians [Moldavians] are fulfilling servant duties; they need to build and protect bridges, and if they failed at their work, if they fall under their burden, they are severely punished. Turks are allowed to kill Christian not only at the battlefield but also those that are peaceful peasants living at [the Ottoman] land.

Tatars

In 1578 Italian soldier Alessandro Guagnini, who in 1571 was ennobled in Poland as Aleksander Gwagnin for his military deeds, published a book *Sarmatiae Europeae Descriptio...*, which in 1611 was translated from Latin

---

41   Jakub Sobieski, *Pamiętnik wojny chocimskiej xiąg troje*, p.63.

to Polish by Marcin Paszkowski and published in Cracow.[42] Amongst many countries and nations described by Gaugnini, there were of course also Tatars. He mentioned their history and all their hordes active in the second part of the sixteenth century, but for us the most interesting is the description of the Tatar warfare. He said that Tatar youths learnt to ride a horse and use a bow from a very young age, riding many miles every day. Their horses are not big and rather ugly but full of stamina and resilient, with each warrior taking two or three horses with him for a raid or campaign. Tatars used a light saddle, 'on which they sit well', with simple tack, they did not have stirrups or whips. As for the weapons used by Tatars 'these are bow and an arrow case full of arrows, *kiścień*,[43] axe and sabre; their arrows are so dipped in poison that it is indeed incredible.' They lacked armour, helmets and shields, which made them vulnerable when fighting in narrow passages or in close combat against experienced soldiers. In battle they would often use ruses, pretending to flee while still shooting at the chasing enemy, which they do with great expertise. Once their opponent is weakened, they will turn back and, still firing many arrows, counter-attack. They normally draw up in curved battle line, which is to help to protect them against the enemy's black powder weapons. When attacking, they send so many arrows 'like a sudden hail, that they can cover with them the nearest clouds.' According to Guagnini, they cannot set up siege operations, as they do not have infantry; if they managed to capture the castle, they will pillage and burn it.[44]

In 1588 Giles Fletcher was sent to Muscovy as an ambassador of Queen Elizabeth I of England. In 1591 he published his observations from the time spent in the country, under the title *Of the Russe common wealth. Or, Maner of gouernement of the Russe emperour, (commonly called the Emperour of Moskouia) with the manners, and fashions of the people of that countrey*. Amongst the many interesting details about Muscovy, there is also information about neighbouring countries, including the Crimean Khanate. Fletcher wrote some interesting details about Tatar warfare, and it is worth giving what he thought about the Khan's forces and their abilities:[45]

Well-armed Tatar, equipped with bow, dagger and mace. Abraham de Bruyn, 1581 (Rijksmuseum, Amsterdam)

Their manner of fight, or ordering of their forces, is much after the *Russe* manner (spoken of before) save that they are all horsemen, and carrie nothing els but a bow, a sheafe of arrowes, and a falcon sword after the *Turkish* fashion. They are very expert horsemen & vse to shoot as readily backward, as forward. Some wil haue a horsmans staffe like to a bore speare, besides their other weapons. The comon souldier hath no other armour then his ordinary apparel, vz: a blacke sheeps skin with the wooll side outward in the day time, & inward in the night time, with a cap of the same. But their *Morseys* or Noblemen imitate the *Turke*

42   Alessandro Gaugnini, *Kronika Sarmacyey Europeyskiey* (Kraków: Drukarnia Mikołaja Loba, 1611).

43   In this context most likely a mace, the word could also be used to describe a *masłak* which was a horse or cow jaw attached to a wooden stick, sometimes the only weapon of a poorer Tatars.

44   Alessandro Gaugnini, *Kronika Sarmacyey Europeyskiey*, book VIII, part II, pp.8–11.

45   Giles Fletcher, *Of the Russe common wealth. Or, Maner of gouernement of the Russe emperour, (commonly called the Emperour of Moskouia) with the manners, and fashions of the people of that countrey* (London: Printed by TD for Thomas Charde, 1591), pp.67-69.

both in apparel, & armour. When they are to passe ouer a riuer with their armie, they tie three or foure horses together, & taking long poles or pieces of wood, bind them fast to the tails of their horse: so sitting on the poles they driue their horse ouer. At handie strokes (when they come to ioyne battaile) they are accounted farre better men then the *Russe* people, fearse by nature, but more hardie & blouddy by continuall practise of warre: as men knowing no artes of peace, nor any ciuill practise.

…

The chiefe bootie the *Tartars* seeke for in all their warres, is to get store of captives, specially yong boyes, and girls, whom they sell to the *Turkes,* or other their neighbors. To this purpose they take with them great baskets made like bakers panniers to carrie them tenderly, and if any of them happen to tyer, or to be sicke on the way, they dash him against the ground, or some tree, and so leaue him dead: The souldiers are not troubled with keeping the captiues, and the other bootie, for hindering the execution of their warres, but they haue certein bands that intend nothing els, appointed of purpose to receiue, and keepe the captiues and the other praye.

According to the previously quoted French engineer Beauplan, Tatars were armed with sabres, bows and an arrow case of 18 to 20 arrows, and a knife. An important part of their equipment was 'five to six fathoms of leather *arkan* [lasso] that they use to bind prisoners'. Only the wealthiest were equipped with mail, with the majority fighting in whatever clothing they had. The Frenchman commented on the way they ride horses as well, admitting that Tatars are 'very agile and brave on their horses' but criticised the way that riders sat on the horse's back, 'with their legs totally crouched and themselves very much leaning', leading to the remark that they looked like a 'monkey on the hound'. He praised the skill of the riders though, mentioning that they are able to jump from one horse to another at full gallop. Beauplan added that, if forced by the enemy, Tatars would often withdraw from melee, 'scattering like flies, everyone running for their lives'. They would continue to shoot from their bows during a retreat though, and after this feigned retreat they would gather together again and return to the attack. Tatars would continue employing such tactics until the enemy was tired and forced to retreat. They also tended to avoid the fight if they did not have a good numerous advantage over their opponents. 'In other situations they just shoot from the distance, without closing too much.'[46] In the right circumstances Tatars could be very dangerous opponents, even when facing Polish hussars. In June 1618, when fighting against a Crimean and Nogay raider force, the 'black' hussar banner of Hetman Stanisław Żółkiewski took heavy losses. The Poles lost seven companions and 34 retainers, in return killing just eight Tatars and capturing three others.[47]

The ruler of the Crimean Khanate was known as Khan, he was also the overall commander of the Tatar military force. Between 1431 and 1781

---

46   *Eryka Lasoty i Wilhelma Beauplana opisy Ukrainy*, pp.128–129, 137.
47   'Dwa Dyaryusze Najazdów Tatarskich na Ruś z r. 1618 i 1624', *Kwartalnik Historyczny*, year VI (Lwów: Towarzystwo Historyczne, 1892), p.95.

Khan of the Crimean Tatars.
Rålambska dräktboken,
mid-seventeenth century
(National Library of Sweden)

the Khanate was ruled by the House of Giray. The first in line of succession and command of the army was known as Kalga-Sultan (*Qalgha Sultan*), usually the Khan's brother. The third most important commander, also often a brother of the ruler, was known as Nurredin Sultan (*nuradyn-sołtan*). Both Kalga and Nurredin Sultans often commanded larger contingents of the Crimean army, either as an independent force or as wings of the main army when the Khan was present. Smaller expeditions or raids would be normally led by *mirza*, from the noble families of the Khanate.

Military forces of the Crimean Khanate could be divided into categories or formations:[48]

The Khan's household cavalry, which in the seventeenth century were called, in Turkish style, *kapikulu*. It was, depending on the period, a corps of between 1,500 and 3,000 well equipped horsemen, mostly armed as horse archers. They accompanied the Khan during the war, serving both as a bodyguard and as elite cavalry

Household infantry, that could be called *tufekci*, janissaries or *segbans*; some of those formations existed at the same time. Some of them were units provided by Ottomans, others were recruited locally on the Crimea but trained by the janissaries. Throughout the sixteenth and seventeenth centuries, there were probably never more than 1,000 in the service at any given time. They were used mostly as garrison troops, although sometimes they could accompany the Khan during the campaign. Such infantry was armed in the same way as the Ottomans, with firearms (usually Turkish-made) and sabres

A small artillery corps, known as *topcu*. As with the infantry, it was mostly used for the garrison duties, responsible for cannon in the Crimean fortresses and outposts. In the seventeenth century it was rarely employed during the campaigns

The Household troops of Tatar nobles, this formation was known as *nöker*, with its soldiers known as *nökerler*. It was composed of volunteers, and was probably the best part of the Tatar cavalry. They might be considered as the regular army, as warfare was their main occupation. Both their equipment and horses were provided by their noble patron, and as such it could be of a better quality than those used by ordinary warriors; it could even include some armour and firearms. They were used as bodyguards of noblebeys or *mirzas* and during raids or campaigns they formed the core of their armed force. Of course, the size of *nöker* varied, depending on the wealth of the noble; some *mirzas* might have just few men, while the Khan's brothers could employ a few hundreds

The levy of the able-bodied population, known as *seferlu*. While in time of need they would compose a large part of the armed force, they would normally be raised on a quota system, i.e., a small number of households would join together to provide horse and equipment for just one *seferlu*. Even in a situation when the Khan with a large part of 'standing' armed forces was leaving the Crimea for a campaign, a big part of *seferlu* had to be left behind, to defend the country.

---

48 Amet-chan A. Szejchumierow, *Armia Chanatu Krymskiego. Organizacja i taktyka (XV-XVIII w.)* (Zabrze-Tarnowskie Góry: Wydawnictwo Inforteditions, 2021), pp.26–99.

Probably a large part of the fighting force would be provided by nobles, gathered from amongst their subjects and vassals, to support *nökerler* and *kapikulu* units

Camp servants, known as *kazinji*. Poorly armed and equipped, they could sometimes be used to support regular troops and *seferlu* during a battle, but their main role was taking care of the horses, gathering and preparing food and keeping an eye on captives during the return from raids.

Nogays did not have kapikulu forces, instead they relied on *nökerler* of their *mirzas'* household, supported by *seferlu* and servants. They were known as very good horsemen, honing their skills in the constant raids and skirmishes. It seems that in the 1620s and 1630s they even used more black powder weapons that their Crimean cousins. They purchased them from Ottomans or in Moldavia and Transylvania, and a further source was battle loot captured from the Polish soldiers, especially during the 'Magnate Wars'.

Based on different primary sources and the most up-to-date modern research[49] we can identify four levels of units' structure:

Smallest section size, that had between five and 10 men. It was known as *dziesiątka* (10 men), *kazan* (meaning cauldron, thus it was group of Tatars that would eat from one cauldron) or *kosz* (literally meaning 'basket' but here used in a sense of group of people)

Boluk, in the case of Tatar infantry this was a unit of 50 men but in the case of cavalry it could means anything from a few dozen men to more than 100. It was roughly the equivalent of a company or banner in other armies

Bayrak, that contains all troops of one clan/family led by the bey. Thus its size could vary, depends on the wealth and power of each bey, having from a few hundred to more than 1,000 warriors

The largest form of the organisation was the regiment, known as an *alay*. While some could be the size of *bayrak*, others could be much larger with a few thousand men. For example all the Khan's household troops that accompanied him during campaign were grouped into a single *alay*. A number of *bayraks* could be also grouped together to act as a wing of the Crimean army or to fulfil a mission as a detached force.

There are also a number of details about the composition of a Tatar raider force in Beauplan's writings, based on his observation during the time in the Polish service. He mentioned a specific order of march, used during attacks on Ukraine and Podolia:[50]

Tatars move in this way: 100 horses as vanguard, which is in fact 300 as each man – as we already said – had with him two spare horses. This vanguard can go as far as between 800 and 1,000 paces ahead, and after them there will be 800 to 1,000 horses, spreading over a good three miles [if] squeezed into four ranks. Usually such ranks spread for more than 10 miles though. For someone who has

---

49 Amet-chan A. Szejchumierow, *Armia Chanatu Krymskiego. Organizacja i Taktyka (XV-XVIII w.)*, pp.83–97.

50 *Eryka Lasoty i Wilhelma Beauplana opisy Ukrainy*, pp.131-132.

Tatar cavalry crossing a river, showing different ways in which mounted troops could cross such obstacles without using bridges. From Luigi Ferdinando Marsigli's *Stato Militare dell'Imperio Ottomanno*, published in 1732 (Author's collection)

not seen it with his own eyes, it is amazing spectacle, as 80,000 Tatars means more than 200,000 horses and even trees in the forest do not grow as close as those horses marching there. And if you see them from the distance, it looks like a huge cloud is rising on the horizon, getting bigger as they approach closer, which strikes fear in even the bravest, not used to seeing such a number of legions [troops] of this kind.

As excellent horsemen, equipped with spare mounts, Tatars were always a very mobile army, often able to avoid fighting if facing an enemy too strong for them. They could often dictate how and when to engage the enemy, as they did during fights against Żółkiewski's expedition in 1620. In the unique conditions of a campaign like that of Khotyn in 1621, Tatar horsemen were not of much use as a part of a direct attack on the Commonwealth's positions. Instead they were ideally suited to cut off the logistic supply lines and in disrupting any potential relief action by raiding Polish territories and terrorising the local population. If not intercepted during the approach before a raid, a Tatar force tended to be the most vulnerable when returning to the Crimea or Budjak with captured prisoners (known as *jasyr*). Often, the main weapon of the Tatars was the psychological effect of their raids. Rumours spread by panicked survivors fleeing from the ravaged regions tended to exaggerate the strength and disposition of the Tatar army, paralysing the defenders and weakening their resolve in the face of the danger. On the other side though, if facing determined and well-led opponents, Tatars could be force to abandon their plans and leave the raiding territory, as they tended to avoid direct combat if possible when the ratio of loss to gains was not favourable.

4

Commanders

Lithuanian Grand Hetman Jan Karol Chodkiewicz
(1570/1571[1] – 24 September 1621)

Jan Karol Chodkiewicz was born into a wealthy Lithuanian magnate family, with his father Jan Hieronimowicz Chodkiewicz serving between 1566 and 1577 as an administrator of Livonia. Jan Karol Chodkiewicz was well-educated, studying in Germany and Italy. He started his military career in 1596, leading a banner of 100 horses of cossack cavalry, fighting against Zaporozhian Cossacks during Nalyvaiko's Uprising. In 1599, he was one of the Polish and Lithuanian nobles supporting Andrew Báthory in his failed attempt to claim the Transylvanian throne. The next year he was again fighting against Michael the Brave, this time under the command of Jan Zamoyski, and playing an important role in the victorious battle of Bucov (Bukowo) on 20 October 1600. In spring 1601 he was sent to Livonia, where he took command of the Polish and Lithuanian forces fighting against the Swedes. It led to a conflict with Lithuanian Grand Hetman Krzysztof Mikołaj 'Thunderbolt' (*Piorun*) Radziwiłł, who previously had some personal rivalry with Chodkiewicz. Despite some animosities, both

Lithuanian Grand Hetman, Jan Karol Chodkiewicz (1570/1571–1621). Portrait by Willem Hondius, 1648 (Muzeum Narodowe, Kraków)

---

1 In older Polish historiography his year of birth was often mistakenly described as 1560 or 1561. For the published research into the correct year, see: Marian Chachaj, 'O dacie urodzenia i o edukacji hetmana Jana Karola Chodkiewicza', *Studia z dziejów Wielkiego Księstwa Litewskiego (XVI-XVIII wieku)*, Sławomir Górzyński, Mirosław Nagielski (ed.) (Warszawa: Wydawnictwo DiG, 2014), pp.49-58.

commanders joined forces and Chodkiewcz, at least for the time being, served under the Hetman's orders.

On 23 June 1601, Radziwiłł's army defeated Carl Carlsson Gyllenhielm at Kokenhausen (Koknese), inflicting severe losses on the Swedish troops. Chodkiewicz led his cavalry regiment with distinction, although after the battle his conflict with the Hetman escalated further, as the former accused him of leading his men to massacre the surrendering Swedish garrison of Kokenhausen. Enraged Chodkiewicz took his men and left the Hetman's camp, for some time fighting as an independent force. He did rejoin the main army when facing a new Swedish counteroffensive and then was later fighting alongside the Polish army of Jan Zamoyski that arrived at Livonia in September. Soon after, Radziwiłł left the theatre of war, while Zamoyski, suffering due to illnesses and weary of campaigning, departed from Livonia in October 1602. Chodkiewcz remained in command, leading the field army as informal Lithuanian Field Hetman. His official nomination was not ratified because of the abrupt end of *Sejm* in winter 1603, so while unofficially holding the office of Hetman, he used the title of 'General Commissioner of the army in Livonia' or just his civil title of *Starosta* of Samogitia (Żmudź). With a small and unpaid army, his soldiers suffering from hunger and desertion, he was facing a very difficult task of confronting much stronger and better prepared Swedish troops. Chodkiewicz, always a supporter of aggressive tactics and strategy, did not sit idle though and managed to successfully besiege, and on 13 April 1603 force the surrender of, the Swedish garrison of Tartu (Dorpat). Being short of money to keep the army in being, he supplemented his soldiers' pay from his own pocket. The rest of the campaign year of 1603 was focused on 'small war', with Lithuanian cavalry harassing Swedes and even burning the suburbs of Tallinn (Reval). Chodkiewicz was not able to start siege operations against Narva, as his army was in such a poor condition. He even thought about resigning from his post, although, probably encouraged by Sigismund III, decided to remain in Livonia. In June he was reinforced by a few banners sent from Poland, allowing him to attempt some limited offensive action against the Swedes. His cavalry pillaged areas around Narva and Tartu but the campaigning of that year ended without any military movement from the Swedish side.

In spring 1604 both sides prepared to renew their operations, and in September the Swedish army led by Arvid Eriksson Stålarm opened the siege of Biały Kamień (Rakvere, Wesenborg) but the initial assaults were repulsed by defenders. Chodkiewicz with 2,000–2,300 soldiers arrived to relieve the city and on 24 September destroyed the Swedish army of between 6,000 and 7,000 men. Chodkiewicz used his hussars to break through the Swedish left flank and scatter their cavalry, the Swedish infantry resisted for a while but was also finally broken and scattered by the combined Lithuanian forces. With the loss of 81 killed and over 100 wounded soldiers, Chodkiewicz's army killed up to 3,000 Swedish soldiers, capturing 21 flags, six cannon and the tabor with much-needed supplies. Chodkiewicz was not able to exploit this victory however, as his unpaid soldiers mutinied and left Livonia. Only a few hundred men remained under his command so again there was no chance for further offensive operations. Later, at the *Sejm* of winter 1605

Chodkiewicz, as a reward for his victories in Livonia, received the office of the Lithuanian Grand Hetman, although it was only officially confirmed at the next *Sejm*, two years later. In spring 1605 he was already back in Livonia, where his troops had to face the Swedes again. The situation was desperate, as the unpaid soldiers were close to mutiny and Chodkiewicz had to again use his own funds to convince them to stay and to fight. In August 1605, the Swedish army under Joachim Frederik von Mansfeld opened the siege of the crucial port of Riga, and a month later it was reinforced by troops led by Karl IX himself. Chodkiewicz managed to gather just over 3,000 Lithuanian and Polish troops, reinforced by a few hundred from Courland. At Kircholm on 27 September 1605, the Lithuanian Hetman won his greatest victory, annihilating the Swedish army of 10,000–12,000 men. With the loss of just 100 killed and 200 wounded, the Commonwealth's troops inflicted huge losses on the Swedes, including between 6,000 and 8,000 killed. The victorious troops captured 60 standards and colours and the entire Swedish camp. While the victory saved Riga from the siege, it did not change the progress of the war. As on many previous occasions, the unpaid troops in Livonia mutinied, organised confederation and left for Lithuania. In autumn 1606 Chodkiewcz and Mansfeld signed a truce, which was expected to last until October 1608.

Polish hussars accompanied by musicians escorting captured Muscovites at Smoleńsk in 1611. The soldiers are armoured, with exotic cat pelts worn over their armour. Nineteenth century copy made from the photographic negative of the original etching by Tomasz Dolabella from 1609 (National Museum, Warsaw. Photo by Tomasz Ratyński)

The Lithuanian Hetman, as a supporter of King Sigismund III, participated in the fighting of the civil war, known as Zebrzydowski's rebellion. It was a movement of a part of the nobility against the King, demanding more rights for Protestants, the expulsion of Jesuits and the abandonment of certain internal policies of the monarch. In July 1607 he was one of the principal commanders of the Royal army at Guzów, where during the short battle they defeated the rebels. The rebellion ended in 1608 with an amnesty for most of its participants, something that Chodkiewicz himself supported.

In Livonia in the spring of 1607, the Swedes tried to recapture some of the main strategic positions, temporarily breaking the truce. They managed to force the fortress of Biały Kamień to surrender but failed to capture Dorpat. Chodkiewicz returned to the Livonian theatre of war in summer 1608, again facing Mansfeld. He was slowly gathering a new army, while the Swedes continued retaking castles and fortresses. At the end of February Chodkiewicz led a swift counteroffensive, recapturing Pernau (Parnawa, currently Pärnu) in a surprise and bloody assault and using an improvised fleet to attack and destroy the Swedish naval squadron as Salis, thus lifting the sea blockade of Riga. In April 1609, despite his army suffering from desertions over the lack of pay, he again defeated Mansfeld near Riga, where the Lithuanians captured 18 standards and colours and accounted for up to 2,000 Swedish dead. Chodkiewicz continue his campaign against the Swedish general near Pernau and at Dünamünde (Dynemunt, currently Daugavgrīva) defeating him in yet another battle, at the River Gawia on 6 October 1609. Both Sweden and the Commonwealth were at that point turning their attention towards Muscovy however; trying to use the opportunities provided by the 'Time of Troubles'. In April 1611. Chodkiewcz signed a nine-month truce with the Swedes, which was later extended on a few occasions, until 1616. After 1611, the Lithuanian Hetman was needed elsewhere, as Sigismund III convinced him to take part in the intervention in Muscovy. In his letter to his wife Zofia, written in July 1611, Chodkiewicz admitted that during the feast with the King he got completely drunk, even breaking a glass over his own head and riding a horse in front of the King. Sigismund assured him of his trust and that he did not listen to rumours spread by Chodkiewicz's enemies. Thus, with tears of joy in his eyes, he agreed to Sigismund's requests. With complete honesty the Hetman admitted to his wife 'I do not remember it all, as I was shamelessly drunk, but the other courtiers told me all of it later.'[2]

In autumn 1611 Hetman Chodkiewicz led a relief force to Moscow, trying to break through to relieve the Polish garrison of the Kremlin. During a fierce battle on 12 October his troops were repulsed by Muscovites, although they managed to get some supplies to the garrison and convinced the soldiers at the Kremlin to continue the fight. He was again at Moscow in the summer of 1612, bringing more supplies and trying to break through to the Kremlin. Between 1 and 3 September, in series of attacks and counter-attacks, Chodkiewicz's troops were defeated by the Muscovites under Dmitry Pozharsky and Kuzma Minin with the loss of some 500 men and forced to retreat. Starving, and no hopes of the arrival of a relief force, the garrison of the Kremlin surrendered on 22 October 1612. Chodkiewicz remained in Muscovy with a small army (the main force had yet again mutinied over the lack of pay) protecting the vital fortress of Smoleńsk, which had been captured in 1611 by King Sigismund's army. Between 1613 and 1615 the Lithuanian Hetman led his soldiers in 'small war', sending raiding forces, including the infamous *lisowczycy*, deep into Muscovite territory. By then he was already struggling with his health, being affected by a number of illnesses as well as mental fatigue. In autumn 1617 Chodkiewicz led the Lithuanian contingent as a part of Royal Prince Władysław's attempt to capture the throne of Moscow. The campaign was unsuccessful however, and harsh disciplinarian Chodkiewicz frequently clashed with young courtiers from Władysław's inner circle. The most famous incident was on 5 July 1618, when the Hetman, in front of the whole army, chastised Marcin Kazanowski

---

2   *Korrespondencye Jana Karola Chodkiewicza* (Warszawa: Drukarnia Jana Jaworskiego, 1875), p.83.

for not following orders regarding the distribution of banners between the regiments. Chodkiewicz, swearing and shouting, threw his mace at the fleeing magnate, hitting him in the back. Such a display of the Hetman's wrath did miracles for the army's discipline, as soldiers quickly took their designated places in the regiments they had been assigned to, unwilling to risk being the next target of the Hetman's displeasure. Royal Prince Władysław had to approach the Lithuanian commander to calm him down, afraid that he would lose Chodkiewicz's support, and knowing that the Hetman's presence was vital for the expedition. Despite reinforcements from a strong contingent of Zaporozhian Cossacks, Władysław and Chodkiewicz were unable to capture Moscow, their night attack of 10/11 October 1618 was repulsed by the defenders. Exhausted and ill, Chodkiewicz was also concerned with the poor health of his wife Zofia and retired to his estates in Lithuania. Nonetheless, when the country needed him after the Moldavian disaster of 1620, he returned to take the field again.

Throughout his life Chodkiewicz suffered from many health issues: gout, kidney stones, sciatica; and he often complained about waves of nausea, and about a cough and chest pains. Chodkiewicz's mental health was deeply affected by losses in his family. In 1613 his beloved son Hieronim, who was only 15 years old, died. In May 1619 Chodkiewicz's wife, Zofia, his close companion and friend, died after a long illness. He took it very hard and became so unwell in mid–1620 that there were concerns that he would soon follow his wife to the grave. He recovered though, and in November 1620 married again, this time with the just 20 years old Anna Alojza Ostrogska (1600–1654). He seems to have been influenced by advice from his brother Aleksander, who used the Hetman's poor mental condition and sheer loneliness, hoping that after the Hetman's death he would become caretaker of his estates. Chodkiewicz did not spend much time with his new wife however, as straight after the wedding he left for Warsaw, to take part in the *Sejm*. He did visit her again in February 1621, when he returned home to resolve some personal issues before leading the Polish-Lithuanian army against the Ottomans. After a month there he said farewell to Anna and travelled to the army, never to see her again. It is worthwhile to note that after the Hetman's death she did not remarry, instead focusing on charity work and her own religious beliefs. In 1648, fleeing mutinous Cossacks, she

Mounted Polish officer accompanied by two haiduks. From the front cover of Bartłomiej Paprocki's *Hetman Hetman Albo Własny Konterfekt Hetmański Skąd sye Siła Woiennych Postępków Każdy Nauczyć Może* (Cracow: 1578). (Jagiellonian Library, Cracow)

took with her the body of her dead husband, Hetman Chodkiewicz, saving it from possible destruction.

Jan Karol Chodkiewicz was one of the most talented and successful commanders of the seventeenth century Polish-Lithuanian Commonwealth. Despite usually leading small, unruly and unpaid armies, on many occasions he managed to win against overwhelming odds. The Hetman was the master of using his cavalry, especially the hussars, in quick and surprising attacks, often able to lure the enemy into an ambush. He also had a flair for unusual tactics, as he showed at Salis by employing an improvised fleet against the Swedes. While he was often in conflict with other magnates, he was valued by King Sigismund III for his military mind, bravery and also his loyalty. Chodkiewicz had a good relationship with his soldiers; they respected him but were also often afraid of him as the Hetman was known as a strict disciplinarian. But he tended to share his men's miseries and hardships during the campaigns. He was often able to raise the morale of his troops with a well prepared speech, encouraging them to face overwhelming odds and then leading them to victory. It is of no surprise that he was able to use those skills in 1621 as well. In 1627 Father Fabian Birkowski, Court Preacher of Royal Prince Władysław Waza, published two funeral eulogies: for Hetman Jan Chodkiewicz and for Jan Wehyer (1580–1626). In the one written for the funeral of Chodkiewicz, there is a very interesting speech that Birkowski claimed to have been said by Chodkiewicz during the early stage of the Battle of Khotyn. As Father Fabian was present in the Polish-Lithuanian camp in 1621, it is possible that at least some of the speech was based on the words of the overall commander of the Commonwealth's army. It is an interesting example of the general trying to raise the morale of his troops, at the same time downplaying the strength of the enemy:[3]

I have high hopes [of victory] as we wage the just war, as it is always when fighting against pagans: in virtue of each one of you and in your brave hands lies the health of our Homeland. You should not be afraid of those tents that Turks set up to show their might and to frighten you; they have tents but there are no men in them. Camels and elephants are of no use on the battlefield, they are just to carry the burden under which they will fall sooner than they will scare you. Those masses [of men] that arrived here from Asia, they are not worth much, are effeminate, spoiled with delicacies, pleasures and silken clothes; once they will hear the sound of Polish trumpets and [once the] whisper of your armour reaches them, they will flee for sure, not able to stand against Sarmatians, real sons of Mars.

---

3   Fabian Birkowski, *Ian Karol Chodkiewicz et Ian Weyher, Wielmożni, Waleczni, Pobożni, Woiewodowie; Pamięcią pogrzebną wspomnieni* (Kraków: Drukarnia Andrzeja Piotrkowczyka, 1627), pp.6-7.

Crown *Regimentarz* Stanisław Lubomirski (1583–1649)

Lubomirski was a wealthy magnate who, from 1620, held the Court office of the Crown Cup Bearer. He was a much better courtier and politician than soldier, although he had seen some military service. Lubomirski took part in the battle of Guzów in 1607, fighting in the ranks of the Royal army against Zebrzydowski's mutineers. He accompanied King Sigismund during the siege of Smoleńsk in 1609 and even gained some experience fighting against Tatars in 1618 and post-Cecora in 1620, when he was preparing a relief force to support Żółkiewski's expedition. In early 1620, in his capacity as a colonel of the district troops from the Cracow Voivodeship, he forced marauding *lisowczycy* to stop their pillaging of the voivodeship and to return to Silesia. As a confidante of the King, he was tasked with organising the preparation of the Polish army for the Khotyn campaign. Some sources claim that he held the rank of *regimentarz* (temporary Hetman), although it seems that in fact he was nominated as an ad hoc Field Hetman.[4] He fought bravely at Khotyn, leading one of the largest regiments in the army and taking the overall command after Chodkiewicz's death. He played a crucial role in encouraging the troops and keeping the army together, he was also in command of the Polish army until Hetman Koniecpolski returned from Turkish captivity in 1623. From time to time he participated in the defence of the border against Tatar raids, when his private troops supported the 'quarter army' in 1626 and 1629. In later years Lubomirski focused on his political career and personal affairs, reaching the prestigious offices of Voivode of Ruthenia (1629–1638) and Voivode of Cracow (from 1638 until his death).

Stanisław Lubomirski (1583–1649), during the campaign of 1621 he served as temporary Crown Field Hetman. Here he can be seen with Turkish envoys. The young Polish knight on his right is sometimes identified as Royal Prince Władysław. Portrait by an unknown artist, after 1621. (Museum of King Jan III's Palace at Wilanów)

---

4   Stanisław Koniecpolski, who held the office at the time, was still in Ottoman captivity.

Portrait of Royal Prince Władysław, in the background is the Battle of Khotyn in 1621. Painting by Pieter Claesz Soutman, between 1624 and 1625 (Wawel Royal Castle, Cracow)

Royal Prince Władysław Zygmunt Waza (1595–1648)

Władysław Zygmunt Waza was the only child of King Sigismund III and Queen Anne of Austria that survived to adulthood. From an early age he was groomed as the heir to the throne, and as a 16-year-old was allowed to take part in the proceedings of the *Sejm*. The King ensured that his son was well educated and by 1612 the Prince already spoke four languages (Polish, Latin, German and Italian). In 1610, after the Polish victory at the battle of Klushino (Kłuszyn) and due to the agreement between Crown Grand Hetman Żółkiewski and the Muscovite Boyars, Władysław was offered the throne of the Tsars. King Sigismund III, for many reasons – including the safety of his heir – did not allow the Prince to travel to Moscow. Despite that, until 1635 Władysław was officially using the title of Grand Duke of Muscovy (*electus magnus dux Moschoviae*). In the campaign of 1617–1618 he accompanied Hetman Żółkiewski during the failed attempt to capture Moscow. In 1621 King Sigismund decided to send Władysław to accompany the army facing the Ottomans. It was also useful that Władysław was liked by the Cossacks and had a good relationship with Konashevych-Sahaidachny, who in 1618 led a strong Cossack contingent supporting the attack on Moscow. Due to illness, either malaria or serious rheumatic pains, the Prince did not take an active part in leading the defence, but his presence helped to keep up the morale of the joint armies and prevented the breakdown of discipline and internal clashes after Chodkiewicz's death. The fact that Władysław took part in the fighting against the Ottomans was exploited by Polish court propaganda, which presented the young Royal Prince as a defender of Christendom. Between 1624 and 1625, under the fake name Snopek/Snopkowski (from Vasa's coat of arms, known as *Snopek*) he took part in a so-called 'grand tour' of Western Europe. Accompanied by small group of courtiers, he visited Emperor Ferdinand II and while in The Netherlands had an opportunity to witness the siege of Breda, spending some time in

Ambrogio Spinola's camp. In Rome, Władysław was greeted with honour by Pope Urban VII. The Prince also travelled to the famous sanctuary of Santa Casa in Loreto, where as part of his pilgrimage he thanked the Blessed Virgin Mary for the victory at Khotyn and for his recovery from his illness. The 'Grand tour' had a huge influence on Władysław, as he had the opportunity to observe Western military, culture, economy and the Royal and Princely Courts – all of those influenced him in later years, when he became King. During the 1625–1629 war against Sweden he was present a few times with his father in Prussia, but played no important military role. He was very upset at the fact and complained about it in letters written to officials such as Lithuanian Field Hetman Krzysztof II Radziwiłł. When King Sigismund III died on 30 April 1632, Władysław was easily able to defeat the other candidates to the Polish throne, and on 8 November was elected King – he was crowned King in Cracow on 6 February 1633. All this took place in the shadow of a new war against Muscovy, which in late 1632 attacked the Commonwealth's border strongholds and besieged the crucial fortress of Smoleńsk. While Krzysztof II Radziwiłł with a small field army was harassing the besieging forces and Crown Grand Hetman Stanisław Koniecpolski protected the Polish borders against Tatars and Turks, newly elected King Władysław IV was at the centre of raising and preparing a strong relief army that he was to lead to Smoleńsk. Based on the experiences of both the 'grand tour' and the war against Sweden, a large part of the Polish-Lithuanian army was to be composed of Western-style troops: infantry, dragoons and reiters, mostly raised within the Commonwealth but trained in the Western way. The relief of Smoleńsk was successful and the Muscovite army was defeated and forced to surrender. The Treaty of Polyanovka was signed on 14 June 1634, with the Commonwealth to receive a war indemnity of 20,000 roubles in gold and Władysław surrendering his claims to Muscovite throne. At the same time Hetman Koniecpolski in the two campaigns of 1633 and of 1634, defeated Turkish and Tatars attacks and prevented a full-scale war with the Ottomans. Władysław was hoping to reclaim his ancestral Swedish Crown, so in 1635 he led a well prepared army to Prussia, where he was trying to pressure the Swedes into acceding to his wishes. England, France, Brandenburg and the United Provinces sent their envoys to take part in the Polish-Swedish negotiations. On 12 September 1635 both sides signed the Treaty of Sztumska Wieś (Stuhmsdorf), agreeing to a truce for 26½ years. The Swedes, heavily engaged in Germany, returned the Prussian territories kept after the 1626–1629 war, and ceded the right to collect valuable tariffs from the Polish Baltic sea-trade but they kept Livonia and Riga. The claim of Władysław to the Swedish throne was not discussed.

For the next 13 years the Commonwealth could enjoy a, very unusual for the seventeenth century, period of near-constant peace, with only two short-lived Cossack mutinies (in 1637 and 1638) and occasional Tatar raids. King Władysław, with the help of Hetman Koniecpolski, played a crucial role in introducing many changes into the Polish and Lithuanian armies, by introducing the division of troops into two contingents known as *autoramenty* (national and foreign), the reform and modernisation of the artillery corps, and changes in the organisation of the 'quarter army' and the Zaporozhian Cossack register. The King had far-reaching plans, planning to invade the Crimea, defeat the Tatars and later even march towards the heart of the Ottoman Empire. His military plans were thwarted by the mass of the nobility, content with the period of peace and unwilling to raise large taxes for royal military adventures. In 1646 Władysław started a large mobilisation, focused on recruiting Western-style troops and negotiating with Zaporozhian Cossacks. *Sejm* strongly opposed those plans however, forcing the King to disband the troops already raised and allowing him to keep only a small Household Guard. The nobles also prevented an increase in the Cossacks' register, which became one of the starting points for the mutiny of 1648. King Władysław, who throughout his life had suffered from many illnesses, died on 20 May 1648. His half-brother Jan II Kazimierz was elected as the new King and had to immediately face a Cossack rebellion, that plunged the country into a new series of military conflicts.

Władysław IV was a very ambiguous monarch. For years he lived in the shadow of his father, he could not be officially treated as heir apparent because of the election system in the Commonwealth. Once he took the throne, in the first few years he achieved a number of military successes, although it is worthwhile to mention that the core of his army was the hardened veterans of Sigismund's wars, which definitely helped to strengthen his forces. Władysław introduced in the 1630s and 1640s many military reforms, that were the basis for the new Polish and Lithuanian armies that were to be fighting in the never-ending conflicts in future decades. He was also a famed patron of the arts and of music, introducing opera to Poland. Many nobles who valued him for the period of prosperity and, after 1635, relatively peaceful time, also liked his easy-going persona that loved hunting and enjoyed love trysts. On the other hand he antagonised many magnates and nobles with his wartime plans and over-reaching dreams of conquest. The fact that he was not willing to resign from the Swedish throne, provided one of the main reasons for the constant conflicts between the Commonwealth and Sweden, it also did not bring him much support within the country. The King always lived on credit, spending huge amounts of money on his court, arts and hobbies such as hunting. To make matters worse, he also indirectly led to the outbreak of the Cossack rebellion of 1648, with some vague promises made by him to the Cossack elders – all in the name of the planned wars against Tatars and the Ottomans.

Władysław was married twice. His first wife was Cecilia Renata of Austria (1611–1644), whom he married in September 1637. They had three children, the oldest – Sigismund Casimir born in 1640 – died when he was seven years old, which was a very painful blow for the King, who had seen in him a potential heir. The second child, Maria Anna Isabella, born in January 1642, died a month later. Cecilia herself died on 24 March 1644, one day after an unnamed daughter, who was stillborn. Władysław's second wife was Marie Louise Gonzaga, known in Poland as Ludwika Maria. She married Władysław by proxy in France in November 1645 and in person, in Warsaw, in March of the following year. It appears that the King married her primarily for her dowry and a large loan (700,000zl) needed for his planned war against the Tatars. Unlike the marriage with Cecilia Renata, the relationship with

Haiduk and Haiduk NCO (10th man) from the scene of the triumph of King Zygmunt III at Smoleńsk in 1612. Tommaso Dolabella and Tomasz Makowski, 1612 (Muzeum Narodowe, Kraków, MNK XV-R-6908)

Ludwika Maria was not successful. Interestingly enough, after Władysław's death, Ludwika Maria married his brother, Jan II Kazimierz and in this marriage she found a much better partner and relationship. During their short marriage, Władysław and Ludwika did not have any children.

Cossack Hetman Petro Konashevych-Sahaidachny
(Piotr Konaszewicz-Sahajdaczny) (1570–1622)

By the time of the Khotyn campaign Konashevych-Sahaidachny was already a very experienced Cossack commander, fighting in their ranks through the first two decades of the seventeenth century. He was active during the Cossack campaign in Muscovy during the 'Time of Troubles'. Between 1614 and 1616 he led many raids against Turkish ports – Trabzon, Sinop (Sinope), the outskirts of Constantinople and Kaffa (captured in 1616). As Cossack Hetman he led 20,000 Zaporozhians in support of Royal Prince Władysław's expedition to Muscovy in 1618, taking part in the unsuccessful assault on Moscow. In late 1619 he led a raid into the Crimea, fighting Tatars at Perekop. Because of the inter-Cossack conflict, as he was seen as a pro-Polish Hetman in 1620 he was removed by the Cossacks from his position and replaced by Jakub Nerodowicz Borodawka. Sahaidachny was still seen as useful however, and was sent as a Cossack envoy to negotiate with Sigismund III. He was later despatched to Khotyn and from there Chodkiewicz sent him to locate the marching Cossack army and to ensure it would reach the Polish-Lithuanian camp. Wounded in a skirmish near Mogilev (Mohylew), he managed to rejoin the Cossack main force and arrive with them on 1 September at the camp at Khotyn. Sahaidachny convinced the Cossacks to mutiny against Borodawka so he could be put in charge of the Zaporozhians, and he led them during the whole siege. In early September he ordered the execution of Borodawka, in this way getting rid of his main rival. The wound he had taken earlier in the war and the hardships of the campaign led to his death few months after the end of the Khotyn War. He died in Kiev on 20 April 1622 and was buried in the monastery of the city.

Cossack Hetman Petro Konashevych-Sahaidachny (Piotr Konaszewicz-Sahajdaczny) (1570–1622). From Kasjan Sakowicz's *Wiersz na Żałosny Pogrzeb Zacnego Rycerza Piotra Konaszewicza Sahajdacznego, hetmana wojsk jego Królewskiej Mości zaporoskich...* A poem read during the Hetman's funeral in Kiev in 1622 and published the same year. (Author's collection)

Stanisław Kobierzycki, often so critical of Cossacks, was full of praise for Konashevych-Sahaidachny and wrote a very interesting character study of the Zaporozhian leader:[5]

It is indeed true that Konashevych was one of the best warriors and it is certain that he should be mentioned amongst the most famous commanders. (…) Like the majority of Cossacks, Konashevych did not have any refinement but stood out for his sharp mind and well thought through judgments, visible every time when he

---

5   Stanisław Kobierzycki, *Historia Władysława, królewicza polskiego i szwedzkiego*, pp.348-349.

had to speak in public. Matters that other [people] know from theory rather than practice, he was able to discuss with some sort of natural sense, offering very good solutions. He was extremely resistant to hardship and very strong. Was generous, despised dangers and death, could practically go without sleep, was mindful of the words he used, he was not a drunkard like the majority of Cossacks, kept strict military discipline and that is why frequently, when there was a [Cossack] mutiny, he was removed from command [by them]. His sea raids brought him lots of fame – he looted and pillaged European and Asian merchant cities, sank many Turkish ships, moving quickly across the Black Sea coast, frightening the Turks. Many time he defeated the Tatars, while his glorious deeds during the Muscovite expedition [of 1618] we described earlier.

Sultan Osman II (1604–1622)

Sultan Osman II (1604–1622) an engraved portrait by Eberhard Kieser, published between 1622 and 1625 (Herzog Anton Ulrich-Museum, E Kieser Verlag AB 3.37)

In 1617, after the death of his father Ahmed I (1590–1617), he was unable to take over the throne as heir apparent. Instead his uncle, known as Mustafa I (1600–1639), was put on the throne by a cabal of Court politicians. Known for his odd behaviour, that earned him the nickname of 'the Mad', Mustafa was quickly dethroned in 1618 and imprisoned in the Old Palace in Constantinople. Osman, well-educated and full of plans for strengthening the power of the Ottoman Empire, became the new the Sultan at the very young age of 14. While heavily influenced by a group of Court politicians, he did not have support from the very important harem faction, which was under the control of Halime Sultan, Mustafa's mother. Osman's reign started from the signing of the Treaty of Serav (26 September 1618), which ended the Ottoman-Persian war fought between 1615 and 1618. With the eastern border of the empire secured at least temporarily, the Sultan turned towards the Polish-Lithuanian Commonwealth. Encouraged by the initial success of 1620 and the death of Hetman Żółkiewski at Cecora, Osman decided to lead the strength of the Ottoman Empire in a new campaign. It is possible that the Sultan was planning to venture further into the Polish interior, once Chodkiewicz's army was defeated. Baki Tezcan theorised, that the further steps of the campaign could lead him to Kamianets-Podilskyi or even as far as towards Cracow. Despite the initial lack of success in 1621, the Sultan made plans for the renewal of hostilities in 1622, although the army opposed such ideas.[6] Lacking victory over the Polish-Lithuanian-Cossack armies, the Sultan decided to focus on the internal situation of the country. Once Osman II was forced to forget about renewal of the operations against the Commonwealth in 1622, he decided to switch his interest to the eastern borders. Officially, he and his Court were to take hajj to Mecca, although

---

6   Baki Tezcan, 'Khotin 1621, or how the Poles changed the course of Ottoman History', *Acta Orientalia Academiae Scentiarum Hungaricae*, volume 62 (2), 2009 (Budapest: Akadémiai Kiadó, 2009), p.191.

there were rumours that he would, in fact, march against the rebels in the Lebanon, maybe would even attempt to provoke the Persians to a renewal of the hostilities between the two countries. Unhappy with the below expected performance of his janissaries during the war, he started to plan to replace the corps, or at least their main position within the army, with Anatolian *sekbans* who were seen as more loyal to the throne. There were even rumours that he wanted to disband the Janissary Corps altogether, shifting the blame for the unsuccessful campaign onto them. The famine that affected even soldiers based in the capital itself, could also play a part in changing of the mood of the army. Scholar Bostanzade Yahya Efendi (d.1639) wrote about the soldiers' displeasure of Osman II's plans. 'What sort of Sultan goes wandering around every part of the country...? And is this any time for a campaign? Or for a hajj? After the Polish campaign, what fool among the soldiers would go now?'[7] A change of mood amongst the soldiers and the weakening of their relationship with the Sultan led to a palace uprising organised by janissaries, Osman was dethroned in May 1622 and imprisoned in Yedikule Fortress. On 20 May he was strangled to death by Kara Davud Pasha, who was awarded with the office of Grand Vizier for this deed. The janissaries delivered Osman's ear to Mustafa I as a sign that the young monarch was indeed dead. Osman II became the first Sultan executed by his own janissaries and his tragic death was the direct consequence of the lack of success during the Khotyn campaign and his attempt to shift the blame of this failure onto his own elite soldiers.

Ottoman Grand Viziers

During whole of 1621 there were a few changes in the office of Grand Vizier, the most important official in the Ottoman Empire. Until March 1621 it was **Güzelce Ali Pasha**, former Kapudan Pasha (Grand Admiral) and Grand Vizier since 1619. A skilled fleet commander, he quickly became part of the Sultan's inner circle, especially thanks to the way he was able to fill Osman II's private treasury and ensure the collection of large funds that were to be used in the upcoming campaign. He strongly influenced the young Sultan, encouraging him to personally lead the army in the offensive war. Güzelce Ali Pasha was most likely also the author of the plan of the attack against the Commonwealth but he did not live to see his ideas put in place. On 9 March he died suddenly from an inflammation of the gallbladder. He was replaced by **Ohrili Hüseyin Pasha**: former steward of the Sultan's palaces, short-time janissary Agha and Beylerbey of Rumelia. He did not have much military experience and was a typical 'yes man', agreeing with Osman II on all counts. At odds with many other officials of the Court and army commanders, he lost his office during Khotyn campaign, after the failure of the general assault on 15 September. After the return from the campaign, Ohrili Hüseyin Pasha was captured and killed by janissaries during their mutiny in May 1622.

---

7   Sam White, *The Climate of Rebellion in the Early Modern Ottoman Empire*, pp.197–198.

The final Grand Vizier during the Khotyn campaign was **Dilaver Pasha**, former Beylerbey of Diyarbakir, who fought against the Persian army in the Yerevan campaign of 1616. It was he that led the negotiations with the Commonwealth's envoys in early 1621 that ended with the signing of the Treaty of Khotyn. He was also captured and killed in May 1622 during the janissaries' revolt against Osman II.

There was one very important absence amongst the Ottoman commanders at Khotyn. **Iskander Pasha**, victorious general from the campaign of 1620, was not able to take part in the new stage of the war. The reason for it was pretty straightforward – he was no longer alive. In some rather suspicious circumstances he was killed in late 1620 or early 1621 by his disgruntled servant. Another rumour was that he was poisoned on the orders of the Grand Vizier, who was probably jealous of the growing fame of the border commander.[8] No matter what really happened, one thing is clear, it was a serious blow for the Ottomans, as they would sorely miss the presence of the talented and energetic Pasha.

Canibek/Janibek Giray, Khan of the Tatar Crimean Khanate (1568–1636)

Tatar, possibly a higher-ranking official of the Crimean Khan's court. *Rålambska dräktboken*, mid-seventeenth century (National Library of Sweden)

Giray in fact reigned twice; the first period was 1610–1623 and the second 1628–1635. Supported by the Ottomans, he took the throne after the death of Selâmet I Giray. He led the Crimeans in the raids against Muscovites during the 'Time of Troubles', and against Poland. On orders from Constantinople, he sent troops to support, with a rather poor result, the Turkish army during the war against Persia in 1616. Living in the constant shadow of the civil war in Crimea, with a candidate to the throne in the person of the exile Shahin Giray always looking for an opportunity to strike, Janibek rarely left his own land, sending his brother or other commanders to lead the raids against the Poles instead. For example, in 1620 it was his brother, Dewlet, that led the Crimean contingent during battle of Cecora. However, in 1621, with Sultan Osman II himself leading the Ottoman army against Khotyn, Janibek decided to take part in the campaign. Nonetheless, he seems to be very reluctant to fight, especially when compared with the much more active Khan Temir of the Budjak Horde. After the change of monarch in Constantinople and the shift in the internal politics, Janibek was replaced on the Crimean throne by Mehmed III Giray but was allowed to settle peacefully in Edirne. The new Khan was very bellicose and ended up in conflicts with practically everyone, especially his Turkish patrons. In 1628 he was removed from the Crimea and Janibek returned to take over as Khan. He held the throne until 1635, when he was again removed by the decision of the Ottoman Sultan Murad IV. He fled the country and finally ended up in exile on Rhodes, where he died in 1636.

---

8   Miron Costin, *Latopis ziemi mołdawskiej i inne utwory historyczne*, p.135.

Khan Temir (?–1637)

Known in Poland as Kantymir Murza or 'Bloody Sword' (*Krwawy Miecz*), he was the bellicose and independent chieftain of the Budjak (Belgorod) Horde of the Nogay Tatars. From the early years of the seventeenth century he was active in leading raids against Podolia and Red Ruthenia (*Ruś Czerwona*) in Poland. He was the main force behind Turkish-Tatar victory at Cecora in 1620. In 1621 he was very active in the operations around Khotyn, where he led his Horde in raids against Poland. As a reward for his service during this war he received the governorship of Silistra Eyalet, although the office was taken from him in July 1623 due to constant raids and lootings committed against the Ottoman orders. After 1623 he again led many raids against Poland although he was defeated by Crown Field Hetman Stanisław Koniecpolski at Martynów on 20 June 1624. In 1626 Khan Temir was again attacking Polish lands, plundering Volhynia and Podolia. From 1628 he was engaged in the civil war in Crimea, fighting against Mehmed III Giray. In 1629 Khan Temir tried another raid against Poland but his forces were defeated by Poles and Zaporozhian Cossacks under the command of Stefan Chmielecki. In 1633, alongside the Turkish army, Khan Temir and the Budjak Horde were defeated by Stanisław Koniecpolski when attempting another invasion of the Commonwealth. From 1635 he was again fighting against the Crimean Tatars, he was defeated in 1637 and fled into exile in Constantinople. There he was strangled in July 1637 on the orders of the Sultan Murad IV.

5

Preparations and Strength of the Armies in 1621

Polish-Lithuanian Commonwealth

The event that would completely change the situation and the Commonwealth's preparation for war post-Cecora was the assassination attempt on King Sigismund III. On 15 November 1620, in front of St John's Cathedral in Warsaw, a noble, Michał Piekarski, attacked the King, hitting him twice with his *nadziak* (horseman's-pick). Sigismund was slightly wounded in the back and face, while the would-be assassin was stopped by Royal Prince Władysław and Crown Court Marshal Łukasz Opaliński from causing further harm. After a short chase, Piekarski was caught and imprisoned in the Royal Castle. Rumours that the King was attacked and killed by Tatar assassins were spreading so quickly, that Sigismund had soon after to show himself to crowds, to assure his subjects that he was alive and well. Piekarski seems to have been suffering from mental illness – assumed to be schizophrenia – which combined with his disgruntled feelings towards Sigismund over lost land holdings led him to an unsuccessful murder attempt. While the King officially announced that he forgave him and he was asking for mercy, the Court did not want to create a precedent. A special dispensation was given for the torture of the captured noble, but unfortunately all documents from this court enquiry were lost during the Second World War. Piekarski was sentenced to a unique type of infamy, losing his rights as both a noble and as a human being; with his family punished as well. The Court even issued a so-called *damniato memoriae*, 'condemnation of the memory', as the nobility wanted to forget about both the attempt and the assassin. On 27 November 1620, in the Warsaw's New Town, Piekarski was tortured and killed during a prolonged, seven hours execution. Both of his hands were cut off, then his body was torn apart by four horses and cut up with an axe by the executioner, after which all the pieces were burnt and the ashes fired out of a cannon. Because of Piekarski's attempt, all nobles were forbidden from carrying popular weapons such as the *nadziak* and the *czekan* in public, with those that were caught carrying them fined an amount of 200zl. When issuing this ban, the *Sejm* made exception for soldiers, as 'we allow them to use *czekan* and other weapons during the war against enemies of the Crown.'[1] One can only imagine the repercussions of the King's death at such a difficult time for the country, luckily he survived and continued to reign until 1632.

In May 1621 Cardinal Ludovico Ludovisi wrote the special instruction to the new Papal Nuncio in Poland, Cosimo de Torres. Amongst the advice and the explanations of the situation and the role of the Polish clergy, he also said that the Commonwealth was preparing for war, 'as there is nothing on this world that is more frightening than the Ottoman might.' As the primary reason for the outbreak of the conflict he pointed to constant Cossack raids in the area of the Black Sea, 'up to the gates of Constantinople.' The Cardinal said that for the last three years Osman II had been preparing for war 'to avenge new harms and old grudges,' and that he would have at his disposal 'countless cavalry, the bravery of the janissaries and the blind obedience of the Muslims, who are willing to give their life in front of their master.' At the same time Ludovisi highlighted his worries about the Polish preparations, as there are 'no impassable mountains, no fortresses that could stop [the Ottomans] for a while, no strong infantry that could face the janissaries, but just open plains and, what was more, no good defensive preparations, no consensus [amongst the Poles] or willingness to obey their commanders.' He placed his hope in God's mercy that He would protect 'His Majesty the King [Sigismund III] and a nation that is mostly Catholic' and in the 'indomitable bravery of Poles, who would rather be cut to pieces than retreat.' Ludovisi advised de Torres to help to support the Poles as much as he could.[2] Those observations were astute as they clearly show the many problems connected with organising the defence of the Commonwealth and in raising an army to fight Osman II.

It is not surprising that as a part of the preparation for open conflict with the Ottomans, the Polish-Lithuanian Commonwealth started to look for support from other countries. Sigismund III was hoping to obtain financial aid, the right of recruitment, and supplies, and so a large number of envoys were despatched on special diplomatic missions. After the defeat at Cecora, Maksymilian Przerębski, castellan of Sieradz, had already been sent to Ferdinand II. He was to congratulate the Emperor for his victory at White Mountain (Biała Góra) and ask for help against the Ottomans.[3] Despite the previous support provided to The Empire by the Poles, such as sending *lisowczycy* to attack Transylvania and allowing for recruitment on Polish soil, the Emperor was not keen to help against Osman II. The Imperial armies were busy fighting in the early stages of what later would be known as the Thirty Years' War, so Ferdinand did not want to risk breaking the truce with the Turks. Therefore he refused to provide financial aid and forbade recruitment of his subjects into the Polish army. In October 1620 he did sent

1   *Volumina Legum,* volume III, p.185.
2   Erazm Rykaczewski (ed.), *Relacye nuncyuszów apostolskich i innych osób o Polsce od roku 1548 do 1690,* volume I, pp.128-129.
3   BK 326, *Acta cancellariatus anni 1616 usque ad 1643 in manuscriptis,* pp.697-705.

his own envoys – Count Michael Adolf von Althan, Bishop of Transylvania István Szentandrássy, and Franz Gansneb Tengnagel – to take part in the Polish Sejm and to discuss further Polish help against the Transylvanians.[4] The Imperial diplomats met with King Sigismund III in a private audience on 17 December 1620 but the Poles were too busy with preparations to defend against Osman II to offer any support to Ferdinand.[5] The Emperor did at least decide to release *lisowczycy* from his service, although it was more likely caused by the troubles they caused by looting the local population during the campaigns against the Protestant armies. Despite the ban on recruitment in Imperial lands, some officers did in fact find a number of volunteers in Silesia, although it was not a practice officially supported by either Imperial or Polish officials. The lack of help from the Imperials was disappointing and limited the range of recruitment of Western-style troops for the Polish armies. In summer 1621, Krzysztof Turczyński, castellan of Nowy Sącz, was sent with a new embassy mission to Emperor Ferdinand II. He was also to take part, in his diplomatic capacity, in the Imperial Diet in Regensburg. Turczyński took with him letters from King Sigismund III to various important officials taking part in the Diet, amongst them Ferdinand of Bavaria, the Prince-Elector Archbishop of Cologne; Johann Schweikard von Cronberg, Prince-Elector Archbishop of Mainz; Johann Gottfried von Aschhausen, Prince-Bishop of Bamberg; the Elector of Saxony Duke Johann Georg I, and the Duke of Bavaria Maximilian I.[6] No help was obtained this way however as the Imperial Diet did not assemble in that year.

The priest and Royal Secretary, Achacy Grochowski was sent to Rome, in the hope that Pope Gregory XV would support the Commonwealth in its fight against the 'enemies of the Cross'. The Holy See, however, was much more engaged in helping Ferdinand II in his fight against Protestants, so provided only scant support to the Poles. The Pope offered 10,000 ducats per month for the period of conflict, but by February 1622 only one monthly payment had been made, although with another 30,000 ducats to be paid soon, and a further 34,000 ducats being delayed, possibly up to April 1622.[7] The diplomatic mission to King Louis XIII, King of France, was half-hearted, with royal courtier Miłoszewski bringing with him a rather generic appeal that if unsupported the Polish-Lithuanian Commonwealth would be defeated by Ottomans, which would allow the Ottomans to attack other Christian monarchs.[8] Probably officials in the Polish court, knowing of

Nadziak-armed hussar, with a leopardskin pelt worn over his armour. From the so-called 'Gołuchów table' (*tablica gołuchowska*), circa 1620 (National Museum in Poznań)

4   *The House of Vasa and the House of Austria. Correspondence from years 1587–1668.* Part I. *The Times of Sigismund III, 1587–1632,* volume I, ed. R. Skowron in collaboration with K. Pawłowski, R. Szmydki, A. Barwicka, M. Conde Pazos, F. Edelmayer, R. González Cuerva, J. Martínez Millán, T. Poznański, M. Rivero(Katowice: Wydawnictwo Uniwersytetu Śląskiego, 2016), no.329, pp.707–708, Emperor Ferdinand II to King Sigismund III, Vienna, 10 October 1620.
5   *The House of Vasa and the House of Austria. Correspondence from the years 1587–1668.* Part I. *The Times of Sigismund III, 1587–1632,* volume I, no.334, pp.714–715, King Sigismund III to Emperor Ferdinand II, Warsaw, [8] January 1621.
6   BK 326, *Acta cancellariatus anni 1616 usque ad 1643 in manuscriptis,* pp.883-891.
7   BK 292, *Panowanie Zygmunta III. Akta od 1613 do 1632 roku,* pp.227-228.
8   BK 326, *Acta cancellariatus anni 1616 usque ad 1643 in manuscriptis,* pp.708-709.

the existing alliance between France and the Ottoman Empire, understood that such an embassy had no chance of succeeding. It is thus no surprise that no support was obtained this way. It also antagonised the Imperials, unhappy with the fact that Poles were looking for help from their old enemies. Royal Secretary and courtier Piotr Żeromski had a rather unusual mission: he was to visit both Archduke Albert in the Habsburg Netherlands and *Stadholder* Maurice of Orange in the United Provinces. On his way from Poland to the Low Countries he was also to visit the Duke of Pomerania, Bogislaw XIV, to advise him of current events.[9] It is possible that Sigismund III was hoping that his officers would be allowed to recruit soldiers in Pomerania. Żeromski was to report the Polish-Ottoman conflict to the City Councils in Hamburg and Lübeck, another two regions known as frequently used recruitment areas.[10] While Żeromski was welcomed in each town and Court he visited during his diplomatic mission, he was unable to ensure that any help would be provided to the Commonwealth in this time of need.

In January 1621 the courtier Jerzy Ossoliński was dispatched to London, to ask King James I[11] for support and troops.[12] He received a very detailed list of instructions from Sigismund III, specifying that the King was asking for 8,000 infantry and that 'let England provide [us] with men experienced in warfare, Scotland gallant and Ireland brave ones'.[13] While Ossoliński was warmly welcomed at the English court, his discussions took a very long time, with James unwilling to provide financial help or engage English diplomacy in the negotiations between the Polish-Lithuanian Commonwealth and the Ottomans. However, he could not object to the numbers of volunteers going to serve against the Turks, and many men were willing to join the Polish army and take part in a war on the Continent. The Polish envoy remarked that it is 'my opinion is that Irish are the best, as they are tough and [are] good Catholics; Scots are also tough but they are really serious heretics. Amongst the English [there are] plenty of Catholics but [they are] soft.'[14] Additionally, there was problem in finding a suitable candidate to command the British contingent. Sir Robert Stuart was Scottish, so there was a good chance that English and Irish soldiers would not follow him. Arthur Aston Senior was English, so there was a concern that the Scots would not be happy with such a commander. Finally Ossoliński decided to nominate Arthur Aston, mostly due to the fact that he was Catholic and that he had previous experience of fighting in Poland and in Muscovy. Unfortunately only a very small part of the recruited contingent arrived in Poland. In mid-September 1621 Aston Junior arrived in Gdańsk with approximately 300 men. Further ships, transporting companies raised in England and Ireland, were stopped by the Danes and never arrived in Poland. Some soldiers decided to return to England and Ireland, others chose to sail to Flanders to fight there. The

---

9   BK 326, *Acta cancellariatus anni 1616 usque ad 1643 in manuscriptis,* pp.709-715, 733-735.

10   BK 326, *Acta cancellariatus anni 1616 usque ad 1643 in manuscriptis,* pp.735-736.

11   Known as James VI in Scotland.

12   BK 326, *Acta cancellariatus anni 1616 usque ad 1643 in manuscriptis,* pp.715-721.

13   *Jerzego Ossolińskiego, kanclerza wielkiego koronnego autobiografia,* p.92.

14   *Jerzego Ossolińskiego, kanclerza wielkiego koronnego autobiografia,* p.141.

company led by Arthur Aston Junior was too late to be sent against the Turks, and it was despatched to Livonia to oppose Gustav II Adolf's army instead. A very interesting list of troops recruited by Ossoliński and Aston is in Appendix IV.

The envoy to the Republic of Venice, Royal Secretary Mikołaj Starzyński, was sent very late, in early September 1621.[15] He was unable to get any support or the promise of a Venetian fleet to engage the Turks. Help was even sought from as far away as Tuscany, with Sigismund III writing to Grand Duke Ferdinando II de Medici asking for support in fighting the Ottomans by using the Tuscan navy for diversionary attacks against Turkish territories.[16] What is really surprising, and for years baffled historians researching the Polish-Ottoman war of 1620–1621, is the fact that no diplomatic mission was sent to two long-term enemies of the Ottomans: Spain and Persia. In the case of the former it was probably expected that the mission to Archduke Albert in The Netherlands and diplomatic help from Rome would be enough. Another possible reason was the lack of any Spanish help during previous conflicts between the Commonwealth and the Ottomans or Muscovites. Spanish involvement in supporting the Austrian Hapsburgs against the revolt in Bohemia was another fact – the financial strain on the Spanish treasury meant that the chances of receiving any money from Madrid were close to nil. As such, Sigismund III decided not to send a separate ambassador to Spain. Instead his envoy in Naples, Adam Mąkowski, was negotiating with Viceroy Antonio de Zapata for the sending of a fleet that would threaten the Turks and convince them to cease hostilities against the Commonwealth. In July 1621 de Zapata even confirmed to Mąkowski that a large allied fleet was getting ready to sail to Constantinople. There were supposed to be 87 ships under the command of the Duke of Savoy: 18 from Naples, 12 from Sicily, 24 from Genoa, 6 from Florence, 5 from Malta, 4 from the Papal navy, 12 from Spain and 6 provided by the Duke of Osuna.[17] Such promised support looked good on paper but it was not fulfilled and did not help the Commonwealth in its struggle against the Ottomans. The lack of contact with Persia could be connected with something as trivial as the dangers and costs involved in the long journey to Isfahan[18]. It could also be that, since Persia signed a truce with the Ottomans in 1618, Shah Abbas I would not be willing to restart hostilities so quickly after the end of the previous conflict. It seems that on both occasions it was really a lost opportunity since support from both Spain and Persia could have been invaluable, especially if the conflict against Osman II had taken longer than it actually did.

There were two ordinary gatherings of the *Sejm*, after the battle of Cecora. The first took part between November and December 1620, while the second was between late August and early September 1621. The former was

---

15   BK 326, *Acta cancellariatus anni 1616 usque ad 1643 in manuscriptis,* pp.721-727.

16   BK 326, *Acta cancellariatus anni 1616 usque ad 1643 in manuscriptis,* pp.741-743.

17   Ryszard Skowron, *Olivares, Wazowie i Bałtyk. Polska w polityce zagranicznej Hiszpanii w latach 1621-1632* (Kraków: Towarzystwo Wydawnicze „Historia Iagellonica", 2002), pp.63-64.

18   Especially as diplomatic envoys tended to pay the majority of the cost of their mission from their own pocket.

Polish haiduks, armed with *rusznica* firearms and sabres. In the centre a servant boy is carrying a large sword belonging to the *rotmistrz* leading the unit. Illustration from the so-called *Sztambuch gdański*, owned by Michael von Heindenreich, dated between 1601 and 1612. (Kórnik Library)

supposed to be longer but 'due to suddenly approaching war with the Turkish Emperor … it was agreed that the normal [time of it] was shorter, to hasten the defensive preparations.'[19] One of the acts of the *Sejm* of 1620 specifically forbade the use of expensive equipment during the upcoming conflict. It stated that none of the soldiers should have gold or silver on their horses' furniture, only iron and leather, under penalty of losing of [the soldier's] pay.[20] Further acts forbade the export of horses and saltpetre, as these were required 'for this time of war against the Turkish Emperor.'[21] Officers were allowed two months to raise their units but once mustered, banners had just two weeks to arrive at the muster place. In order to strengthen discipline, 'a companion that enlists in the service of the Commonwealth should stay with his *rotmistrz*, a retainer with [his] companion and servants with volunteers, as in the orders of the Hetman or *rotmistrz* [and] not to change between banners until this [war] expedition is over.' The breaking of these rules was to be punished with *wytrąbienie* (trumpeting out), which was the disciplinary discharge from the service, and his retinue (*poczet*) would be disbanded without him receiving pay for it.[22] The recruitment and raising of this new army became a huge logistical headache and caused many problems in the country both during and after the campaign.

The mercenary cavalry known as *lisowczycy* that were returning in the early 1621 from Imperial service were also eager to join the Polish army. Some magnates and nobles, such as Prince Jerzy Zasławski, were opposed to the idea; afraid that a long period of staying in Poland would end with these infamous troops being a huge burden on and nuisance to the local population. Zasławski even went so far as to suggest that all units should be disbanded and only the best men be taken into the ranks of the regular army by the royal officers. He had many concerns regarding the soldiery serving

---

19   *Volumina Legum*, volume III, p.176.
20   *Volumina Legum*, volume III, p.177.
21   *Volumina Legum*, volume III, pp.181, 185.
22   *Volumina Legum*, volume III, p.177.

in the returning regiments, stating that 'as they said, there are not many Poles amongst them, as the best died [during the campaign], and [instead] there are many Croats, French and Walloons.' The Prince also added that they may be inefficient as an independent force, since in the Imperial service they relied on cooperation with reiters, while previously they worked with the support of Polish hussars and infantry. The primary concern was the thought of the looting and pillaging however, where the *lisowczycy* might cause more trouble than they were worth.[23] As such the returning regiment of Idzi Kalinowski was disbanded and only some of its soldiers taken into the ranks of the Polish army. At least four units, each of 100 horses, were planned, under the command of Idzi Kalinowski, Mikołaj Moczarski, Marcin Jaskólki and Samuel Mszalski (Miszalski). Jaskólski died in early June and his soldiers were then moved under the command of Kalinowski. In the letter to the companions of this unit, King Sigismund III wrote that 'with all severity' he was ordering them to obey new the *rotmistrz* and immediately follow his orders.[24] It may explain why some of surviving army lists mentioned Kalinowski's banner as 200 horses, double the strength of a normal banner. Those banners of *lisowczycy* that served within the structure of the regular army with the units of Kalinowski and Moczarski being part of Lubomirski's regiment and possibly moving to Opaliński's regiment during the course of the campaign.[25] Another large unit of *lisowczycy*, the regiment led by Colonel Stanisław Rusinowski, came back to Poland in the early summer of 1621 and was taken, complete, into the Polish army. It was composed of at least 12 banners of cavalry and was kept under the command of Rusinowski. As was the custom in this formation, he was also in charge of two banners: the black and the red (probably named after the colour of their standards). We know the names of a further 10 officers of *rotmistrz* rank: Jakuszewski, Stanisław Jędrzejowski, Paweł Mojsławski, Piotrowski, Jędrzej Ryszkowski, Jan Sławecki, Sebastian Stępczyński, Stanisław Stroynowski, Wojciech Sulimirski and Hieronim Swarczewski. It would indicate that there were at least 12 banners in this regiment, although the estimate of its strength – between 1,200 and 5,000 men – indicates that there may have been even more banners.[26] Most researchers tend to agree with a lower estimate of up to 1,400 fighting men, as this is the number given in some primary sources,[27] although another account mentions 'a few thousand men' under the command of Rusinowski.[28] That number could be supplemented by volunteers and armed servants attached to the banners, often confusing eyewitnesses as to the overall strength of the formation.

23   *Listy księcia Jerzego Zbaraskiego, kasztelana krakowskiego, z lat 1621-1631* (Kraków: Nakład Akademii Umiejętności, 1878), pp.24-25.

24   BK 330, *Akta Zygmunta III od roku 1618 do 1621,* no 503, p.811.

25   Emil Kalinowski, 'Z dziejów elearów polskich – Idzi Kalinowski. Część I: od Moskwy do Chocimia' in Zbigniew Hundert, Karol Żojdź, Jan Jerzy Sowa (ed.), *Studia nad staropolską sztuką wojenną,* volume IV (Oświęcim: Wydawnictwo NapoleonV, 2015), pp.65-68.

26   Henryk Wisner, *Lisowczycy* (Warszawa: Dom Wydawniczy Bellona, 2004), p.124,

27   Biblioteka Uniwersytetu Wrocławskiego (BUWr), Oddział Rękopisów, Akc. 1949.439, Steinwehr II F 37 vol. 2, p.102.

28   Stanisław Kobierzycki, *Historia Władysława, królewicza polskiego i szwedzkiego,* p.327.

A plan to raise Polish-Lithuanian troops to fight against the Ottomans in 1621 suggested that the Commonwealth should prepare a regular army of 60,000 horses and portions, not counting Zaporozhian Cossacks. It was to be divided as follows:

15,000 hussars
10,000 reiters
20,000 cossack cavalry
10,000 German (foreign) infantry
5,000 Polish (and Hungarian) infantry

The total pay for such a large army was to be 1,540,000zloty per quarter, 6,160,000zloty per year (in case of a longer campaign). An additional 100,000zloty was to be paid to the Zaporozhian Cossacks for their support in the war. 560,000zloty was planned to be used to prepare the artillery and pay for ammunition and powder for the army for the whole year of service.[29] It was a very ambitious idea that of course, due to many factors – ranging from the available manpower, through equipment to money that could be raised via taxes – was unrealistic. The army actually gathered was much smaller, never reaching the expected numbers, although when researching Polish and Lithuanian troops in the Khotyn campaign, one quickly realises that a large number of the surviving army lists, known as *komput* or registers, makes it very difficult to confirm the correct number of soldiers present under the command of Chodkiewicz. There are at least 16 separate documents of this type, with many differences in names, strength and even formation assignment of individual units.[30] (Some of these are reprinted in Appendix II, to show composition of the regiments and their estimated strengths.) We also need to remember that all such sources provide us with the 'paper strength' of the banners and regiments, which would need to be reduced by removing 'dead pays' at 10 percent, and an unknown number of non-combat losses, such as desertions, men that did not show up for musters, were sick or simply died en route to Khotyn. Additionally some of the units present on some army lists were not actually raised – their officers just taking the advance payment for raising the troops – or were too late to take part in the fighting at Khotyn and instead accompanied King Sigismund III to Lviv. When comparing different primary and secondary sources, taking into consideration the researches of Jan Wimmer, Leszek

Very interesting but slightly confusing 'Tatar' from Abraham Booth's journal. Booth, a Dutchman, drew this figure while observing the Polish army in Prussia in 1627, but there were no units there that could be designated as 'Tatar cavalry'. An unarmoured horseman, armed with a bow could indicate cossack cavalry or *lisowczyk*, but the pair of wings looks more like a parade item. It is possible that this individual belonged to a banner of hussars and was part of a 'showing off' to foreign diplomats during negotiations with the Swedes. Abraham Booth, *Journeal van de Legatie in Jaren 1627 en 1628*, Amsterdam, 1632 (National Archive, Gdańsk)

---

29 Biblioteka Uniwersytetu Wrocławskiego (BUWr), Oddział Rękopisów, Akc. 1949.439, Steinwehr II F 37 vol. 2, f.93v.

30 For the most detailed list, see: Sławomir Augusiewcz, 'Werbunki Hansa Georga von Arnima, Georga Friedricha von Kreytzena i Ernsta Georga von Sparra na kampanię chocimską 1621 roku, *Echa Przeszłości*, XXII/2, 2021 (Olsztyn: Wydawnictwo Uniwersytetu Warmińsko-Mazurskiego w Olsztynie, 2021), pp.87–88.

Podhorodecki, Ryszard Majewski and Wiesław Majewski, a reasonable estimate of the 'paper strength' of the Polish-Lithuanian force at Khotyn is:

Formation	Number of units	Total 'paper strength'
Hussars	53	8,520 horses
Cossack cavalry and *lisowczycy*	66	8,450 horses
Reiters	10	2,160 horses
German infantry	5	6,450 portions
Polish and Hungarian infantry	29	7,600 portions
Total:		33,180 horses and portions

Reducing it by the typical number of 'dead pays' lowers the available strength to around 30,000 men, which then need to be further reduced even further, as previously mentioned, by non-combat factors. While the percentage of these is unknown, researchers tend to agree that they were significant, especially in the light of first-hand accounts mentioning that many units arrived well below their expected strength. It seems that the actual maximum available number of Polish and Lithuanian soldiers available for Chodkiewicz at the start of the siege was around 25,000–26,000 men.

The fact that an army gathered to defend a fortified camp had more than 55 percent of its overall strength in cavalry units may be surprising. However, we need to understand that a pitched battle leading to the destruction of the enemy's manpower was always an important part of the Polish and Lithuanian campaign strategy, which explains such a strong presence of hussars and other mounted troops. It was also Chodkiewicz's favourite and preferred tactic, which he used many times during his campaigns in Livonia against the Swedes. He tried to employ it on a number of occasions during the early stages of the Khotyn campaign, although on at least one occasion his plan was vetoed by the commissioners who did not want to endanger the Polish-Lithuanian army in a risky battle.

Estimates of the overall strength of the Commonwealth's forces deployed during the campaign vary, and are often highly exaggerated. The *Nieuwe Tijdinghen*, a newspaper published in Antwerp by Abraham Verhoeven in the 1620s[31] provides much interesting information received from Poland, usually via Gdańsk, about the campaign and battles against the Turks. The numbers of troops, of both sides, often tend to be on the very high side however. For example, the issue from 10 November 1621 (it is necessary to take into consideration the delay in receiving the information) states 'from Cracow they write that they have information from Wallachia that the two armies, the Grand Turk's with 200,000 soldiers and the King of Poland's with 100,000 soldiers were only a mile apart. The King of Poland himself was in

---

31   *Nieuwe Tijdinghen*, Antwerp, Erfgoedbiblioth. English translation by Paul Alblaster available on https://www.facebook.com/NieuweTijdinghen (last entry 01/06/2023). Translation used with permission (all rights reserved).

Podolia with 18,000 noblemen and 20 big guns.'[32] Another issue, published two days later, gave even higher numbers: 'From Warsaw, 8 October: On 15, 16 and 17 September the Poles gave battle to the Turks and Tatars in Wallachia. The enemy is said to have been over 400,000 strong, with Osman, the emperor of the Turks, personally present. The Poles had about 200,000 men, commanded in person by Vladislaus, son of Sigismund, the present King of Poland.'[33] Sir Thomas Roe in his report from January 1622 wrote that the army defending Khotyn had '40,000 Polacks and Cossacques, and 8,000 High Dutch,' the latter term is used to described German mercenaries. While these number do not sound so inaccurate, Roe then wrote that at the same time 'Prince [Władysław Waza] was encamped at Caminitza and strongly entrenched with 60,000 souldiers' which is of course completely inaccurate.[34] Even when both armies clashed at Khotyn, their estimated strength was still very high. According to Mehmet of Anatolia, a *sipahi* captured during the fighting on 2 September, the Ottomans believed that the allied army had 'all together 100,000 the best Crown [Polish] and Lithuanian men' and that once this force was defeated, they did not expect further resistance.[35]

Units of the Polish and Lithuanian armies were raised for the campaign in a number of ways. Firstly, there were those of 'quarter army' banners that did not take part in the ill-fated Żółkiewski expedition, and also the remnants of the depleted units that could be now brought back to full strength. Newly enlisted units were to be raised, in the same way as normal supplementary troops were created to strengthen the 'quarter army' during time of need. As many officers travelled to the neighbouring countries on a recruiting mission, it is not surprising that Sigismund III sent numerous letters to various monarchs, asking for their permission in raising troops. Amongst these were King Christian IV of Denmark, the Emperor Ferdinand II and Johann Georg I Elector-Duke of Saxony, with the latter being asked to allow Colonel Ernest Denhoff to recruit 3,000 infantry in Saxony.[36] Even Royal Prince Władysław was involved in this correspondence; for example in March 1621 he wrote to Ferdinand II, advising him that Christoph Ernst von

Examples of hussars from the early 1620s. Decoration from Hetman Stanisław Żółkiewski's sarcophagus, c.1621 (National Museum, Cracow)

---

32   *Nieuwe Tijdinghen*, issue 162 (10 November 1621).

33   *Nieuwe Tijdinghen*, issue 164 (12 November 1621).

34   *The Negotiations of Sir Thomas Roe, in his Embassy to the Ottoman Porte, from the year 1621 to 1628* (London: Samuel Richardson, 1740), p.11.

35   *Zherela do istoriï Ukraïny-Rusy*, volume VIII, p.234.

36   BK 326, *Acta cancellariatus anni 1616 usque ad 1643 in manuscriptis*, pp.736-739.

Puchheim had received a commission for the raising of 500 reiters (*equites sclopatarios Germanos*).[37]

Another source of manpower was the district troops, raised by the various provinces. They were created in the same way and with the same structure as other troops, although as their pay was provided by the recruiting province and was often higher than the rates agreed on by the *Sejm*, it could led to internal conflicts within the army. Another problem with troops raised in this way was that each voivodeship could offer to raise certain number of troops but in reality the exact strength of those that were put in service relied on the available money gathered as taxes within the province. An example of this is the Cracow Voivodeship which planned to raise 1,100 hussars, 250 cossack cavalry, 250 dragoons and an unspecified number of infantry plus some artillerymen. However, the actual recruitment numbers were to be assessed by the colonel of district troops, in this case Stanisław Lubomirski, who was to recruit as many soldiers as '[collected] taxes will allow for three quarters of the service'.[38] It seems that the actual size of the contingent from this region was rather different, at around 660 hussars, 625 cossack cavalry and 1,000 Polish infantry.[39] Two voivodeships from Wielkopolska, (Poznań and Kalisz) declared they would raise between 950 and 1,050 horses (hussars, *arkabuzeria* and cossack cavalry) but finally managed to send only 550 horses (450 hussars and 100 cossack cavalry).[40] Smaller contingents of hussars arrived from Bełz, Volhynia and Łęczyca voivodeships, with some *arkabuzeria* from Łęczyca and cossack cavalry from the Kiev voivodeship as well. Most of the district troops served in the regiment of Stanisław Lubomirski, with some banners in the regiments of Piotr Opaliński and Maciej Leśniowski.[41]

Finally, powerful and wealthy magnates, that already had some private troops and units in the 'quarter army' could be asked to participate in the military effort. Some magnates not only took part in the recruiting effort and raised troops, paying for them from their own coffers, but were also present during the campaign, playing important roles in the Polish-Lithuanian army. Chief amongst these were Chodkiewicz and Lubomirski, next to them Jakub Sobieski, Mikołaj Sieniawski, Prokop Sieniawski, Michał Tarnowski, Jan Rozrażewski and Jerzy Czartoryski. Others were not present at Khotyn but sent their troops. Below are further details of the recruiting made by Tomasz Zamoyski but it is also worthwhile to mention magnates such as Prince

37   *The House of Vasa and the House of Austria. Correspondence from years 1587–1668*. Part I. *The Times of Sigismund III, 1587–1632*, volume I, no.343, p.727, Prince Władysław to Emperor Ferdinand II, Warsaw, 6 March 1621.

38   Dariusz Kupisz, *Wojska powiatowe samorządów Małopolski i Rusi Czerwonej w latach 1572-1717* (Lublin: Wydawnictwo Uniwersytetu Marii Curie-Skłodowskiej, 2008), p.96.

39   Dariusz Kupisz, *Wojska powiatowe samorządów Małopolski i Rusi Czerwonej w latach 1572-1717*, pp.236-237.

40   Bartosz Staręgowski, *Formacje zbrojne samorządu szlacheckiego województw poznańskiego i kaliskiego w okresie panowania Jana Kazimierza (1648-1668)* (Warszawa: Wydawnictwo DiG, 2022), pp.39-40, 291.

41   Dariusz Kupisz, *Wojska powiatowe samorządów Małopolski i Rusi Czerwonej w latach 1572-1717*, pp.236-237; Bartosz Staręgowski, *Formacje zbrojne samorządu szlacheckiego województw poznańskiego i kaliskiego w okresie panowania Jana Kazimierza (1648-1668)*, pp.40-41.

Janusz Ostrogski (600 cavalry and infantry), Rafał Leszczyński (an hussar banner), Krzysztof Sapieha (an hussar banner) or Jan Sapieha ('elite banners of infantry').[42] Amongst those that received direct letters from the King asking for recruits, were even representatives of the clergy. The Bishop of Warmia, Szymon Rudnicki, was asked to raise 'with all haste' a few hundred reiters from Pomerania. Sigismund III also requested as many infantry as could be recruited and for them to be despatched to defend Polish borders. Bishop Rudnicki was expected to pay all expenses from his own pocket, for which he was to be reimbursed during the next *Sejm*.[43]

As mentioned above, it is worth looking more closely into the recruitments made by Tomasz Zamoyski as we have access to quite detailed information, giving some ideas about the process of raising such private troops as part of the army.

In January 1621 Zamoyski received recruitment letters for a strong regiment of cavalry: 1,000 hussars and 500 reiters. Zamoyski already had 400 hussars in his service, as a part of his private troops, so he was allowed to include them as a part of the newly created regiment. With regards to the recruiting of reiters, Crown chancellor Andrzej Lipski said in the letter '[they should not be] some poor local ones but [instead] some good foreigners or Walloons, experienced and well equipped.'[44] Zamoyski

Another example of how the Polish and Lithuanian reiters at Khotyn could have been equipped. Mounted arquebusier, with helmet, back and breast plate; armed with arquebus, pistols and sword. Johann Jacobi von Wallhausen, *Ritterknst*, 1616 (Author's collection)

found some captains that were eager to serve under his command and they were sent out 'both to Livonia … and to Silesia, near the Hungarian and German border, where those troops can be raised.'[45] As newly created units could receive better pay, especially in a situation when a magnate or district was willing to pay an additional incentive just to encourage experienced men to serve under their banners, it led to many issues, and added to the chaos of raising the army. Up to 200 hussars serving under Tomasz Zamoyski, hearing about the higher rate of pay in the service of other commanders, left the ranks and switched to the banner of Sieniawski. It was a serious blow to Zamoyski, who had previously received a recruitment letter for 1,000 hussars and the 400 hussars in his service were to be the core of the newly created regiment. Now he had suddenly lost half of his men, making his own recruiting operations even more complicated and difficult.[46] The Magnate complained that it was very difficult to find enough suitable men, especially as they wanted the even higher rate of pay of 50zl. He assured Chancellor Lipski that he would provide at least 600 hussars and 500 reiters. With the

42   Stanisław Kobierzycki, *Historia Władysława, królewicza polskiego i szwedzkiego*, p.331.
43   BK 330, *Akta Zygmunta III od roku 1618 do 1621*, no 224, pp.340–341.
44   Stanisław Żurkowski, *Żywot Tomasza Zamoyskiego*, pp.69–70.
45   Stanisław Żurkowski, *Żywot Tomasza Zamoyskiego*, p 74.
46   Stanisław Żurkowski, *Żywot Tomasza Zamoyskiego*, p.72.

latter he was hoping for better recruiting in Livonia and Silesia, where 300 horses should be found in each of those regions. 'I understand that it will not be an issue with [the additional] 100 horses, even though I do not have a recruitment letter for them.'[47] He appointed two of his trusted followers, the nobles Wojciech Średziński (Średzicki) and Jan Świeżyński (Świdziński), to raise banners of 200 hussars each. Mikołaj Kołaczkowski was sent to Silesia to enlist 400 reiters there. Finally Walenty Kossobucki was sent 'with money and letters' to Livonia, where captains Andrzej (Anzel) Kietlicz and Wilhelm De la Barre were to raise banners of 100 reiters each.[48]

A very important part of the preparation of the Polish army was the creation of the regiment of Royal Prince Władysław. The presence of the King's son was to play an important role in the morale of the troops, despite Władysław's youth and lack of military experience. In order to highlight his position in the army, it was crucial that his regiment – in fact division – was of a considerable size. As such it was to compose almost a third of the entire army, depending on which source you read it was between 8,000 to 12,000 soldiers, with a strong contingent of hussars and three regiments of the German infantry.

The composition of the military contingents under Władysław's command is also very interesting.[49] Firstly he was provided with a very strong contingent of the Household units, both volunteer and paid troops. There was a very large 'court' banner of hussars, with 500 horses and composed of both Sigismund III's and Władysław's courtiers, who volunteered with their retinues. Amongst them were many friends and confidantes of the Royal Prince: Prince Konstanty Wiśniowiecki, Adam Przyjemski, Andrzej Firlej, Stefan Koniecpolski, Zygmunt Tarło and Tomasz Sobieski, all under the command of a survivor of the Cecora campaign, Marcin Kazanowski. Another 'court' banner, raised in the same way as the hussars, was composed of 200 horses of cossack cavalry. The Royal edict issued to the courtiers, asking them to take part in the military expedition in 1621 as a part of these 'court' banners, specified that they should 'prepare well, with good horses and military equipment not of silver but of iron.' It was a clear indication that they should forget about parades and ceremonies and be prepared for war instead.[50] From Sigismund III's Household Guard, there were 600 Royal haiduks under *rotmistrz* Mikołaj Kochanowski. Finally Władysław had his small unit of Scottish and Irish bodyguards, 'veterans that were not only distinguished by their noble birth, excellent armament but also a bravery shaped in many wars.'[51] The next part was the foreign troops raised as part of the regular army. Among these Jan Weyher was in command of the regiment of German infantry and a banner of reiters, Gerhard Denhoff with a regiment of German infantry, Ernest Denhoff with a regiment of German infantry and a banner of reiters, while Almady (another survivor

47 Stanisław Żurkowski, *Żywot Tomasza Zamoyskiego*, pp.73–74.
48 Stanisław Żurkowski, *Żywot Tomasza Zamoyskiego*,p. 81.
49 Stanisław Kobierzycki, *Historia Władysława, królewicza polskiego i szwedzkiego*, pp.322-323.
50 BK 330, *Akta Zygmunta III od roku 1618 do 1621*, no 516, p.830.
51 Stanisław Kobierzycki, *Historia Władysława, królewicza polskiego i szwedzkiego*, p.323.

of the Cecora campaign) and Bartoszewski were each leading a banner of Hungarian haiduks. There were also at least three banners of hussars and one banner of cossack cavalry from amongst the regular units. The final part of Władysław's regiment was composed of the units that were part of the recruitment organised by magnates and usually paid for from their own funds. Amongst these were one or two banners of Tomasz Zamoyski's reiters, a banner of hussars and a banner of cossack cavalry of the Bishop of Kujawy and Pomerania Paweł Wołucki, under command of his brother Filip Wołucki, a banner of hussars, a banner of cossack cavalry and between one and three (the sources differ) banners of Polish infantry sent by Ludwik Aleksander Radziwiłł, and lastly a banner of cossack cavalry under Mikołaj Gniewosz. The soldiers brought with them 16 cannon, comprising the majority of the Polish artillery park during the campaign. They are mentioned as being 'of a large calibre', indicating probably some *kartouwen* (*kartauny*) field pieces.[52] The regiment was to play a crucial role in the defence of the camp in Khotyn, and with its strong infantry contingent it was to defend the centre of the battle line, with the German units manning the main earthwork in front of the camp. According to the Armenian Chronicle of Joannis (Owanis), Royal Prince Władysław's division had 12,000 soldiers, 'fortified by courageous zeal and warrior bravery.' Joannis had a chance to see them with his own eyes when the troops marched through Lviv and he recorded that they were well equipped with weapons and armour, 'dressed in precious garments dyed in spring colours, so everyone [seeing them] was amazed by the great splendour of the warriors,' and their horses had golden ornaments.[53]

The logistics of raising such a large army in a fairly short period of time, combined with the different ways that the men were to be raised and financed, quickly led to organisational chaos and a shortage of both suitable men and war materials. As early as January 1621, Prince Jerzy Zasławski had already complained in his letter to King Sigismund, that there were problems in equipping soldiers with the proper weapons.

Hussar-style nobles from the Court of King Sigismund III, early seventeenth century. All 'wear' animal pelts, *magierka* hats and have a single wing attached to the saddle. From volume IV of *Civitates Orbis Terrarum* by Georg Braun and Franz Hogenberg, published in 1617 (National Library, Warsaw)

He said that there was a lack of *rusznica* calivers, of carbines and of pistols, so even when soldiers wanted to receive them as a part of their normal pay, such weaponry could not be supplied.[54] In June 1621 King Sigismund III wrote to Hetman Chodkiewicz that the soldiers are very unruly, ignoring both resolutions from the *Sejm* and recruitment letters. They set their own rates of pay, which was very problematic. It led to the situation where Sigismund III did not want to allow district soldiers from Volhynia to begin their service with a rate of pay higher than the one agreed by the *Sejm*. He was aware that such demands could start some sort of chain reaction, causing the rest of the army to also ask for higher pay. It would be a huge problem, as the agreed

52 Jakub Sobieski, *Pamiętnik wojny chocimskiej xiąg troje*, pp.17-18.
53 'Istoriya Khotinksoy voyny Ioannesa Kamenetskogo', pp.276-268.
54 *Listy księcia Jerzego Zbaraskiego, kasztelana krakowskiego, z lat 1621-1631*, p.19.

taxes would not allow for the sustained planned recruitments for a half a year of service.[55] Jakub Sobieski complained about the way that recruitment letters were issued without the agreement of Hetman Chodkiewicz. Many officers that were to raise banners of infantry and cossack cavalry were 'of poor quality', indicating issue with a proper cadre after the losses at Cecora. The number and strength of the created units also was not according to Chodkiewicz's plans.[56] At the end of June, Hetman Chodkiewicz was complaining to the King that soldiers were gathering very slowly and that they lacked proper discipline.[57] In late July he wrote to King Sigismund III, advising that many banners were below the required strength, and were also lacking horses and equipment. It appears that prior to musters, some officers were borrowing 'armour, firearms, swords, [even] almost horses and retainers [as well]' from each other to show their units in proper shape. The Lithuanian Hetman was very unhappy with this and stated that 'it would be waste to give money from His Royal Majesty's treasury for such retinues.' It seems that many *rotmistrz*-level officers used allocated advance funds for their private affairs, recruiting companions to their units without an initial pay. According to Chodkiewicz, it explained why many companions took away their retinues and deserted from the ranks of units on the march. The issue was not only with the cavalry however and it seems that the situation in the units of Polish infantry was even worse. Some officers 'gave neither money, nor proper equipment, nor even powder, so barely every tenth soldier has powder and due to hunger they beg, swell and die.' It led to a large number of desertions, as from banner of *rotmistrz* Grajewski that 'on paper' had 400 portions, but had had 70 haiduks desert.[58] In early August 1621 Papal Nuncio Diotallevi was concerned that the Poles had managed to gather barely 30,000 men, who were constantly bickering and arguing with each other, to the point where '30 to 40 men are killed each day'.[59] While information about these self-inflicted losses seems like an exaggeration, it nonetheless supports Chodkiewicz's statements. There are many indications that units arriving at Khotyn were understrength, with a number of companions and their retinues absent at the initial musters or late for the campaign. Worse, there were also cases of desertion during the fighting, with soldiers fleeing from the army. While deserters from the infantry would be more or less untraceable, it was a completely different matter with companions, and it was much easier to track their absence. A document entitled *Delata towarzysztwa co uciekli oprócz co nie stawili pocztów* [A Report of [those] Companions That Fled, Except [those] That did not Show up with Their Retinues] recorded almost 40 companions, mostly from cossack style cavalry but also some from the

55 Hanna Malewska, *Listy staropolskie z epoki Wazów* (Warszawa: Państwowy Instytut Wydawniczy, 1977), p.197.

56 'Jakóba Sobieskiego Dziennik wyprawy chocimskiej', p.109.

57 Biblioteca Apostolica Vaticana (BAV), Barberiniari Latini, vol.6579, f.134r, F. Diotallevi to L. Ludovisi, Warsaw, 2 VIII 1621.

58 Artur Goszczyński, 'Nieszczęścia gorsze od wroga. Głód i niedostatki w armii Rzeczypospolitej podczas kampanii chocimskiej z 1621 r., *Wschodni Rocznik Humanistyczny*, volume XVIII (2021), number 3 (Lublin: Towarzystwo Nauki i Kultury „Libra", 2021), pp.32-33.

59 BAV, Barberiniari Latini, vol. 6579 f.166r, F. Diotallevi to L. Ludovisi, Warsaw, 2 VIII 1621.

hussars and *lisowczycy*. There was even a *rotmistrz* of Polish infantry that disbanded his banner and then deserted.[60] By the end of the campaign, close to 500 companions across the whole army were counted among the deserters, an alarming number considering that when they left the ranks, they tended to take their retinues with them, further weakening the strength of their banners. By 10 September Jakub Sobieski had already noted that the army was suffering due to sickness and because of desertion, 'diminishing every hour'. He added that their horses were starving, that there was no pay for the men and that the important factor was uncertainty of the relief from the siege.[61] When describing the day-by-day activities during September 1621, even more examples of such non-combat losses are recorded.

The main Polish-Lithuanian army fighting at Khotyn was divided into 12 regiments (*pułki*); and this structure is mentioned in practically all surviving army lists. Eleven of them were composed of regular army troops, supplemented by some district and private troops, and the final regiment were *lisowczycy* under Colonel Rusinowski, who acted as a semi-independent force. The nominal commanders of those regiments were as follows:

Royal Prince Władysław Waza
Lithuanian Grand Hetman Jan Karol Chodkiewicz
Crown Field Hetman Stanisław Lubomirski
Maciej Leśniowski, Vice-Chamberlain of Bełz
Jan Mikołaj Boratyński, *starosta* of Lipnik
Mikołaj Zenowicz, castellan of Połock
Aleksander Sapieha, *starosta* of Orsza
Piotr Opaliński, castellan of Poznań
Stefan Potocki, *starosta* of Kamieniec
Mikołaj Kossakowski, *starosta* of Wizna
Mikołaj Sieniawski (Crown *Krajczy*[62]) and Prokop Sieniawski
Stanisław Rusinowski (regiment of *lisowczycy*)

The structure of these regiments was not in any way uniform. The majority of them, nine, were a mix of units of both cavalry and infantry, with only three, including *lisowczycy*, as cavalry only. More than a half of the entire army was contained within three main regiments: Royal Prince Władysław's, Chodkiewicz's and Lubomirski's – they were also the focus for the crucial point of the defence. German infantry was present only in Władysław's and Lubomirski's regiments, with some additional units that arrived later either operating outside of the regimental structure or being attached ad hoc under the command of a colonel. It is important to explain the rather confusing issue about regiments serving as a part of other regiments. As mentioned

---

60 Zakład Narodowy im. Ossolińskich, unit 4, section 1, manuscript 198, *Miscellanea historyczne z lat 1606-1676*, p.169.

61 'Jakóba Sobieskiego Dziennik wyprawy chocimskiej', p.140.

62 *Krajczy* means 'carver' and in Medieval times he was the court official responsible for carving the royal meals and passing them to the monarch. By the seventeenth century the role was defunct and had become just an honorary title.

above, the Polish word for cavalry regiment was *pułk* (plural: *pułki*) while larger units of reiters and foreign infantry were also called *regiment* (plural: *regimenty*). Because national units, especially hussars, were seen as more important in the hierarchy of the army, foreign regiments could be included as a part of a Polish *pułk*, on some occasions making it almost division-size. We can especially see that with Royal Prince Władysław's regiment, that as well as a large number of cavalry banners also had two or three (depending on the source) regiments of foreign infantry.

Due to the absence of the Polish Grand and Field Hetman – with Żółkiewski killed and Koniecpolski captured – it was decided that Lithuanian Grand Hetman Jan Karol Chodkiewicz would command the Polish-Lithuanian army. He was to act as Crown Grand Hetman as well, which was very unusual but was fully understood and accepted in such difficult circumstances. Stanisław Lubomirski was nominated as a temporary Crown Field Hetman. Lithuanian Field Hetman Krzysztof II Radziwiłł did not take part in Khotyn campaign, and he remained to command the defence of Livonia against a possible Swedish attack. Due to the severity of the situation and the unusual chain of command of the Polish-Lithuanian forces, it was decided that Chodkiewicz would be accompanied by a war council composed of 11 commissioners chosen from amongst *Sejm* envoys. They were: Mikołaj Sieniawski, Crown *krajczy*; Maciej Leśniowski, Chamberlain of Bełz; Marek Stadnicki, vice-Cup-Bearer of Cracow; Jakub Sobieski, *wojewodzic*[63] of Lublin; Michał Tarnowski; Jan Działyński, *starosta* of Pokrzywnica; Paweł Działyński, *starosta* of Bratian, Mikołaj Kossawski, *starosta* of Wizna; Jan Pukszta, Standard-Bearer of Wołkowysk; Baltazar Strawiński, *starosta* of Mozyrz; Daniel Narownik.[64] Their primary role was to assist him in the decision making (from organising to deploying troops), controlling military spending and during the eventual peace negotiations. They had the main voice in deciding whether the Ottomans could be engaged in open battle, a situation which was not much to Chodkiewicz's liking, as he was rather used to independent command. He seems to have found common ground with them at some point however, as the Hetman realised that he could rely on them for many administrative (and rather burdensome) tasks; especially when facing unpaid troops. It is worthwhile mentioning that Sieniawski and Kossakowski were in charge of their own regiments, clearly showing that not all commissioners were just civilians sent to control the actions of the Lithuanian commander.

Raising a large army and the relocation of numerous units through different areas of the country was a severe burden on the local population. As always in such situations, the soldiers committed many crimes – from stealing food to assaulting locals. Przemysław Gawron in his excellent study[65]

---

63   Son of voivode, a word used as an official office name during the seventeenth century.

64   *Volumina Legum, volume III*, p.176; 'Stanisława Lubomirskiego Dziennik wyprawy chocimskiej', p.109.

65   Przemysław Gawron, 'Dyscyplina w szeregach armii polsko-litewskiej na terenie Małopolski i Rusi Czerwonej w czasie przygotowań do wyprawy chocimskiej w 1621 r., *Czasopismo Prawno-Historyczne*, volume LXXI, 2019, part 2 (Poznań: Instytut Historii Polskiej Akademii Nauk and Wydział Prawa i Administracji Uniwersytetu im. Adama Mickiewicza w Poznaniu, 2019),

analysed the complaints regarding such activities brought to the territorial courts in the regions of Małopolska and Ruś Czerwoną (Red Ruthenia). These areas included the main routes of the marching armies when they travelled to the camp in Gliniany and to Kamianets-Podilskyi. Amongst the towns in the area are important locations such as Lublin and Lviv, operating as sorts of logistics hubs, often used to purchase equipment, horses, clothing and supplies. Gawron found 190 cases registered in the courts, with complaints mentioning 78 different army units – from banners of hussars to foreign infantry regiments. Altogether there were 8 main towns and 76 cities, villages and estates that were mentioned in various court cases.

Polish haiduks from the period of the Khotyn war. Officer with mace and *haiduk* armed with *rusznica*, both in distinctive *magierka* caps. From Jakub Sobieski's *Commentariorum Chotinensis Belli Libri Tres*, published in 1646 (National Library, Warsaw)

The most common cases were those where soldiers took provisions without paying – everything from grain, flour, butter, and eggs to livestock such as pigs, cattle, rams, sheep and poultry. There were even cases where soldiers drained the water from ponds to take all fish that could be found there. The marching troops took axes, spades, blacksmiths' tools, weapons (especially sabres and firearms), clothing and shoes. To carry away the loot, they also often confiscated horses and carts. Locals that were trying to defend their possessions were beaten up, some even tortured to reveal where they may have hidden their valuables. There were also a few cases of rape, murder and kidnapping for ransom. The soldiers did not focus only on the local population, there were incidents when men from different units clashed with each other about quarters or loot. In some situations the locals attacked small groups of soldiers, e.g. a single retinue travelling alone without the rest of its banner. Amongst the recorded complaints there were also cases where deserters fleeing from their unit stole the possessions of companions, usually their horses and weapons.

The cases analysed by Przemysław Gawron are just a part of the issue that in fact affected a much wider area and population. Firstly, he investigated only two regions of Poland, and secondly even in those regions not all cases were reported and registered in the courts. Many units were marching from as far away as Prussia, meaning they had a long journey before them and they had to take care of themselves. It is worthwhile to point out, that – as on many occasions both before and after the Khotyn war – Polish and Lithuanian soldiers were left to their own devices to acquire supplies during the march to the army camp. There was no organised logistic schedule and no designated army quartermasters, who could coordinate supply for the troops. The troops had to find their own way to purchase horses, weapons, equipment and food, as there were no pre-setup warehouses or storage area for the army's needs. Thus it was inevitable that marching troops would be such a big menace to the local population wherever they went, often behaving like an occupying army, without any concern for the locals. King Sigismund III bitterly complained to Jan Weyher about his foreign troops marching

---

pp.89-111. All information in this part of the book, unless where noted, is based on this article.

to Warsaw from Prussia: 'Wherever they went, they behave towards our subjects like they are on the enemy's land, [and] they did not leave anything remaining in the houses, throwing themselves into rooms, chests and other hiding places, taking by force everything they found and they were let loose so much that even priests could not remain in their vicarages and churches were not safe [from them].'[66] There were numerous complaints about the troops of Hans Georg von Arnim, that were a trouble to the local population in Prussia, as they were confiscating food, robbing people on the streets and even attacking churches.[67] Part of the problem, as often with the case of the Polish-Lithuanian Commonwealth's military efforts, was the lack of available funds. Poor coordination in gathering taxes meant that there was never enough cash to make it available for troops and their needs.

Despite all the troubles and the numerous issues, Polish troops were slowly gathering under the command of Lubomirski, while Chodkiewicz was marching to meet them with the Lithuanian contingent.

Zaporozhian Cossacks

The support of the Zaporozhian Cossacks in a war against Osman II's forces was crucial and Sigismund III spared no effort to ensure that they would arrive in Moldavia to help Chodkiewicz. There were some worries, that religious factors might play a part in the absence of the Cossacks. Since 1596, after the Union of Brześć, some of the Orthodox population of the Commonwealth, as the Greek Catholic Church was known, became a part of the Roman Catholic Church. The Cossacks remained part of the Orthodox Church and still saw the Patriarch of Constantinople as their spiritual leader. Konashevych-Sahaidachny was a strong supporter of allegiance to the Eastern Orthodox Church and in August 1620 he managed to convince Patriarch Theophanes III to re-establish Orthodox archeparchy in the Commonwealth, with Job Boretsky (Borecki) as the Metropolitan of Kiev, Galicia and all Ruthenia. From the point of view of the Polish court, it was an illegal move, as there was already a Greek Catholic Metropolitan of Kiev, Józef Welamin Rucki. Sigismund III wrote to Theophanes III, asking him to convince the Cossacks to support the military effort against the Ottomans. The Patriarch agreed with the Polish King, and wrote, in a special proclamation to the Zaporozhians, that 'your homeland is being threatened by the worst enemy of the whole Christendom, [a vision] of the yoke of the Turkish slavery.' Lack of information about the Cossacks' progress and, more importantly, their suspected unwillingness to take part in the campaign, was worrying to King Sigismund III. In June 1621 he wrote about his concerns to Hetman Chodkiewicz, mentioning that he doubted that the Cossacks would listen to the requests he had already sent them. As he did not have anyone suitable to

---

66 Jerzy Pietrzak, *Po Cecorze i podczas wojny chocimskiej. Sejmy z lat 1620-1621* (Wrocław: Wydawnictwo Uniwersytetu Wrocławskiego, 1983) p.119.
67 Józef Tretiak, *Historya wojny chocimskiej 1621 r.*, pp.74-75.

send as a messenger to the Cossacks, he asked Chodkiewicz to send someone trustworthy, who could instil discipline, arrange the raising of units, provide them with flags and money and finally encourage them to march wherever the Hetman ordered them to. The King was also concerned about the current leadership of the Cossack troops, 'as long as Borodawka is their elder, the Commonwealth will not have any service from them.' Therefore he suggested that Borodowka be replaced by Sahaidachny or another known supporter of Poland.[68] On 15 June 1621, a letter from Theophanes was read on the great gathering of Cossacks near Kiev and despite initial Polish concerns, they did show a willingness to take part in the war. Their primary condition however was that Sigismund had to accept the new hierarchy of the Orthodox Church. Cossack envoys, led by Konashevych-Sahaidachny, travelled to Warsaw, to negotiate with the King. Two months of talks ended up with a compromise: while Sigismund III did not officially approve the new Orthodox Church, he did agree to its continued existence and cancelled his proclamation that would have named all new Orthodox bishops as enemies of the Commonwealth. In the meantime, the Cossack army gathered in Ukraine and started to march towards the Dniester.

Depending on the primary source or the work of the modern researcher, there is a wide range in the overall number of Zaporozhian Cossacks given as taking part in the campaign of 1621, usually with figures between 20,000 and 45,000 armed men. In June, the Cossack army assembled near Kaharlyk and was supposed to number 50,600 able-bodied men.[69] However, not all of them would end up fighting at Khotyn: some took part in sea raids against the Ottomans, while many died during the march through Moldavia. Additionally some were more than likely 'dead pays', added to the register but not actually representing real men. Two more detailed army lists, where the names of colonels and the, at least theoretical, strength of their regiments is reprinted in Appendix III. One list has 44,100 men, while the other has 38,820 men.

The Armenian, Auxent wrote about a strong force of 45,000 men, although he added that the advance guard of 4,000 Cossacks was surprised on its way to Khotyn and massacred, which would indicate that his overall strength of the marching army would be 49,000 soldiers.[70] 40,000 Cossacks is mentioned by Joannis, another Armenian author of the chronicle from the period.[71] From the Polish diarists, very interesting and confusing at the same time is a note from Jan Czapliński who wrote about the arrival of 40,000 mounted and 30,000 infantry Cossacks. The problem seems to be due to the error of the scribe who copied the letter and changed the original number 'one' into a 'four'. Therefore, the more plausible figure is 10,000 mounted and 30,000 foot Cossacks.[72] Albrycht Stanisław Radziwiłł,

Zaporozhian Cossack armed with *rusznica* and sabre. From Beauplan's map of Ukraine (Author's collection)

---

68 Hanna Malewska, *Listy staropolskie z epoki Wazów*, p.198.
69 Petro Sas, *The Khotyn War of 1621*, p.118.
70 Ödön (Edmund) Schütz (ed.), *An Armeno-Kipchakc Chronicle of the Polish-Turkish Wars in 1620–1621*, p.53.
71 'Istoriya Khotinksoy voyny Ioannesa Kamenetskogo', p.268.
72 'Kopia listu od pana [Jana] Czaplińskiego do Jerzego Radzimińskiego 1 Octobris z obozu pisanego', p.207.

who had access to good information from the Polish court, also stated that there were 40,000 Cossacks at Khotyn.[73] According to the author of *News from Wallachia,* at the end of the campaign there were still 40,000 Cossacks in the camp.[74] Two anonymous diaries, probably written by soldiers present in the camp, mention 40,000 Cossacks that arrived in the army camp.[75] Numbers for Cossacks are also often mentioned in the registers of the overall army strength. In those that are given in Appendix II, are figures of 21,260 in one, while in another the author mentions 'at least 30,000'. The figure of 'about 30,000' is also repeated in at least two further documents and it can be also be found in Piasecki's chronicle.[76] Miron Costin provides a rather low estimate, with a vanguard of 1,000 men followed by the main army of 20,000 men.[77] Taking into consideration so many different sources, especially those written by soldiers present in the camp, I think that we can safely assume that 30,000 Cossacks were present at Khotyn as a minimum and perhaps a maximum of 40,000 seems plausible.

The Ottoman Empire and The Tatars

Once the war against the Commonwealth was decided, the Ottoman war machine started to slowly gather speed. On 1 March 1621 orders were sent out to all provinces: troops from Asia were to join the Sultan and his guard near Constantinople, while European troops were to join during the march to the Polish border. Some of the latter, supported by Moldavians, were to act as a vanguard, protecting the main army during its arrival in Moldavia. *Kapikulu* troops, both cavalry and janissaries, were gathered at Davutpaşa Sahrası (Davutpaşa Field) near Constantinople, where they were to be joined by the contingents from the provinces of the Empire. The Sultan's orders sent to Anatolia and Rumelia stated that war preparations needed to be started immediately, highlighting the fact that Osman II would supervise the concentration of the troops and lead the army himself. His orders were to be obeyed without hesitation and any provincial *sipahi* that would not attend would be punished and stripped of their land holdings.[78] Food, powder and weapons were being collected, while siege artillery, equipment and more provisions were transported from Constantinople in galleys. Part of Osman II's preparation for the war against the Commonwealth was to collect funds for the prolonged campaign. According to Rhoads Murphey, the war effort was one-third financed from the Sultan's own Inner Treasury, with the rest provided in gold from Egypt's treasury (arrears payments from

---

73 Albrycht Stanisław Radziwiłł, *Rys panowania Zygmunta,* p.73.

74 *Zeitung aus der Walachei,* p.19. 'Relacya prawdziwa o expediciey przeciwko Turkom, na którey sam cesarz turecki był Ao 1621, Woyska koronnego y W. X. Litte pod regimentem Pana Karola Chodkiewicza W. X. Litte które pod Chocimiem leżało', p.219.

75 'Opisanie wyprawy chocimskiej', p.211.

76 *Kronika Pawła Piaseckiego biskupa przemyślskiego,* p.292.

77 Miron Costin, *Latopis ziemi mołdawskiej i inne utwory historyczne,* p.138.

78 Kadir Kazalak, Tufan Gündüz, 'Osman'in Hotin Seferi (1621)', p.132.

1617 and 1619) and from Yemen's treasury. In total, Osman II had amassed the equivalent of at least 150,000,000 akçes. It seems that a large part of it was used towards preparing troops, purchasing equipment and giving out advance pay and cash advances at the beginning of the campaign.[79] A large amount of cash was to be carried on camels travelling with the army to Khotyn and on many occasions the Sultan paid special bonus money to his soldiers for brave deeds on the battlefield.

A Polish spy present in the Ottoman capital in the spring of 1621 provided a very detailed description of the Sultan's court, guard units and other entourage leaving the City and marching towards Adrianople (Edirne), where *kapikulu* and Asian contingents were to gather for the expedition against the Commonwealth. He also noted many Asian provincial troops marching through the capital in order to reach Adrianople. Some of these Asian contingents had to travel vast distances to arrive at the army's assembly location. Those from Damascus had 1,250km to travel, those from Tripoli in Lebanon 1175km and those from Sivas almost 700km. On the way the contingents struggled with the weather, from the early spring frosts to the torrential rains. Therefore, once they arrived near Constantinople they were forced to rest for a few days, before they were able to continue with the journey to Adrianople.[80] Despite some exaggerations, typical in such reports, it may be useful to look into the report of a Polish spy, as it provides a great deal of interesting information about the assembling army.[81] Between 26 and 28 April a large artillery park was transported towards the camp. There were 150 field cannon, most of them transported by two horses, some by three. Other heavier pieces were 'transported by sea and land.' From 29 April the Sultan and his main guards started their march from Constantinople, initially moving to the camp outside of the city, where they stayed for nine days. Osman II was accompanied by janissaries, who were marching 'without ranks, so it could look like they were countless of them.' They had with them four flags 'brimmed with red cloth' and three tugs (*buńczuk*). Following from the number of those battle ensigns, there should have been 20,000 men under banners and 15,000 under tugs but the spy counted no more than 12,000. Some of them were carrying 'huge sword, maces, ostrich feathers, armour.' His information about the 'paper strength' of the *kapikuli* cavalry seems to be exaggerated, as he mentioned that under six banners and four tugs there should have been 32,000 of them but only 10,000 were present. There were also different units of cavalry, including a small group of 60 horsemen under a green banner and a larger one of 400 without any banners. The armourers, known as *cebeci*, marched under three tugs, while the *topçu* artillerymen were grouped in units under two tugs. The Sultan was preceded by pilgrims

Three Turkish officers. Johan Wilhelm Bauer, 1641. (Herzog Anton Ulrich-Museum, J W Baur AB 3.55)

---

79   Rhoads Murphey, *Ottoman warfare 1500-1700*, pp.59-60.
80   Leszek Podhorodecki, Noj Raszba, *Wojna chocimska 1621 roku* (Kraków: Wydawnictwo Literackie Kraków, 1979), p.72.
81   BK 333, ff.2r–4v.

and dervishes, some of them were shouting, while others were singing and playing on instruments. After him, marched servants with packs of hunting dogs, including scent hounds and sight hounds. After them, a group of *peyks* armed with bows and arrows; they were leading 13 horses 'with beautiful and expensive ornaments'. Osman II was wearing a *ferezja* garment, made of red satin, with a lining of ermine. Over it, he had a red satin, striped dolman. On his turban he had two large feather crests; one was 'two fingers wide, with a feather [falling] down on his forehead', while the other was 'a hand wide, attached with expensive clasp'. The Sultan was riding a dun (yellow) horse. He was followed by *kapikulu sipahi* under 10 banners, however, no number of soldiers is given. They were escorting the Sultan's two large flags. One was white, made from so-called *altembas*: heavy silk with golden thread. The witness noted that there many 'superstitions or mysterious [objects]' attached to the standard pole and sewn into the fabric of the flag. He did not elaborate what they were, but they were probably prayer scrolls and charms. The second flag was green and made from silk. The *sipahi* were accompanied by 'all kind of music, trumpets, drums, etc.' There were also two *deli* cavalrymen, 'dressed in bear's pelts' who were present to improve morale, 'shouting and raising the hearts of [the Ottoman] knights.' After the cavalry, the spy described and counted the Sultan's court, which was led by two mounted servants, dressed in the Circassian way: one was carrying a sabre, the other a very expensive *sahajdak* (bow and arrow case), adorned with precious gems. The Court numbered 4,000 men, accompanied by 24 carts, pulled by four grey horses each. Then one banner of 200 janissaries, travelling mounted, 'with lances and sabres in the style of Hungarian hussars.' After them, came four elephants carrying beautiful tents, 'of which each could allow 15 men [inside]' and 400 camels transporting money, with a further 6,000 camels, carrying all other items for the Court and the troops. After some rest, on 7 May, the assembled army left the camp outside Constantinople and started their journey to Adrianople. They did not force the pace as it took them two weeks to travel through the Thracian Lowland to a new army assembly location. Here they rested again, awaiting the rest of the forces. After the muster of troops, Osman II nominated some new officers and on 21 May ordered the provincial troops to march towards the border with Poland. The slowly arriving Asian troops finally reached that camp on 8 June, although here the Polish spy's account seems to greatly exaggerate the number of available troops. He did not have the opportunity to even attempt to count the arriving troops, instead he assumed that each banner meant the presence of 5,000 soldiers. As such he calculated that the 31 banners that had arrived had in total 155,000 men, which, when estimating the real strength of the Ottoman army, appears far too high. On 9 June the Sultan, his guards and court followed the main body of the army.

When looking into primary sources about the Khotyn campaign of 1621 you can always find rather exaggerated relations about the strength of the fighting armies – something already noted from the Polish spy's account quoted above. It can be seen as well in reports describing the Ottoman army, where some accurate information is usually mixed with huge, rather impossible numbers. Amongst such sources are reports from spies and also the testimony of the captured soldiers. As there are quite a few such surviving documents, it is interesting to look at them and compare the numbers provided by the different witnesses. Even later accounts can provide rather confusing numbers. Sir Thomas Roe, the English ambassador that arrived in Constantinople at the end of December 1621, wrote that the Sultan had with him an army of 300,000 soldiers, although he mentioned that some estimates reported it as 600,000.[82] The Swedish diplomatic envoy in Helsingør, Anders Svensson, regularly sent updates about the war to Stockholm, based on the news received from Gdańsk. Of course such despatches were full of incorrect information and exaggerated numbers of troops involved in the campaign. In one of his letters, Svensson wrote that Osman II was leading 400,000 soldiers, then in another letter he mentioned that the Ottoman army had 500,000

Janissaries with parade clothing and equipment, like the large ceremonial mace. From *Icones Habitus Monumenta Turcarum*, between 1586 and 1650. (Jagiellonian Library, Cracow)

soldiers. Equally interesting, although also false, was the information that the Turks had brought with them a large number of elephants, which they were hoping to use to strike panic in the Polish army (although there were four elephants used for carrying baggage). At some point the Swedish envoy wrote to Stockholm that Royal Prince Władysław had been captured during the fighting. Interestingly enough though, Svensson provided a very detailed and accurate description of the peace treaty between the Commonwealth and the Ottoman Empire.[83] To show how outnumbered the Polish-Lithuanian-Cossack army was and to praise the victory, Albrycht Stanisław Radziwiłł wrote that Osman II had with him 500,000 men, who 'set up the tents in a way that due their numbers and variety they were to frighten us.'[84] Bishop Paweł Piasecki in his chronicle described Osman II's army as '300,000 Turkish cavalry, 12,000 janissaries and 180,000 Tatars'.[85] The first two figures are repeated by Miron Costin but he lowered the number of Tatars to 80,000.[86] The Armenian Joannis also wrote highly exaggerated information about the size of the Ottoman and Tatar forces. According to him there were 'uncountable numbers of men and horses' in Osman II's armies, alongside up to 300 cannon, with 14 of them so large that they had to be pulled by 20 oxen each. The Ottomans were supported by 100,000 Crimean and 80,000 Nogay Tatars – again such numbers are far too high.[87] Estimates provided by Polish diarists taking part (directly or indirectly) in the war vary greatly. Jan Ostroróg initially mentioned 300,000 men, not counting Tatars.[88] In a later part of his diary, based on the observations of the Polish

82 *The Negotiations of Sir Thomas Roe, in his Embassy to the Ottoman Porte, From the Year 1621 to 1628*, p.11.

83 Władysław Czapliński, 'Cień Polski nad Sundem 1621–1626', *Kwartalnik Historyczny*, year LXXXVI, volume 2 (Warszawa: Instytut Historii Polskiej Akademii Nauk, 1979) p.325.

84 Albrycht Stanisław Radziwiłł, *Rys panowania Zygmunta*, p.73.

85 *Kronika Pawła Piaseckiego biskupa przemyślskiego*, p.294.

86 Miron Costin, *Latopis ziemi mołdawskiej i inne utwory historyczne*, p.137.

87 'Istoriya Khotinksoy voyny Ioannesa Kamenetskogo', pp.268-269.

88 'Jana hrabi z Ostroroga Dziennik wyprawy chocimskiej', p.19.

envoy in the Ottoman camp, he lowered those estimates to 150,000 Turks and 60,000 Tatars.[89] Prokop Zbigniewski, despite describing the campaign in much detail, did not mention the size of the Ottoman army. In the diary of Stanisław Lubomirski is more detailed information, and he mentions a letter from Teofil Szemberg, who on 26 August 1621 was in the Ottoman camp. According to the account of this soldier, diplomat and spy, there were 300,000 'souls' in the Ottoman army but only 160,000 of them, including 30,000 janissaries, were battle-worthy. Szemberg also counted 62 cannon in the camp.[90] Stanisław Kobierzycki in his well-researched history of the life of Royal Prince Władysław, published in 1655, mentioned that many authors give different numbers of the Ottoman soldiers but according to 'prisoners, deserters and other sources' there were at least 300,000 soldiers, supported by 100,000 Tatars. While these numbers are clearly exaggerated, the Polish politician and historian provides a very interesting description of Osman II's army, based on the eyewitnesses' accounts:[91]

> The biggest part of it [the army] is composed from the European troops. Those soldiers were very impressive, with their posture, resilience to hardships and skill with which they used their weapons. Amongst them were many Hungarians, exceptionally experienced through [many] wars, who many times before fought against Christians. These veterans not only fought with great valour but also with indomitable bravery. From Asia arrived a large crowd of people, who most focused on being merchants [in the camp, rather] than warriors; others, recruited in [areas] near [Rivers] Euphrates and Tigris, were confused what they are doing in this strange world, where even air is different. They were there just to make up numbers – their usefulness in the fight was insignificant. Also arrived regiments of janissaries, without whom the Turks could never be victorious. Their numbers were much lower than usual though, due to the greed of the officials, who instead of really having the soldiers were just taking [stealing] the money for them.

When researching the Ottoman army of the period, it is also important to remember the observation made by Polish envoy Zieliński, who during the Khotyn campaign visited Osman II's camp as a part of preparations for the peace negotiations. Ostroróg wrote these comments in his diary:[92]

> In the Turkish army they count as a separate each one that is alive, so when [their] soldier is on horse but also has a second horse, mule or a camel, they will count each [animal] separately and [adding it together] is the reason why the strength of the their army is [always] so big, but of them only one is fighting after all ...
> In the overall strength of the army they count every mouth that needs feeding, which makes [their army] so huge; in the Polish army we do not add anything else except musicians; and so if there is a Polish army of 10,000 [men] it will have more soldiers than in a Turkish [army] of 20.000 or maybe even 30,000 [men].

---

89 'Jana hrabi z Ostroroga Dziennik wyprawy chocimskiej', p.38.
90 'Stanisława Lubomirskiego Dziennik wyprawy chocimskiej', p.72.
91 Stanisław Kobierzycki, *Historia Władysława, królewicza polskiego i szwedzkiego*, pp.333-334.
92 'Jana hrabi z Ostroroga Dziennik wyprawy chocimskiej', pp.38–39.

Looking into details provided by other sources during the campaign, I want to start with the fragment from the relation given by Jerzy Worocki. Worocki served in Żółkiewski's army at Cecora in 1620, was captured by Turks and imprisoned at Constantinople, from where he managed to escape in June 1621. He recorded, about the Ottoman army:

Ottoman musicians: drummers and trumpeters, from the Turkish embassy entering Prague in 1609. Samuel Suhuduller/ Schuduller, c.1609 (National Museum, Prague)

with the Sultan [there are] 75,000 Turks, 30,000 Arabs, of Greeks, Armenians, Bulgars, Serbs and other Christian people 47,000, 10,000 janissaries. 260 cannon for which it is very hard [to get] cannoneers; from the regiment of 700 foreigners, French and German, that were in Sultan's service, all deserted as soon as they heard that there would be war against the Poles; only 60 of them stayed. He said that there are many camels, although he could not count them all, with the Sultan alone there are 6,000 of them. Each had a saddle in the shape of the man, with each saddle there is a lance with pennons, so from far away one would though that there's lance-armed army marching. On 60 of those camels they are carrying Sultan's money … [There are] Four elephants, which for now are carrying tents. Once they cross the Danube, those elephants are to carry large tent set up on them, so it is ready for both day and night.[93]

Information that arrived in early August to the Polish Court in Warsaw indicated that the Sultan's army had 200,000 men and up to 80,000 Tatars. The numbers were confirmed by a few sources, such as the report by a Pole named Gołdepski who travelled with the Ottoman army from Constantinople and in despatches sent by Hetman Chodkiewicz.[94] It is not a surprise that this news about the Ottoman strength was a rather shocking revelation to the Polish court leading to a great consternation there. While previously there had been hopes that Osman II would send only a part of his army against

---

93   *Zherela do istoriï Ukraïny-Rusy,* volume VIII, pp.225-226.
94   BAV, Barberiniari Latini, vol.6579, f.148r, F. Diotallevi to L. Ludovisi, Warsaw, 16 VII 1621; BAV, Barberiniari Latini, vol.6579, f.158r, F. Diotallevi to L. Ludovisi, Warsaw, 6 VIII 1621; BAV, Barberiniari Latini, vol.6579, f.166r, F. Diotallevi to L. Ludovisi, Warsaw, 2 VIII 1621.

the Commonwealth, it was now clear that he was leading the army in person, and it was a large part of the Ottoman military force.[95] In a letter written to King Sigismund III, dated 4 August 1621, Hetman Jan Karol Chodkiewicz wrote about the approaching Ottomans:[96] 'We can ignore what [other] spies told us before, that up to two million armed men are there [in the Sultan's army] but the one [spy] that has seen them with his own eyes and marched with them, gives us assurances that they have 90,000 lancers [*sipahi*], 50,000 Tatars [and] 30,000 janissaries.'

The Hungarian spy employed by Lubomirski arrived in the Polish-Lithuanian camp on 27 August and brought more information about the Ottoman army. According to him, the Sultan's army was 300,000 men strong, not counting Tatars. He mentioned 15 very large cannon and 'more than 200 of those that were drawn by one horse'. The spy did not forget about the splendour of Osman II's court and testified about four elephants, many thousands of transport camels and a large number of oxen.[97] On 28 August Istvan Radagi, another spy in Polish service, arrived at Khotyn from the Ottoman army, although considering frequent mix-ups in sources and a one day difference between dates, he may be in fact the Hungarian spy mentioned above. According to him, Osman II was directly leading up to 150,000 men, with the overall strength of the Ottoman force 'no more than 300,000 but very miserable and dolorous', including no more than 30,000 janissaries. The artillery park was very large though, estimated as near 500 pieces, which of course is an obvious exaggeration. Rumelian troops were marching in the vanguard, followed by Moldavians and Wallachians, who were mending the roads for the rest of the army.[98] Jakub Sobieski, who took part in the campaign and was a frequent visitor to the Ottoman camp during truce negotiations, greatly exaggerated the numbers of the enemy, most likely in order to highlight the importance of battle. According to him there were 300,000 Ottoman soldiers, supported by 100,000 Tatars. Additionally they were supported by way more than 100,000 servants, who were taking care 'of tents, camels and other belongings'.[99]

Budjak Tatar Czegar, who was captured by Polish cavalry and brought to Khotyn on 31 August, provided more information about the approaching enemies. His estimate of the Tatar force was very high, and he stated 100,000 men. Amongst them 10,000 with the Khan (possibly a guard force), 10,000 Circassians, 10,000 Nogay (from Budjak), while the rest were from the Crimea. The prisoner said that the Khan did not have his infantry, 'shooters equipped with *rusznica*', with him. Czegar estimated the Ottoman army as 200,000 men, including 10,000 janissaries, supported by 230 cannon.[100]

Further information about the strength of the Ottoman army comes from the testimony of Mehmet of Anatolia, *sipahi* 'serving in one horse' and

95   BAV, Barberiniari Latini, vol.6579 f.166r, F. Diotallevi to L. Ludovisi, Warsaw, 2 VIII 1621.
96   *Zherela do istorii Ukraïny-Rusy,* volume VIII, p.229.
97   'Jakóba Sobieskiego Dziennik wyprawy chocimskiej', pp.121-122.
98   *Zherela do istorii Ukraïny-Rusy,* volume VIII, pp.230-231.
99   'Jakóba Sobieskiego Dziennik wyprawy chocimskiej', p.177.
100   *Zherela do istorii Ukraïny-Rusy,* volume VIII, pp.231-232.

captured during the fight on 2 September. Numbers given by him are very high, although some parts of his relation provides some interesting details. He was not sure of the strength of the Ottoman cavalry, although he estimated it as 'combined with Tatars [there are] three or four time of one hundred thousand ready to fight, excluding servants.' The core of the infantry was provided by 'not more than 30,000 janissaries' but they were supported by other troops as well. The prisoner mentioned that there were over a dozen thousands of non-janissary infantry, serving under pashas and beylerbeys. The army had up to 300 cannon, although they required 'powder, cannonballs and cannoneers.' The Ottomans were supposed to be well supplied with food for themselves and their horses, as they brought provisions on 500 galleys and they managed to gather further supplies when marching through Moldavia. As often in such relations, four elephants are mentioned as being present, 'on which they carry large bells to let know that the army is on march and on which [now] some small field cannon can be carried.' There are up to 50,000 camels that brought food and tents; also many oxen-pulled carts with food.[101]

Ottoman *Topçu* artilleryman. *Rålambska dräktboken*, mid-seventeenth century (National Library of Sweden)

Auxent in his chronicle provides some information about the strength of the Ottoman forces, although he seems to exaggerate a lot. His estimate of the overall number of the Ottoman army is very high, stated as '250 times 1,000 men, with 250 cannon.' Among the cannon were 14 heavy pieces drawn by 30 pair of oxen each, with others drawn by 9 or 10 pairs, smaller pieces were drawn by 4 pairs.[102] In a similar way, his numbers for the Tatars are far too high as well, as the Crimean contingent is described as 130,000 men led by the Khan, while the Budjak Tatars were 80,000 strong under Khan Temir.[103] Qaraqash Pash, leading the provincial troops from Buda, is mentioned arriving with a force of 4,000 men. When attacking the camps of the allied army, he was supported by 6,000 janissaries, 5,000 provincial *sipahi* from Anatolia and 12,000 from Rumelia.[104]

Another captured Ottoman cavalryman, named as Alliarnard from *kapikulu sipahi*, gave some additional information about Osman II's army. His testimony comes from 4 September, when he was captured during the fighting. The *sipahi* played down the strength and readiness of the Turkish force. He estimated that were there just 20,000 'worthy *sipahi*', no more than 8,000 janissaries and some *semeni* infantry serving with pashas and other officials but mostly 'to take care of food and taking care of horses.' A further 3,000 *kapikulu sipahi* were guarding the Sultan himself. The army had around 150 cannon 'both small and large'. He did say, however, that at that time when he was captured, there were 10 pashas (beylerbeys) present at Khotyn. They were officials from provinces of Rumelia, Anatolia, Karaman, Sivas, Maras,

101 *Zherela do istoriï Ukraïny-Rusy*, volume VIII, p.233-234.
102 Ödön (Edmund) Schütz (ed.), *An Armeno-Kipchak Chronicle of the Polish-Turkish Wars in 1620–1621*, p.53.
103 Ödön (Edmund) Schütz (ed.), *An Armeno-Kipchak Chronicle of the Polish-Turkish Wars in 1620–1621*, p.53.
104 Ödön (Edmund) Schütz (ed.), *An Armeno-Kipchak Chronicle of the Polish-Turkish Wars in 1620–1621*, pp.61–63.

Aleppo, Diarbakir, Kefe, Bosnia and *Rutella* (Al-Raqqah?).[105] Mustafa Naima confirmed in his chronicle the presence of provincial troops from Diarbakir, Anatolia, Karaman, Sivas, Aleppo, Damascus, Bosnia[106] and Anatolia, with troops from Buda arriving later, during the siege.[107]

A final piece of information, again much-exaggerated, came near the end of the campaign. A Moravian captive, who had been held for 40 years by the Turks, managed to escape and at the end of September fled to the positions of Colonel Denhoff's infantry regiment. 'He reported as an indisputable fact that the young Turkish Sultan was personally in the camp; that he was barely 17 years old; that his terrible forces are 200,000 Turks and 107,000 Tatars.'[108]

Ottoman tabor wagons. Sebastiano de'Valentinis, 1558. (Rijksmuseum, Amsterdam)

It is clear that many primary sources often provided greatly exaggerated figures in order to highlight the danger of the Ottoman invasion and the serious odds that that Commonwealth's army was facing.

It is worthwhile to examine what previous historians working on the Khotyn campaign have had to say about Osman II's army and its size. Józef Sękowski, who in 1824 published two volumes of Ottoman accounts relating to the conflicts with Poland and, later, with the Commonwealth, was the first researcher who tried to estimate the strength of Osman II's army at Khotyn. His estimate was based on the registers of all Ottoman provinces and on information from Mustafa Naima's chronicle.[109] Numbers given by Sękowski were:[110]

---

105 *Zherela do istorii Ukraïny-Rusy,* volume VIII, p.235.
106 Mustafa Naima (Naima Efendi), *Dziennik wyprawy chocimskiey,* p.158.
107 Mustafa Naima (Naima Efendi), *Dziennik wyprawy chocimskiey,* p.164
108 *Zeitung aus der Walachei,* pp.15–16.
109 Mustafa Naima (Naima Efendi), *Dziennik wyprawy chocimskiey,* pp.145-182.
110 Józef Sękowski, *Collectanea z dziejów tureckich,* volume I, pp.234-238.

Turkish Provincial Forces Taking Part in the Campaign		
Province/Region	Commander	Estimated strength
Rumelia	Yousuf Pasha	22,000
Anatolia	Hassan Pasha	25,000
Silistra	Kior Hussein Pasha	8000
Buda	Qaraqash (Karakash) Pasha	10,000
Bosnia	?	14,000
Aleppo	Tayhar Pasha	3000
Diyarbakir	Dylewar Pasha	10,000
Sivas	Ibasanly Hassan Pasha	6000
Karaman	Mustafa Pasha	3000
Aleppo	Tayjar Bey Pasha	3000
Damascus (Syria)	Nogay Pasha	5000
Kefe	Circassian Hussein Pasha	5000

It gives a total of 114,000 troops from the provinces. Janissaries were to have a maximum of 30,000, *kapikulu* cavalry up to 25,000, while all other *kapikula* troops, including artillerymen (including those left in Constantinople) up to 14,000. Amongst the allied and vassal contingents were 10,000 Crimean Tatars of Khan Janibek Giray, 5,000 men of the Budjak and Dobruja Hordes under Khan Temir and 6,000 Walachians. While the data provided by Sękowski give some basis for further research, his numbers seem to be high, as they are based on maximum strength at muster of the provinces and *kapikulu* troops, without any reduction due to vacancies, or to losses during the march to Khotyn or the need to leave some garrison troops.

Leszek Podhorodecki researched the Khotyn conflict in great depth, publishing in 1979 a study of the battle, co-written with Ukrainian historian Noj Raszba[111] and three years later a biography of Hetman Jan Karol Chodkiewicz, in which he updated some of his earlier findings.[112] As the basis of his estimates of the strength of the Ottoman army he used information from Mustafa Naima's chronicle and the testimonies of the soldiers captured during the battle. It provided him with an identification of the provincial forces present during the campaign, while for the overall strength of those provinces he used two further sources. One was the relation of the state of the Ottoman Empire during the reign of Sultan Ahmed I (1590–1617), while the other was the book by Paul Rycaut *The Present State of the Ottoman Empire*, published for the first time in 1665.[113] Podhorodecki compared the

---

111 Leszek Podhorodecki, Noj Raszba, *Wojna Chocimska 1621 roku* (Kraków: Wydawnictwo Literackie, 1979).

112 Leszek Podhorodecki, *Jan Karol Chodkiewicz 1560–1621* (Warszawa: Wydawnictwo Ministerstwa Obrony Narodowej, 1982).

113 Leszek Podhorodecki, *Jan Karol Chodkiewicz 1560–1621*, p.417. Podhorodecki used the Polish translation of Rycaut's work, published in 1678.

numbers from these two, so for a period just before Khotyn and for 40 years after it, noting that the differences between them were very low. He lowered them by a percentage, indicating that some of the *sipahi* did not take part in the expedition for a number of reasons (e.g. sickness). His final estimate of the strength of the Ottoman provincial forces taking part in the campaign is as follows:[114]

Province/Region	Commander	Estimate strength
Anatolia	Hassan Pasha	14,000
Rumelia	Yousuf Pasha	18,000
Buda (arrived at Kotyn during the siege)	Qaraqash (Karakash) Pasha	4,000
Aleppo	Tayhar Pasha	2,000
Diyarbakir	Dylewar Pasha	1,400
Bosnia	Hussein Pasha	5,000-6,000
Tripoli (Lebanon)	?	1,000
Sivas	?	6,000
Maras	Abazy Pasha	1,000
Kefe	?	2,500
Volunteers from Dobruja	?	1,000
Contingent from Al-Raqqah	?	2,000-3,000
Local private troops and tribal auxiliaries	-	5,000

Mounted officer of janissaries.
Abraham de Bruyn, 1577.
(Rijksmuseum, Amsterdam)

In total, his provincial troops were estimated as up to 70,000 but Podhorodecki assumed that due to desertion and non-combat losses their strength at Khotyn was much lower, probably around 50,000 or 55,000 men. This force was also reinforced by up to 8,000 cavalry of *kapikulu sipahi* although he did not provide a source from which he took this number. The strength of the janissary force varies between 12,000 and 18,000. While the latter may be close to the initial strength, when the troops were leaving Constantinople, because of losses en route and the high rate of desertion he assumed that it was likely that the former was closer to the actual number of men that started the siege. The artillery corps was represented by at least a few hundred men, with some estimates of up to 1,300. As for the Ottoman allies, Podhorodecki presented them in the following way: the Crimean Tatars, led by Khan Janibek Giray, arrived with at least 10,000 men. Khan Temir brought 5,000 Tatars from the Budjak and the Dobruja Hordes. There were also between 1,000 and 2,000 mercenary Tatars directly in the service of the Sultan. Stefan IX

---

114 Leszek Podhorodecki, Noj Raszba, *Wojna chocimska 1621 roku*, pp.167-171; Leszek Podhorodecki, *Jan Karol Chodkiewicz 1560-1621*, pp.334-337.

Tomșa had with him around 5,000 Moldavians, while Radu Mihnea led up to 7,000 Wallachians.

Wiesław Majewski in his article[115] disputed some of the numbers provided by Podhorodecki. He was especially against lowering the number of available troops, pointing out that Osman II had to be accompanied by up to three-fifths of the military strength of the Ottoman Empire in such an important campaign. Majewski also disputed the high level of attrition amongst the janissaries, especially that due to desertion, during the journey towards Khotyn. As such his estimates are:[116]

Formation	Strength	Notes
Provincial *sipahi*	60,000	
Kapikulu cavalry	12,000	
Janissaries	30,000	12,000 from Constantinople, the remainder from the provinces
Other *kapikulu*	Up to 8000	
Other infantry	'a few thousand'	
Crimean Tatars	10,000	
Budjak Tatars	5,000	
Moldavians	12,000-13,000	Possibly counting both Moldavians and Wallachians

Ukrainian researcher Petro Sas in his work from 2011 quoted a number of estimates of the Ottoman strength from the period, commenting about how some of them were greatly exaggerated. He also looked into figures provided by Russian and Polish historians, comparing them with the primary sources. In general while he agreed with Podhorodecki's findings, he felt that the overall numbers were actually slightly higher, with at least 150,000–160,000 men including allied forces and 'tens of thousands' of camp servants.[117]

The most recent Polish research into this subject was published in 2021 by Andrzej Witkowicz.[118] He decided to rather drastically lower the overall numbers of troops available to Osman II, stating that there were only 40,000–45,000 provincial troops, including barely 10,000 cavalry. *Kapikulu* formations were 8,000–12,000 janissaries, 12,000 cavalry, a few thousand 'technical troops' (e.g. artillery crews) and a few thousand guard soldiers of different courtiers, including the Grand Vizier's. Finally auxiliary forces were composed of 9,000 Crimean Khanate Tatars, 5,000 Budjak Tatars, between 2,000 and 6,000 Moldavians and 4,000 to 5,000 Wallachians. So in total, according to Witkowicz, there were between 90,000 and 100,000 soldiers at

---

115 Wiesław Majewski, 'Chocim 1621 rok' in *Wojny polsko-tureckie w XVII w.* (Przemyśl: Wydawnictwo Towarzystwa Przyjaciół Nauk w Przemyślu, 2000), pp.9-22.

116 Wiesław Majewski, 'Chocim 1621 rok', p.13.

117 Petro Sas, *Khotyn War of 1621*, pp.225–230.

118 Andrzej Witkowicz, *Bułat i koncerz. Poprawki do obrazu wielkich bitew polsko-tureckich (1620-1683)*, volume I (Zabrze: Wydawnictwo Inforteditions, 2021), pp.100-107.

Khotyn, with a few thousand Tatars detached from this number to conduct raids against Poland.

I would be inclined to agree with higher estimates of the provincial troops though, especially cavalry, putting it closer to 60,000 men in total, with at least a few thousand firearms-armed infantry. *Kapikulu* seems to be at least 10,000 janissaries and up to 12,000 cavalry. There were also thousands of camp servants, some of which were used to reinforce troops during the fighting. All the the Tatar contingents were probably no more than 15,000 men in total, although they were of minimal use in the direct attacks on the Commonwealth's camp, and were much better employed in cutting logistic lines and in raiding Polish territories. Moldavian and Wallachian troops were practically not a factor, and used as engineering support. The Ottoman artillery park was much stronger than that of the Commonwealth, with the initial estimates of Szemberg, who counted 60 plus cannon probably being too low. It is certain that more cannon were brought to Osman II's camp during the campaign, with a final count of a minimum 100–120 pieces being present. There were at least 15–20 heavy cannon, with rest being smaller, lighter pieces. Amongst the Ottoman artillery park taken to Moldavia were heavy cannon 'able to destroy the strongest walls', shooting cannonballs weighting 55 pounds.[119] Rudomina, who mentioned the rather exaggerated number of 200 Ottoman cannon, wrote that some of the heavy pieces were using 50 pounds cannonballs.[120]

Turkish camp during siege operation in 1593. Engraver unknown, dated between 1594 and 1650. (Herzog August Bibliothek, Graph. *c.*1687)

So at least when comparing the number and size, the Ottoman army had a massive advantage, although it appears that the training and skill of Turkish gunners left much to be desired. The artillery train was well supplied with ball and powder though, as the Ottomans were able to continue with long barrages on a daily basis – on many occasions giving fire few hundred times a day.

---

119 Jakub Sobieski, *Pamiętnik wojny chocimskiej xiąg troje*, p.23.

120 Fridrich Warzuchtig (Jan Rudomina), *Diariusz prawdziwy expediciey Korony Polskiey, y Wielkiego Xięstwa Litewskiego przeciw Osmanowi Cesarzowi Tureckiemu w roku 1621 pod Chocimiem w Wołoszech Fortunnie odprawioney. Fridrych Warzuchtig Bawarczyk Zoldath ubogi będąc przytomny opisał*, p.48.

This massive army was accompanied by thousands of horses, used as battle mounts; many oxen, buffaloes and camels that were employed as beasts of burden and were ever-present with the Ottoman army as part of its supply train. The presence of such animals, especially camels – always seen as very desirable battle plunder – is often mentioned by diarists describing the campaign. For example, Jan Czapliński, serving as a volunteer at Khotyn, claimed that the Ottomans had a large number of camels and oxen in their camp. Perhaps even more interesting, is that he records that there were eight elephants (while all other sources mentioned four) and that one was killed by the Polish-Lithuanian artillery.[121] Unfortunately no other primary source that I know of corroborates his comment about an elephant being killed, so it cannot be verified. Elephants were used for extra heavy transport duties, while during the fighting itself they could be used as a sort of morale-booster, with Ottoman musicians sitting on top of them encouraging soldiers to greater bravery during the assaults.

---

121 'Kopia listu od pana [Jana] Czaplińskiego do Jerzego Radzimińskiego 1 Octobris z obozu pisanego', p.213.

6

The Initial Stages of the Campaign (summer 1621)

Polish troops were initially gathering at the camp in Gliniany, near Lviv. In mid-May Lubomirski organised the advance corps, slowly reinforced by district troops arriving from Polish provinces and marched with them to set up an advance camp in Podolia, in Skała at the River Zbruch (Zbrucz), 80km north of Khotyn. It was well a protected outpost, from which the Poles sent frequent reconnaissances to check on the progress of the Ottoman army and clash with marauding Tatars. It also served as a place to collect and store provisions. The camp in Skała became a very important staging point for the rest of the army before moving on to Khotyn, as regiments and individual banners were now arriving here on an almost daily basis.[1] In mid-June, Chodkiewicz, while staying in Ostroh (Ostróg) wrote to King Sigismund III, informing him of the progress in organising the troops. As he was in constant contact with Lubomirski, the Lithuanian Hetman had good insight into the situation. In his letter to the King he mentioned that he was gathering Lithuanian troops, 'so I can have them with me when I arrive at the [army] camp', although he complained that the Polish units were arriving slowly. Chodkiewicz asked Sigismund to dispatch cannon 'that we badly need here' and to hurry the Germans (foreign troops) so they arrived before the main army would have to march against the Ottomans. The Hetman mentioned his plan to march to Moldavia, where he wanted to set up a defensive camp, as a more advantageous strategy than facing the enemy in Poland.[2] Jerzy Rudomina, himself *rotmistrz* of one of the Lithuanian hussar banners, mentioned that the units under Chodkiewicz's command were well equipped 'without any gold [ornaments]', with good horses, and that there were also plenty of veterans of the Livonian and Muscovite wars in the ranks.[3] On 18 July

---

1   Stanisław Kobierzycki, *Historia Władysława, królewicza polskiego i szwedzkiego,* pp.320-321.
2   *Korrespondencye Jana Karola Chodkiewicza,* pp.181–183.
3   Fridrich Warzuchtig (Jan Rudomina), *Diariusz prawdziwy expediciey Korony Polskiey, y Wielkiego Xięstwa Litewskiego przeciw Osmanowi Cesarzowi Tureckiemu w roku 1621 pod Chocimiem w Wołoszech Fortunnie odprawioney. Fridrych Warzuchtig Bawarczyk Zoldath ubogi będąc przytomny opisał,* p.27.

a rather unexpected visitor arrived in the Polish camp at Skała. His name was Constantine Baptiste Vevelli (Konstanty Baptysta Wewelli) and he was an Italian from Crete in the service of new Moldavian Voivode, Alexandru Iliaș. He brought with him letters from the Voivode and from some high-ranking Ottoman court officials, urging peace talks and trying to convince the Poles that Osman II would be willing to negotiate. Modern researchers believe that the Ottoman letters were fakes, created at Iliaș' court as a part of the plan to avoid conflict on Moldavian soil. Lubomirski, at this point in charge of the army at Skała, was rightly suspicious of both Vevelli and his mission, seeing him as a potential Turkish spy, so he ordered him to wait in Orynin for the arrival of Chodkiewicz. He was kept under guard but was well treated. He met with Lubomirski at a feast and was invited to take part in Holy Mass.[4] Once Hetman Chodkiewicz arrived in the camp, after a few days he spoke with Vevelli who, probably to his own surprise, was warmly welcomed and the Lithuanian commander discussed with him the letters that were brought from Voivode Iliaș. Chodkiewicz and Lubomirski decided to send the Moldavian envoy back but in the company of a Polish representative. It was all done with the full support of Sigismund III, who did not trust Moldavians and their offer of being the middle-man in the negotiations but at the same time he was willing to open talks with the Ottomans. Chodkiewicz had the perfect candidate for the Polish emissary in Teofil Szemberg, a survivor of Żółkiewski's expedition of 1620, during which he had been in command of the artillery. He was an experienced soldier, with a good knowledge of both Ottoman and Tatar warfare. He was to serve not only as a diplomat but also as a spy, to report on the strength and the preparations of Osman II's army. Both envoys left the Polish-Lithuanian army camp on 4 August and started the slow journey towards the marching Ottoman army.

Officer and standard-bearer of Polish infantry. Abraham de Bruyn, 1581. (Rijksmuseum, Amsterdam)

In the meantime, the combined Polish-Lithuanian army, now divided into 10 regiments, marched from Kamianets-Podiskyi via Orynin. It was led by a vanguard under the command of Lubomirski, who had with him three regiments. The remaining seven, led by Chodkiewicz, slowly travel towards the Dniester River. There were issues with supplies during the march, as the Hetman strictly forbade his soldiers from plundering the local population. Officers were ordered to enforce this decree in their own units. The problem was that the army was already lacking funds, so there was no opportunity to purchase food locally and discontent was growing.[5] By the end of July the

---

4 'Opisanie wyprawy chocimskiej', pp.209-210; under incorrect date of 18 June in 'Stanisława Lubomirskiego Dziennik wyprawy chocimskiej', pp.69-70; 'Jakóba Sobieskiego Dziennik wyprawy chocimskiej', pp.109-110.

5 Fridrich Warzuchtig (Jan Rudomina), *Diariusz prawdziwy expediciey Korony Polskiey, y Wielkiego Xięstwa Litewskiego przeciw Osmanowi Cesarzowi Tureckiemu w roku 1621 pod*

troops started to arrive at the planned crossing place over the Dniester River near the village of Braha, next to Khotyn. Some banners of cossack cavalry crossed the river, to secure the area around Khotyn and reconnoitre the terrain. Here the army encountered its first major crisis. Chodkiewcz wanted all troops to cross to the Moldavian side, in order to set up camp at Khotyn, where he planned to wait for the Cossacks and together they would face the approaching enemy. The soldiers did not want to do this, preferring to stay on the Polish bank of the river, with better logistic lines and ways to more easily retreat into the Polish interior under the expected Ottoman pressure. Chodkiewcz made four main points in support of his idea of moving into Moldavia:[6]

> First, it was the will and order of His Royal Highness to move across the border; second, is not to be burden to [Polish] citizens; third, [Chodkiewicz] liked this place to fight a battle [at Khotyn], as thanks to ruses [that could be employed] the battle would be on our, not the enemy's terms, as we had good place for the camp, ideal for defence and for fortification; fourth, and the most important, that the Zaporozhian Cossacks were approaching and, if they heard that we had not crossed the Dniester [to Moldavian side] and not trusting our soldiers to face the Turks, they might not come here as it is not hard for such men as they to be suspicious.

While clearly unhappy, the soldiers followed the orders and the first regiments started to cross the river, although it appears that morale was low and the men were disgruntled. They were not eager to march into Moldavia, probably the fate of Żółkiewski's expedition was still a raw wound. In the first days of August, the rumour was spreading among troops that there was an order issued to pillage the Polish town of Żwaniec. The men did not need to be told twice and masses of soldiers and camp servants alike threw themselves at the town, plundering it as well as some of the neighbourhood villages. Chodkiewicz was unwell and could not react, but Lubomirski accompanied by some colonels and other officers managed to quickly stop the chaos. A few looters were captured and were immediately sentenced to death and hanged. Another issue was linked with the bridge built by the Poles over the Dniester. It was made of connected boats but the task was difficult, as there were 260m between the two banks and the water levels were very high due to the summer rains. On 3 August the bridge was already broken, so each regiment was ordered to arrange its own crossing of the river using ferries gathered along the banks. Lastly, the soldiers were grumbling as they were still awaiting confirmation of their term of service and pay, while 'many [were full] of fear, hunger and misery.'[7] The crossing was very slow, the repaired bridge was broken again during the night of 7/8 August. However, by the morning of 8 August Lubomirski and three regiments of his vanguard force

---

Chocimiem w Wołoszech Fortunnie odprawioney. Fridrych Warzuchtig Bawarczyk Zoldath ubogi będąc przytomny opisał, p.22.

6   'Jakóba Sobieskiego Dziennik wyprawy chocimskiej', p.111.
7   'Jakóba Sobieskiego Dziennik wyprawy chocimskiej', p.112.

were safely on the Moldavian bank of the river and they were setting up camp next to Khotyn castle. Here the Field Hetman was joined by Chodkiewicz and the army's principal engineer, the Dutchman Wilhelm Appelman, to start planning the fortifications and preparations for the defence works.

The issue of the soldiers' pay was a growing concern however, as their representatives were continuously asking Chodkiewicz for confirmation of the period of service, which was directly linked with the amount of pay that they were due. They were asking for a longer term, which would include the time of their journey from the area where the unit was raised to the army camp. In a rather vivid description, Sobieski wrote that 'both newly-recruited and veteran, native and foreigners, common soldiers and nobles, horsemen and infantrymen, all of them were screaming to the heavens that they do not have money and food, that without any reward they are to face grave dangers.'[8] The Hetman sent them to the commissioners, arguing that it was their prerogative to deal with financial matters. After a few days of checking army registers and units' muster rolls, it was agreed:[9]

> Except district [troops] that are paid by their districts, and soldiers of the Grand
> Duchy of Lithuania, who receive their pay from the Treasury, Crown units will
> count as starting their service either from the day when they entered the camp or
> were mustered in front of the Crown Field Clerk,[10] or when they announced that
> they are ready to be mustered. Additional time for the arrival [that was included
> in pay] was four weeks for those travelling from Silesia, Prussia and Kujawy; those
> from Mazovia and Podlasie three weeks and those from Małopolska two weeks.

On 10 August Lubomirski sent a large party to gather food in Moldavia. *Rotmistrz* Lipnicki (Lipiński) took 150 horses of cossack cavalry, 50 dragoons and a few hundred camp servants armed with *rusznica* firearms. They travelled as far as the town of Seret on the Prut River, where they clashed with the Moldavians. The Poles managed to capture a few hundred head of cattle and returned to camp on 13 August, having suffered only two wounded through the whole escapade. It seems that Chodkiewicz was not happy with Lubomirski's decision to send out the mission however. He wanted to prevent any hostilities with the Moldavians, possibly hoping that they could help Szemberg in his mission and in negotiations with the Ottomans. In the meantime, the conditions of the crossing over the Dniester improved. Some local Ruthenian volunteered, for pay of 100zl, to swiftly build a new, and solid, bridge. 'Pairs of heavy [wooden] legs were put diagonally in the water, with a fairly thin third [piece of wood] connecting them at the bottom.'[11] It sped up the process of moving rest of the units, and the large tabor, across. By 19 August the whole army assembled under Chodkiewicz and

---

8   Jakub Sobieski, *Pamiętnik wojny chocimskiej xiąg troje*, p.12.

9   'Jakóba Sobieskiego Dziennik wyprawy chocimskiej', p.114.

10   One of the army's officials, *pisarz polny* (*notaries campestris* in Latin); his role was to deal with the administrative aspects of the army, such as checking muster rolls and dealing with pay and reports about the state of the army, which could be submitted to the King and *Sejm*.

11   'Jakóba Sobieskiego Dziennik wyprawy chocimskiej', p.115.

Lubomirski was finally safely on the Moldavian bank of the Dniester, with the soldiers now focused on building field fortifications and setting up camp. They were eagerly awaiting reinforcements: the strong regiment of Royal Prince Władysław, the Zaporozhian Cossacks and the other delayed Polish units. On 23 August Colonel Rusinowski brought in a regiment of *lisowczycy* cavalry, composed of '11 banners of cossack cavalry, fairly well equipped'.[12] They were to set up their own separate camp and fight as a semi-independent force during the entire battle.

The march of Władysław's regiment was hampered by many issues, and his troops assembled very slowly. Cannon had to be brought from Gdańsk and Smoleńsk, as there were no suitable ones in the arsenal in Warsaw. On 7 June the main body of the regiment left Warsaw, with the Royal Prince following them a few days later. It took his troops a month to arrive at Lviv, where they stayed for an extended rest. One of the main problems they had was linked to the artillery train that was to accompany the troops to Khotyn. Many guns had to have their carriages replaced or repaired, and some of them arrived at Lviv very late. Another issue was caused by the exhaustion of the German infantry as the regiments had had to march from Prussia to Lviv under the strong summer sun. The infantry 'was so tired by the long march and sweltering heat that one would have thought that it was not walking but crawling instead. Many men fall on the ground and were breathing heavily.'[13] The Royal Prince received a very warm welcome in Lviv, with a parade of city militia and even some equestrian exhibitions presented by the local Armenians, dressed in Ottoman style. While Władysław and his entourage were honoured by the burghers, his soldiers were setting up camp outside of the city, recovering after the long journey.[14] Nervous, Chodkiewicz sent messengers to the Royal Prince, encouraging him to hasten the march – he wanted to ensure that the regiment would join the army before the arrival of the Ottomans.

Two of the most important envoys despatched by the Hetman were Jakub Sobieski and Rafał Leszczyński, they were to ask Władysław 'for his honour and for the wellbeing of the Homeland' to hurry his troops to Khotyn. On 29 August Władysław's troops arrived at Kamianets-Podiskyi and from there they moved in a defensive tabor, protecting themselves from Tatars. On the morning of 30 August the troops moved towards Żwaniec and arrived there by evening. During the night they had to defend themselves against

Rather unusual depiction of the infantry in the Polish army in 1611. The unit is armed with both firearms and pikes, indicating foreign troops, while the clothing and hussar-like mounted officer in front of the unit seems to point to its Polish character. From the portrait of King Sigismund III by Wolfgang Kilian, based on the composition by Tomasz Dolabella, 1609–1611. (Print Room of the University of Warsaw Library. Photo by Tomasz Ratyński)

---

12 'Jakóba Sobieskiego Dziennik wyprawy chocimskiej', p.119.
13 Stanisław Kobierzycki, *Historia Władysława, królewicza polskiego i szwedzkiego*, p.327.
14 Józef Bartłomiej Zimorowic, *Historya miasta Lwowa, Królestw Galicyi i Lodomeryi stolicy; z opisaniem dokładnem okolic i potróynego oblężenia*, p.304.

harassing Tatars, who managed to capture some wagons carrying provisions. From 31 August Władysław's troops started the crossing, racing against time to arrive at camp before the main body of the Ottoman army.

The Cossacks' plan was to march through Moldavia and to join the main Polish and Lithuanian forces. On its way Borodawka's men were to gather as many supplies as they could, denying them to Osman II's army. Their route towards Moldavia presented, as always, a very heavy burden to the local population of the Polish lands they had to travel through. Tomasz Zamoyski was forced to keep some of his private troops on his estates, under the command of Stefan Chmielecki, in order to protect them from the marching allies.[15] On 8 August the Zaporozhian army crossed the Dniester near Mogilev and started their march through Moldavia. Cossack regiments and *sotnias* spread out far and wide, pillaging and destroying on their way. Their passage frightened the Moldavians and Voivode Alexandru Iliaş 'fled with all men from Iaşi, leaving it full of many belongings, including the palace full of cannon.'[16] Even Szemberg, travelling to meet the Ottoman army, reported in one of his letters that 'all Wallachians [Moldavians] from Dniester and Prut had fled [as far as] to Suceava and Transylvanian mountains.'[17] While the scorched earth policy that accompanied their march seems cruel, it can be clearly explained by the necessities of the war. The Moldavians, allied with the Ottomans, were seen by Cossacks as an enemy; pillaging their supplies on one side helped the Cossack army, and on the other made such materials unavailable to the Ottomans. The fact that the Moldavians were unable to adequately supply Osman II's troops during the campaign was one of the main reasons why, by the end of August 1621, Alexandru Iliaş was dethroned by the Turks and replaced with Stefan Tomşa. Alexandru was blamed for acting negligently: not preparing bridges on time and not gathering enough supplies, all of which affected the proper march of the Ottoman army. It seems that Osman II was also not happy with the Voivode's attempts to start negotiations with Chodkiewicz and wanted to avoid having another pro-Polish Moldavian on the throne in Iaşi.[18]

Some Cossacks troops did not venture to Moldavia however, instead they focused on sea raids, attacking both the Crimean and the Ottoman coasts. They managed to defeat a galley fleet at Trabzon (Trebizond) and their boats were even striking fear into the population near Constantinople. Only in a raid against the port of Riza near Trabzon were the Zaporozhians, supported by their Don Cossack brethren, unsuccessful as the raiders were defeated by an Ottoman squadron. Other attacks met with much more luck though, with the Cossacks able, to some degree, to disorganise the Ottoman supply lines because the Turks were often reliant on provisions and weapons delivered by their galleys. At the same time, it is very difficult, because of the very general information given in surviving sources, to estimate how many Cossacks and Turkish soldiers died during those naval episodes of the war.

---

15   Stanisław Żurkowski, *Żywot Tomasza Zamoyskiego*, p.82.
16   'Stanisława Lubomirskiego Dziennik wyprawy chocimskiej', p.71.
17   'Stanisława Lubomirskiego Dziennik wyprawy chocimskiej', p.71.
18   Mustafa Naima (Naima Efendi), *Dziennik wyprawy chocimskiey*, p.154.

Cossack attack on the Black Sea, plundering Turkish towns in 1624. Romeyn de Hooghe, 1699 (Herzog August Bibliothek, Graph. Res. C: 145.37)

The Cossacks that were marching to meet the Polish-Lithuanian army faced growing pressure from Turkish and Tatar cavalry, with both small reconnaissance parties and larger bodies of raiders often clashing throughout the second half of August 1621. According to Budjak Tatar Czeger, captured by the Poles on 31 August, the Crimean troops fighting the Cossack forces on 26 August took heavy losses attacking the Zaporozhian tabor. It seems that the Tatars, initially clashing with Cossack patrols, were lured inside the tabor, where they lost 'their best men' and were then forced to retreat. Osman II was allegedly angry with the Khan for being unable to defeat the Cossacks.[19] The story about this fight seems to be confirmed by Naima, who wrote that while the Tatars managed to kill some Cossacks and plunder a few wagons, they lost 1,000 men themselves. The Khan asked Osman II for the support of Ottoman troops and their artillery although the detachment under Nogay Pasha and Ilbasanly Hassan Pasha arrived too late and the Cossacks managed to leave the battlefield safely.[20] The main army under Borodawka was at risk of being cut off from Khotyn by the Ottomans, so the Polish and Lithuanian command was eager to know more about the whereabouts of its allies. On 24 August one Cossack regiment, under Mykhailo Doroshenko (Michał Doroszenko), arrived at Khotyn but the rest of the army was still trying to break through strong Ottoman and Tatar forces. Two Polish cavalry banners, under Kuliczkowski and Liske, sent on a reconnaissance mission on 27 August were not able to link with the Cossacks because of a high number of Tatars troops in the area. The fighting between the Cossacks rushing to Khotyn and the Turkish and Tatar forces attempting to stop them were often fierce and bloody. The Zaporozhians struck from ambushes, hiding in caves, on hills and by 'giving strong fire' causing losses amongst Osman II's troops. Probably the most famous episode is that where a group of 200 or 300

---

19   *Zherela do istoriï Ukraïny-Rusy,* volume VIII, p.231.
20   Mustafa Naima (Naima Efendi), *Dziennik wyprawy chocimskiey,* p.154.

Cossacks managed to delay the main Ottoman army near the River Prut for the whole day. When the Sultan himself arrived at the site of skirmish, he was unhappy that the Zaporzhians, well placed in woods and makeshift trenches, were still able to resist his men. Even the janissaries were not successful in their attacks, although some of them managed to bring the Sultan the severed heads of their dead enemy. Under the cover of darkness, fighting against constantly attacking Turks, the Cossacks tried to retreat but most of them were killed in the uneven fight.[21] Szemberg, who as Polish envoy was at that time with the Ottoman army, said in his dispatch that there were 260 Cossacks, who initially defeated the Tatar attacks and then through the whole of 27 August defended against the 'might of the Sultan and his whole army'. On 28 August the remnants of the Cossack unit were still fighting, covering their wagons with earth and digging trenches with their sabres; with the last 30 men selling their lives dearly. Such stubborn resistance affected the morale of the Ottoman army and so enraged Osman II that he ordered his *kapikulu sipahi* to cut the Cossacks' bodies to pieces.

Worried about the approaching Ottoman army and concerned that his allies might not arrive on time, Chodkiewicz despatched Konashevych-Sahaidachny with strong group of Polish cavalry, ordering him to find the Cossacks and lead them to Khotyn. In the meantime, Borodawka's forces managed to repel strong enemy attacks and continue their journey to meet Chodkiewicz's. The Polish cavalry, in constant clashes with Tatars, was finally able to find the marching Cossacks, although during those skirmishes Konashevych-Sahaidachny had lost his horse and was severely wounded in his hand. Wandering through the forest, the Cossack commander managed to find the Zaporozhian army. He was warmly welcomed by his men, who quickly decided that it was time for a change of the leadership. Borodowka, 'man slothful and constantly drunk' was by acclamation voted to be

Sultan Osman II with his court and guard units travelling towards Khotyn, spring 1621. Illustration from Ġanizāde Nādirī's *Şehnāme-iNādirī* (Topkapı Palace Museum Library)

---

21   Mustafa Naima (Naima Efendi), *Dziennik wyprawy chocimskiey*, p.154.

replaced by Konashevych-Sahaidachny.[22] It is probable that the Cossacks, facing overwhelming numbers of Tatars and Turks, were eager to have an experienced and brave leader in charge of the army. In a quick march, fending off Tatars attacks, the Zaporozhian force moved towards Khotyn where they arrived on 1 September. Chodkiewicz must have been relieved and pleased not only because of their arrival but also because of the change in the leadership. Konashevych-Sahaidachny, seen as the leader of the pro-Polish faction, also had a good relationship with Royal Prince Władysław, which was a good omen for their future cooperation. The Commonwealth's armies were finally together at the designated place and preparing to face the invaders.

As mentioned above, the Ottoman army began to leave the camp in Adrianople in late May, with the Sultan and his court following on 9 June. The Ottoman army, divided into at least two corps marched along separate but parallel routes, through modern-day Bulgaria. The journey through the Balkan Mountains was not without danger, as due to the constant rain and muddy ground the Ottomans lost a lot of baggage. Mustafa Naima wrote that even camels were useless in such conditions, so four elephants that accompanied the army had to carry the burden of a large kettle-drum and the majority of the tents.[23] By the end of July the army arrived at Isaccea where it was to cross over a newly built bridge to the left bank of the Danube. It was a specifically chosen point, being one of those rare places where, in the right conditions, the Lower Danube could be forded. However, only some of the troops could cross this way, others, including the artillery park and the vast tabor, had to patiently wait until the bridge construction was finished. While waiting for the engineers to complete their work, the Sultan mustered his janissaries and paid them a special bonus; after which he mustered the other troops as well. He also daily practised his archery, encouraging the soldiery to exercise with their weapons as well in preparation for fighting the Commonwealth's troops.

At the same time on the Black Sea Kapudan Pasha (Grand Admiral of the Ottoman Fleet) captured some Cossacks attempting a raid using their *chaika* boats. He brought the prisoners along the Danube to present them to Osman II at Isaccea. For his victory, the Pasha was rewarded with two magnificent fur coats, but the fate of the captives was horrifying. Some were used for archery target practice, 'a few of them shot by the Sultan himself'. Others were ripped to pieces by elephants; others cut in half or ripped with hooks. One 'who was formerly of Islamic faith, was cut into very small pieces'.[24] This bloody spectacle was not something unusual in the relations between the Ottomans and the Cossacks, the latter were often brutally killed when captured in revenge for their raids. On this occasion it is also possible that the young Sultan was keen to show the army his determination and eagerness to fight against 'the enemies of the faithful'.

---

22 Stanisław Kobierzycki, *Historia Władysława, królewicza polskiego i szwedzkiego*, pp.328-329.
23 Mustafa Naima (Naima Efendi), *Dziennik wyprawy chocimskiey*, p.148.
24 Mustafa Naima (Naima Efendi), *Dziennik wyprawy chocimskiey*, p.151.

Plate A
Polish or Lithuanian hussar
(Illustration by Sergey Shamenkov © Helion & Company 2023)
See Colour Plate Commentaries for further information.

I

Plate B
Unarmoured cossack or *lisowczyk*
(Illustration by Sergey Shamenkov © Helion & Company 2023)
See Colour Plate Commentaries for further information.

Plate C
German infantryman in Polish service
(Illustration by Sergey Shamenkov © Helion & Company 2023)
See Colour Plate Commentaries for further information.

Plate D
Zaporozhian Cossack
(Illustration by Sergey Shamenkov © Helion & Company 2023)
See Colour Plate Commentaries for further information.

Plate E
Ottoman janissary
(Illustration by Sergey Shamenkov © Helion & Company 2023)
See Colour Plate Commentaries for further information.

Plate F
Ottoman *sipahi*
(Illustration by Sergey Shamenkov © Helion & Company 2023)
See Colour Plate Commentaries for further information.

Plate G
Ottoman *serdengeçti* volunteer
(Illustration by Sergey Shamenkov © Helion & Company 2023)
See Colour Plate Commentaries for further information.

Plate H
Crimean or Nogay Tatar
(Illustration by Sergey Shamenkov © Helion & Company 2023)
See Colour Plate Commentaries for further information.

Plate I
See Colour Plate
Commentaries for further
information.

1

2

Plate J
*See Colour Plate Commentaries
for further information.*

X

1

2

Plate K
See Colour Plate Commentaries for further information.

1

2

Plate L
*See Colour Plate Commentaries for
further information.*

XII

The fact that Osman II took so much interest in the construction of the bridge – he spent days sitting in his tent overlooking the place of the construction – definitely motivated the crews to speed up the work.

Once the bridge was finished, the first to cross were troops from Rumelia, then those from Anatolia, followed by the rest of the contingents. Troops were moving day and night for around a week. Each crossing 'division' set up their own camp, to await the rest of the troops before the continuation of the march. Of course, moving such a large number of troops and supplies across the Danube was not the easiest task. A Polish spy noted that during the crossing of the Ottoman artillery park the bridge broke and six cannon, up to 200 oxen and many men were lost in the river. The maintenance workers responsible for the bridge were punished with a death sentence and impaled.[25] The new working crews, ordered to repair the bridge, seem to have been highly motivated to do their job quickly and efficiently. Once all available troops, tabors and supplies had finally safely

Sultan Osman II executing captured Cossacks. Illustration from Ġanizāde Nādirī's *Şehnāme-i Nādirī*. (Topkapı Palace Museum Library)

crossed the Danube, the Ottoman commanders started preparations for the march through Moldavia. Some public executions of prisoners, mostly probably Cossacks, were organised again. 100 of them were beheaded, while a few hundred more were given to janissaries, who over a few days tortured them to death. While campaign allowances were customarily paid at this point, it seems that not all the *kapikulu* soldiers received them. The official explanation was that they were late for the concentration of the army, but it is possible that Osman II was also punishing those units that were well below expected strength. It definitely affected the morale of the unpaid troops and would have had a bearing on their later unwillingness to fight.[26] Dilaver Pasha arrived at Isaccea, leading his delayed contingent from Diyarbakir. He brought with him a force of which 'most of [soldiers] were horsemen, well dressed and armoured.'[27] After the successful crossing, the army moved on to the River Prut, preceded by a strong vanguard of cavalry from Rumelia,

---

25 *Zherela do istoriï Ukraïny-Rusy*, volume VIII, p.228.
26 Kadir Kazalak, Tufan Gündüz, 'Osman'in Hotin Seferi (1621)', p.137.
27 Kadir Kazalak, Tufan Gündüz, 'Osman'in Hotin Seferi (1621)', p.139.

supported by Tatars and auxiliary troops of both Moldavian and Wallachian voivodes. By then, thanks to frequent reconnaissance missions and the 'interviewing' of captured prisoners, Osman II and his commanders were aware of the overall deployment of the enemy. They knew that the main Polish-Lithuanian army was preparing its defences at Khotyn but also that the march of Royal Prince Władysław's force was delayed and they had not reached the camp yet. The Ottomans were also painfully aware of the presence of the Cossack army in Moldavia so it was decided that the army needed to speed up its march. The weather, and the terrain through which they now had to travel, made progress much easier, so by mid-August the Ottoman vanguard was at Cecora, meaning that they had travelled 180km in less than three weeks. Here they met with the rest of the troops from European provinces and the supporting Tatars. The Ottoman army now had 200km of road to Khotyn and its commanders were eager to engage the Cossacks and prevent them from joining with Chodkiewicz's forces. As mentioned though, Osman II's troops were unable to stop Borodowka's army and the Zaporozhians, despite some losses during the constant skirmishes, arrived at Khotyn on 1 September, just ahead of the Turks.

7

The Battle of Khotyn
(2 September – 9 October 1621)

The Camp and the Deployment of the Polish-Lithuanian and Cossack Armies

The town of Khotyn could not be used as a part of the defensive line, so the houses were burnt by Polish soldiers before the start of the fighting. Only the brick building of the Orthodox Church was not destroyed and was instead garrisoned by infantry, and set up as an armed outpost reinforced with earthworks built around it. With the old fortress of Khotyn, also garrisoned by Polish troops, they were to be the first points on the western approach to the camp. Next to Khotyn Castle was the bridge over the Dniester, making it the only open supply line with Poland. The Castle was connected with the Polish camp by a drawbridge over the nearest ravine. While the Ottomans did not attack the Castle directly, it played the role of a prison, where captured Turkish soldiers and deserters that fled from their army were kept after being interrogated in the camp. The vital bridge over the Dniester was defended by more earthworks, on both banks of the river. That on the Polish side was an important staging point for supply convoys travelling to and from Kamianets-Podilskyi during the period of siege. The northern and southern approaches to the camp were protected by further ravines, with many hills and forests, ideal for skirmishing and for setting ambushes, making it very difficult terrain for a possible attack, so the defenders did not even build proper fortifications there. One part of the southern approach was easier to reach and it was here that the Cossacks, who arrived at Khotyn at the very last moment, initially set up their camp. The River Dniester protected the eastern side of the camp, with its high and rocky banks creating a natural defence line. The main line of fortification was to protect western side of the camp, where the plain terrain was ideal for an Ottoman attack. Field fortifications in the Polish-Lithuanian camp could take many forms. Next to some purposely built sconces and blockhouses, tabor wagons were used as well as impromptu defences. 'Our men fortified the camp in any way they could: infantry set up near the gates [of the camp] sorts of small tabors, setting up wagons filled with manure and earth and surrounding them with earthworks. Both the German and our [Polish] infantry was set up in woods and trenches as well.'[1]

Engineers prepared two lines of ramparts protecting the main Polish-Lithuanian camp, with earthworks, trenches and blockhouses, and reinforced by roundels manned mostly by the German infantry. The outer rampart was additionally protected by a deep moat. There were also additional redoubts built in front of the main line, garrisoned by further units of infantry. On the plain in front of the camp, in order to have an open line of sight and fire, trees were cut and bushes were removed. The felled trees were put to good use, as wood was utilised to reinforce the fortifications. As Chodkiewicz's army did not have sufficiently powerful artillery, the defenders had to rely on the fire from their muskets and *rusznica* calivers, with just a few small batteries of guns set up in a few important locations, mostly on the western approach.

There were two gates out of the camp, both protected by additional earthworks. They were to be used to allow cavalry sallies to reinforce any endangered part of the defensive line or to lead the troops out to deploy for a pitched battle. One gate was set up near the northern part of the camp and was known as Lubomirski's gate, the other was in the southern part and was called Chodkiewicz's (or the Lithuanian) gate. Additionally, as the last line of the defence, each regiment had their own smaller camp within the main camp, each protected by lines of tabor wagons. As mentioned before, the Cossacks arrived very late so they had little time to prepare their own defensive position. They relied on their tabor wagons, set up in two rows, reinforced by some trenches and hastily erected improvised earthworks. Worse was the separate camp of the *lisowczycy* cavalry, set up between Chodkiewicz's and the Cossacks' positions. Light cavalry, without much tabor, lacking infantry support, was not suitable for a defensive role, and at times during the battle they were indeed very hard-pressed.

The Polish-Lithuanian army was divided into three 'divisions', which were defending different sections of the camp. It was a deployment that included troops from Royal Prince Władysław's regiment and was arranged even before the arrival of his troops, so for the first few days of the siege these new arrivals were gradually filling in the appointed positions. The right wing (northern part of the camp) was under the command of Stanisław Lubomirski, who had his own regiment and those of Maciej Leśniowski, Stefan Potocki and Jan Mikołaj Boratyński. It seems

Polish, Lithuanian and Cossack army camps during the Battle of Khotyn. Giacomo Lauro, between 1621 and 1624 (National Library, Warsaw)

---

1   'Jakóba Sobieskiego Dziennik wyprawy chocimskiej', p.129.

that all his units were Polish and that some part of them were district troops. The left wing (southern part of the camp) was under the command of Jan Karol Chodkiewicz, who had with him his own regiment and the two other Lithuanian regiments of Mikołaj Zenowicz (his son-in-law) and Aleksander Sapieha. The large regiment of Royal Prince Władysław Waza, with its strong force of both foreign and Polish infantry, was defending the centre of the line, supported by the Polish regiments of the Sieniawski brothers (Mikołaj and Prokop) and Mikołaj Kossakowski. The main force of German infantry was deployed in the outer fortifications in front of the gates and the main line of ramparts. Next to Chodkiewicz's Lithuanians were the separate positions of the *lisowczycy* and the Zaporozhian Cossacks. The camp of the latter was near the River Dniester. The sources do not mention to which 'division' the regiment of Piotr Opaliński was attached, but it is possible that it was either serving under Lubomirski or in the centre of the camp. As many banners of cavalry and infantry arrived after the concentration of the main army, they did not form new regiments but it seems instead that they were just attached ad hoc to whichever regiment or position was required. Regimental structure was very fluid, as units were detached to different tasks (e.g. supply missions) and could serve for a longer period away from their initial regiment. It was similar with the Cossacks, as their units could be detached and serve as far away as on Lubomirski's wing.

End of August

The last days of August had seen a race with time between the two armies approaching Khotyn. While Chodkiewicz's troops were frantically working on the field fortifications of the camp, they were still awaiting the arrival of Władysław's regiment and the Cossacks. The Royal Prince, assisted by a few banners of cavalry, crossed the Dniester River on 31 August; his troops set up a defended camp near Żwaniec and from there they were to move over the bridge to the main army camp near Khotyn. Unfortunately the bridge broke and while it was being fixed, a new solution had to be found. Locally gathered ferries and quickly built rafts were used, so the troops started crossing during the night of 31 August / 1 September. It was a risky business however, as sometimes, due to bad weather, boats capsized and men were drowned. Small groups of Tatars and Moldavians were harassing camp servants taking horses for grazing on pastures, with many men killed and horses captured. It would be an issue that plagued the allied army through the whole period of siege. The vanguard of the enemy army was also in the vicinity, with Khan Temir leading 5,000 Tatars to attack the Polish-Lithuanian forces at dawn on 31 August. He divided his force in two parts, sending 2,000 men led by his brother to skirmish with the Polish cavalry near Lubomirski's positions, while 3,000 under his own command

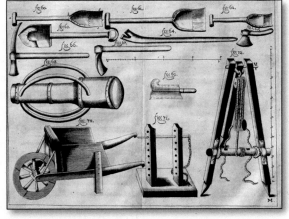

Examples of different engineering tools used to build field fortifications such as those that defended the camps at Khotyn. Adam Freitag (Freytag), *Architectura Militaris Nova et Aucta Oder Newe Vermehrte Fortification…*, (Leiden: 1631). (National Library, Warsaw)

struck on the other flank. Here they encountered the cossack cavalry banner of *rotmistrz* Hrehory Piotrowski. This unit was resting outside of the main camp, returning from the previous day's reconnaissance mission. Its soldiers were surprised by the Tatars, the banner's small tabor was completely overwhelmed, 'horses taken and many sleeping [men] cut down.'[2] The Commonwealth's commanders quickly reacted to the attack, well aware that the camp, with its fortifications still not finished and the infantry contingents from Royal Prince Władysław's regiment not present, was vulnerable. Lubomirski sent some banners of cavalry towards the Tatars, while some Polish and German infantry set an ambush in the ravines and woods. The majority of the Polish and Lithuanian cavalry left the camp and deployed into a crescent-shaped line of battle, ready for the arrival of the Tatars. Temir Khan's men were soon engaged in skirmishing with the defenders of the camp, and were being attacked by cossack cavalry and reiters from ambush. Kobierzycki mentions one Tatar, 'whose bravery and height was above anyone else' who fought near the Polish ramparts, until one of the defenders hit him in the head with a stone, shattering his skull and killing him instantly.[3] The Tatars quickly decided that discretion was the better part of the valour and retreated from the field. Losses were fairly small, although considering the fate of Piotrowski's banner, it seems that Chodkiewicz's army probably lost more men than the Tatar attackers. The Polish-Lithuanian command reacted quickly to the threat and despite some initial surprise managed to control the situation. Overnight the soldiers resumed working on the fortifications, while Royal Prince Władysław's regiment continued its crossing of the river. As already mentioned the bridge was damaged and the soldiers were forced to use ferries and rafts, so priority was given to the infantry that was badly needed on the first line of the defence. The first to arrive was the Hungarian infantry, followed by 3,000 German infantry, that crossed 'silently, without a [beat of] drum.'[4] It seems that the German regiments of Ernest Denhoff and Gerhard Denhoff were immediately after the crossing deployed onto the ramparts and into the blockhouses, followed next day by that of Jan Weyher.[5] Because of the size of Władysław's regiment and the complication with moving all of its men across the Dniester, it was not until on 5 September that all his troops arrived on the Moldavian side.

1 September

The full strength of the defenders was finally gathering at Khotyn. While Władysław's troops were crossing the Dniester day and night, it was the Cossacks that were now the final piece of the puzzle. As only one regiment

---

2   'Jakóba Sobieskiego Dziennik wyprawy chocimskiej', p.124.

3   Stanisław Kobierzycki, *Historia Władysława, królewicza polskiego i szwedzkiego*, p.328.

4   *Diarius expeditiey królewicza polskiego Władysława przeciwko Osmanowi II, cesarzowi tureckiemu y chanowi tatarskiemu w osobach swych na woynie będących w Wołoszech pod Chociniem roku 1621, BK 342, f.50v.*

5   *Zeitung aus der Walachei*, p.3.

of 3,000 men had arrived by the end of August, a great amount of hope was placed on Konashevych-Sahaidachny and his mission. The Cossack commander did not disappoint and he brought the main Cossack Army to Khotyn in the evening on 1 September. During their march they still had to defend themselves against harassing Tatars but these attacks did not stop the well defended tabor. The strong Cossack force set up their own camp near Chodkiewicz's and the *lisowczycy* positions. Due to a lack of time however, the Zaporozhians could not fortify their position properly. Over the next few days their camp, protected by two lines of tabor wagons and some improving earthworks, would be frequently attacked by Ottoman forces. Initially the sight of the marching Cossacks was mistaken for the approaching Turkish and Tatar troops so it raised the alarm. The Polish and Lithuanian banners were marched in front of the camp to deploy for battle. It had to be a great relief for both the commanders and their soldiers when they discovered that the new arrivals were in fact their long awaited allies, reinforcing the defence of the camp.[6]

In the shadow of the appearance of the Cossacks, two other important men came to Khotyn: Szemberg and Vevelli were finally released from the Ottoman camp and brought news of their mission back to the Polish-Lithuanian camp. The Turkish officials that were allegedly the authors of the letters brought to Lubomirski and Chodkiewicz by Vevelli of course immediately denied that they were attempting to contact them. Grand Vizier Ohrili Hüseyin Pasha refused the Polish envoy the right of an audience with Osman II. It is possible that Szemberg's and Vevelli's presence in the Ottoman camp may even have been kept from the Sultan. The Grand Vizier wrote to Chodkiewcz, advising that there would be no peace without justice for the Cossack raids.[7] The reaction of the Lithuanian Hetman was unusual, showing that he was not only a great army commander but also a rather shrewd politician. Claiming that no one in the Polish-Lithuanian army was able to read the Turkish letter, he despatched Vevelli back to the Ottoman army, with his own letter written in Latin:[8]

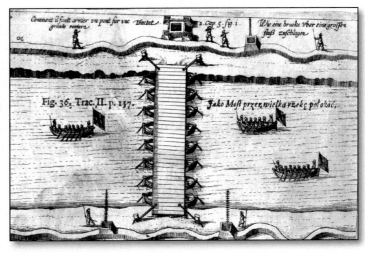

Bridge protected on both banks of the river by earthworks, in similar way that Polish-Lithuanian one was set up near Khotyn in 1621. Diego Ufano, *Archelia albo artilleria to iest fvndamentalna y doskonała informacya o strzelbie…* Original book in German was published in 1614, Polish translation in 1643 (National Library, Warsaw)

---

6   Fridrich Warzuchtig (Jan Rudomina), *Diariusz prawdziwy expediciey Korony Polskiey, y Wielkiego Xięstwa Litewskiego przeciw Osmanowi Cesarzowi Tureckiemu w roku 1621 pod Chocimiem w Wołoszech Fortunnie odprawioney. Fridrych Warzuchtig Bawarczyk Zoldath ubogi będąc przytomny opisał*, p.45.

7   'Jakóba Sobieskiego Dziennik wyprawy chocimskiej', p.125.

8   'Stanisława Lubomirskiego Dziennik wyprawy chocimskiej', pp.75-76.

I find it pleasing that, as I understand, Your Lordship[9] showed to my envoy Szemberg such caring kindness towards renewal of the old friendship [as it was] with our old kings and to confirm the peace; as it is our duty to deal with such matters by council than by blade, so our world can flourish thanks to the peace than be destroyed due to wars. I will do my utmost best in this matter and I do hope that Your Lordship will also make the best efforts towards it. As I do not have [here] anyone that could translate to me the letter of Your Lordship, I am asking, for the common good, that if you will attempt for further contacts [in future], Your Lordship should write to me in European language. I bid you Your Lordship good help, for the joint benefit of the king and the kingdom, offering you my services.

[Signed]

From the camp at Khotyn

The diplomatic solution was no longer an option, and it was time for a clash of arms. The next day, 2 September, the Ottoman army arrived at Khotyn and the fighting would begin in its earnest.

Ottoman cavalry fighting against Western-style arquebusiers/reiters in 1593. Engraver unknown, dated between 1601 and 1675 (Herzog August Bibliothek, Graph. C: 1085)

2 September

The strong vanguard of the Ottoman army started to arrive at Khotyn around midday on 2 September. It was up to 20,000 *sipahi* and janissaries, under the command of Hussein of Anatolia. Sultan Osman II, probably with a contingent of his *kapikulu* cavalry, arrived as well. The rest of the large army was marching slowly towards the area of the Commonwealth camp. The first units of cavalry started skirmishing against Chodkiewicz's troops, allowing the rest of the vanguard to deploy into line of battle. The Lithuanian Hetman moved the majority of his troops outside of the camp, trying to provoke the approaching Turks into meeting him in battle. This plan did not work

---

9   The Latin term used by Chodkiewicz was *Illustrissimae Dominationis Vestrae* so probably a little more elaborate, more like 'Your Illustrious Lordship'. In this translation I have decided to simplify it.

however, as his troops were only facing some Ottoman and Tatar cavalry, while the main body of the vanguard, supported by artillery, struck against the Cossack camp. The combined force of *sipahi* and janissaries clashed with the Zaporozhians, pressing them hard in their not yet fully prepared defensive position. Under cover of the fighting, the Ottomans start to set up their own camp on the hills in front of the Polish-Lithuanian positions and near the Dniester next to the Cossacks. Chodkiewicz was in control of the situation and quickly despatched support to the Zaporozhians. 4,000 German and Polish infantry joined the Cossacks, striking at the enemy from ambush within the woods. A strong cavalry force, including the regiment of *lisowczycy*, some banners of reiters and some volunteers from other cavalry units, also arrived to support their allies. It seems that initially the allied army was hard-pressed, as Rudomina mentions that, due to losses, some Lithuanian cossack cavalry banners were pushed back and that one of the reiter units was also forced to flee. The arrival of further reinforcements helped to blunt the Ottoman attacks, although the continuing firefight and cavalry skirmishing took place into the evening. Mustafa Naima noted that the Ottomans, in order to set up their campsite, had to first push back the Cossacks from the hill, indicating that some Zaporozhian infantry may have awaited the enemy in ambush and did not retreat without a fight. As these preliminary clashes continued for a long time, Osman II ordered his tent to be set up on one of the hills, so that he could have a good position from which to watch the fighting. Soldiers from the vanguard, encouraged by being under the watchful eye of the Sultan, brought in up to 40 prisoners and some severed heads. Even in the evening, when Chodkiewicz's infantry supported the Cossacks and 'fought stubbornly', the Ottoman soldiers continued providing Osman with prisoners and the heads of the dead defenders, and in turn he 'rewarded them and encouraged [them] with praise.' Mehmet of Anatolia, captured by the Poles the next day, testified that the Sultan did not leave the tabor during the fight 'even though he badly wanted to, but they [his courtiers] prevented him from doing it'. This seems reasonable, as no one in the Ottoman camp wanted to risk his life, especially in the dangerous early phase of the battle. According to Sobieski, the victorious allies, especially the infantry, captured a great deal of loot from the battle, 'many Turkish horses, ornate horse tack and sabres, six tigers [pelts] and other beautiful things, as well as other weapons, lances, spears.' The Tatars that were sent to the left flank of the fight, were not eager to engage Lubomirski's forces deployed there. They seemed happy to simply hide on the hills and between the woods, 'entertaining us [just] with their passage.' Despite such an uninspiring effort, Khan Janibek Giray received an audience with Osman II, where he was allowed to kiss the hand of the Sultan. He also received rich gifts, 'a beautiful fur, a bow and arrow case and a pallasch, [all] encrusted with gems, also a beautiful horse with expensive furniture, all of which really caused Tatars to rejoice.' A large force of Crimean Tatars crossed the Dniester via the ford and 'like locusts' arrived in the area between Khotyn and Kamianets. They captured a few merchants travelling to Khotyn, taking their goods. Amongst the loot seized were 140 oxen, some cattle and a few hundred sheep.

Ottoman cavalryman carrying the severed head of an enemy. It is worth noting the distinctive pelt of a big cat. *Rålambska dräktboken*, mid-seventeenth century (National Library of Sweden)

Estimates of losses taken during this fighting vary depending on the diarist. Ostroróg says up to 800 Turks were killed and many more wounded. Among his own losses he wrote about two officers of Lithuanian cossack cavalry, Czarowicz and Bohdan. Based on army registers the first named can be identified as having served in Hetman Chodkiewicz's regiment, and the second in Mikołaj Zenowicz's regiment; each was *rotmistrz* of a cossack cavalry banner. Other losses amongst the Poles and Lithuanians were recorded as up to 30 killed and many wounded. Zbigniewski also wrote about a few hundred Ottomans killed, but he gives a more detailed list of Polish losses. He confirmed the two officers of cossack cavalry killed, Czarowicz and Bohdan, also 'thanks to God, just 20 killed' including at least eight companions. The *Lisowczycy* had one killed *rotmistrz* – Jędrzejowski – while Colonel Rusinowski (shot in the heel) and *rotmistrz* Jakuszewski (shot in the knee) were wounded. Rusinowski's injuries were so serious, that he was out of action for the remainder of the campaign, and his regiment was under the command of *rotmistrz* Stanisław Stroynowski.[10] Many horses, especially from among the reiter units, were lost; it seems that most of those losses were caused by Turkish firepower and cannon. Pseudo-Lubomirski recorded the same names and the same number of dead, twenty, but he seems to indicate that these were just the losses among the companions. Earlier in his description of the fight he mentioned that the Ottomans 'killed up to 30 of our good retainers' from the volunteers supporting the Cossacks, which would indicate that the losses of Chodkiewicz's army could be in fact higher than just the 20 killed. Sobieski clarified that Czarowicz and Bohdan who died during the fighting were 'Lithuanian Tatars, valiant men and for a long time serving the Commonwealth.' He also confirmed that the Ottoman artillery caused some serious losses, especially among the hussar and reiter banners, where many horses were shot and killed. Among the wounded was *rotmistrz* Kłuski from the cossack cavalry ('shot in the face') and infantry *rotmistrz* Ratowski. Auxent provides much lower estimates, as according to him and contrary to the other already mentioned sources, it was a fairly low-key fight, and only 12 Turks and 20 Poles were killed. Czapliński wrote in his letter that 'many enemies were killed' but he admitted that allied losses were also severe, with many killed, amongst them seven officers of *rotmistrz* rank, and many wounded.

After the battle the Cossacks focused on improving their defensive positions, with work taking place throughout the night. Morale in the allied camp was very good, boosted by the victorious day. In the meantime, while the Ottomans were preparing the camp for their army, the Tatars were harassing the troops remaining on the other bank of the Dniester. The tabor of Royal Prince Władysław's regiment was attacked, with a number of men and some supplies being captured, including cattle from Władysław's own kitchen. The cavalry banner of Prince Jerzy Czartoryski, a volunteer private unit, that was marching towards Khotyn from Kamianets, was surprised by

---

10 Władysław Magnuszewski, *Z dziejów elearów polskicj* (Warszawa-Poznań: Państwowe Wydawnictwo Naukowe, 1978), pp.35-36.

Moldavians or Tatars, losing a few companions, most of its horses and many camp servants.[11]

3 September

The war council that took place in Chodkiewicz's tent during the night of 2/3 September discussed the next course of action for the allied armies. The Lithuanian Hetman was trying to convince the council to attempt a pitched battle. Chodkiewicz wanted to engage the enemy while the Ottoman army had not yet assembled in full. He seemed to prefer this course of action, as he was concerned that the Turks might push back the defenders from the still unfinished fortifications. However, the rest of the council, including Lubomirski and the commissioners, opposed this plan. 'We need to use cunctation rather than playing dice with the [fate of the] Commonwealth.' This faction wanted to focus on finishing the fortifications and trenches, and also waiting for Royal Prince Władysław to cross the River with his entire regiment, to provide a strong infantry force. While Władysław did not take part in the initial council, he arrived later and spoke directly with Chodkiewicz, supporting the idea of avoiding a risky fight and focusing on the defence instead.[12] Unfortunately, soon after his arrival the Royal Prince fell ill and spent the majority of September bedridden with a fever. His biographer Stanisław Kobierzycki explained in great detail what happened and how it affected the Prince:

> [Władysław's] illness was caused by his massive effort [of leading troops] that he undertook both day and night, also from the unbearable heat during the march from Kamianets to the camp. He was travelling in full armour under the burning rays of the sun. Then he suffered greatly due to heavy and unwholesome Wallachian [Moldavian] air. He was affected by the sudden bouts of fever, that left him only at the end of the war – by then he recovered. He was also plagued by a

---

11 'Jana hrabi z Ostroroga Dziennik wyprawy chocimskiej', p.20, 'Prokopa Zbigniewskiego Dziennik wyprawy chocimskiej', pp.44-45, 'Stanisława Lubomirskiego Dziennik wyprawy chocimskiej', pp.77-78, 'Jakóba Sobieskiego Dziennik wyprawy chocimskiej', pp.127-128, Jakub Sobieski, *Pamiętnik wojny chocimskiej xiąg troje*, p.9, 'List z cyfer przełożony Pana Jakóba Sobieskiego do Xiążęcia Zbaraskiego Pana Koniuszego Koronnego z obozu pod Chocimiem 22 Septembris 1621 roku', p.204, 'Opisanie wyprawy chocimskiej', pp.211-212, 'Relacya prawdziwa o expediciey przeciwko Turkom, na którey sam cesarz turecki był Ao 1621, Woyska koronnego y W. X. Litte pod regimentem Pana Karola Chodkiewicza W. X. Litte które pod Chocimiem leżało', pp.219-220, *Diarius expeditiey królewicza polskiego Władysława przeciwko Osmanowi II, cesarzowi tureckiemu y chanowi tatarskiemu w osobach swych na woynie będących w Wołoszech pod Chociniem roku 1621*, BK 342, ff.51r-51v, Mustafa Naima (Naima Efendi), *Dziennik wyprawy chocimskiey*, pp.157-158, *Zherela do istoriï Ukraïny-Rusy*, volume VIII, p.233, Ödön (Edmund) Schütz (ed), *An Armeno-Kipchak Chronicle of the Polish-Turkish Wars in 1620-1621*, p.53, 'Kopia listu od pana [Jana] Czaplińskiego do Jerzego Radzimińskiego 1 Octobris z obozu pisanego', p.207, Fridrich Warzuchtig (Jan Rudomina), *Diariusz prawdziwy expediciey Korony Polskiey, y Wielkiego Xięstwa Litewskiego przeciw Osmanowi Cesarzowi Tureckiemu w roku 1621 pod Chocimiem w Wołoszech Fortunnie odprawioney. Fridrych Warzuchtig Bawarczyk Zoldath ubogi będąc przytomny opisał*, pp.49-51.
12 'Jakóba Sobieskiego Dziennik wyprawy chocimskiej', pp.128-129.

Baltaci guard, dressed as a janissary and wearing a leopard pelt. *Rålambskadräktboken,* mid-seventeenth century (National Library of Sweden)

lack of patience. He complained that he was bedridden at the time when every man and his strength would matter.[13]

The Ottoman army was slowly setting up their camp and preparing positions in front of the allied defensive lines. A large contingent of Tatars, initially supported by Moldavians and Wallachians, was deployed on the northern side, near the Khotyn fortress. In front of Lubomirski's and Władysław's lines were the provincial contingents from Europe supported by janissaries and artillery – creating the left flank of the Ottoman army. The Turkish centre, facing Chodkiewicz's and the *lisowczycy* camp, were further units of janissaries, *kapikulu* cavalry and more artillery. Finally the right flank of the Ottoman army was deployed south from the allies' defences, through the Dniester, and composed of provincial troops from the Asian provinces, also with some artillery support.[14] Their main task during the battle would be focused on the Cossacks and their camp. Further contingents of Tatars crossed the river and were harassing Polish supply lines, and also later taking part in raids deeper into Polish territory. At this stage no Ottoman forces had moved to the Polish side of the Dniester, and it seems that the Turkish command did not see it as necessary.

From early morning a new series of clashes started, with the Ottomans probing the defences in a few places. The Turkish cavalry, possibly supported by Tatars, was skirmishing in front of Lubomirski's positions. The Polish horsemen were riding out of their lines for individual fights, in the old tradition of pre-battle combat known as *harce*. Chodkiewicz and Lubomirski did not allow more cavalry to deploy far from the ramparts however, eager to protect the camp. At the same time the troops (mostly infantry) continued working on the field fortifications, strengthening the defences. The German infantry built earthworks next to the camp gates, reinforcing the previously improvised defences that utilised tabor wagons. In the meantime, combat soon focused on the fortified Orthodox Church in the north. Lubomirski sent more and more of his men, both cavalry and infantry, to reinforce the initial force deployed in the area. The janissaries pressed the defenders hard here, 'fighting bravely and moving forward. They even crawled near to the rampart and the moat, being close to capturing them.' Here they were met with a furious Polish counter-attack that managed to force them back. An important role in repulsing the attack was played by units of infantry from Royal Prince Władysław's command: 300 Hungarian haiduks under Mikołaj Kochanowski and a few companies of German infantry from Jan Weyher's regiment. The German officer taking part in the fight noted that 'there was a fierce battle on both sides.' The position around the Orthodox Church was saved and infantry started to work on reinforcing the earthworks there. There

---

13   Stanisław Kobierzycki, *Historia Władysława, królewicza polskiego i szwedzkiego*, p.340.
14   Mustafa Naima (Naima Efendi), *Dziennik wyprawy chocimskiey*, p. 158, Andrzej Witkowicz, *Bułat i koncerz. Poprawki do obrazu wielkich bitew polsko-tureckich (1620-1683)*, volume I, pp.161-164.

were also three assaults against the Cossack positions, all were repulsed by the defenders. Jan Weyher, who was in command of Royal Prince's troops left on the Polish bank of Dniester, set up a battery of three cannon that supported the Cossacks with its fire across the river. The Zaporozhians took a heavy toll of the attacking janissaries and *sipahi*, although some Polish estimates claiming that up to 1,000 Turks were killed seem too high. Encouraged by Chodkiewicz, Polish and Lithuanian camp servants took part in the fighting as well, supporting the cavalry during the counter-attacks and taking a large amount of booty from the battlefield. 'They returned to the camp with decorated sabres, with horses, with spears and with turbans.' Three janissaries were captured by the Cossacks, providing information about the attacking army, and others were taken prisoner by the Poles and Lithuanians. From their testimony came some rather anecdotal information, that 'the Turks promised themselves not to eat this day, until they captured the Polish camp.'[15] Describing this day of fighting, Mustafa Naima had to admit that 'with their cannon and guns, the enemy killed many of our men.' The Bey of Bosnia, Hussein, who was shot in the face during the assaults on 2 September, died of wounds this day as well. As often in such situations, Polish estimates of their own losses seem very low, with Zbigniewski mentioning only six killed companions and some shot (so killed and wounded) infantry. Reiter *rotmistrz* Oporowski was killed by a cannonball, amongst the dead was also one lieutenant from Denhoff's infantry regiment. The Cossacks lost a colonel named Zmudzik and a few dozen men.[16] Darkness brought an end of the fighting, although both sides were bracing for renewing hostilities the next day.

4 September

During the night the Commonwealth's soldiers continued their work of reinforcing the fortifications, with newly arrived contingents from Royal Prince Władysław's regiment deployed into the first line. As the bridge over the Dniester was still damaged, the troops were ferried across. Denhoff's Germans were busy with working on the earthworks outside of Chodkiewicz's gate from where they could support the *lisowczycy* and the Cossacks.

---

15 *Kronika Pawła Piaseckiego biskupa przemyślskiego*, p.294.

16 'Jana hrabi z Ostroroga Dziennik wyprawy chocimskiej', p.20, 'Prokopa Zbigniewskiego Dziennik wyprawy chocimskiej', pp.46-47, 'Stanisława Lubomirskiego Dziennik wyprawy chocimskiej', pp.78-79, 'Jakóba Sobieskiego Dziennik wyprawy chocimskiej', pp.129-130, 'List z cyfer przełożony Pana Jakóba Sobieskiego do Xiążęcia Zbaraskiego Pana Koniuszego Koronnego z obozu pod Chocimiem 22 Septembris 1621 roku', p.204, 'Opisanie wyprawy chocimskiej', pp.211-212, 'Relacya prawdziwa o expediciey przeciwko Turkom, na której sam cesarz turecki był Ao 1621, Woyska koronnego y W. X. Litte pod regimentem Pana Karola Chodkiewicza W. X. Litte które pod Chocimiem leżało', pp.219-220, Mustafa Naima (Naima Efendi), *Dziennik wyprawy chocimskiey*, p.158, Stanisław Kobierzycki, *Historia Władysława, królewicza polskiego i szwedzkiego*, pp.340-342, *Zeitung aus der Walachei*, p.3, *Diarius expeditiey królewicza polskiego Władysława przeciwko Osmanowi II, cesarzowi tureckiemu y chanowi tatarskiemu w osobach swych na woynie będących w Wołoszech pod Chocimiem roku 1621*, BK 342, ff.51v-52r.

Gerhard Denhoff (1589–1648). During the Khotyn campaign he served as Colonel of a German infantry regiment, part of Royal Prince Władysław's troops. Engraving by Wilhelm Hondius, 1643 (National Library, Warsaw)

Rotmistrz Kochanowski and his Royal Guard haiduks were placed in the Orthodox Church, which was now seen as a vital component of the defence of the southern approach to Polish lines. The defenders received some interesting information from the Ottoman camp, brought by a defector named Timofey. He was a Cossack from Korsun captured as a young boy, and who for 12 years was a servant of a Turkish *sipahi*. While he did not know anything about the size and disposition of the Sultan's army, he had overheard that many Turks had been killed and wounded during the previous day's fighting and he described the morale of the attacking troops. Ottoman soldiers were talking and saying to one another that 'we never before fought against giaurs like those before, those are not afraid of us … [The Turks] were astonished by bravery and courage of our men although they are saying that no matter how well giaurs fight, they all will be ours [defeated].'[17]

In the morning, the Ottomans started their assaults, initially sending some troops against Lubomirski's flank. That seems to have been just a feint, as the main attacks, spearheaded by janissaries, again focused on the Cossack camp. It seems that Osman II and his commanders saw this as a weak point of the defence, probably due to the improvised nature of the Zaporozhian defences (see above). The Sultan ordered the setting up of a small tent on one of the hills closer to the fight, so that he could observe and motivate his army. He allegedly said, 'I shall not ear nor drink until you bring me this grey dog Sahaidachny.' Naima mentioned a well known ritual, where warriors that brought prisoners and the heads of dead Cossacks received 'rewards and encouragements', four prisoners and eight heads were brought to the Sultan. The Turks attacked again in the early afternoon and continued with their assaults for two hours. As on the previous day, the Cossacks seemed to be hard pressed by the constant attacks, but Chodkiewicz, as always keeping a close eye on the developments of the situation, reacted quickly. A strong infantry force was despatched to support the Zaporozhians: German infantry from Learmont's and Jan Weyher's regiments, supported by the Polish infantry banners of Prince Franciszek Zasławski, Łukasz Jelski and Rakowski. Additionally, some cavalry, with the help of armed camp servants – always eager to seize loot

---

17 *Zherela do istoriï Ukraïny-Rusy*, volume VIII, p.234-235.

from the battlefield – were sent out as well. Another series of attacks against the Cossack camp started in the early evening and this time continued for some hours. Both sides exchanged a constant fire of cannon and firearms, creating vast clouds of smoke 'that covered the sun' and an overwhelming noise, prompting Chodkiewicz to comment that in his whole military career he had never heard such a cannonade. The Poles counted 1,100 shots from the Turkish cannon, so even taking into consideration the usual exaggeration of diarists, it appears that it was genuinely a long and serious barrage. According to contemporary accounts though, despite such heavy Ottoman firepower, it did not cause significant harm to the Cossack position, and thus later in the evening some cannon were relocated to new batteries, with a better field of fire to shoot at the fortified camp. Facing constant attacks from the Ottomans, the Cossacks received more reinforcements, this time in the form of cavalry: *lisowczycy* and reiters. The stubborn defence yet again forced the janissaries and *sipahi* to return to their camp without success. As it was nearing supper time, it might be expected that the fighting would now calm down.

It was not the case though, as the Zaporozhians decided to follow up their successful defence and in the late evening counter-attacked, completely surprising the Turks in their camp. They were hoping to capture or spike some cannon, which is why Chodkiewicz sent them Teofil Szemberg, who was to use his expertise as an artilleryman in this venture. Some banners of Polish infantry, under the command of *rotmistrz* Morenda, arrived in support as well. In the first captured battery they did not find any cannon, as these had been relocated earlier. The attacking Cossacks began looting the Ottoman tents, taking a rich booty. In another captured battery, the Cossacks found seven cannon. However, the victorious *moloitsy* could not take them back to their camp as the cannon 'were bound by iron-rings to the oak trees and the cannon were fastened to each other by chains.' The Cossacks had a good idea as they had brought axes from their own positions, they 'cut the wheels of the guns to pieces and dragged two cannon to their camp.' They also captured many horses and baskets used for moving earth during field works, something that they later put to good use when working on their own defences. Encouraged by their success, the Zaporozhians despatched messengers to Chodkiewicz, asking for more reinforcements and possibly a full-scale attack of the whole army against the Ottomans. Chodkiewicz did not want to risk such an attack in the approaching darkness, and was concerned that the soldiers would break ranks and focus on looting, so he refused to send more of his men out. The Ottomans managed to pull themselves together and organised a counter-attack, led by *kapikulu* cavalry. The Cossacks and the supporting Poles and Lithuanians were pushed out and with heavy losses had to retire to their own positions. Naima wrote that the Turks captured three standards and killed or took prisoner 800 Cossacks. While such losses cannot be verified from Polish sources, diarists

Polish haiduk, armed with *rusznica* caliver, axe and sabre. From the 'Gołuchów table' (*tablica gołuchowska*), *c.*1620 (National Museum in Poznań)

say that 'many were lost' during the retreat to the camp and that Morenda lost two colours, indicating that the Polish infantry took a serious beating. The sources record that Cossack Colonel Wasyl was among those killed; this is probably Vasyl Luchkov (Wasyl Łuczkowicz). The German officer in his *News from Wallachia* said that the Cossacks, while grateful to the German infantry for their support, were not happy with their Polish and Lithuanian allies. One Zaporozhian was heard to say 'Germans are good but Poles are sons of whores', indicating that Chodkiewicz's decision of not supporting the Cossacks during the night fight was upsetting for the *moloitsy*. Despite the losses, the day was definitely a success for the Polish-Lithuanian-Cossack army, with all of the attacks against their positions repulsed and the defensive lines intact. The Tatars continued to harass the part of Władysław's regiment that was still stationed on the Polish bank of Dniester. They succeeded in capturing a small supply tabor, perhaps indicating that the Polish soldiers had problems trying to defend against the swift Crimean and Nogay horsemen.[18]

5 September

After three days of near-constant fighting, 5 September was a day of very low intensity combat, at least if you consider military matters. The Ottomans were moving their camp closer to that of the Cossacks, building more batteries and getting better positioning for further assaults. There was some cannon fire and cavalry skirmishing but more as posturing than as a serious action. Chodkiewicz was well aware of the ogistical problems of his army, especially not having sufficient supplies of powder. He was hoping that once the remainder of Royal Prince Władysław's regiment crossed the river, it would provide the opportunity to engage the Ottomans in open battle. As the lack of food started to be an issue, a convoy protected by 200 infantry and 300 cossack cavalry was despatched to Kamianets, to bring back some supplies.

Unfortunately an event that took place day that day was to become a shameful stain on the reputation of Polish and Lithuanian troops. In the small camp next to Khotyn fortress, thus within the Polish fortifications, was a group of Moldavian merchants with their wives, children and servants; in

---

18 'Jana hrabi z Ostroroga Dziennik wyprawy chocimskiej', pp.20-21, 'Prokopa Zbigniewskiego Dziennik wyprawy chocimskiej', pp.47-48, 'Stanisława Lubomirskiego Dziennik wyprawy chocimskiej', pp.79-80, 'Jakóba Sobieskiego Dziennik wyprawy chocimskiej', pp.131-132, Mustafa Naima (Naima Efendi), *Dziennik wyprawy chocimskiey*, pp.158-160, Stanisław Kobierzycki, *Historia Władysława, królewica polskiego i szwedzkiego*, pp.342-343, *Zeitung aus der Walachei*, p.4, Ödön (Edmund) Schütz (ed), *An Armeno-Kipchak Chronicle of the Polish-Turkish Wars in 1620-1621*, p.55-56, 'List z cyfer przełożony Pana Jakóba Sobieskiego do Xiążęcia Zbaraskiego Pana Koniuszego Koronnego z obozu pod Chocimiem 22 Septembris 1621 roku', p. 205, 'Opisanie wyprawy chocimskiej', p.212, 'Relacya prawdziwa o expediciey przeciwko Turkom, na której sam cesarz turecki był Ao 1621, Woyska koronnego y W. X. Litte pod regimentem Pana Karola Chodkiewicza W. X. Litte które pod Chocimiem leżało', p.221, *Diarius expeditiey królewicza polskiego Władysława przeciwko Osmanowi II, cesarzowi tureckiemu y chanowi tatarskiemu w osobach swych na woynie będących w Wołoszech pod Chociniem roku 1621*, BK 342, ff..52v-53r.

total perhaps 200 civilians. They were selling alcohol and food to the troops and also buying battle loot from the soldiers and camp servants. Some of them may even have loaned money to those in the camps, which may have led those already in debt to get the idea of getting rid of the Moldavians. Rumours were spread that the Moldavians were in league with the Ottomans, that they were planning to set fire to the Polish camp and that Chodkiewicz and Lubomirski had ordered their punishment. An angry mob attacked the Moldavian camp and massacred everyone present. Virtually every Polish diarist, clearly shocked by the event, left a description of this pogrom. Innocent people were cut down or shot, 'no mercy was shown to women or children.' Some, with their hands and legs tied, were thrown into the Dniester or from the bridge into the ravine. As some still 'managed to swim very well', soldiers started to shoot at them. Toddlers were ripped from their mothers' arms and drowned. Some women were raped before being murdered. 'It was horrifying sight: the massacre and looting, mothers pushed into chasms alongside their children. Pleas and pleading cries were of no use here – there was no room for mercy in this madness.' Chodkiewicz was upset at this news and some captured perpetrators were hanged on the spot. The Hetman's health problems and the focus on fighting against the Ottomans meant that there was no proper investigation, thus many more of those involved in the massacre got away with it and were not prosecuted afterwards.

It is worth considering that the danger of arson in the camp was not just an idle threat. The same day the Cossacks captured a Ruthenian peasant from the village of Rzepnica, who was bribed by Ottomans to set a fire in the camp. When tortured, he gave the names of some other peasants that had been sent with the same mission. He was executed next day in front of the whole army, to serve as a warning and 'to show the troops that they need to be attentive'[19] to their duties.

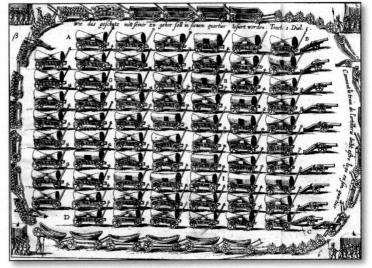

Tabor wagon and artillery park, surrounded by one line of wagons. Diego Ufano, *Archelia albo artilleria to iest fvndamentalna y doskonała informacya o strzelbie…* Original book in German was published in 1614, Polish translation in 1643 (National Library, Warsaw)

19 'Prokopa Zbigniewskiego Dziennik wyprawy chocimskiej', pp.48-49, 'Stanisława Lubomirskiego Dziennik wyprawy chocimskiej', p.81, 'Jakóba Sobieskiego Dziennik wyprawy chocimskiej', p.133, Stanisław Kobierzycki, *Historia Władysława, królewica polskiego i szwedzkiego*, pp.343-344, 'Relacya prawdziwa o expediciey przeciwko Turkom, na którey sam cesarz turecki był Ao 1621, Woyska koronnego y W. X. Litte pod regimentem Pana Karola Chodkiewicza W. X. Litte które pod Chocimiem leżało', pp. 221-222, Jakub Sobieski, *Pamiętnik wojny chocimskiej xiąg troje*, pp.32-33, *Diarius expediitey królewicza polskiego Władysława przeciwko Osmanowi II, cesarzowi tureckiemu y chanowi tatarskiemu w osobach swych na woynie będących w Wołoszech pod Chociniem roku 1621*, BK 342, p.53.

6 September

It was another day of low intensity actions without attacks, with both sides focused on preparing their camps and resting. The Ottomans were preparing for the assaults that were planned for the next day, so a call out was made for *serdengeçti* from among the ranks. These were a famous volunteer 'forlorn hope' used to spearhead the attacks where insane bravery was required and losses were expected to be high. Osman II also ordered the building of a bridge over the Dniester, below the Cossack camp, in order to move some troops and artillery onto the other bank of the river. Vassal Moldavian soldiers were moved to a new position on the right flank of the Ottoman army, to build this bridge. In the meantime, Hetman Chodkiewicz again sent Vevelli to the Grand Vizier, claiming that he was unable to directly answer the Turkish letter as 'he do not have good translators' but that he was willing to negotiate for peace. Three Ottoman soldiers deserted to the Polish camp, claiming that the Sultan himself had started to have doubts and that the morale of the army was falling. At the same time they testified about the power and strength of Osman II's army, but as such they were not seen as reliable witnesses, and had possibly been sent out to frighten the defenders. Two more fugitives that fled from the Ottomans provided more information. One of them was Cossack that had been held in captivity for seven years. According to him, during the previous assault the Turks had lost 2,000 janissaries killed, which appears to be a rather exaggerated number. He also said about the rising price of food in the Ottoman camp, indicating early problems with supplies. The second fugitive was a German soldier, who had previously served with Prince Korecki during the campaign of 1620. In his testimony, he confirmed a decrease in the morale of the Turkish army but also the fact that the Sultan was giving 'assault money' to his soldiers, preparing for the next day's attacks. It seems to be confirmation of preparing *serdengeçti* to lead the army against the defensive lines.[20]

Example (upper bridge of the illustration) of a bridge of boats, of the type often used during the crossing of the Dniester River. Andrea (Andrzej) dell'Aqua, *Praxis ręczna działa na trzy xięgi podzielona*, 1630 (Kórnik Library)

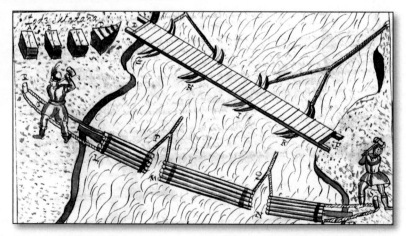

---

20   'Jana hrabi z Ostroroga Dziennik wyprawy chocimskiej', p.21, 'Prokopa Zbigniewskiego Dziennik wyprawy chocimskiej', p.49, 'Stanisława Lubomirskiego Dziennik wyprawy chocimskiej', pp.81-82, 'Jakóba Sobieskiego Dziennik wyprawy chocimskiej', p.134, Mustafa Naima (Naima Efendi), *Dziennik wyprawy chocimskiey*, p.160.

7 September

The Polish bridge over the Dniester was mended, which sped up the crossing of Władysław's troops. Zbigniewski recorded that it improved the method of transport, as when ferrying troops across, because of the overloading of boats and also suffering from the heavy wind during the crossing, many men, especially German infantry, had drowned. Starting during the morning, the Ottoman forces prepared a new series of assaults, Naima stated that all provincial troops, janissaries and even *silahdars* of the *kapikulu* cavalry were preparing for action. The attack was spearheaded by 1,000 men of the serdengeçti, with the initial focus on the Cossack camp with some secondary probing attacks against the Polish and Lithuanian positions. Despite the fact that earthworks around the Zaporozhian camp were not finished, the stubborn Cossacks managed to repulse four consecutive assaults during five hours of fighting. The German infantry of Denhoff and Learmont defended their own positions as well, despite heavy cannon fire targeted at them. The Ottoman artillery hit some hussar cavalry in Lubomirski's camp and even Royal Prince Władysław's tent was in danger but there was no follow-up assault against this part of the line.

Just after midday the Turks struck on what appears to have been a vulnerable position near Chodkiewicz's gate, on the point between the Lithuanian lines and those of Royal Prince Władysław's troops. A small earthwork outside of the gate was manned by two banners of *wybraniecka* infantry, under the command of *rotmistrz* Życzewski and *rotmistrz* Śladkowski. Despite the Hetman's orders, the position was not prepared properly, as it lacked a large rampart and there was only a moat or trench around it. What was worse, the soldiers were unprepared, with many sleeping and resting after the midday meal 'as it was Polish custom'. The janissaries and *sipahi* completely surprised the *wybraniecka* infantry, taking their position. Both infantry banners were nearly wiped out, with up to 150 men dead, including both commanding officers; their colours were captured, along with two tabor wagons with some hook-guns or *śmigownica* light guns on them. As was their custom, the Turkish soldiers cut off the heads of the dead, in order that they could claim a reward from the Sultan.

Seeing this initial Ottoman victory, the other defenders started to waver, with some infantry abandoning their positions. Mikołaj Sieniawski, who was in charge of the guard duties that day, 'by threatening and hitting [the men]' stopped the retreat and restored some order. The Ottoman troops managed to cross the main ramparts and even entered the defensive tabors of some Lithuanian regiments, where the looting started. Hetman Chodkiewcz reacted quickly however, with volunteers from among the units of cavalry sent out in a counter-attack sally. They managed to push the Ottomans away from the camp and then from Życzewski's and Śladkowski's positions, while more infantry was sent to again defend this place. Naima complained that the janissaries focused on looting instead of fighting and this led to their defeat. Another Turkish attack was stopped by Weyher's German infantry, when the assaulting Ottoman troops came under heavy fire from muskets and cannon and had to abandon their attempt to reach the earthworks. The

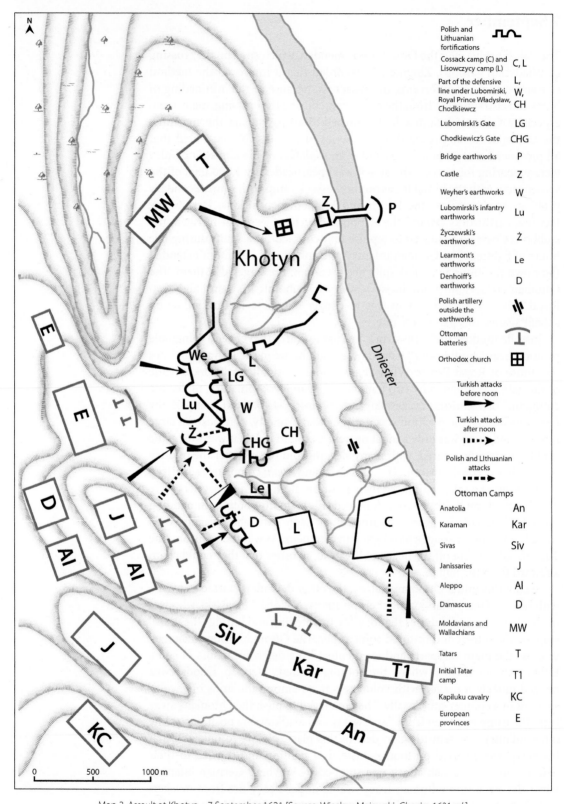

Map 3. Assault at Khotyn – 7 September 1621 [Source: Wiesław Majewski, *Chocim 1621 rok*]

next attack took place at the Orthodox Church, where Lubomirski controlled the situation though and quickly counter-attacked with cavalry from the regiments under his command.

Hussars fighting Turkish *sipahi*. Detail from the sarcophagus of King Sigismund III at the Wawel Castle in Cracow (Author's archive)

After both sides had paused to reorganise and rest their troops, in the evening the Ottomans made another assault attempt. Their attack focused on the area of their previous success, so the previous position of Życzewski and Śladkowski. A strong 'division' of several thousand *sipahi* supported by janissaries, some Polish sources claimed this force was 10,000 to 15,000 men, approached the earthworks. This time the Lithuanians and Poles were much better prepared however. More infantry were placed in the defended position, and Hetman Chodkiewicz took four regiments of cavalry to in front of the camp. Three of them were Lithuanian: his own, Mikołaj Zienowicz's and Aleksander Sapieha's, with the fourth one Polish, under Piotr Opaliński. Seeing the mass of Ottoman cavalry, Chodkiewicz decided to prevent the attempt with a charge of his hussars. Four banners were chosen: the Hetman's own, Mikołaj Zienowicz's, Jan Rudomina's and Mikołaj Sieniawski's. In all around 600 men, with each unit set up in two ranks, to maximise the impact of the charge. It is worthwhile to note that Rudomina's banner did not have lances, and thus was fighting 'in reiter style' – relying on pistols and hand weapons. The hussars charged against the right flank of the approaching Ottomans, striking the *sipahi*. 'With God's Mercy each lance was broken on them [Turks],' with soldiers quickly discarding broken weapons and switching to sabres, estocs and pallasch swords. Rotmistrz Rudomina claimed that some hussars managed to kill three or four Turks with one lance thrust. The Lithuanian and Polish soldiers were under heavy fire from the janissaries supporting the *sipahi*, but they pushed on despite the losses, forcing the

Ottoman cavalry to retreat. Chodkiewicz's hussars lost their standard, it was an 'expensive white damask, [with, on it] eagle's wing with one black leg', when Standard-Bearer Jankowski was killed. The Hetman was upset at the loss, as the standard had been carried by his troops in previous campaigns in Moscow. While leading the attack, Mikołaj Zienowicz lost his horse and was surrounded by Turks. His *szyszak* helmet was dislodged and the Lithuanian officer received numerous cuts to his face and head. His soldiers managed to save their grievously wounded commander from the battlefield but he succumbed to his wounds a few days later. The Ottoman cavalry broke and fled through its own infantry, allowing the badly battered hussars to gather their wounded and return to their camp. Chodkiewicz was prepared for the further fighting and he ordered Lubomirski to bring some cavalry regiments to support him, but the Turks lost the heart to continue their attacks. The Tatars were sent out to skirmish against the Commonwealth army's lines but the Hetman sent out *lisowczycy* against them. The Polish mercenary cavalry forced the Tatars to retreat back to their own positions, ending the fighting for the day. While Polish and Lithuanian infantry focused on reinforcing their earthworks and ramparts, and Lubomirski's cavalry protected the camp, the surviving soldiers from the hussar banners and their camp servants were busy recovering their wounded colleagues and the bodies of their dead. The same was happening with the Turks, who, throughout the night, 'with torches and night lamps,' were searching the battlefield, looking for the most important among their dead, 'they left the others on the spot as [one might] dogs'. In order to get a reward from the Sultan, Ottoman soldiers were also cutting off the heads of Polish and Lithuanian bodies; it appears that all of the dead companions from Jan Rudomina's banner met with this fate.

Memorial in the church in Navahrudak (Nowogródek, today in Belarus), funded in 1643 by Jan Rudomina to commemorate his brother Jerzy and eight other companions from his hussar banner that died at Khotyn on 7 September 1621. All hussars are shown kneeling in prayer, dressed in full armour. What is striking, however, is that they are all shown headless, as their bodies were beheaded on the battlefield and the heads taken as trophies by Ottoman soldiers (Author's collection)

As always in such situations, it is very difficult to estimate the losses of both sides. Naima mentions '1,000 infidels were killed', although that seems too high a number. We do not know the losses among the Cossacks, who faced numerous Turkish assaults beginning in the morning. As for Polish and Lithuanian troops, there were at least 150 to 200 infantry lost, mostly from the two banners of *wybraniecka* destroyed during the afternoon attack. For the cavalry, we can put together estimates of the losses amongst four units of hussars that took part in the counter-attack. The Hetman's banner had seven companions and 15 retainers killed, including Standard-Bearer Janowski. The unit also had 10 horses killed, and many retainers were shot and wounded. Zenowicz's banner had its *rotmistrz* mortally wounded and most of the sources mention that only three companions were killed. One detailed relation provides a much higher list of losses in this unit though, with 17 companions killed, 18 killed and wounded retainers, and 20 killed and wounded horses. Rudomina's unit also took severe losses, with 9 companions dead, and many other companions (including the *rotmistrz*), retainers and horses wounded. Amongst the killed was the brother of *rotmistrz* Jan Rudomina, Jerzy. Finally Sieniawski's unit had 3 companions killed. Taking into consideration that around 600 men took part in the charge, the losses were high and they paid dearly for their success. It is even more difficult to estimate the losses amongst the Ottoman troops, as the majority of diarists mention the very general 'many perished'. One anonymous diary gives a figure of '4,000 killed janissaries counted on the battlefield,' which can be easily discredited as unreliable. Auxent gives 1,200 'more or less' killed during the evening's fighting, although we do not know where he would have received such information from. Zbigniewski seems to be more cautious with his numbers, estimated that during the hussars' charge up to 500 Turks were killed, with many others wounded.

Polish hussars against Ottoman *sipahi*. Decorations from Hetman Stanisław Żółkiewski's sarcophagus, circa1621 (Sergey Shamenkov's archive)

The decisive action by Chodkiewicz stopped the Turkish attack and prevented the Ottomans from getting any foothold within the Polish-Lithuanian defensive lines. The stubborn resistance shown by the Cossacks repulsed all assaults aimed against their camp. The Polish and Lithuanian hussars, despite severe losses, yet again showed their skill and mastery of the battlefield. It is possible that if the charge had taken place during the day, Chodkiewicz and Lubomirski would have deployed more troops – especially cavalry – and tried to follow up on the success of the initial charge. As the fight took place in the evening, the Lithuanian Hetman did not want to risk a battle during the hours of darkness, where the Turks could ambush his men. But the day was won by the defenders and yet another series of Ottoman attacks had failed.[21]

---

21   'Jana hrabi z Ostroroga Dziennik wyprawy chocimskiej', p.22, 'Prokopa Zbigniewskiego Dziennik wyprawy chocimskiej', pp.49-50, 'Stanisława Lubomirskiego Dziennik wyprawy chocimskiej', pp.82-83, 'Jakóba Sobieskiego Dziennik wyprawy chocimskiej', pp.134-137, Mustafa Naima (Naima Efendi), *Dziennik wyprawy chocimskiey*, pp.160-161, Stanisław Kobierzycki, *Historia*

8 September

Learning from the last day's mistake, the Polish and Lithuanian infantry worked on reinforcing the positions previously manned by Życzewski and Śladkowski. The Polish bridge over the Dniester was finally mended, so the remainder of Royal Prince Władysław's regiment, including the supply wagons, managed to cross over to the Moldavian bank and join the rest of the army. Feeling that the morale of his troops was high and that there was a good chance in engaging the Turks in another pitched battle, Chodkiewicz decided to deploy the majority of the cavalry regiments through both gates, hoping for a chance of a new combat. The Ottomans were unwilling to engage, focusing on the artillery cannonade instead. The Lithuanian Hetman would not risk an attack against Ottoman positions in the woods and on the hills, so he kept his army next to the camp. In the afternoon, the Tatars made some advances in the area of the Orthodox Church but were not eager to assault such a well defended position. Instead, they managed to capture or kill a number of camp servants, also taking many horses from the pastures outside of the Polish lines. It was on this day that Auxent mentioned the reorganisation of the Ottoman forces, when losses amongst janissaries had to be filled in with men drawn from the ranks of *serhaddkulu*, where '4,000 Janissaries were recruited from among the *segbans* and *bostanjis*'.

Another crucial event took place in the Cossack camp. During the final approach to Khotyn, Jakub Nerodowicz Borodawka had been replaced by Konashevych-Sahaidachny but now Borodawka was to meet his fate. For the losses taken during the march through Moldavia and poor leadership, he was now sentenced to death by his fellow Cossacks. Kobierzycki provides us with a rather one-sided character of Borodawka, indicating why he was removed from the command and executed:[22]

> He was the most slothful man amongst all rebels[23] and completely given over to his desires. He arrived late with his troops and the delay was caused by crimes and pillaging, committed both in his homeland and abroad. Because of that

---

Władysława, królewicza polskiego i szwedzkiego, pp.344-347, Ödön (Edmund) Schütz (ed), *An Armeno-Kipchak Chronicle of the Polish-Turkish Wars in 1620-1621*, pp.57-59, 'List z cyfer przełożony Pana Jakóba Sobieskiego do Xiążęcia Zbaraskiego Pana Koniuszego Koronnego z obozu pod Chocimiem 22 Septembris 1621 roku', p.205, 'Opisanie wyprawy chocimskiej', pp.213-214, 'Relacya prawdziwa o expediciey przeciwko Turkom, na którey sam cesarz turecki był Ao 1621, Woyska koronnego y W. X. Litte pod regimentem Pana Karola Chodkiewicza W. X. Litte które pod Chocimiem leżało', p.222, Fridrich Warzuchtig (Jan Rudomina), *Diariusz prawdziwy expediciey Korony Polskiey, y Wielkiego Xięstwa Litewskiego przeciw Osmanowi Cesarzowi Tureckiemu w roku 1621 pod Chocimiem w Wołoszech Fortunnie odprawioney. Fridrych Warzuchtig Bawarczyk Zoldath ubogi będąc przytomny opisał*, pp.55-62, *Zherela do istoriï Ukraïny-Rusy*, volume VIII, p.237, Jakub Sobieski, *Pamiętnik wojny chocimskiej xiąg troje*, pp.34-38, *Diarius expeditiey królewicza polskiego Władysława przeciwko Osmanowi II, cesarzowi tureckiemu y chanowi tatarskiemu w osobach swych na woynie będących w Wołoszech pod Chociniem roku 1621*, BK 342, ff.53r-53v.

22 Stanisław Kobierzycki, *Historia Władysława, królewicza polskiego i szwedzkiego*, p.348.

23 Kobierzycki published his book in 1655, so he had no sympathy towards the Cossacks that by then already waged a war against the Commonwealth for seven years.

he completely neglected gathering food [needed] during the wartime. When everything that was looted was eaten and there was no other opportunity to pillage, the Cossacks decided that they would redeem their crimes with the life of one man. They demoted Borodawka and chose Konashevych-Sahaidachny to take his previous command. He ordered that Borodawka be taken to a place of execution and beheaded. In this way he enforced the military discipline.

Despite the words of the Polish seventeenth century historian, other diarists indicate that Borodawka was sentenced by the gathering of Cossacks, in a similar way in which Beauplan described their customs during the campaign. It is almost certain however that Konashevych-Sahaidachny played some part in both removing his rival from the command and in his execution. He got rid of his main opponent, blaming him for any problems that the Cossacks had encountered during the initial stages of the campaign. He was warned by his *moloitsy* that he had to be careful that 'if he changes anything (in this order of things), then he will suffer the same fate'.[24]

A unit of janissaries engaged in the fight against Christian forces. Workshop of Frans Hogenberg, between 1595 and 1597 (Rijksmuseum, Amsterdam)

9 September

Remaining troops from Royal Prince Władysław's regiment finally arrived in the camp, leaving just some infantry manning the earthworks protecting the bridge on the Polish bank of the river. In the morning the Ottoman army deployed outside of its camp, ready to start a new wave of attacks. Chodkiewicz was ready though and he took a large part of the Polish and Lithuanian cavalry through the gates, outside the main defence line. Units of hussars, cossack cavalry and reiters were standing in rank in front of the

---

24 'Jana hrabi z Ostroroga Dziennik wyprawy chocimskiej', pp.22-23, 'Prokopa Zbigniewskiego Dziennik wyprawy chocimskiej', p.50, 'Stanisława Lubomirskiego Dziennik wyprawy chocimskiej', pp.83-84, 'Jakóba Sobieskiego Dziennik wyprawy chocimskiej', pp.137-138, Mustafa Naima (Naima Efendi), *Dziennik wyprawy chocimskiey*, pp.161-162, Ödön (Edmund) Schütz (ed), *An Armeno-Kipchak Chronicle of the Polish-Turkish Wars in 1620-1621*, p.59, *Zeitung aus der Walachei*, p.5, , *Diarius expeditiey królewicza polskiego Władysława przeciwko Osmanowi II, cesarzowi tureckiemu y chanowi tatarskiemu w osobach swych na woynie będących w Wołoszech pod Chociniem roku 1621*, BK 342, f.53v.

ramparts, protected by infantry manning the earthworks. 2,000 Zaporozhian Cossacks were redeployed from their camp to the northern part of the Polish camp, where they were 'set up [in ambushes] in the woods', in order to stop further incursions of Tatars near the Orthodox Church. The Turks were not keen to engage in an open fight though, so while they kept some part of their forces in front of the Polish-Lithuanian line, with the usual skirmishing between cavalry, their assaults focused yet again on the Cossack camp. Osman II and his commanders seemed to hope that this time Chodkiewicz would not be able to properly support Zaporozhians and will keep his forces to himself, in the anticipation of attacks against other parts of the camp. Starting just after noon, after a one-and-half hour artillery and firearms barrage, for the next four hours masses of janissaries were throwing themselves at the Cossack camp, every time forced to retreat though. As with previous assaults, Zaporozhians were supported by German infantry, mostly from Denhoff's and Learmont's regiments. Some secondary attacks by Tatars, Wallachians and Moldavians took place in the north but Cossacks that were laying there in ambushes and 100 haiduks defending the Orthodox Church did not have any problems in forcing the attackers to retreat. At the evening, Chodkiewicz sent out *lisowczycy* to flush out the Turkish skirmish screen, as the Hetman was hoping to engage the enemy in an open fight. The Ottoman

forces decided that they had enough for one day though and retreated to their own positions. Polish sources estimated that between 1,500 and 2,000 Turks, mostly janissaries, were killed during this day's attacks, although as always it is very difficult to know how accurate such figures are. In the meantime, on the other bank of the Dniester, Tatars continued to harass Polish logistic lines. Infantry defending the bridge managed to force them to retreat but not before Tatars were able to capture many horses left there on pastures.[25]

10 September

After two days of heavy fighting, Ottomans decided to take some rest, with no further assaults on the camp on that day. As Naima described it 'day was idle'. It was not exactly the case though, as Osman II's army or rather, to be precise, its Moldavian allies, were working on the bridge over the Dniester, which would allow them to set up batteries

Polish haiduk from 1620's, armed with sabre, axe and *rusznica*. Abraham Booth, *Journael van de Legatie in Jaren 1627 en 1628*, Amsterdam, 1632 (National Archive, Gdańsk)

25 'Jana hrabi z Ostroroga Dziennik wyprawy chocimskiej', p.23, 'Prokopa Zbigniewskiego Dziennik wyprawy chocimskiej', pp.50-51, 'Stanisława Lubomirskiego Dziennik wyprawy chocimskiej', p.84, 'Jakóba Sobieskiego Dziennik wyprawy chocimskiej', pp.138-140, Mustafa Naima (Naima Efendi), *Dziennik wyprawy chocimskiey*, pp.162-163, Ödön (Edmund) Schütz (ed), *An Armeno-Kipchak chronicle of the Polish-Turkish wars in 1620-1621*, p.61, 'Opisanie wyprawy chocimskiej', p.214, 'Relacya prawdziwa o expediciey przeciwko Turkom, na którey sam cesarz turecki był Ao 1621, Woyska koronnego y W. X. Litte pod regimentem Pana Karola Chodkiewicza W. X. Litte które pod Chocimiem leżało', pp.222-223, *Zherela do istoriï Ukraïny-Rusy*, volume VIII, p.238, , *Diarius expeditiey królewicza polskiego Władysława przeciwko Osmanowi II, cesarzowi tureckiemu y chanowi tatarskiemu w osobach swych na woynie będących w Wołoszech pod Chociniem roku 1621*, BK 342, ff.53v-54r.

and aim cannon over the river on the Cossack camp. The Tatars were also very active on the Polish side of the Dniester, attacking, 'like bandits or rapacious wolves,' any merchants or supply convoys attempting to travel to the besieged Commonwealth's forces. They also continued their raids into Polish inland, capturing many prisoners and a large quantity of food. Tatar raids in Polish land were very successful, they brought so many captives that the price of slaves sold in the Ottoman army became very cheap. Cossacks asked for permission to cross the river and attack them but were refused so as not to weaken the defences of the camp. In the evening, Hetman Chodkiewicz called out the war council, to discuss further courses of action. Commanders of the joint army were concerned that every day hunger, sickness and desertion was taking their toll on their men. Sobieski wrote about it in great detail:

> Bad air, maybe [also] due to unhealthy water, was decimating every day Polish ranks. From the noblest [commander] to the common soldier, many men died suddenly; some suffered from diarrhoea and in awful pain gave up the ghost; others were sick, unable to bear arms, without the strength, were dying in the camp. (…) During this campaign there were many of those, that fled during the day and night, leaving their banners, preferring to rather die in the river's currents than bravely face the danger threatening the Homeland. Many of those fleeing, who did not want to stand against the enemy, were captured by Tatars. (…) Many of the nobles from the good families were found hiding amongst the supply carts, they were dragged out from their hiding place and paraded in shame through the camp. Others, who shamed themselves with cowardice, had their names added to the list and, to be remembered with more disgust by posterity, their possessions were confiscated and *Sejm* sentenced them to infamy.

To try to improve the morale and overall strategic situation, commanders decided to attempt some offensive action. It was agreed that on the night from 11 to 12 September a strong Polish-Lithuanian-Cossack force would leave the camp and attack the Ottoman position. It seems that Konashevych-Sahaidachny was the most vocal in choosing this course of action, possibly in order to strengthen his position amongst the Cossacks. He was supported by Jan Weyher, who had previous experience in fighting against the Turks in Hungary. Royal Prince Władysław also gave his blessing to the planned action. Chodkiewicz was not so keen for such a venture though, 'afraid of the Cossacks' greed of looting' but not wanting to antagonise his officers, he agreed to support the plan and allow them to carry on with the mission.[26]

---

26 'Jana hrabi z Ostroroga Dziennik wyprawy chocimskiej', p.23, 'Prokopa Zbigniewskiego Dziennik wyprawy chocimskiej', p.51, 'Stanisława Lubomirskiego Dziennik wyprawy chocimskiej', p.84, 'Jakóba Sobieskiego Dziennik wyprawy chocimskiej', p.140, Mustafa Naima (Naima Efendi), *Dziennik wyprawy chocimskiey*, p.163, Kadir Kazalak, Tufan Gündüz, 'Osman'in Hotin Seferi (1621)', p.143, Jakub Sobieski, *Pamiętnik wojny chocimskiej xiąg troje*, pp.38-40.

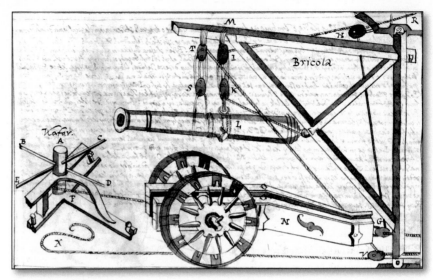

Setting a cannon on its carriage. Andrea (Andrzej) dell'Aqua, *Praxis Ręczna Działa na trzy Xięgi Podzielona*, 1630. (Kórnik Library)

11 September

Finishing the bridge over the Dniester allowed the Ottoman forces to move troops and four to six cannon to the other side of the river. They set up a battery from which they were able to open fire on the Cossack camp. The barrage continued through the whole day, killing many horses, although only a few Cossacks were killed, but amongst them was Colonel Jarczek. While most of the diarists played down the accuracy of the Turkish artillery, Czapliński mentioned that cannon fire was causing a lot of trouble to the Cossacks, as batteries were being moved closer to the camp and the barrage took place 'every day, without a break, so cannon balls are flying through the camp like a bumblebees'. The Poles redirected some of their cannon into counter-battery fire and the Ottomans had to cease their cannonading across the Dniester. The bridge itself seems to have been a feat of engineering, especially when compared with the Polish one. It clearly impressed the German officer, the author of *News from Wallachia*, who saw it later after the end of the campaign. He described it in great detail and it is worthwhile to read his description, as a good example of the skill of the Ottoman engineers, who seem to have supervised the Moldavian troops actually building it:

> The Turk, on the other hand, built such a strong bridge to his camp that he could transport guns to his side along it, which were dragged by 18 and 24 pairs of oxen. A lot of people, cattle and provisions looted in Podolia were driven across the Turkish bridge by the Tatars. The Turkish bridge was built in the following way: powerful pillars were driven across the entire width of the Dniester at a distance of no more than three feet from each other. In the middle of the bridge, as well as at its two ends, six powerful oak trunks were driven in, on top of which the same ones were fastened crosswise. It was not long before a worthy building appears on the Dniester. When the Dniester rose so high that it flooded the bridge, it did not do him much harm. Powerful oak logs were laid on the bridge, firmly hammered together with solid nails, and earth, sand and, finally, small pebbles were laid on the logs. At each end of the bridge they made powerful and strong

gates, upholstered with strong iron bands. They were made from a hard and rough-hewn oak logs. Two powerful oak logs were also dug here, between which strong steel chains were stretched. All this was both in front of one and in front of the other gates (on both sides of the Dniester). There is no doubt that thousands of bridges cannot compare with this structure. [27]

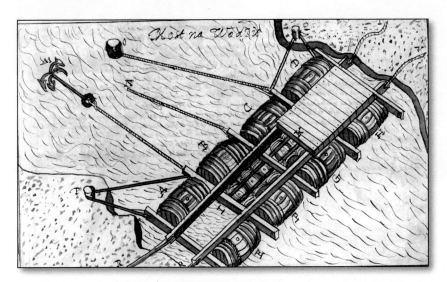

Example of the bridge set up on large wooden barrels. Andrea (Andrzej) dell'Aqua, *Praxis Ręczna Działa na trzy Xięgi Podzielona*, 1630 (Kórnik Library)

Not much happened along the main lines, with Chodkiewicz and Lubomirski again taking their cavalry outside the defensive ramparts but thr Turkish forces were not in the mood for more serious fighting. As on previous occasions, there was only some skirmishing between the cavalry volunteers from both sides. In the evening, a few thousand Tatars tried to attack the defensive position protecting the bridge on the Polish bank of the Dniester. The 200 haiduks defending it managed to easily repulse this attempt, however. Hetman Chodkiewicz's health began to get worse, with the hardships of the campaign and the mental strain taking its toll. Soon his activities were to be very much affected by bouts of illness, reducing his ability to coordinate and command the joint armies.[28]

---

27 *Zeitung aus der Walachei*, pp.9–10.
28 'Jana hrabi z Ostroroga Dziennik wyprawy chocimskiej', p.24, 'Prokopa Zbigniewskiego Dziennik wyprawy chocimskiej', p.51, 'Stanisława Lubomirskiego Dziennik wyprawy chocimskiej', p.84, 'Jakóba Sobieskiego Dziennik wyprawy chocimskiej', pp.140–141, 'Relacya prawdziwa o expediciey przeciwko Turkom, na któréy sam cesarz turecki był Ao 1621, Woyska koronnego y W. X. Litte pod regimentem Pana Karola Chodkiewicza W. X. Litte które pod Chocimiem leżało', p.223, 'Kopia listu od pana [Jana] Czaplińskiego do Jerzego Radzimińskiego 1 Octobris z obozu pisanego', p.208.

Thousands of oxen and camels were present in the Ottoman camp and many accounts mentioned them as valuable loot captured by Cossacks, Poles and Lithuanians during the night sallies. Romeyn de Hooghe, 1694 (Rijksmuseum, Amsterdam)

Night of 11/12 September

Just after midnight, on the night of 11/12 September, the majority of troops from both camps were to leave in silence and proceed towards the Ottoman lines. 20,000 Cossacks supported by at least four banners of Polish-Hungarian infantry and part of two regiments of German infantry were to attack the right flank of the Turkish lines, from the side of the Dniester River. A strong contingent of Lithuanian cavalry, with the support of further units of German infantry under command of the Chodkiewicz himself was to march behind them as reserve. Lubomirski with Polish cavalry and further units of infantry was to protect his side of the camp and block any possible action by the Ottoman left flank and the Tatars. The Commonwealth's commanders were hoping to surprise the Ottoman soldiers, who – it was believed – were not used to fighting during the night and tended to set rather weak guards. The Cossacks and the infantry were to cause panic and confusion in the Ottoman camp, while during the attack the cavalry kept in reserve was to make a 'very loud noise, both from men and from their military music, trumpets, drums, zurnas (*surmy*)'. If the Turks forced the attackers outside of their camp, Chodkiewicz wanted to charge with hussars and reiters on a confused Ottoman soldiery. The plan seems risky, as the coordination of such large groups of attacking soldiers would be practically impossible. It had the potential to cause a high level of losses among Osman II's men, although in the case of failure it could also spell disaster for the Polish, Lithuanian and Cossack troops. The soldiers were to be woken just after midnight and assembled in their banners and regiments as quietly as possible and march through the gates of the camps. The Cossacks moved first and despite the fact that so many thousands of them were closing-in on the Ottoman camps, none of the guards noticed them. The Polish and Lithuanian troops were much slower however and it is possibly that the soldiers were not as enthusiastic about the idea of night attacks as their Zaporozhian brothers-in-arms. The other theory is that only the Cossacks knew about the attack, while the rest of the Commonwealth troops were later told that their commanders had information about an upcoming morning Ottoman attack and the units were moved outside the camp to face them. No matter what the real explanation was, it took many hours to get the units in positions outside the camp, so it was close to dawn when the attackers were ready. But before the fighting could begin torrential rain hit the area. With damp match and powder, the troops would not be able to use their firearms, so Chodkiewicz had to cancel the sally and ordered all troops back to camp. They managed to return safely, as it seems that the Turks and Tatars never saw the attempt. Sobieski, writing about the aborted action, says that it was perhaps for the better that the attack did not take place. As he later had a chance to see the Ottoman camp during peace negotiations, he noted that it appeared to be much better defensively prepared than the Poles had expected it to be. In front of each important tent there were lamps that were kept lit throughout the night. Within the camp, tents were connected by ropes, so in the confusing night melee 'not only cavalry but also infantry would not be able to find their way, getting stuck and falling down due to the ropes'. The Turks were also very active during the night, with councils, feasts, meetings between friends and were often woken up for prayers. The most pragmatic comment was that 'considering the wealth seen in the Ottoman camp, I do not believe that Polish troops, especially common soldiers, would be able to stop themselves from looting, and once focused on the pillaging, it would bring us shameful defeat and eternal disgrace'.[29]

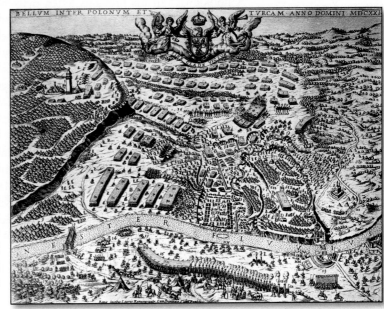

Plan of the Battle of Khotyn. Giacomo Lauro, between 1621 and 1624 (National Library, Warsaw)

---

29   'Jana hrabi z Ostroroga Dziennik wyprawy chocimskiej', p.24, 'Prokopa Zbigniewskiego Dziennik wyprawy chocimskiej', p.52, 'Stanisława Lubomirskiego Dziennik wyprawy chocimskiej', pp.84-85, 'Jakóba Sobieskiego Dziennik wyprawy chocimskiej', pp.141-143, 'List z cyfer przełożony Pana Jakóba Sobieskiego do Xiążęcia Zbaraskiego Pana Koniuszego Koronnego z obozu pod Chocimiem 22 Septembris 1621 roku' in: Józef Tretiak, *Historya wojny chocimskiej 1621 r.*, p.206, 'Opisanie wyprawy chocimskiej', p.215, 'Relacya prawdziwa o expediciey przeciwko Turkom, na której sam cesarz turecki był Ao 1621, Woyska koronnego y W. X. Litte pod regimentem Pana Karola Chodkiewicza W. X. Litte które pod Chocimiem leżało', p.223, *Zherela do istoriï Ukraïny-Rusy*, volume VIII, p.238, Jakub Sobieski, *Pamiętnik wojny chocimskiej xiąg troje*, pp.41-42, *Diarius expeditiey królewicza polskiego Władysława przeciwko Osmanowi II, cesarzowi tureckiemu y chanowi tatarskiemu w osobach swych na woynie będących w Wołoszech pod Chociniem roku 1621*, BK 342, f.54v.

12 September

Both sides were unwilling to attempt any major actions, with the Commonwealth troops resting after a sleepless night. Disappointed with the performance of his soldiers so far, Sultan Osman II decided on a change in the command of the Janissary Corps. The current commander, Nigdeli Mustapha, was replaced with Ali Agha. Naima does not give the reason for this change but, considering the rather lacklustre performance of the janissaries so far, this move was probably intended to improve their behaviour on the battlefield. There was also another attempt to restart negotiations. With the Grand Vizier's permission, Voivode Stefan Tomşa sent Vevelli to the Polish camp again. In a letter addressed to Chodkiewicz, the Voivode lamented that his country was being destroyed by the warring sides and he implored the Lithuanian Hetman to start peace negotiations. Tomşa wrote that the Vizier was not happy with the rather general statements and comments made by Chodkiewicz in his previous letter, delivered by Vevelli. He offered to be an intermediary in any talks that took place between the Commonwealth and the Ottomans, asking the Hetman to send a 'wise and smart man, who will have, in your name, all [the necessary] instructions to negotiate'. The Moldavian also guaranteed the safety of such an envoy, even if the talks were unsuccessful. It is possible that Tomşa's initiative was ordered by the Ottomans, who wanted to check if the Commonwealth's commanders were uncertain about the, for them, positive outcome of the war and were willing to negotiate instead of fighting. It is worthy of note that the correspondence from the Voivode was written in Hungarian, so at least Chodkiewicz had his wish that letter addressed to him was 'in a Christian language'. The war council that gathered in the evening decided that the defence would continue, although messengers needed to be sent to Kamianiets and to the local Polish magnates and nobles, to gather food to be delivered to the Polish-Lithuanian camp. The only military action of 12 September took place in the night, when a group of Cossacks crossed the Dniester and ambushed some Tatars guarding horses on the pastures. In a sudden attack, using their *rohatyna* spears and sabres, they killed several dozen sleeping Tatars and forced the others to flee in panic.[30]

13 September

While the Polish-Lithuanian army planned another night sally for 12/13 September, a few Hungarians from Moszyński's and Fekiety's banners deserted to the Turks and made them aware of the possible attack. The

---

30   'Jana hrabi z Ostroroga Dziennik wyprawy chocimskiej', p.24, 'Prokopa Zbigniewskiego Dziennik wyprawy chocimskiej', p.52, 'Stanisława Lubomirskiego Dziennik wyprawy chocimskiej', pp.84-87, 'Jakóba Sobieskiego Dziennik wyprawy chocimskiej', p.143, Mustafa Naima (Naima Efendi), *Dziennik wyprawy chocimskiey,* p.164, 'Relacya prawdziwa o expediciey przeciwko Turkom, na którey sam cesarz turecki był Ao 1621, Woyska koronnego y W. X. Litte pod regimentem Pana Karola Chodkiewicza W. X. Litte które pod Chocimiem leżało', p.223.

Ottoman army was deployed ready for battle, so any idea of a sally from the camp was abandoned. It led to what was one of the 'quiet' days of that stage of the siege, with some skirmishing between individual horsemen from both armies but lacking in any serious actions or assaults. The Ottoman artillery deployed on the other bank of the Dniester continued to fire on the Cossack camp but did not cause any damage.

By that time the supply crisis was affecting the Zaporozhians badly, as it seems that during their march to Moldavia they had not gathered enough food and provisions for their horses. Sobieski mentioned that complaining Cossacks were walking 'from tent to tent' in the Polish and Lithuanian camp, asking for hay for their horses, and the soldiery was sharing what bread and fodder each one could. Lubomirski supplied provision for 300 horses of the Cossack artillery train, while 'feeding his own horses with leaves and oak barks.' The unhappy Cossacks were close to mutiny and many of them approached Konashevych-Sahaidachny demanding that the Zaporozhian army needed to leave Khotyn. Despite his illness, Royal Prince Władysław played an important role in pacifying the mood of the rebellious *moloitsy*. He sent his envoys – Lubomirski, Sobieski and Opaliński – to negotiate with the Cossacks, 'giving them his word, that their service, full of sacrifice, was worthy and that they had the Commonwealth's gratitude.' He asked them to stay and continue their brave service. As was often the case in such a situation, the Cossack colonels were promised rewards for calming the situation, while the assembly of Zaporozhians was offered an 'award of 50,000 florins, to cover their losses, and the promise of receiving even larger rewards in the future.' The Polish envoys had to confirm this promise in writing, with their signatures and seals on the official document. It seems that the crucial point here was that this offer was approved by Royal Prince Władysław, who was highly respected by the Cossacks and they trusted his word. The crisis was averted, at least for now.[31]

Hungarian infantryman armed with *rusznica* caliver and sabre. Abraham de Bruyn, 1581 (Rijksmuseum, Amsterdam)

14 September

During the further meetings of the war council, Chodkiewicz agreed with the overall assessment that the situation in the allied camp was difficult, realising that the hardships of the campaign and the lack of supplies were badly affecting the army. However, he pointed out that the Ottomans were suffering even more, losing many men in unsuccessful assaults as well as because of hunger and desertion. 'What about [the fact] that cowards are fleeing [from the allied

---

31 'Jana hrabi z Ostroroga Dziennik wyprawy chocimskiej', p.25, 'Prokopa Zbigniewskiego Dziennik wyprawy chocimskiej', p.52, 'Stanisława Lubomirskiego Dziennik wyprawy chocimskiej', p.87, 'Jakóba Sobieskiego Dziennik wyprawy chocimskiej', p.144, Stanisław Kobierzycki, *Historia Władysława, królewicza polskiego i szwedzkiego*, pp.348-350, 'Opisanie wyprawy chocimskiej', p.215, 'Relacya prawdziwa o expediciey przeciwko Turkom, na którey sam cesarz turecki był Ao 1621, Woyska koronnego y W. X. Litte pod regimentem Pana Karola Chodkiewicza W. X. Litte które pod Chocimiem leżało', p.223, *Zherela do istoriï Ukraïny-Rusy*, volume VIII, p.238.

camp], I prefer it [happening] now than during the battle; but I also know that pagans [Ottomans] are losing even more men [than us]'. The soldiers were clearly unhappy with the situation, complaining about losses, problems with food, dying horses and the Tatars that were raiding Polish lands with impunity. The Hetman was determined to continue the fight but listened to the voices of his council that asked him to try negotiating. Chodkiewicz sent Vevelli back to the Ottoman camp and the Italian was accompanied by a Polish envoy, Jakub Zieliński, one of Lubomirski's courtiers. They were to deliver two letters written in Latin, one to Voivode Tomşa and one to the Grand Vizier. In the correspondence to the Moldavian Voivode, the Hetman stated that he understood very well how badly the country was affected by the war but pointed out that 'I only took up my arms to defend my [own] Homeland and to keep up the peace, not to start and wage the war'. He was grateful for the offer of mediation during negotiations, hoping that it was sincere. The Hetman asked the Voivode to take good care of Zieliński and help him during the negotiations. In the correspondence to Ohrili Hüseyin Pasha, the Hetman wrote that he did not understand why both sides were still engaged in a military struggle and why they were not looking for peace. Chodkiewicz said that he was willing to open negotiations and that was why he was sending Zieliński, 'a man of good judgment and immaculate loyalty'. The envoy was authorised to discuss peace on Chodkiewicz's behalf 'as if I was there in person'. It seems that Chodkiewicz was cautiously unoptimistic that peace talks would even start, but wanted to assure his war council that he was taking all the necessary steps.

Ottoman artillery during the siege operation. Next to the battery are Turkish *sipahi* cavalrymen. Studio of Frans Hogenber, 1594–1596 (Rijksmuseum, Amsterdam)

In the meantime there was finally a reason for rejoicing in the Ottoman camp. Qaraqash (Karakash) Pasha arrived with a few thousand troops from Buda. His soldiers were eager to fight and Qaraqash himself 'had very skilful hands and so the Turkish Sultan liked him well and knew he was a Pasha of fortunate constellation.' He asked for permission to attack the Polish-Lithuanian camp the next day, promising that he would be victorious. Osman II was happy to agree to such a request and the Ottomans started their preparation for a new assault. Negotiations had to wait, as fighting was about to recommence.[32]

15 September

In the morning, Ottoman forces started to harass the defensive lines with skirmishers, while their cannon continued their usual barrage. Osman II took to the field this day, setting up an observation position to watch the day's fighting. Qaraqash Pasha assembled a strong assault force for the main attack. According to Auxent he had with him 4,000 troops from Buda, 6,000 janissaries, 12,000 Rumelian and 5,000 Anatolian *sipahi*; other diarists give, clearly exaggerated, numbers of between 36,000 and 70,000 men. Around noon, he led his men towards the Commonwealth camp. He was planning to strike against that part of the ramparts between Lubomirski's and Royal Prince Władysław's positions. From a Hungarian deserter he knew that this position was manned only by *rotmistrz* Moszyński's infantry banner. 'here there are neither any bulwarks, nor cannon, so you will be able to take them easily'. Ottoman infantry and dismounted cavalrymen, guided by the turncoat haiduk, marched around the forward earthwork of Weyher's German infantry and in a surprise attack struck directly at the ramparts. Facing overwhelming numbers, Moszyński's haiduks quickly broke and started to flee, with the victorious Turks chasing them across the ramparts directly into the camp. Despite his poor health, Chodkiewicz accompanied his troops in the fight and so he was able to react quickly to the situation. Lubomirski was also nearby and both commanders organised a counter-attack. Hundreds of volunteers from regular army units – both cavalry and infantry – clashed with the Turks and forced them out of camp and back across the ramparts. The Ottoman morale collapsed when Qaraqash was mortally wounded, depending on the source hit by musket ball either in the chest or the stomach. Even worse for the mass of Turkish troops, is that they were attacked from behind by Weyher's German infantry and from the flank by a charge of hussars, and Lubomirski ordered a few hundred Polish and German infantry to move through his gate, outflanking Qaraqash's men. The Ottoman attack was repulsed, with losses amongst the assault troops estimated as at least several hundred dead. Osman II was so upset at the death of Qaraqash Pasha that in retaliation he ordered the execution of the

---

32 'Jana hrabi z Ostroroga Dziennik wyprawy chocimskiej', p.25, 'Prokopa Zbigniewskiego Dziennik wyprawy chocimskiej', p.52, 'Stanisława Lubomirskiego Dziennik wyprawy chocimskiej', pp.87-93, Mustafa Naima (Naima Efendi), *Dziennik wyprawy chocimskiey*, p.164, Stanisław Kobierzycki, *Historia Władysława, królewicza polskiego i szwedzkiego*, pp.351-352, Ödön (Edmund) Schütz (ed), An Armeno-Kipchak Chronicle of the Polish-Turkish Wars in 1620-1621, pp.61-63, 'Opisanie wyprawy chocimskiej', p.215, 'Relacya prawdziwa o expediciey przeciwko Turkom, na którey sam cesarz turecki był Ao 1621, Woyska koronnego y W. X. Litte pod regimentem Pana Karola Chodkiewicza W. X. Litte które pod Chocimiem leżało', p.223, *Diarius expeditiey królewicza polskiego Władysława przeciwko Osmanowi II, cesarzowi tureckiemu y chanowi tatarskiemu w osobach swych na woynie będących w Wołoszech pod Chociniem roku 1621*, BK 342, ff.54v-55r.

Hungarian deserter who had pointed out the place for the attack. '[Sultan] on this day did not eat nor drink, he just lamented the loss of the one in whom he put so much faith'. The Polish and Lithuanian soldiers and camp servants looted the battlefield, bringing into camp 'the cut off Turkish heads, rings on the cut off fingers, bags full of coins, and decorated sabres'. *Rotmistrz* Fekiety with some men of his cavalry banner even managed to even capture some *sipahi* horses left behind after the attack.

Janissaries assaulting the fortress. In front of them is a battery of light cannon and some skirmishing infantry, equipped with firearms and bows. Studio of Frans Hogenber, 1594–1596 (Rijksmuseum, Amsterdam)

Despite a good opportunity to strike against the Polish-Lithuanian positions, the Ottoman attack ended in total failure and the death of its commanding officer. It appears Qaraqash Pasha did not receive the proper support from the other high-ranking officials, as there were no secondary assaults that could have diverted the Polish and Lithuanian defenders. It allowed Chodkiewicz and Lubomirski to move reinforcements and deal with the dangerous event in the camp. Osman II immediately started to look for a scapegoat to blame for the defeat, which over the next few days led to important changes in the command structure of the Ottoman army and a shift in the strategic plan of campaign. At the same time failure to properly prepare and coordinate the day's attacks could be also partially blamed on the Sultan himself, who simply enthusiastically agreed to Qaraqash Pasha's idea of an attack but did not ensure that other army commanders were prepared to take part in the assault to engage the defenders along the other parts of the line.[33]

33 'Jana hrabi z Ostroroga Dziennik wyprawy chocimskiej', pp.25-26, 'Prokopa Zbigniewskiego Dziennik wyprawy chocimskiej', p.53, 'Stanisława Lubomirskiego Dziennik wyprawy chocimskiej', pp.93-94, 'Jakóba Sobieskiego Dziennik wyprawy chocimskiej', pp.144-146, Mustafa Naima (Naima Efendi), *Dziennik wyprawy chocimskiey*, p.164, Stanisław Kobierzycki, *Historia Władysława, królewicza polskiego i szwedzkiego*, pp.352-353, Ödön (Edmund) Schütz (ed), *An Armeno-Kipchak Chronicle of the Polish-Turkish Wars in 1620-1621*, p.63-65, 'List z cyfer przełożony Pana Jakóba Sobieskiego do Xiążęcia Zbaraskiego Pana Koniuszego Koronnego z obozu pod Chocimiem 22 Septembris 1621 roku', p.206, 'Opisanie wyprawy chocimskiej', pp.215-216, 'Relacya prawdziwa o expediciey przeciwko Turkom, na którey sam cesarz turecki był Ao 1621, Woyska koronnego y W. X. Litte pod regimentem Pana Karola Chodkiewicza W. X. Litte które pod Chocimiem leżało', pp.223-224, *Zeitung aus der Walachei*, pp.7-8, *Zherela do istoriï Ukraïny-Rusy*, volume VIII, p.239, *Diarius expeditiey królewicza polskiego Władysława przeciwko Osmanowi II, cesarzowi tureckiemu y chanowi tatarskiemu w osobach swych na woynie będących w Wołoszech pod Chociniem roku 1621*, BK 342, p.55, Fridrich Warzuchtig (Jan Rudomina), *Diariusz prawdziwy expediciey Korony Polskiey, y Wielkiego Xięstwa Litewskiego przeciw Osmanowi Cesarzowi Tureckiemu w roku 1621 pod Chocimiem w Wołoszech Fortunnie odprawioney. Fridrych Warzuchtig Bawarczyk Zoldath ubogi będąc przytomny opisał*, pp.67-68.

16 September

During the day there were no assaults although the Ottomans were planning for a surprise attack during the night. One of their soldiers deserted to the Polish-Lithuanian camp, revealing the plan, so the assault was abandoned. Hunger had started to be an issue in the allied camp, affecting both men and horses. Camp servants venturing outside the camp to look for fodder for mounts often had to fight with marauding Tatars. 'Even for bark from oak trees, that we were giving to horses instead of hay, we had to pay with blood'. According to the author of *News from Wallachia*, by mid-September Weyher's infantry regiment was down to between 500 and 600 men, half of its original strength, 'since our poor soldiers were dying, mainly from hunger'. As it was often the case, the infantry were the worst affected, especially as the soldiers were not allowed to leave their positions to look for food. On an almost daily basis the Cossacks were crossing the Dniester and fighting with Tatars for provisions, trying to resupply in this way. Jan Czapliński says that up to 50,000 horses were dead by then, with the remaining mounts being fed with leaves but 'there is maybe 1/10 [of the original number of horses] left by now'.[34]

17 September

While again not much happened so far as fighting, there was an unexpected development in the Ottoman army. Osman II decided on a major change as an afterthought of the failed assault of 15 September. Grand Vizier Ohrili Hüseyin Pasha was demoted and his office taken over by Dilaver Pasha, former Beylerbey of Diyarbakir. Ohrili Hüseyin was blamed for the lack of coordination of the Ottoman army on 15 September; there were rumours that he was jealous of Qaraqash Pasha and did not support him in order to stop him succeeding in defeating Chodkiewicz's troops. While there may be some truth in such gossips, it was more likely a lack of experience in leading a large army that should be blamed here. Jakub Sobieski, who later had a chance to meet and talk to the new Vizier during the peace negotiations, described him as 'old, wise, very experienced, with a healthy and simple common sense, not much sly or rough like pagans usually are by [their] nature'. Dilaver Pasha used his wealth to bribe many of the Sultan's courtiers, he also had good and close relationships with officials like the Chief Eunuch and the chief Muslim clerics. It seems that, unlike previous viziers, he was more amicable towards the Poles and would play an important part in the negotiations for peace. The Ottomans were planning to continue with military operations however, although with the main focus on a regular blockade of the defenders' camp and a daily artillery barrage. They were also working on fixing the damaged

---

34 'Jana hrabi z Ostroroga Dziennik wyprawy chocimskiej', p.26, 'Prokopa Zbigniewskiego Dziennik wyprawy chocimskiej', pp.53-55, *Zeitung aus der Walachei*, p.7, 'Kopia listu od pana [Jana] Czaplińskiego do Jerzego Radzimińskiego 1 Octobris z obozu pisanego', p.209.

bridge over the Dniester, to move more troops and cannon to the Polish bank of the river. From there, their focus was to concentrate fire on the Cossack camp, to 'soften' it before further assaults. Tatars were to continue their raids into Podolia and prevent any supply convoys moving to and from Kamianets.[35]

Engineers in charge of the fortifications in Polish-Lithuanian camp were foreigners, like Dutchman Wilhelm Appelman, so they would look very similar to the officers shown on Salomon Savery's etching of the siege of 's-Hertogenbosch in 1629 (Rijksmuseum, Amsterdam)

18 September

Despite their military successes from 15 September, the mood in the Polish-Lithuanian camp was not good. The lack of supplies, the rising losses on a daily basis and the hordes of Tatars cutting off the lines of supply on the Polish bank of the Dniester badly affected the morale of the troops. Desertion was rife, as Zbigniewski mentioned that 'being in camp for three Sundays [weeks] we did not have bread, nor beer, nor oats'. Two Hungarians from Moszyński's banner were captured and executed while attempting to desert in the morning of the 18th. The worsening situation was well summarised by a German officer:[36]

> At that time, we were sitting in the fortification in mortal danger, and hunger was especially harassing us. We had two options: either to fight the Turks, or to leave across the Dniester for those who can swim, but on the other side of the river everyone was killed by the Tatars. We no longer expected to leave here alive. But

---

35 'Jakóba Sobieskiego Dziennik wyprawy chocimskiej', pp.146-147, 149, Mustafa Naima (Naima Efendi), *Dziennik wyprawy chocimskiey,* p.165-166.

36 *Zeitung aus der Walachei,* p.10.

the Almighty, who held the fate of the enemies in his hands, showed us the surest means – to fight the enemy. For this, eternal gratitude to the Lord!

As Hetman Chodkewicz's health was getting worse, and probably aware of his incoming death, he decided to test the resolve of his officers and soldiers. He called for the first general assembly of the army, in the presence of the commissioners, and with the officers of Polish, Lithuanian and foreign troops, as well as senior Cossack commanders. Some sources indicate that assembly took place on 17 September but it is more likely that on that day Chodkiewicz only met with the war council, while the meeting with the larger number of officers in fact took place on 18 September. The Hetman was aware of the growing discontent among the troops, so wanted to approach them in his usual direct way. He said that supplies were low, that men and horses lacked food and that there was a problem with powder for the cannon and the firearms. Then he asked if soldiers wanted to continue fighting from the defended camp, 'holding our ground and until the last drop of blood protect [the way to our] Homeland' or did they prefer to retreat from Khotyn to look for a new position elsewhere? The suggestion of a retreat while facing a large Ottoman and Tatar army was probably to frighten many of his men, with the vision of a repeat of Żółkiewski's defeat of the previous year. It is possible, that this was in fact Chodkiewicz's real goal, to show his soldiers that the stubborn defence of the fortified camp was the only viable option, no matter the hardships and the situation. It was no surprise that all present quickly assured him that they would keep fighting from the camp, staying as long as needed and awaiting the relief army of King Sigismund III. The soldiers pledged that they would 'under penalty of death' remain under his command and defend against the enemy, and if anyone wanted to disobey the oath by fleeing, he would be killed by the others. They did ask, however, for some support for their hardships, especially as the cavalry had lost so many precious horses. The Hetman, with the agreement of the commissioners, agreed an additional quarter of pay (so-called *ćwierć darowana*) to be given to the soldiers after the end of the campaign. The morale of the army was improved thus, if it really was Chodkiewicz's plan, it seemed that it worked and the soldiers were eager to continue the campaign.

To show their willingness and eagerness to fight, the Zaporozhian Cossacks organised another sally, this time during the night of 18/19 September. The sources vary as to the numbers taking part in the attack, although the largest figure of 8,000 men seems to be a bit high. It is more probable that the attacking force was between a few hundred and 1,500 *moloitsy*. The Cossacks managed to either avoid the Ottoman guards or 'talked to them in Turkish' and crawling silently approached the camp of the provincial troops from Karaman and Sivas near the Dniester. Under cover of the darkness, armed with *rohatyna* spears and scythes, they attacked the sleeping Ottomans. In the ensuing panic they managed to capture some impressive booty and bring it back to their own camp. Sources mention close to 200 horses, 20 to 30 camels, some tents, some clothes and weapons. Two janissary flags were delivered by them to Royal Prince Władysław. They even surprised an Ottoman

Janissary loading his musket. Another example of an Ottoman infantryman wearing a leopard skin. *Rålambska dräktboken*, mid-seventeenth century (National Library of Sweden)

Pasha, taking from his tent 'registers and army lists, [and also the] chain that more important pashas wear as a symbol of their office.' The Cossacks also took a large red standard 'of the regiment of this Pasha', although it is possible that it was one of the already mentioned janissary flags. Naima mentioned that *sanjakbey* of Kayseri in Sivas province 'died a martyr' so it is possible that he was the Pasha whose possessions were looted by the Zaporozhians. It appears that the whole attack was a quick 'smash and grab', since the Cossacks did not stay to fight but hastily returned to their positions. It was an example of the typical harassment tactics, that they employed during the campaign, positively affecting the morale of the defenders and keeping the wary Ottomans awake and restless during the nights.[37]

Beasts of burden and wagons used in Ottoman tabor. Two types of wagons (covered and open) pulled by oxen or buffalo, a camel, and a mule. From *Stato Militare dell'Imperio Ottomanno*, Luigi Ferdinando Marsigli, published in 1732 (Author's collection)

19 September

On this day Ostroróg recorded that 'there was peace on both sides'[38] although other diarists, those present at the camp, saw the situation quite differently. During the night of 18/19 September, a few hundred Cossacks had made a successful raid against the Turkish camp (see above). To help with the dwindling supplies, a convoy under the command of Lewikowski was despatched to Kamianets. Each cavalry banner sent two companions, and 15 servants to take care of the provisions. Unfortunately, this improvised unit had to return empty-handed, as a large number of Tatars on the roads prevented the Poles from reaching the fortress. Naima recorded either this fight or one that perhaps took place either the day before or the day after. According to him, the main role in stopping Polish supply attempts was played by Khan Temir, who stopped a convoy of 100 wagons from reaching Khotyn. Seeing an increase in the number of convoys, the Tatars asked for Ottoman reinforcements, and Osman II sent Ohrili Hüseyin Pasha and Hajeki Pasha with some troops and cannon to help in the blockade on the Polish bank of the Dniester.[39]

37 'Jana hrabi z Ostroroga Dziennik wyprawy chocimskiej', pp.26-27, 'Prokopa Zbigniewskiego Dziennik wyprawy chocimskiej', p.54, 'Stanisława Lubomirskiego Dziennik wyprawy chocimskiej', pp.94-95, 'Jakóba Sobieskiego Dziennik wyprawy chocimskiej', pp.146-147, Mustafa Naima (Naima Efendi), *Dziennik wyprawy chocimskiey*, p.166, Stanisław Kobierzycki, *Historia Władysława, królewicza polskiego i szwedzkiego*, p.355, 'Opisanie wyprawy chocimskiej', pp.216-217, 'Relacya prawdziwa o expediciey przeciwko Turkom, na którey sam cesarz turecki był Ao 1621, Woyska koronnego y W. X. Litte pod regimentem Pana Karola Chodkiewicza W. X. Litte które pod Chocimiem leżało', p.224, *Zherela do istoriï Ukraïny-Rusy*, volume VIII, p.239, *Diarius expeditiey królewicza polskiego Władysława przeciwko Osmanowi II, cesarzowi tureckiemu y chanowi tatarskiemu w osobach swych na woynie będących w Wołoszech pod Chociniem roku 1621,* BK 342, pp.55-55v.
38 'Jana hrabi z Ostroroga Dziennik wyprawy chocimskiej', p.27.
39 'Prokopa Zbigniewskiego Dziennik wyprawy chocimskiej', p.54, 'Stanisława Lubomirskiego Dziennik wyprawy chocimskiej', p.95, 'Jakóba Sobieskiego Dziennik wyprawy chocimskiej', pp.147-148, Mustafa Naima (Naima Efendi), *Dziennik wyprawy chocimskiey*, p.165.

20 September

Both sides continued their exchange of artillery fire, but no assaults were attempted. The Ottoman guns shot up to 40 times but only managed to kill one haiduk. A Polish convoy sent for supplies managed to sneak past the Tatars and get to Kamianets. During the night the *lisowczycy* made a sally, capturing some horses and oxen from the Tatars. Chodkiewicz sent a messenger to the Moldavian Voivode, asking for the whereabouts and the wellbeing of envoy Zieliński. Osman II left the camp and travelled to the Prut River, where with Halil Pasha and the Khan they discussed a diversionary attack against Kamianets and other Polish-held castles. It would allow them to completely cut off supply lines to Khotyn and thus worsen the situation in the Commonwealth camp.[40]

Ottoman army during the battle of Khotyn. Giacomo Lauro, between 1621 and 1624. (National Library, Warsaw)

21 September

During the day the main activities focused on skirmishes between individual horsemen, with many Polish officers taking part in the fighting. Relentless, the Cossacks attacked Turkish camp servants on pasture, capturing horses and oxen. Royal Prince Władysław, seeing that Chodkiewicz was very ill, discussed the situation with the commissioners and senators present at the camp. It was agreed that a messenger needed to be sent to King Sigismund with an update on the current state of the campaign. The officials also started to plan to shorten the lines of the defence, as because of losses there were not enough soldiers to man all fortifications in the camp. Hungarian *rotmistrz* Fekiety, one of the most active officers in Polish service during the whole campaign, took his men in a raid across the Dniester, capturing 50 horses, many mules, and a few oxen.[41]

---

40 'Prokopa Zbigniewskiego Dziennik wyprawy chocimskiej', p.55, 'Jakóba Sobieskiego Dziennik wyprawy chocimskiej', p.148.

41 'Prokopa Zbigniewskiego Dziennik wyprawy chocimskiej', p.55, 'Stanisława Lubomirskiego Dziennik wyprawy chocimskiej', p.96, 'Jakóba Sobieskiego Dziennik wyprawy chocimskiej', pp.148–149.

22 September

As the campaign progressed, the situation in the Polish-Lithuanian camp worsened, with the lack of fresh water and proper food decimating men and horses alike. Volunteer Jan Czapliński noted that due to a lack of supplies the price of the food doubled, soldiers also ran out of beer (normally drunk instead of water). He did say that the Cossacks were bringing in food captured from the Turks, 'but what of it? You cannot buy it. As one cabbage costs 10gr, one egg 5gr, all you have [left] is to get sick'.[42] The German officer in his *News from Wallachia* provides a very detailed, and at the same time depressingly upsetting, description of the soldiers' suffering. Under the dates between 22 and 29 September 1621 he recorded:[43]

> Since there was no way to get provisions for the unfortunate, starving soldiers, and because of this, and also because of thirst, [they drunk] unhealthy poisonous lime water, [and] bloody dysentery broke out among the troops, aggravating all the troubles. The faces of the poor soldiers were so damaged by the water that many could not see. Their genitals were swollen like bull bladders and would not let out the urine.
>
> For eight or ten, twelve, fourteen days there was neither bread nor beer. Soldiers had to fry horse liver and eat it instead of bread. True, boiled horse meat, which was eaten instead of beef, was very good. Instead of beer, they drank bad lime water. It got to the point that bread could not be delivered to the camp for four weeks and several more days. Some of the soldiers for ten, twelve days did not have a piece of bread in their mouths. The commanders were not in the best position [either], having only cereals and some crackers. Some of them did not escape a miserable fate.
>
> Rarely in wars [one] had to experience such hardships as they were in Wallachia [Moldavia], when they ate dogs and cats. Many honest soldiers and commanders were convinced of this. Some said that in besieged Smolensk in Muscovy,[44] although one had to eat dogs and cats and not have bread for ten or twelve days, one could at least get good drink there. There was no good water here for four weeks.
>
> Mention should be made of the death of a terribly starving musketeer. Before his death, he asked the Lord [for] only a piece of bread. When his lieutenant gave him a piece of biscuit, he still could not eat it due to severe exhaustion. He only bit off a piece of cracker, holding another in his hand, and died like that. Once, when I was walking through the camp, a soldier greedily asked me for water. I gave him lime water and he drank it with great greed. I had not gone twenty steps before he died. Many others died the same way.
>
> I omit the story of the great shortage of food for the unfortunate horses, who for four weeks did not eat hay or straw. There was grief here. Good horses

---

42 'Kopia listu od pana [Jana] Czaplińskiego do Jerzego Radzimińskiego 1 Octobris z obozu pisanego', p.213.
43 *Zeitung aus der Walachei*, pp.11–13.
44 Indicating that the soldiers in questions were part of the Muscovite garrison, defending the City between 1609 and 1611.

ate branches in an oak forest, because of hunger they had to gnaw on the stakes to which they were tied, to eat each other's withers. The horses, like many hundreds of soldiers, were dying of hunger. According to knowledgeable people from the camp, 24,000 horses perished inside and outside the great fortification.

As I was reliably informed, two soldiers committed suicide due to severe hunger. They went to the middle of the bridge, shouted "Jesus" twice, jumped down and drowned.

Western European officers in the service of the Polish army at Khotyn in 1621. From the front page of *Zeitung aus der Walachei*, an account written by an officer who took part in the battle, published in 1622 (National Library, Warsaw)

Auxent wrote about the severe problems with supplies, mentioning how expensive food was in both the Commonwealth and the Ottoman camps. He also described the way that Cossacks were able to obtain provisions from the Polish bank of the Dniester:[45]

In the Polish camp prices were very high and there was a [terrible] need, because the Turks and Tatars held all the surroundings of the camp, so that we could have no victuals supplied for us or for our horses, so that I myself, Auxent, who were in the camp, saw for what price [did victuals] were sold, and also I myself bought of it. One loaf of bread [formerly] worth of 1 akçe was sold for 20gr, 1 onion 1gr, 1 egg 1gr, 1 gallon [*garniec*] honey 24gr, 1 quart of raqi [raki[46]] 3 florins, 1 *seledec* [lardo] 12gr, 1 quart of vinegar 20gr, 1 bulb of garlic 1gr, 1 madrik-cheese 1 florin, 1 cheese 24gr, 2 *kvasnicas* [kvass] 1gr, 1 cabbage 10gr. And all other food was also very dear. But beef was cheap. 1 slab of meat was 3–4gr, because the Cossacks frequently got some and sold both the cattle and the Turkish buffaloes in the Polish camp. In any case, in the beginning the Cossacks were starving. But later they went upstream as far as Śniatyń and brought back a rich booty of all kinds

---

45 Ödön (Edmund) Schütz (ed.), *An Armeno-Kipchak Chronicle of the Polish-Turkish Wars in 1620–1621*, p.83.

46 Alcoholic drink made from twice-distilled grapes, very popular in Turkey and also in some Balkan regions.

of food. They bound 3–4 tree trunks together, loaded [the booty] on it and so they brought it downstream. So the famine lasted for 5 weeks. This way we pulled through the period, until peasants came on foot, bringing bread and brandy on their back and sold it in the camp. 100–200 men agreed to go at night through the forest to Żwaniec, but many of them were caught by the Tatars.

As for the shortage of provisions in the camp of the infidel Turks: the camp of the infidel was free of access and they were not blocked by anybody as was the camp of the Poles. To begin with: 1 Wallach bag of oats cost 6 gold florin, 1 oqa[47] biscuit 80 akçes, 1 oqa salt 60 akçes, 1 bread 6 akçes, 1 oqa rice 60 akçes, 1 oqa raisins 50 akçes, 1 hen 80 akçes, 1 egg 8 akçes, 1 onion 5 akçes, 1 bulb of garlic 10 akçes, 1 oqa raw honey 1 gold, 1 oqa olive oil 150 akçes and all the other victuals were also very dear with the infidel. But meat was likewise cheap, because the infidel Tatars seized [much cattle] in Poland and they sold them cheap to the Turks.

Polish infantry armed with sabres and *rusznica* calivers. Detail from the restoration copy of the sarcophagus of King Sigismund III at the Wawel Castle in Cracow (Author's archive)

The situation was very bad, affecting both the soldiers' morale and their ability to fight. To makes things even worse, Chodkiewicz's health deteriorated further, and during the night he was so unwell that the other commanders were afraid that he would not last until the morning. When Zieliński and Vevelli finally returned from the Ottoman camp with letters from the Grand Vizier, 'wrapped in the red silk', they had to hand the correspondence to Lubomirski, as the Lithuanian Hetman was unable to deal with it any more. Dilaver Pasha was showing willingness to negotiate but it did not stop hostilities between the armies. The Tatars struck yet again at the Polish camp servants protecting horses on the pastures, 'killing many and capturing many horses'.

The Cossacks continued their nighttime sallies, this time crossing the Dniester and striking against Turkish forces protecting the bridge. 1,200 *moloitsy* supported by 300 of Lubomirski's haiduks completely surprised the sleeping Ottoman soldiers, who were probably not expecting such a strong incursion on that side of the river. The attackers killed some Turks, others fled in the ensuing panic. Ohrili Hüseyin Pasha barely survived, hiding from the Cossacks and only returning to his camp in the morning. Another Ottoman commander, Toganjy Pasha, was killed. As with previous sallies, the

---

47 Ottoman measure of mass, known as *oka, okka* or *oke*. It varied from region to region but roughly it was 1.2 kg.

Cossacks and haiduks quickly looted the camp and then returned to their own positions.[48]

23 September

Facing a constant barrage from the Ottoman guns, the Commonwealth's commanders decided to redeploy their troops and change the defensive set up of the camps. The majority of earthworks set up outside of the main ramparts were abandoned, 'since most of our people died and could not hold on any further.' The remaining infantry was moved to the ramparts, with the only outer work still manned with troops being held by Denhoff's regiment. As the Turks moved even more guns to the Polish side of the Dniester, it was decided that the Cossack camp would be moved uphill, to be included as a part of the Lithuanian camp. The Zaporozhians moved their tabor wagons and destroyed their temporary earthworks. Those changes left the campsite of the regiment of *lisowczycy* as the most vulnerable position still outside of the main defensive lines. As the Turks and Tatars were focused on the movement of Polish and Cossack troops, it allowed a supply convoy to leave towards Kamianets. Under the command of Mikołaj Kossakowski, it was protected by up to 1,000 cavalry, including the district troops of cossack cavalry from Kiev and Volhynia, and 100 or 200 Hungarian haiduks from Royal Prince Władysław's unit. The convoy managed to safely avoid marauding invaders and after reaching Kamianets it returned to Khotyn on 1 October.

In the meantime, Chodkiewicz was already on the point of death, and everyone in the Polish-Lithuanian command realised it. During the last meeting with officers and commissioners he was not even able to speak any longer, and with a symbolic gesture he passed his Hetman's mace into the hands of Lubomirski, nominating him as the new general commander. The Lithuanian officers, upset with losing their Hetman, grudgingly accepted Lubomirski but also asked Royal Prince Władysław 'to take them under his wing', looking for his protection and support. He agreed, 'offering them his help and his assistance'. As rumours of Chodkiewicz's condition were spreading through the army camp, he was taken in a horse-drawn cart to Khotyn Castle, to be kept away from the soldiers, but it was impossible to keep his condition a secret, and most probably everyone in the ranks was expecting the bad news at any moment.[49]

---

48 'Jana hrabi z Ostroroga Dziennik wyprawy chocimskiej', pp.27-28, 'Prokopa Zbigniewskiego Dziennik wyprawy chocimskiej', pp.55-56, 'Stanisława Lubomirskiego Dziennik wyprawy chocimskiej', p.97, 'Jakóba Sobieskiego Dziennik wyprawy chocimskiej', p.149, Mustafa Naima (Naima Efendi), *Dziennik wyprawy chocimskiey*, p.167, Ödön (Edmund) Schütz (ed), *An Armeno-Kipchak Chronicle of the Polish-Turkish Wars in 1620-1621*, p.65, *Zherela do istoriï Ukraïny-Rusy*, volume VIII, p.241, *Diarius expeditiey królewicza polskiego Władysława przeciwko Osmanowi II, cesarzowi tureckiemu y chanowi tatarskiemu w osobach swych na woynie będących w Wołoszech pod Chociniem roku 1621*, BK 342, f.56r.

49 'Prokopa Zbigniewskiego Dziennik wyprawy chocimskiej', pp.56-57, 'Stanisława Lubomirskiego Dziennik wyprawy chocimskiej', p.97, 'Jakóba Sobieskiego Dziennik wyprawy chocimskiej', p.150, Mustafa Naima (Naima Efendi), *Dziennik wyprawy chocimskiey*, p.167, Stanisław

24 September

The day brought the biggest loss for the Polish-Lithuanian army. The numerous illnesses, the stress and hardships of the campaign finally prevailed and Grand Lithuanian Hetman Jan Karol Chodkiewicz died at Khotyn Castle. He died in the afternoon or the early evening (different sources give different times) and the news of his death quickly spread between the soldiers of both armies. The German officer recorded in *News from Wallachia*, 'Chodkiewicz treated the Germans like their own father, and therefore enjoyed great fame among them', thus clearly even foreign soldiers were upset at his death. Following the dying Hetman's nomination, Lubomirski was now in overall command of the joint armies, and Aleksander Sapieha probably took over the Lithuanian troops. Royal Prince Władysław, whose health was by then improving, was not in direct command but his voice was heard by officers and his position amongst Zaporozhian Cossacks was also of importance.

An interesting scene from the battle of Khotyn. Osman II is observing the battle, we can see Ottoman artillery, cavalry and soldiers of the guard units are shown in front and each side of him. Drums placed on the elephant are used to raise the morale of the troops. In the centre of the picture, Polish and Cossack prisoners are being executed. Illustration from Ġanizāde Nādirī's *Şehnāme-i Nādirī* (Topkapı Palace Museum Library)

As news of Chodkiewicz's death quickly reached the Ottoman army, Osman II decided to organise a new assault. Both he and the Turkish commanders were probably expecting that the defenders' morale would be badly hit by the loss of the Hetman. For the new attacks planned against the Commonwealth's camp, the Sultan looked into raising more *serdengeçti*, as had previously happened on 6 September. This time they were recruited from amongst Osman II's court servants, and also probably from camp followers. Auxent provides us with a very interesting description, although the numbers given by him seem to be, as is usual, far too high. 'Also that day [24 September] were enrolled 14,000 men, who had come from the Court, that is to say volunteers and *serdengeçti* in the camp of the Turks. These volunteers, as infantrymen, have to go in front on foot in encounters and attacks. Of this kind of people anybody wanting to get enrolled is suitable, all he needs to have is armour, no matter who he is, he gets soldier's pay. There

Kobierzycki, *Historia Władysława, królewicza polskiego i szwedzkiego*, pp.355-356, 'Opisanie wyprawy chocimskiej', pp.217, 'Relacya prawdziwa o expediciey przeciwko Turkom, na którey sam cesarz turecki był Ao 1621, Woyska koronnego y W. X. Litte pod regimentem Pana Karola Chodkiewicza W. X. Litte które pod Chocimiem leżało', pp.224-225, *Zherela do istoriï Ukraïny-Rusy*, volume VIII, p.241, *Zeitung aus der Walachei*, pp.10-11, *Diarius expeditiey królewicza polskiego Władysława przeciwko Osmanowi II, cesarzowi tureckiemu y chanowi tatarskiemu w osobach swych na woynie będących w Wołoszech pod Chociniem roku 1621*, BK 342, ff.56r-56v.

were enrolled in order to go into the attack against the Poles; if any of them showed special abilities, he was given spahiship'. While the assault did not take place until the next day, there was still the usual artillery cannonade and skirmishing between cavalry. The barrage was concentrated on the Cossacks and *lisowczycy*. The janissaries took over the abandoned earthworks of the German infantry and the former Cossack camp, moving their own positions closer to the defenders. Both sides were preparing for the next day's assaults.[50]

Western-style officers of infantry, the mounted figure would probably be higher-ranking (possibly commanding the regiment). The half-pike and halberd were both used as weapons and symbol of the rank. Simon Frisius, after Antonio Tempesta, between 1595 and 1628 (Rijksmuseum, Amsterdam)

25 September

The Ottomans attacked along the whole front, with cavalry, provincial infantry and janissaries attacking the Polish and Lithuanian lines and the Cossack and *lisowczycy* camp. Probably serdengeçti spearheaded the attack and in some places they even managed reach the ramparts. In the ensuing chaos, there were even cases of 'friendly fire' when Polish gunners killed some of their own men. Officially it was explained by their using low quality black powder. A few banners of Polish infantry began to flee from their positions but Lubomirski reacted quickly, supporting them with reserve units and volunteers from amongst the cavalry units. According to Naima, the Ottoman troops managed to twice enter the interior of the Polish-Lithuanian camp, they even took and sent some prisoners to the Sultan, although on each occasion 'the janissaries' incompetence took the near victory out from our hands.' Polish and Lithuanian reinforcements managed to push them back after a hard-fought close combat, and it seems that dismounted cavalrymen supporting haiduks and German infantry were very useful in such melee. The *lisowczycy* were very hard pressed, as they were only a regiment of cossack cavalry and their camp does not seem to be well protected with earthworks. Seeing their situation, Lubomirski timely reinforced them with his own Polish infantry under *rotmistrz* Bobowski. The haiduks managed to stabilise the situation and stopped the Turks and Tatars. Czapliński mentioned that the Ottomans were 'throwing janissaries like a cattle during the assaults, so we were [shooting] at the naked[51] men

---

50   'Jana hrabi z Ostroroga Dziennik wyprawy chocimskiej', p.28, 'Prokopa Zbigniewskiego Dziennik wyprawy chocimskiej', p.57, 'Stanisława Lubomirskiego Dziennik wyprawy chocimskiej', p.97, 'Jakóba Sobieskiego Dziennik wyprawy chocimskiej', pp.150-151, Stanisław Kobierzycki, *Historia Władysława, królewicza polskiego i szwedzkiego*, p.356, Ödön (Edmund) Schütz (ed), *An Armeno-Kipchak Chronicle of the Polish-Turkish Wars in 1620-1621*, p.67, 'Relacya prawdziwa o expediciey przeciwko Turkom, na którey sam cesarz turecki był Ao 1621, Woyska koronnego y W. X. Litte pod regimentem Pana Karola Chodkiewicza W. X. Litte które pod Chocimiem leżało', p.225, *Zherela do istoriï Ukraïny-Rusy*, volume VIII, p.241, *Zeitung aus der Walachei*, p.15.
51   Unarmoured.

Two *solak,* bow-armed janissaries. *Rålambska dräktboken*, mid-seventeenth century (National Library of Sweden)

like at bison[52]. As it is often the case, the sources lack details about losses of both sides, with the Commonwealth's soldiers claiming to kill 'many' and taking little loss themselves. *Rotmistrz Łoś,* leading one of haiduk banners in Stefan Potocki's regiment, was shot and killed, Colonel Learmont of the German infantry and cossack cavalry *rotmistrz* Kopaczewski were wounded. Assaults ended in the evening, with the Ottomans returning to the recently abandoned outer earthworks of the Polish-Lithuanian camp.[53]

26 and 27 September

The weather turned worse, as according to Naima 'a dark fog covered the horizon; the ground was covered with snow and you could feel the beginnings of the northern cold.' Such conditions were difficult for both sides but especially badly affected were the Asian contingents of the Ottoman army, not used to such weather. There were no assaults through those two days but the Turks moved more cannon across the Dniester, and the artillery barrage continued, focused mostly on the Cossack and *lisowczycy* camp. On 26 September there was some skirmishing in front of Lubomirski's part of the camp but it did not develop into a more serious fight. Vevelli was travelling between the Polish and the Ottoman camps, bringing letters written by Lubomirski and the Grand Vizier. Both sides seemed to be open to negotiations although the Turks were insisting that the Polish negotiators were required to go to their camp, but they gave assurances of their safety during the peace talks.[54]

---

52   He used word *żubry*, as he had European bison (*Bison bonasus*) in mind.
53   'Jana hrabi z Ostroroga Dziennik wyprawy chocimskiej', p.28, 'Prokopa Zbigniewskiego Dziennik wyprawy chocimskiej', p.57, 'Stanisława Lubomirskiego Dziennik wyprawy chocimskiej', p.98, 'Jakóba Sobieskiego Dziennik wyprawy chocimskiej', pp.151-152, Mustafa Naima (Naima Efendi), *Dziennik wyprawy chocimskiey*, pp.167-168, Ödön (Edmund) Schütz (ed), *An Armeno-Kipchak Chronicle of the Polish-Turkish Wars in 1620-1621*, p.67, 'Opisanie wyprawy chocimskiej', p.217, 'Relacya prawdziwa o expediciey przeciwko Turkom, na którey sam cesarz turecki był Ao 1621, Woyska koronnego y W. X. Litte pod regimentem Pana Karola Chodkiewicza W. X. Litte które pod Chocimiem leżało', p.225, *Zherela do istoriï Ukraïny-Rusy,* volume VIII, p.241, 'Kopia listu od pana [Jana] Czaplińskiego do Jerzego Radzimińskiego 1 Octobris z obozu pisanego', p.211.
54   'Prokopa Zbigniewskiego Dziennik wyprawy chocimskiej', pp.57-58, 'Stanisława Lubomirskiego Dziennik wyprawy chocimskiej', p.98, 'Jakóba Sobieskiego Dziennik wyprawy chocimskiej', p.153, Mustafa Naima (Naima Efendi), *Dziennik wyprawy chocimskiey*, p.168, 'Relacya prawdziwa o expediciey przeciwko Turkom, na którey sam cesarz turecki był Ao 1621, Woyska koronnego y W. X. Litte pod regimentem Pana Karola Chodkiewicza W. X. Litte które pod Chocimiem leżało', pp.225-226, *Zherela do istoriï Ukraïny-Rusy,* volume VIII, p.241.

28 September

Despite discussions regarding opening the negotiations, Osman II decided on one more all-out assault, hoping that it would either break the resolve of the defenders or at least 'soften them' ready for the peace talks, giving the Ottomans the upper hand. The Sultan issued a proclamation saying 'woe to the man who received soldiers' pay and not go out today to attack the Poles and Cossacks; not a single man in the army's ranks shall stay in

Two janissaries in 'campaign clothes'. From *Icones Habitus Monumenta Turcarum*, between 1586 and 1650. (Jagiellonian Library, Cracow)

the camp, neither a Turk, nor a Wallach,[55] nor a Multanian,[56] all will join the attack against the Polish camp'. A barrage from the Turkish guns, including from the large battery set up on the Polish bank of the Dniester, started in the morning. It seems that the Turks had by now at least 25 field pieces and two heavy siege cannon, 'drawn by 14 pairs of oxen', moved from their main camp to the other bank, to ensure that they could provide heavy fire support from this direction. As during the previous day, the cannonade was focused mostly on the *lisowczycy* and Cossacks. Losses caused by this fire seem to have been fairly low, with just a few killed and wounded recorded by diarists. Once the assaults started in the afternoon, they were all-out attempts: from attacks against the Orthodox Church in the north, through Polish and Lithuanian main lines, to the camps of the Cossacks and of the *lisowczycy*. The latter was especially picked as a target, as it was seen as a weak point of the defence. Unfortunately the defenders did not reinforce the earthworks here and, at least during initial stages of the assaults, the *lisowczycy* were not supported by infantry. Masses of janissaries, provincial infantry and dismounted *sipahi* continually threw themselves onto the defensive lines, with serdengeçti leading the attacks. The Sultan held only a minimal reserve of a few thousand janissaries and *kapikulu* cavalry with him, while the rest of the troops were ordered to continue with the assaults. Even the Tatars deployed on the Polish bank of the river were involved in the fighting, on a number of occasions trying to swim on their horses through the river to at least divert the attention of the defenders. None of their attempts ended with a full crossing of the river though, and it seems they were clearly just planned as a diversion. Osman II himself was observing the battle from one of the hills, 'there a royal seat was made for him with a baldachin, and in front of him 4 musicians mounted on 2 elephants each beating the drum and blowing the pipe'. During the first few assaults the hard-pressed *lisowczycy*

---

55 Moldavian.
56 Wallachian.

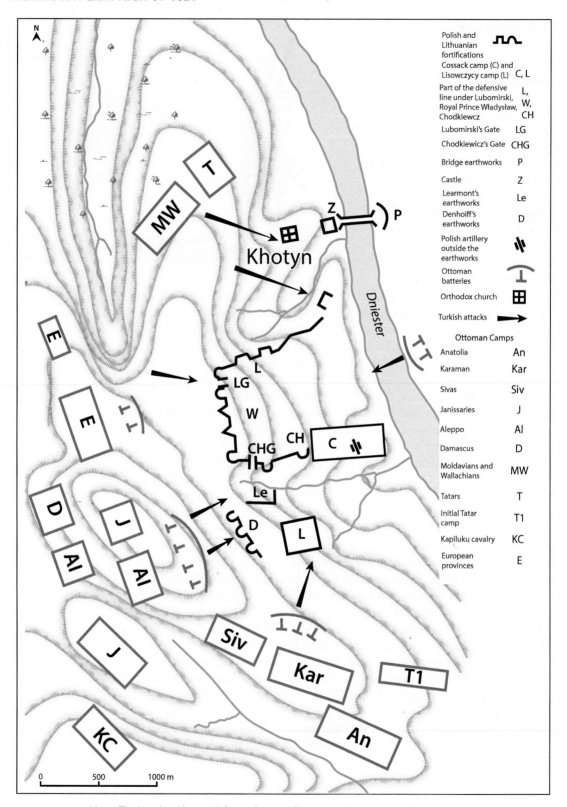

Map 4. The Assault at Khotyn, 28 September 1621 [Source: Wiesław Majewski, *Chocim 1621 rok*]

were supported by the Cossacks, but then the Zaporozhians had to focus on the defence of their own camp being attacked by janissaries and *sipahi*. The *Lisowczycy* started to waver but Lubomirski kept an eye on events and started to reinforce them with infantry. He sent his own Polish unit, then Hungarians under Almady. Royal Prince Władysław was also involved, initially ordering his Polish infantry commanded by *rotmistrz* Mikołaj Kochanowski and later, when the fighting was particularly intense, even his Scottish and Irish lifeguard unit. This infantry support strengthened the defence but in the face of masses of attacking Ottomans it seemed that it might not be enough. Seeing this, Lubomirski asked the Polish cavalry to help and to despatch 10 men from each banner to the *lisowczycy* camp. At least 1,000 men moved to the *lisowczycy* camp and their counter-attack pushed the Turks out. They even pursued the fleeing Ottomans outside the ramparts, preventing further attacks. It is important to note however, that the Polish and Lithuanian cavalry was fighting dismounted, there was no attempt to use their banners to sally out through the gates and charge mounted. The loss of horses throughout the campaign seems to have been so severe that the cavalry was not able to fight in its designated primary role.

While the main thrust of the Ottoman attacks was focused on the *lisowczycy,* another strong push was aimed at Chodkiewicz's gate and the earthworks of Denhoff's and Learmont's German infantry. On the previous day, in anticipation of the new attack, Teofil Szemberg – back at his military duties, after a long diplomatic stint – prepared a new sconce facing the abandoned earthworks previously manned by Wehyer's Germans and Almady's Hungarians. Szemberg had with him a few light cannon, a banner of haiduks (depending on sources, of between 50 and 200 men), Rychter's company of dragoons[57] and a banner of dismounted reiters of Tomasz Zamoyski. This force was also reinforced by some camp servants, probably armed with firearms. The cannon were covered with barks and bushes and the soldiers were ordered to hide, so that the earthwork would look abandoned. When the unsuspecting Turkish soldiers were marching around the sconce, towards the ramparts and the gate, Szemberg gave the order to fire. Sudden salvoes from cannon, muskets and *rusznica* calivers hit the Ottomans, causing numerous losses and smashing the attack. According to Auxent, 'many men fell there, some were torn to pieces, there were people whose head flew off, some lost their legs, some their arms'. After the battle, captured Turks accused the Poles of using magic, with 'something green [in the cannon fire] that choked us and within a moment killed 400 good Turks'. The Poles laughed at it, as it appears that they had used grass to wad the powder in their guns and while shooting at close distance 'that the grass that did not burnt out and hit the Turks in the face'. It seemed to have had a rather powerful effect, badly shaking the morale of Osman II's men.

The assaults continued until the evening but every time the Ottoman troops were forced to retreat. Clearly, both sides fully understood that it was really the last attempt to resolve the campaign by a feat of arms. This is why

---

57　The only unit of dragoons present in the Polish-Lithuanian army at Khotyn.

German infantry fighting at Khotyn would have used muskets with rests, as shown by this musketeer from Wallhausen's drill book. Johann Jacobi von Wallhausen, *Ritterkunst*, 1616 (Author's collection)

the Sultan kept throwing his men at the ramparts over and over, no matter what their losses. Naima had to admit that 'we lost [killed a] high number of men and horses, also many wounded'. Auxent with an obvious exaggeration wrote that the Turks lost 1,400 janissaries, 3,000 *sipahi* and 5,000 to 6,000 Moldavians killed. In the Polish and Lithuanian camp every able-bodied man took part in the defence in order to defeat the Ottomans; with only the 'sick, wounded and shot [left] in huts and tents, expecting death [any moment]'. Losses amongst the allies are unknown, although it is possible that especially amongst *lisowczycy* there were many killed and wounded. The most notable loss was the Hungarian cavalry *rotmistrz* Fekiety, who was mortally wounded 'by a janissary musket shot just in his elbow'. While Royal Prince Władysław and Hetman Lubomirski ordered that 'any skilled and trained barbers there were should come and cure him', no one was able to safely extract the bullet and the brave officer died within the week.

After a whole day of fighting it was the defenders that were triumphant, with Osman II's soldiers forced to cease their attacks without achieving any success. Both armies were by now exhausted and decimated by the hardships of the campaign. Additionally, in the whole Polish-Lithuanian camp there was only one barrel of powder left. It is therefore not surprising that there were hopes that the hostilities would now stop and both sides could focus on the negotiations.[58]

29 September

In the morning, the Polish envoys Jakub Sobieski and Stanisław Żórawiński travelled to the Ottoman camp, to start the peace negotiations. They were accompanied by 20 to 30 servants and on their way to Osman II's lines were escorted by number of hussars who 'all had leopard or tiger skins

---

58 'Jana hrabi z Ostroroga Dziennik wyprawy chocimskiej', pp.29-30, 'Prokopa Zbigniewskiego Dziennik wyprawy chocimskiej', pp.58-60, 'Stanisława Lubomirskiego Dziennik wyprawy chocimskiej', pp.99-100, 102, 'Jakóba Sobieskiego Dziennik wyprawy chocimskiej', pp.153-156, Mustafa Naima (Naima Efendi), *Dziennik wyprawy chocimskiey*, p.168, Stanisław Kobierzycki, *Historia Władysława, królewicza polskiego i szwedzkiego*, pp.361-363, Ödön (Edmund) Schütz (ed), *An Armeno-Kipchak Chronicle of the Polish-Turkish Wars in 1620-1621*, pp.69-73, 'Opisanie wyprawy chocimskiej', pp.217-218, 'Relacya prawdziwa o expediciey przeciwko Turkom, na którey sam cesarz turecki był Ao 1621, Woyska koronnego y W. X. Litte pod regimentem Pana Karola Chodkiewicza W. X. Litte które pod Chocimiem leżało', p.226, *Zherela do istoriï Ukraïny-Rusy*, volume VIII, p.241, *Diarius expeditiey królewicza polskiego Władysława przeciwko Osmanowi II, cesarzowi tureckiemu y chanowi tatarskiemu w osobach swych na woynie będących w Wołoszech pod Chocimiem roku 1621*, BK 342, ff.57r-57v, 'Kopia listu od pana [Jana] Czaplińskiego do Jerzego Radzimińskiego 1 Octobris z obozu pisanego', pp.211-212.

[thrown over their shoulders]'[59]. At the outskirts of the camp they were greeted by Turkish cavalry – also adorned in full splendour – and escorted into the Turkish positions. Sobieski has left a very detailed description of the mission, with talks taking place up to 9 October.[60] He and Żórawiński received a set of instructions, agreed upon during the long meeting at Royal Prince Władysław's quarters, which took place before their departure on 28 September. The main points were that the Commonwealth would stop Cossack raids, while the Ottomans should, in a similar manner, stop their Tatar allies from attacks on Poland. Khotyn would be returned to Moldavia, although Moldavian voivodes were to stop their attempts to incite a conflict between the neighbouring countries. Envoys were to discuss further negotiations, including despatching ambassadors to both monarchs. Both armies were to return any deserters that changed sides; there was also a set of rules as to how the troops were to retreat through Moldavia – with the Poles planning to insist that the Ottomans were to leave first. During the initial negotiations Vevelli proposed a list of gifts that were to be given to Turkish officials, which was a typical custom in this period. For himself he asked for 4,000zl and Polish *indygenat* (ennoblement). The Poles were satisfied with the idea of paying the Ottomans, they even agreed to compensate Vevelli with 5,000zl, although they were not so keen on his suggestion about giving him a Polish noble title. A special set of gifts for Osman II included 200 sable pelts (50 bundles of 40), 20 marble fox pelts, an expensive chest 'of the exquisite workmanship, worthy of the emperor' and two clocks. The Moldavians also suggested that, at least for the time being, the Polish would not discuss the case of the prisoners taken during Żółkiewski's expedition of 1620. They did not want the Ottomans to know the real worth of many of the captured magnates, so were hoping that this topic could be determined later. Sobieski and Żórawiński were for the next few days moving between the two camps and talking to Turkish court officials, including the Grand Vizier.

Osman II, while aware of the negotiations, was still hoping that his military strength would prevail. During the council of war, he was to say that 'he would not leave until the enemy camp is [finally] captured' and if necessary, the army would spend the winter at Khotyn. It was mere bravado however, as even he had to realise by then how badly exhausted and bloodied his army was. He still tried to break the resolve of the defenders, with large numbers of Tatars sent to Podolia to pillage and to burn anything they could not carry back. Ohrili Hüseyin Pasha with a strong corps, including up to 30 guns, was sent to capture Kamianets, to cut off the main Polish

Examples of officials and commanders at the beginning of seventeenth century, from the copy of the 'Stockholm Roll' showing the Royal entry to Cracow in 1605. Artist unknown. The original painting is currently in the collection of the Royal Castle in Warsaw. (Author's collection)

---

59 Ödön (Edmund) Schütz (ed.), *An Armeno-Kipchak Chronicle of the Polish-Turkish Wars in 1620–1621*, p.75.

60 'Jakóba Sobieskiego Dziennik wyprawy chocimskiej', pp.157-176, Jakub Sobieski, *Pamiętnik wojny chocimskiej xiąg troje*, pp.61-76.

supply base. He did not threaten the fortress however and after a short and uneventful siege of the castle at Panowce, the Ottoman commander returned to the main army. This insignificant action was later exaggerated by Piasecki in his chronicle, giving rise to the myth that even today is often repeated as a truth. He wrote that Osman II led the expedition in person and that upon his arrival at Kamianets, seeing the natural defensive position on which this fortress was built, he asked who made it into such an impressive fortress. When his advisers told him that 'it had to be God that fortified this place', Osman II was said to have answered, 'then it should be God himself that needs to besiege it' and he ordered a retreat to the camp around Khotyn.[61] While very amusing and clearly boosting the morale of Polish readers, this story is simply not true and is not confirmed by other sources. The Sultan did not leave the main army camp and did not lead his troops on the Polish bank of Dniester; he would also not leave camp to participate in a low-scale expedition, while important peace talks were still taking place.

Negotiations (30 September–9 October)

Despite the negotiations, the Ottoman artillery continued its barrage, especially from the other bank of the Dniester. There was some cavalry skirmishing and the Cossacks attempted some sallies against the Tatars and the Turks, but there were no serious assaults on the defence lines. Polish and Lithuanian camp servants, trying to take their masters' horses to pasture, were constantly harassed by Tatars, losing many men and horses over the period of few days. An important event of 1 October was the safe arrival of Mikołaj Kossakowski's supply convoy from Kamianets. The Poles managed to outmanoeuvre the Tatars and the Turks sent to intercept them and reached Khotyn without any fighting. The convoy brought badly needed food but just two barrels of powder. There was also news that a contingent of 20,000 Don Cossacks was marching towards Khotyn, with their envoys already having arrived at the camp to discuss this relief mission with Royal Prince Władysław. This seems to have been no more than a rumour spread to improve the morale in the allied camp at a critical moment of the campaign. At the same time, while Sobieski and Żórawiński were engaged in advanced talks with the Turks, Osman II ordered the public execution of prisoners – a rather unusual decision, considering the timing of it. The German officer in his *News from Wallachia* wrote:

> by order of the Turkish Sultan, all the captured Cossacks, Poles and Germans, as well as those who were caught trying to get something to eat, were taken to a fairly high rock. They stripped them and then cut off the heads of all these 500 people. The rock was located on the opposite bank of the Dniester, in an open area, and everyone saw the Sultan's joy when the severed heads flowed down one after another, and then the bodies of the executed.

---

61   *Kronika Pawła Piaseckiego biskupa przemyślskiego,* p.299.

While one could argue that it was just anti-Ottoman propaganda, in the illustrations from Ġanizāde Nādirī's *Şehnāme-i Nādirī* executed Cossacks and Poles can clearly be seen, confirming that such an event did take place. Auxent also mentioned the mass execution of captured Poles, Lithuanians and Cossacks, who, after interrogation in front of the Sultan, had their throats cut and '[ordered the] killed men to be thrown down from the high hill'. In a similar manner the Ottomans were dealing with deserters from the Commonwealth's camp, 'they had also been interrogated and then slayed'. Finally any Turkish soldier or camp servant caught during desertion was beheaded and thrown down from the hill. The heads of the dead prisoners were placed together in heaps, while the headless bodies were gathered in three places at the foot of the hill. According to the 'Armenian Chronicle', there were more than 700 men killed in this way.[62]

While some small-scale fighting still took place, the Polish and Ottoman negotiators, assisted by Moldavian Voivode and his courtiers, were talking daily trying to find some agreement. The Grand Vizier was trying to frighten the Poles into submission, presenting them with a vision of the Tatars hordes, supported by European Turkish troops, Moldavians and Wallachians, that were to be unleashed on Poland, while Osman II in spring 1622 would gather a 'huge army from Asia and Africa' and follow the trail of destruction towards the Polish interior. The bluff did not work however, as Żórawiński phlegmatically answered, that the 'fate of the war is always uncertain, that defeat and victory are part of the unknown.' He added that so far the Turks had nothing to boast about and the Poles nothing to be afraid of. Both he and Sobieski then decided to leave but the Vizier realised

Deli with his distinctive self-mutilation, painted horse and lack of armour. Note the estoc visible under his left leg. *Icones Habitus Monumenta Turcarum*, between 1586 and 1650. (Jagiellonian Library, Cracow)

that a completely different approach was needed and, 'asking them to stay, since then [it] became much easier to discuss the conditions of peace'. The whole process of negotiations – both verbal and later written as the treaty – was severely hampered by language problems. The Poles were talking to a Moldavian translator Szymon (Simon), who then translated into Romanian for the Voivode, who in turn spoke in Turkish to the Vizier and the other Ottoman officials. It is thus no surprise that the talks took such a long time and that many things had to be repeated and re-checked, as details were misunderstood or lost in translation. Sobieski said that while writing down all the agreed points, 'I dictated in Polish to Multan [the Moldavian], he in Greek to the Greek one and that one to Turk, who was writing down the treaty'. It seems that final versions of agreement in fact had some significant differences between the Polish and the Turkish copies. For example, while the Poles strongly disagreed with the idea of paying a tribute to the Sultan, such a term was included in the Turkish version. The complete exhaustion of the fighting armies, problems with supplies and the worsening weather had to be a factor in 'smoothing out' any potential disagreements however. On 8 October the Polish negotiators were even invited for an audience with

---

62 Ödön (Edmund) Schütz (ed.), *An Armeno-Kipchak Chronicle of the Polish-Turkish Wars in 1620–1621*, p.79.

Sultan Osman II, as a show of his good will. They brought him a letter from Hetman Lubomirski, while Sobieski in short speech, translated by one of the Moldavian courtiers, thanked the Ottoman monarch for ending the war, signing the peace, and renewing friendship with the Polish King. The envoys also delivered gifts sent by Sigismund III, 'a sabre with gold and jewels made in the old fashioned way, a pair of pistols and a finely crafted firearm, as well as a golden goblet, a beautiful silver watering can and a black bandog,[63] quite sightly.'

With constant quarrels over the different terms of the agreement and despite clear language barriers, negotiations finally reached their conclusion. On the evening of 9 October the Polish envoys received a signed copy of the treaty; another copy was to be delivered by the Ottoman envoy to King Sigismund III. In theory none of the sides came out as winners or could be called victorious, with the Poles agreeing to stop Cossack raids and the Ottomans agreeing to control their Tatar vassals. While the Commonwealth managed to stop the Sultan's invasion, the treaty was in fact a confirmation of Turkish control over Moldavia and, at least for the time being, meant that Polish influence there was diminished. (A translation of the full text of the treaty, based on its Polish version, is provided *in extenso* in Appendix VI.) While both sides were finalising their talks, the atmosphere between the two armies started to change. Despite orders forbidding such practices, Polish and Lithuanian soldiers were visiting the Ottoman camp or were meeting Turks outside their own camp, 'drinking vodka together, providing gifts to each other, there were also plenty of trading'. Only the Tatars seemed to be unfazed by any peace talks and they continue to harass Polish camp servants, and in return were attacked by Cossacks. Osman II even despatched one of his pashas to the other side of the Dniester, to punish the Tatars, ordering the execution of anyone caught attacking the Commonwealth's men.[64]

Tin figurines of a Polish officer (hetman) and horseman. Decorations from Hetman Stanisław Żółkiewski's sarcophagus, c.1621 (National Museum, Cracow)

---

63 The Polish word used in the text, *brytan*, indicates a large and strong dog, a bandog or a type of mastiff.

64 'Jana hrabi z Ostroroga Dziennik wyprawy chocimskiej', pp.30-32, 'Prokopa Zbigniewskiego Dziennik wyprawy chocimskiej', pp.60-64, 'Stanisława Lubomirskiego Dziennik wyprawy chocimskiej', pp.100-103, 'Jakóba Sobieskiego Dziennik wyprawy chocimskiej', pp.157-176, Mustafa Naima (Naima Efendi), *Dziennik wyprawy chocimskiey*, pp.168-170, Stanisław Kobierzycki, *Historia Władysława, królewicza polskiego i szwedzkiego*, pp.363-369, Ödön (Edmund) Schütz (ed), *An Armeno-Kipchak Chronicle of the Polish-Turkish Wars in 1620-1621*, p.77, "Relacya prawdziwa o expediciey przeciwko Turkom, na którey sam cesarz turecki był Ao

Sir Thomas Roe, writing after the war was over, provided a few reasons why Osman II was forced to negotiate with the Commonwealth and cease further military action at Khotyn. They all seems very reasonable and were clearly based on the information he received from his Turkish contacts in Constantinople. The Ottoman army was exhausted because of the bad conditions to fight in, especially because of the weather. With the approaching winter, soldiers were suffering 'great extremities of cold and other miseries'. Torrential rains were destroying the camp and ordnance, 'carried away tents, horses, and other cattell, and sum part of his [Ottoman II's] cannon'. There were no provisions for men and horses alike, the latter had to be abandoned or killed by the owners 'for want of means to feed them'. Especially affected were horses of the Asian contingents, not used to cold weather. Roe mentioned that 'many men of quality, that came out with 10 and 12 [horses], were compelled to retorne on foote'. Sickness was spreading through the camp, with many dying 'of fluxes, fever and colds'. The soldiers were unhappy with the lack of the success and, apparently, with the leadership of the young Sultan. As such, 'the army, either for wearinesse or for discontent … not only refuzed to fight but were little lesse then mutined'. It seems that many blamed Osman II, as the one that was pushing for war 'contrary to the counsell of al his viziers, who desired generally a peace'.[65] The weather in the autumn of 1621 did not favour the Ottoman army, with cold spells and heavy rain badly affecting men, mounts and beasts of burden alike. It seems that many Turkish chronicles highlight the especially severe rains as one of the main factors that forced the Ottomans to abandon the campaign and leave Moldavia.[66] Both armies were to lose many men and horses during their retreat from the battlefield, adding to the overall human and financial cost of the conflict. It is very difficult to be precise about the losses of both sides during the campaign (although some information on this is set out in Chapter 9 below).

Final days (10–15 October)

There was a serious argument between the negotiators of both armies about which army should leave their camp first. It was a matter of pride, as whoever left last could claim to be victorious, but it also showed a very pragmatic approach, since there were worries that the army leaving first could be attacked by its opponents. The Commonwealth's envoys pointed out that their army had arrived first, so it needed to be the last to leave. It seems that

---

1621, Woyska koronnego y W. X. Litte pod regimentem Pana Karola Chodkiewicza W. X. Litte które pod Chocimiem leżało', pp.226-228, *Zherela do istoriï Ukraïny-Rusy*, volume VIII, p.241-243, *Zeitung aus der Walachei*, pp.16-19, *Diarius expeditiey królewicza polskiego Władysława przeciwko Osmanowi II, cesarzowi tureckiemu y chanowi tatarskiemu w osobach swych na woynie będących w Wołoszech pod Chociniem roku 1621*, BK 342, ff.58r-59r.

65 *The Negotiations of Sir Thomas Roe, in his Embassy to the Ottoman Porte, from the Year 1621 to 1628*, p.12.

66 Sam White, *The Climate of Rebellion in the Early Modern Ottoman Empire*, pp.194–195.

Osman II and the Grand Vizier did not want to argue too much about this, they knew that their troops had a long way home, and their march would be badly affected by the worsening weather so there was no point in delaying. In the morning of 10 October 'the Turkish army march out very silently, without noises and shouting'. The many wounded and sick were placed on carts, while supplies, tents and weapons were carried by beasts of burden. The army was protected by a strong vanguard, while an equally strong rearguard ensured that everyone left the camp and that marching troops were protected. The Sultan quickly set up a new camp a half a mile from his original one, on the hills that were initially taken by the Ottomans on 2 September. From there he observed the march of his own army leaving its positions, while at the same time waiting for the Poles, Lithuanians and Cossacks to abandon their camp. Lubomirski and Władysław did not want to take risks, so they delayed their own departure. The Polish envoys returned to their own camp, where they were greeted by the Royal Prince who, 'despite still being of poor health' led the soldiers in prayers, thanking God for His protection and the

Osman II returning to Constantinople after the end of Khotyn campaign. An interesting detail is that there are some captured Cossacks being marched alongside the Ottoman troops. Illustration from Ġanizāde Nādirī's *Şehnāme-i Nādirī* (Topkapı Palace Museum Library)

victory, singing *Te Deum Laudamus* and other psalms. Father Szołdrowski was dispatched to Lviv during the night, to carry the message about the end of hostilities.

Only once Osman II had crossed the Prut River and moved a few miles away from the allied camp did Władysław order his troops to leave Khotyn. Jakub Sobieski and Mateusz Leśniowski were sent to the Cossack camp, to advise them about the terms of the peace treaty. The commissioners advised the Zaporozhians, that despite the fact that the Turks were strongly pressing for punishment for the Cossack leader, the Polish envoys had not agreed to that, 'not allowing [the Ottomans] to add any paragraph that would have brought harm and woe to the Zaporozhian army.' They did remind them however, in the name of the Commonwealth, to stop any further raids on the Black Sea. While Konashevych-Sahaidachny promised that, as a faithful servant of his Royal Highness and the Commonwealth, the Cossacks would obey those orders. He was to await further commands, but instead, without checking with Royal Prince Władysław and Hetman Lubomirski, ordered his Cossacks to cross the Dniester and leave the camp. This clearly upset the Poles and Lithuanians, probably most especially Władysław who wanted to ensure that he left Khotyn first, as the vanguard of a victorious army. The Royal Prince's regiment used the Ottoman bridge and marched to Żwaniec, where the soldiers rested on 13 and 14 October. They had to defend themselves and their tabors from marauding Tatars and Moldavians, who had not followed the Ottoman army and were still a constant menace on the Polish bank of the Dniester. Anyone that was left behind the army was at risk of falling victim to robbers and the Tatars, a number of tabor wagons were looted in such attacks, with a large number of camp servants killed. Many soldiers and servants died of cold and exhaustion as well, with dying men '[laying] on the fields and roads, asking for help (that no one would provide).' In the morning of 15 October the Royal Prince moved to Kamianets, where he arrived late in the day. After one week of rest there, he left for Lviv to meet with King Sigismund III. The army that marched behind him suffered greatly during their stay at Kamianets, with hundreds dying daily because of the weather conditions and hunger. 'In the [city's] market place, on the streets, there were plenty of dead bodies, upon which beasts [birds] were feeding'. A bitter German officer wrote about this time in his *News from Wallachia*:

We set out from our Wallachian field camp. Since most of the commanders did not have horses, they were forced to walk, which was painful to look at. A pale, wounded cornet from Colonel Claus von Bruchhausen's unit also had to walk in order not to die. But here one could see excellent beautiful wagons, many hundreds of beautiful Polish carriages, beautiful tents, which cost 200 and 300 florins each. Now the 'Noble Men' rode stately with their lynx pelts, saddles and caparisons, decorously advancing next to us, the Germans, who were on foot.

Since the Tatars undertook robbery raids on this bank of the Dniester and caused great damage, a lot of our wagons remained near the water. The regiment of Mr Colonel Learmont made the crossing in the morning, and then marched under the cover of wagons [to protect them].

Many soldiers along the way were beheaded by the Tatars, frozen, or were killed by Podolian peasants. In Kamianets-Podilskyi, the Poles pushed sick commanders out into the street, like Fenrik Wilhelm von Loben, and soldiers left on the heaps of dung where they could be eaten by pigs.

Jakub Sobieski also wrote about the poor shape of the returning troops:

The sight of the Polish army was upsetting and worthy of pity. Misery and weakness took away any colours from [men's] faces; valiant horses were emaciated or died in the scorcher; cavalry became infantry and a quite strong army became a handful of soldiers. The only thing we had left was to cry. Our wagons were moving without food, without equipment and household items; [instead] they carried dead, wounded and sick. There were many eagles [unit's signs] and flags but not many soldiers [left] serving under them, [and] even less discipline. Not taking care of order or orderly ranks, all of them run to cross the Dniester, so the enemy, when looking at it from the distance, could think that it was shameful escape of some loose bunch, not the retreat of the Polish army. Many of our men were punished for such fickleness, as in the bushes and ravines [next to the river] they were looted or beaten by Tatars and even by Cossacks.

The Tatars continued their attacks every day, and every day killing more camp servants and capturing horses. During the week's stay there, the army commissioners were busy verifying army musters, to ensure they had the correct numbers to provide for the paying off of the free quarter (*donatywa*) previously promised to the soldiers. Lubomirski and other high-ranking commanders were involved in sessions of the military court, in the preparation for disbandment of the majority of the army and the setting up of winter quarters for those troops that were to remain in the service. The ravaged troops were slowly marching to Lviv where they were to receive their final pay, this was soon to cause another serious crisis in the Commonwealth (described in Chapter 9, below).[67]

---

67 'Jana hrabi z Ostroroga Dziennik wyprawy chocimskiej', pp.32-39, 'Stanisława Lubomirskiego Dziennik wyprawy chocimskiej', p.103, 'Jakóba Sobieskiego Dziennik wyprawy chocimskiej', pp.176-180, Stanisław Kobierzycki, *Historia Władysława, królewica polskiego i szwedzkiego*, pp.369-370, Ödön (Edmund) Schütz (ed), *An Armeno-Kipchak Chronicle of the Polish-Turkish Wars in 1620-1621*, pp.77-81, 'Relacya prawdziwa o expediciey przeciwko Turkom, na którey sam cesarz turecki był Ao 1621, Woyska koronnego y W. X. Litte pod regimentem Pana Karola Chodkiewicza W. X. Litte które pod Chocimiem leżało', pp.228-229, *Zherela do istorii Ukraïny-Rusy*, volume VIII, pp.243-244, *Zeitung aus der Walachei*, pp.19-21, Jakub Sobieski, *Pamiętnik wojny chocimskiej xiąg troje*, pp.77-78, *Diarius expeditiey królewica polskiego Władysława przeciwko Osmanowi II, cesarzowi tureckiemu y chanowi tatarskiemu w osobach swych na woynie będących w Wołoszech pod Chociniem roku 1621*, BK 342, f.59r.

8

Other theatres of war: preparations of the relief army and Tatars Raids

Relief army under King Sigismund III

Not all units of the Polish army raised for the Khotyn campaign joined with the Lithuanians and Cossacks in Moldavia. A few vital or strategic points in Poland had garrisons as a precaution against Tatars raids. In Cracow there was a banner of *wybraniecka* infantry of 204 men, under Stanisław Skarbek Celatycki, a German infantry company of 100 men, and 100 horses in one cavalry banner, these were probably cossack cavalry. In Lviv there were around 400 men, including a *wybraniecka* infantry banner under Wojakowski and the cavalry banner of Mniszech, possibly Stanisław Bonifacy. The Garrison of Kamianets-Podilskyi had 400 men (mainly infantry), while Halicz was defended by one banner of Polish infantry of 100 men, under Feliks Kosiński. Further units of *wybraniecka* and Polish infantry were spread out across the minor castles. In total it is estimated that all the garrisons totalled up to 3,000 men: 1,300 *wybraniecka* infantry, 1,200 Polish and German infantry and 500 cavalry.[1] It

Letter from October 1621, in which King Sigismund III confirmed that the City of Lublin took part in the recent levy of nobility, by sending 'three good wagons with some infantry and cavalry'. Lublin was one of the Royal cities in Poland and as such it was obliged to provide well armed haiduks to support the levy of the nobility. Cavalry mentioned in the document would most likely have been cossack cavalry (National Archive, Lublin)

---

1   Jan Wimmer, 'Wojsko i skarb Rzeczypospolitej u schyłku XVI i w pierwszej połowie XVII wieku', *Studia i Materiały do Historii Wojskowości*, volume XIV (Warszawa: Wydawnictwo Ministerstwa Obrony Narodowej, 1968), p.39.

Well equipped cuirassier in three-quarter armour and carrying a sword and a pair of pistols. At least some of the Polish and Lithuanian reiters at Khotyn would have been armed in a similar style. Johann Jacobi von Wallhausen, *Ritterkunst*, 1616. (Author's collection)

was a purely defensive force, so in order to organise the potential relief force King Sigismund III had to look for a combination of those enlisted troops that did not manage to join the main army, those raised by magnates and, especially, the levy of the nobility. This relief force was to gather in Lviv but it took a very long time to arrive there and was not able to move towards Khotyn on time.

The King with a strong force of Household troops and newly raised units left Warsaw in late September, to arrive at Lviv on 13 October. The temporary Papal Nuncio in Poland, Giuseppe Frentanelli, who had replaced the elderly and ill Francesco Diotallevi (who left Poland in mid-September 1621) recorded an interesting list of troops that accompanied King Sigismund III from Warsaw to Kamianets-Podilskyi. In a letter dated 1 October 1621, Frentanelli mentioned 1,700 German infantry, 300 Irish infantry, 700 Hungarian haiduks, more than 300 cossack cavalry, 200 arquebusiers [reiters] and 500 lancers [hussars]. While initially there was a plan to take 12 guns with them, because of the lack of horses the four larger had to be left behind.[2] One of the Polish diarists described the King arriving at Lviv on 13 October and that he was accompanied by 3,000 hussars (clearly far too high a number), his Royal Court, some German and Polish infantry, three banners of cossacks and some banners of reiters.[3] The levy of the nobility, as was its custom, gathered slowly and was not eager to fight. When Sigismund III arrived in Lviv, there were nobles from just three voivodeships there: Sandomierz, Lublin and Ruthenia; all from Małopolska (Lesser Poland) Province. The levy from Sieradz County, part of Sieradz Voivodeship of Wielkopolska (Greater Poland) province, arrived as well, and three other levys were four miles away from town: Volhynia (Wołyń), Bratslav (Bracław) and Kiev (Kijów), also of Małopolska province.[4] It is estimated that up to 20,000 of the levy of nobility gathered mid-October in Lviv, supported by a few thousand men brought by the King.

An anonymous noble from Czchów county (Cracow Voivodeship) left a diary of his participation in the levy of nobility in 1621.[5] He mentioned leaving home on 27 September, the slow gathering of his local levy and marching to meet the rest of the army at Lviv. In his description he paints a picture of unruly men, unwilling to take part in any fighting, and often complaining and bickering with their own commanders. It appears that all

---

2 BAV, Barberiniari Latini, vol. 6580, ff.10r–10v, Giuseppe Frentanelli to L. Ludovisi, Warsaw, 1 X 1621.

3 'Diaryusz wojny tureckiej r. 1621', in: Ambroży Grabowski (ed.) *Starożytności historyczne polskie*, vol , p.133.

4 Albrycht Stanisław Radziwiłł, *Rys panowania Zygmunta III*, p.74.

5 'Dziennik wyjazdy naszego na pospolite ruszenie', in: Hanna Malewska, *Listy staropolskie z epoki Wazów* (Warszawa: Państwowy Instytut Wydawniczy, 1977), pp.216-220.

least some of nobles taking part in this levy were well equipped as he says that they were asked to serve 'in armour, with lances', while others were serving as *arkabuzeria*. They lacked the fighting spirit though and were disheartened by the sight of fires set by the raiding Tatars. When, on 9 October, the Voivode of Cracow, Jan Tęczyński, asked for volunteers to carry out a reconnaissance, only 70 men came forward, 'They went

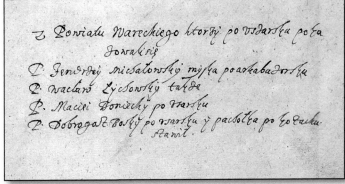

disorderly, without commanders'. What was even worse is that they did not fulfil their mission, with some abandoning the group due to bad roads, others returning mid-mission and the remaining group not eager to engage the Tatars and returning with no success. On 17 October, still quarrelling and refusing the final proper muster, 'not willing to muster on horses, but they did on foot,' the levy dissolved and started their individual journeys home. The noble diarist seems to be totally unfazed by his own lack of involvement in the defence of the country, while his main achievement was that 'by the grace of God, [I] was safe and all horses and all oxen and all possessions [taken for the campaign] were safe'. An Italian diplomat working for the Holy See, Antonio Ratti, who was present in Cracow in September 1621, estimated that there would be between 150,000 and 200,000 men in the levy of nobility (which is a massive exaggeration) but was fairly accurate when describing their attitude. 'This season [of the year] here now is very bad due to continuous rains and extraordinary cold, [which] will make them want to return to their homes soon'.[6] It is obvious from this that nobles from the levy were happy to return home without taking part in any real fighting and thus their contingents quickly started to disperse. As for a regular army, foreign units that were late for the Khotyn campaign and mustered in Lviv also did not take part in any further action, they simply had to be paid off and disbanded. Among them was a unit of reiters under the command of Buchen. King Sigismund III ordered it to be formally mustered, to check that it was 'composed of honest foreigners and if they are all properly [equipped] in reiter style and mounted'. Once that was satisfactory, the unit was to receive one month's pay (15zl) and be disbanded, unless it was so well equipped and ready that it could be kept as part of the reduced army that was to stay under arms at the end of the war.[7] The army returning from Khotyn arrived in Lviv as well, joining with those troops that were gathered there. It had to be a shocking contrast when units from Khotyn, battle-weary and ravaged by war, met those men that had spent the conflict well away from the fighting.

Short fragment of the muster roll of the levy of nobility from Warka district in 1621. The initial part of the muster mentioned nobles that arrived equipped 'in hussar style', although the first two are in fact described as 'arkabuzeria' style', indicating similar armour as hussars but using firearms instead of the lance. The third and fourth are 'in hussar style', although the fourth one additionally had a retainer equipped 'in cossack style'. The additional part of the muster, not visible here, had 25 hussars (including one *arkabuzer*) and 124 cossack cavalry (AGAD, Warsaw)

---

6   BAV, Barberiniari Latini, vol. 6660, f.9r, A. Riatti to L. Ludovisi, Cracow, 26 IX 1621.

7   BK 330, *Akta Zygmunta III od roku 1618 do 1621*, no 287, pp.407–408.

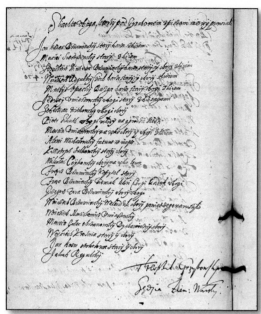

A list of nobles from Warsaw land (part of the Mazowsze Voivodeship) that did not appear at the muster of the levy of the nobility in October 1621. All of them have annotations about the reason for their absence, e.g. old, sick, pauper, et cetera. The list is confirmed with the signature of Teofil Grzybowski, district judge of the Warsaw land (AGAD, Warsaw).

Tatar raids in 1621 and 1622

The constant actions of Tatar forces on the Polish bank of the Dniester, aimed at cutting supply lines to Khotyn and terrorising the local population is mentioned above. As Crimeans and Nogays were of less use during the direct assaults on the defensive camp, Osman II agreed to allow them to venture into the Polish interior as a useful diversion of the slowly gathering relief army. There were two major raids carried out by the Tatars during the Khotyn campaign of 1621. The First, by the Crimean Tatars, took place throughout most of September and was led by Nurredin Sultan Azamet Giray. The second attack happened at the very end of campaign, between 30 September and mid-October, under the command of Khan Janibek Giray himself, involving a majority of Crimean forces, reinforced by a strong contingent of the Nogay Tatars of Khan Temir. Both of them were described in great detail in 2012 by Andrzej Gliwa, in his excellent and well-researched study, focused on the damage caused on the Przemyśl Land (*ziemia przemyska*).[8] Based on his article and some additional primary sources,[9] this is a short summary of those raids, to show the impact that they had on the local population and the region as a whole.

Before larger operations, there was also a smaller raid carried out by the Budjak Horde between 2 and 10 September that ravaged Podolia, especially the areas surrounding Kamianets. It was just a prelude to a much more serious invasion however. After 3 September, Nurredin Sultan Azamet Giray (the Khan's younger brother) led a few thousand horsemen on a deep raid towards the Polish interior. The Crimean Tatars were to strike terror into the local population and gather as many prisoners, cattle and food as possible, in order to bring them all back to the army camp. Another important object was to divert the attention of any Polish relief forces that would be gathering to support Khotyn and, if the opportunity arose, the Tatars were to intercept convoys with supplies to Chodkiewicz's army.

After crossing the Dniester between 2 and 3 September, the Crimeans quickly marched through already pillaged Podolia and by 6 September had reached Ruthenian Voivodeship. The next day they attacked the outskirts of Tarnopol, where Tomasz Zamoyski was slowly gathering the private and regular army troops. Polish soldiers, utilising the firepower of their infantry set up an ambush and, supported by artillery, easily repulsed those attacks however. 'The enemy struck once and twice with all their might. Hit with

---

8   Andrzej Gliwa, 'Dwa najazdy tatarskie na Ruś Czerwoną podczas wojny Rzeczypospolitej z Imperium Osmańskim w 1621 r. Zniszczenia i straty demograficzne na obszarze ziemi przemyskiej', *Rocznik Przemyski*, volume XLVIII, part 1, Historia wojskowości (Przemyśl: Wydawnictwo Towarzystwa Przyjaciół Nauk w Przemyślu, 2012), pp.3-58.

9   All information in this sub-chapter, unless otherwise noted, is based on Andrzej Gliwa's study.

[our] guns, they stopped engaging and moved towards our lands'.[10] The Tatar horsemen were not discouraged by this minor defeat and quickly spread out to attack Volhynia, Ruthenia and the Bełz Voivodeship. With their main camp (*kosz*) set up just over 20km from Tarnopol, their smaller raiding forces spread out through the Polish land, focusing especially on the Przemyśl Land (the western part of Ruthenian Voivodeship), part of the Lviv Land (*ziemia lwowska*) and the Halicz Land (*ziemia halicka*). The Tatars were divided into four main forces: one part protected the camp, while the three others attacked the aforementioned lands. They were practically unopposed, with just a token military force and the armed population trying to stop them. Stefan Chmielecki with some of Zamoyski's private troops (cossack cavalry composed of the magnate's Ukrainian subjects) managed to defeat one Tatar group and release some prisoners, but his men were quickly overwhelmed by the far superior numbers of Crimeans and had to cease any further attempts to stop the raids.[11]

Now practically unopposed, the raiders burned villages and a few small towns, and captured a number of people, killing those that they could not take with them. Cattle, sheep, and horses were also amongst the loot. The Tatars were also taking as many supplies as possible, in order to deliver them to Osman II's army around Khotyn. They looted cheese, butter, vegetables and also vodka and beer. One very important task was to obtain fodder for the horses, including hay. Groups of a few hundred Tatar horsemen burned and pillaged for two weeks, slowly gathering together again before returning to Khotyn. On 21 or 22 September their larger force clashed with the levy of nobility near Przemyśl. Initially the Poles took some losses, including many horses but a counter-attack by some regular private units under the leadership of Franciszek Karol Korniakt forced the Tatars to retreat. By 24 September the main Crimean raiding force was on the move towards Khotyn, bringing a large quantity of loot and many captives. Jakub Sobieski said that the Crimean Tatar force was ruthlessly raiding the Ruthenian, Volhynian and Bełz voivodeships, 'burning villages and towns, taking horses and cattle, capturing nobles and peasants of both genders and of any age, the Turkish camp was full of the cries of the Polish prisoners'.[12]

Tatar horseman. Abraham de Bruyn, 1577 (Rijksmuseum, Amsterdam)

Encouraged by the initial success of the raid, and also hoping to put more pressure on the Poles in the final phase of the siege of Khotyn, the Tatars decided to attempt another attack. Between 7,000 and 9,000 horsemen, including Khan Temir's Nogays, decided to raid through Moldavia, along the so-called Wallachian route (one of the usual Tatar raiding roads towards Poland) to strike against Red Ruthenia (*Ruś Czerwona*). Thousands of Tatars struck against many Polish villages and towns, mercilessly pillaging everything 'with fire and sword'. As mentioned above, the raiders were even

---

10 Stanisław Żurkowski, *Żywot Tomasza Zamoyskiego*, p.82.
11 Stanisław Żurkowski, *Żywot Tomasza Zamoyskiego*, pp.82–83.
12 Jakub Sobieski, *Pamiętnik wojny chocimskiej xiąg troje*, p.78.

close to the Polish levy of nobility marching to the concentration point near Lviv but the Polish nobles were not eager to fight against swift horsemen. When the raiders were near Halicz, Tomasz Zamoyski attempted to stop them, leading his troops from Tarnopol. He had under his command three banners of reiters (at least 300 horses), 600 Ukrainian subjects serving as cossack cavalry, and 600 infantry that were converted into improvised dragoons so that they could keep up with the cavalry. The expedition was a failure however as the Poles failed to catch up with the Tatars and returned to Tarnopol empty-handed.[13] While the main Ottoman army was leaving the area around Khotyn, the Tatars continued their looting and destroyed everything in their path and only from mid-October did the raiding groups start their retreat from Poland, carrying their loot and escorting prisoners.

Andrzej Gliwa, focusing his research on Przemyśl Land, based on reports provided to the land court of the regions, found that at least 20.5 percent of all villages in this area – that is 191 out of 931 – were to some degree affected by these two attacks, and 6 of 31 towns in the area (19.3 percent). As well as vast swathes of cultivated land, important locations such as mills and taverns were burnt by invaders – 90 percent of both had been destroyed by mid-October 1621. At least 1,447 houses in villages were burnt, as well as 9 manor houses (*dworek*) of the nobility and 11 large farms, known as *folwark*. Of course, places of worship were also affected, and 56 Orthodox churches were burnt as well. With the raids of 1620, this all left whole areas of the land barren, without settlements and without people. It was the sad reality in many regions of southern Poland that were so often affected by the almost annual raids by Tatars. Of course, the situation in 1621 was made worse by the larger number of attacking invaders and by lack of a proper defence. Such devastation had also long-term effects on the future of the affected regions, as they often had to seek relief from taxation and support to rebuild and resettle destroyed villages.

---

13 Stanisław Żurkowski, *Żywot Tomasza Zamoyskiego*, pp.84–85.

9

After the War

The Losses of The Warring States

The issue of the losses of all those involved in the campaign of 1621 has always been a matter of discussion and argument among historians. The main problem is the only partial data available for us, based on often contradictory and exaggerated primary sources. Leszek Podhorodecki estimated Polish-Lithuanian losses as around 2,000 killed in battles, 3,000 dead due to illness and hunger, also up to 2,400 deserters and missing. According to him the Cossacks lost 6,000–6,500 men at Khotyn, with a further 2,500–3,000 during their march through Moldavia and the fighting at sea. Ottoman losses were given by this author as around 40,000 men, including both combat and non-combat deaths.[1] Wiesław Majewski lowered Cossack losses to about 8,000 and the Ottoman losses to some 30,000 men, with Polish-Lithuanian losses given as the same as Podhorodecki's estimates.[2] Petro Sas estimated Polish-Lithuanian losses as up to 10,000 men, although he counts both soldiers and camp servants, and also includes deserters. His calculation of Cossack losses is much lower however, putting together only figures from individual days of the siege and giving a very low estimate of the losses due to sickness and hunger. So in total, including killed during the march through Moldavia and the fighting at sea, the Ukrainian researcher assumed just 3,250 Cossack dead. His estimates of Ottoman losses are close to Podhorodecki and given as 40,000 men.[3] Andrzej Witkowicz put the total losses of the Commonwealth's troops as 15,000 dead at Khotyn, including 2,000 Poles and Lithuanians and 3,000 Cossacks killed during the fighting, with the rest dying from sickness and hunger. An additional 5,000, mostly Cossacks, according to him were lost prior to the siege of Khotyn, so the total combat and non-combat loss he gives as 20,000 dead. He disagreed strongly with other researchers' estimates of Ottoman losses however, as he claims that they were much lower. He criticised the high number of Turkish soldiers stated as killed during the

---

1   Leszek Podhorodecki, *Jan Karol Chodkiewicz 1560–1621*, pp.387–388.
2   Wiesław Majewski, 'Chocim 1621 rok', p.22.
3   Petro Sas, *Khotyn War of 1621*, pp.476–477.

fighting, claiming that Polish sources tend to overestimate them. As such he believes that the combat losses of Osman II's troops were only between 8,000 and 9,000 men, not the 15,000–20,000 given by other authors. He also assumed that the Ottoman army did not suffer as much as the Commonwealth army from sickness and hunger, thus non-combat losses had to be fairly low. As such he thinks that the total loss was much lower than the 40,000 given by other authors and that with those lost during the march to Khotyn and the fighting at sea, Osman II's army lost around 25,000 men.[4]

Polish hussars from the beginning of seventeenth century, from the copy of 'Stockholm Roll', showing the Royal entry into Cracow in 1605. Artist unknown. The original painting is currently in collection of the Royal Castle in Warsaw (Author's collection)

Ottoman witnesses who described the events to Sir Thomas Roe, provided shockingly high estimates of the losses in Sultan's army. 'It is reported, that there dyed in the Turks camp, by the sword, famine, sickness and cold, about 80,000 men and about 100,000 horses; and the remayne, at their returne, appearing so naked, poore, and sickly, made evident demonstration of the losse and misery susteyned'.[5] Polish losses were estimated by him as 'about 20,000 by the famine suffered in their besieging'.[6] Lithuanian Vice-Chancellor Albrycht Stanisław Radziwiłł, who accompanied King Sigismund to Lviv, received there news about the events of the war from the officials and soldiers taking part in the campaign. The Ottoman losses that he mentioned are, as in many other accounts, very high. He wrote 'they said that 60,000 enemies were killed, [also] 100,000 camels and uncountable number of horses'. He estimated losses of Polish and Lithuanian armies as 'almost 10,000' but it is not clear if he includes Cossack losses here as well.[7] Bishop Piasecki in his chronicle greatly overestimated Ottoman losses, as according to him up to 60,000 men died 'from blade and from sickness.' Even more were to perish during the journey back from Khotyn, as the Ottoman army was returning

---

4   Andrzej Witkowicz, *Bułat i koncerz. Poprawki do obrazu wielkich bitew polsko-tureckich (1620-1683)*, volume I, pp.199-203.

5   *The Negotiations of Sir Thomas Roe, in his Embassy to the Ottoman Porte, from the year 1621 to 1628*, p.12.

6   *The Negotiations of Sir Thomas Roe, in his Embassy to the Ottoman Porte, from the year 1621 to 1628*, p.12.

7   Albrycht Stanisław Radziwiłł, *Rys panowania Zygmunta III*, p.75.

'during the time of rainy and snowy autumn', and many soldiers, after losing their horses, had to walk the great distance and only one-third of the original army returned to Constantinople. He did admit however, that Polish-Lithuanian losses were heavy as well. While he underestimated those that died in direct fighting, mentioning only 400 killed, he added 'many died due to sickness, even more fled and an uncountable number of horses was lost'.[8] Massive losses amongst horses were even mentioned in the correspondence of the Papal diplomats, with Frentanelli writing in one of his letters that many animals died of hunger, while others were slaughtered by Polish soldiers who did not want them to die slowly from starvation.[9] Józef Bartłomiej Zimorowic, writing in his chronicle of the history of Lviv, described the shocking state of the returning Polish-Lithuanian army, especially the German troops. Soldiers marching from Khotyn arrived in the area of Lviv in early November, preceded by Royal Prince Władysław accompanied by some courtiers and servants. Zimorowic said that the returning Germans were a 'long line of dead men', ravaged by illnesses and weather conditions. Destitute and sick soldiers were laying on the outskirts of the town, begging for food and dying in droves. The City Council ordered that they be brought into the town, where they were to be taken care of. Nonetheless, many still perished and in Saint Lazarus Hospital alone more than 2,000 died due to sickness.[10] Considering the overall number of German troops employed by Poles, this last number seems too high and probably also includes Polish and Lithuanian soldiers and their servants. Prokop Zbigniewski confirmed the high losses amongst both men and horses, 'through the six Sundays [weeks] our army was so worn-out that more than half the banners [of cavalry] marched on foot, as some of their horses died of hunger, while others were captured by Tatars, when they were taken by servants to gather grass and food. The soldiers themselves were very miserable and emaciated by numerous illnesses'.[11] Auxent highlighted the very heavy losses amongst the German infantry, claiming that 5,000 of 8,000 German infantry died during the campaign:[12]

> Some among them died in the camp, others in Kamianets, and some on the road leading to Lviv. So that there remained only [a] few of the Germans able to go back to their country. And the cause of it was that they were a very wretched sort without perseverance. Moreover they had walked all the way and became exhausted, furthermore because for some time they went without bread in the camp.

---

8   *Kronika Pawła Piaseckiego biskupa przemyślskiego*, p.302.

9   BAV, Barberiniari Latini, vol. 6580, ff. 10rv, Giuseppe Frentanelli to L. Ludovisi, Warsaw, 1 X 1621.

10   Józef Bartłomiej Zimorowic, *Historya miasta Lwowa, Królestw Galicyi i Lodomeryi stolicy; z opisaniem dokładnem okolic i potróynego oblężenia*, pp.308–309.

11   *Diarius expeditiey królewicza polskiego Władysława przeciwko Osmanowi II, cesarzowi tureckiemu y chanowi tatarskiemu w osobach swych na woynie będących w Wołoszech pod Chociniem roku 1621*, BK 342, p.59v.

12   Ödön (Edmund) Schütz (ed.), *An Armeno-Kipchak chronicle of the Polish-Turkish Wars in 1620–1621*, p.81.

It is worthwhile noting, that he also added that from amongst 2,500 reiters present at Khotyn, 'only a few died', in contrast with the fate of German foot units. He also says that 1,700 Germans and retainers[13] died during the army's stay in Kamianets, with many men dying every day due to exhaustion. They were buried in mass graves that quickly 'filled with corpses up to the brim'. Some houses outside of the city walls were given to the sick and wounded soldiers as improvised hospitals so 'there they were given medical treatment until they recovered. But only a few recovered'.[14] Another volunteer serving at Khotyn, Grochowicki, did mention that due to the poor conditions of service, the lack of food and the sicknesses, up to half of the German and Hungarian infantry that took part in campaign died in the camp. Many foreigners deserted as well but in the Polish infantry the level of desertion was even higher. One diarist says, 'also many camp servants and retainers fled', indicating that the cavalry was weakened by men leaving its ranks.[15]

The Triumph of King Sigismund III. Engraving by Schelte Adamsz. Boslwert, made after 1621. It presents victory over the Ottoman Turks, represented by the figure on the right (wearing a turban and offering an olive branch) and Muscovy, represented by the figure on the left (presenting the tsar's crown). The King is flanked by the symbolical figures of the Polish-Lithuanian Commonwealth (armed figure, on the left) and Sweden (crowned figure, on the right) (Rijksmuseum, Amsterdam)

---

13 He is using the word *pacholik* which can mean both retainer and camp servant in a cavalry unit.
14 Ödön (Edmund) Schütz (ed.), *An Armeno-Kipchak Chronicle of the Polish-Turkish Wars in 1620–1621*, p.81.
15 Artur Goszczyński, 'Nieszczęścia gorsze od wroga. Głód i niedostatki w armii Rzeczypospolitej podczas kampanii chocimskiej z 1621 r', p.39.

Post War Propaganda

King Sigismund III's court used the victory over the Ottomans – as Khotyn was seen in the Commonwealth – to release many propaganda pieces, praising the King, Royal Prince Władysław and Hetman Chodkiewicz. Engravings and paintings, commemorating the triumph, were ordered from court artists. The King, despite the fact that he was not present at Khotyn, was shown as the victorious monarch, with Ottoman prisoners and captured weapons presented to him. At least two portraits of Władysław seem to have fighting at Khotyn shown in the background, both are attributed to Pieter Claesz Soutman. There were also official accounts of the events that were written in Poland but published in Western Europe. The Benedictine monk Maciej Tytlewski wrote a narrative of the 1620 and 1621 war, based on Szemberg's and Ostroróg's diaries. It was initially published in Latin in Naples in April 1622, under the title *Narratio De Praeliis gestis inter Polonvm, Et Tvrcam Annis 1620. & 1621*[16] and it included a confirmation from the Polish envoy in Italy, Adam Makowski, that it was written based on the official reports received from the Royal Court in Poland. In 1623 both the Latin original and its Spanish version, entitled *Relacion Diaria de las Guerras Tenidas entre Polacos y Turcos por los años 1620 y 1621*[17], were published in Madrid. Of course such accounts always highlighted the religious aspect of the war, clearly indicating that Providence was on the Commonwealth's side. An example of this can be seen in the title of another pamphlet published in Italian in 1622; it was entitled *La Gran Vittoria di Sigismunde III, Re di Polonia, controi Turchinel 1621 (The Great and Wonderful Victory, by the hand of God to the most powerful and godly Sigismund III, King of Pollonia against the Turks in the year 1621).*[18] An anonymous German officer wrote in his *News from Wallachia* that there was a lot of incorrect information circulating in Europe about the war. 'Here in Germany, as well as in Prussia, Kashubia, Pomerania and other places, absolutely incredible rumours about events in Wallachia [Moldavia] are constantly spreading. They talk about various battles that allegedly took place during this campaign, during which the Poles killed 40 thousand Turks, and the Turks – 30 thousand Poles. All of this is inaccurate and untrue. The Poles did not even give the enemy a [formal] battle.'[19] His pamphlet clearly was not a part of any court-related flow of information, as it is often critical of Polish soldiers, instead praising German mercenaries and Zaporozhian Cossacks. A more official account in German was *Kurze Relation was sich in der polnischen Expedition wider den Erbfeind christlichen Namens vom 1. bis auf 24. September 1621 begeben*

---

16 Maciej Tytlewski, *Narratio De Praeliisgestis inter Polonvm, Et Tvrcam Annis 1620. & 1621* (Naples: Ex Typographia Lazari Scorrigij, 1622).

17 Maciej Tytlewski, *Relacion Diaria de las Guerras Tenidas entre Polacos y Turcos por los años 1620 y 1621* (Madrid: Per Tomas Junti, Impressor de Rey, 1623).

18 Sebastiano Farczeuoskhi [name uncertain], *La gran vittoria di Sigismunde III, Re di Polonia, contro i Turchi nel 1621* (Florence: Bartolomeo Sermartelli, 1622).

19 *Zeitung aus der Walachei*, p.2.

hat, (Augsburg: Andreas Aperger, 1621)[20]. Interestingly enough, it covers a period only until 24 September but despite that it was already highlighting the success of the 'Polish' army against the Ottomans. There were also those available in French, like the letter *Copie d'une lettre écrite de Léopol en Pologne, par laquelle se voit l'heureux succcs del'armée contre le Turc,* published by Clovis Eve in Paris[21] or the account La Grande et Memorable Défaite de 150.000 Turcs where the title already indicated victory over a large Ottoman army.[22] News about the war against Osman II was also spread in English, with pamphlets like *Newes from Poland...*[23] and *Newes from Turkie and Poland...*[24] In Appendix V is an English translation of issue 171 (23 November 1621) of Nieuwe Tijdinghen, published in Antwerp. It was a double-length issue with *An Account of the War in Poland from 1 to 21 September* and it is a great example of the way that the description of the conflict was presented in Western Europe.

One of the most interesting examples of the cultural impact of the Khotyn war is an epic poem *Osman,* written between 1621 and 1638 by Croatian poet Ivan Gundulić. It is a story of the life and death of Sultan Osman II and clashes between Christian and Muslim armies at Khotyn, glorifying those that were standing against the Turks. The poet was especially praising of Royal Prince Władysław, seeing in him a symbol of the successful fight against Ottomans and a beacon of hope for those Christians that were suffering under the Turkish yoke. Of course, many Polish poets focused on Khotyn as well; amongst these was Maciej Kazimierz Sarbiewski, whose poetry, written in Latin, was well known and was often published throughout Europe. On this occasion he authored *Poem for the praise of Jan Karola Chodkiewicz – hetman – [and] his victory at Khotyn in 1621,* that was initially published in 1623 and then reprinted in 1625, 1632 and 1634. Even before the Khotyn campaign Stanisław Witkowski in his *Pobudka ludzi rycerskich* wrote about the death of Żółkiewski in 1620 and encouraged Polish nobles to fight under the command of Chodkiewicz. After the campaign, in late 1621, Marcin Paszkowski published his poem *Choragiew Sauromatcką w Wołoszech, to jest Pospolite ruszenie iszczęśliwe zwróceni Polaków z Wołoch,* praising the defensive effort during the war. Józef Bartłomiej Zimorowicz

---

20 *Kurze Relation was sich in der Polnischen Expedition wider den Erbfeind christlichen Namens vom 1. bis auf 24. September 1621 begeben hat* (Augsburg: Andreas Aperger, 1621).

21 *Copie d'une lettre écrite de Léopol en Pologne, par laquelle se voit l'heureux succcs del'armée contre le Turc* (Paris: Clovis Eve, 1621).

22 *La grande et mémorable défaite de 150.000 Turcs* (Paris: Abraham Saugrin, 1621).

23 *Newes from Poland Wherein is truly inlarged the occasion, progression, and interception of the Turks formidable threatning of Europe. And particularly, the inuading of the kingdome of Poland. With many seuerall repulses he hath receiued from that braue and military nation: euen to this present moneth of October: as is truly collected out of the originall.* Published by authority (London: Imprinted by F K[ingston] for B. D[ownes] and Wiliam Lee, 1621).

24 *Nevves from Turkie and Poland. Or A true and compendious declaration of the proceedings betweene the great Turke, and his Maiestie of Poland, from the beginning of the warres, vntill the latter end VVith a relation of their daily millitary actions; shewing plainly how the warre continued and ended, peace was concluded, the troubles appeased, the articles of agreement confirmed, and a full league of amity ratified. Translated out of a Latine copie, written by a gentleman of quality, who was an actor in all the businesse: and now with his consent published* (Hage: Edward Allde, 1622).

was another author celebrating the victory, in *Pamiątka wojny tureckiej w roku MDCXXI od polskiego narodu podniesionej,* published in 1623.[25]

The religious aspect of the Khotyn war was also important and used as a part of the official propaganda. A Papal brief (breve) of George XV from 1621, entitled *Victoriarium gloria,* praised what was seen as the biggest victory of the Christian force over the Ottomans since the battle of Lepanto in 1571. Two years later, the Pope approved the Polish request for a special liturgy regarding the battle. His brief *Decet Romanum Pontificum* from June 1623 introduced 10 October as a holy day to celebrate the signing of the truce under the protection of the Most Holy Virgin Mary and two Polish patron saints: Saint Adalbert (święty Wojciech) and Saint Stanislaus of Szczepanów (święty Stanisław Szczepanowski). The text of the liturgy (so-called *oficjum*) was prepared in 1628 by the Polish synod led by Primate Jan Wężyk, and officially approved by the Holy See in June 1629. It was published as *Officium gratiarum actionis pro Victoria ex Turcis obtenta* in same year.

Front cover of the liturgy *Officium gratiarum actionis pro Victoria ex Turcis obtenta,* officially celebrating 10 October as a holy day in Poland. Published for the first time in 1628, this is from the edition of 1653 (Jagiellonian Library, Cracow)

Political repercussions

Probably the biggest winner of the conflict between the Commonwealth and the Ottoman Empire was actually the Kingdom of Sweden. King Gustav II Adolf took the opportunity of the fact that Commonwealth's military was focused in Moldavia and decided to strike against poorly defended Livonia. On 21 August 1621 the Swedish army began the siege of the vital Baltic port of Riga. Lithuanian Field Hetman Krzysztof II Radziwiłł attempted a relief but his small army was vastly outnumbered by the Swedes so he had no chance to succeed. Despite a valiant defence, Riga surrendered to the Swedes on 25 September. Gustav II Adolf finally achieved what his father, Karl IX, was not able to do during the war of 1600–1611. In October 1621 the Swedes also captured Mitau, the capital of Courland. Krzysztof II Radziwiłł had some more success in 1622, when between January and July he besieged Mitau to recapture it, and the town surrendered to the Lithuanian army on 5 July. The Swedish relief force arrived too late and in July and August waged an unsuccessful series of small-scale actions against the Lithuanians around the town. On 10 August both sides agreed to a ceasefire, which in 1623 was extended into a truce that was to run until March 1625. Riga stayed in Swedish hands though, providing them with a strong, strategic post in Livonia, and the Commonwealth forces were never able to recapture it. The war in Livonia continued from 1625 to 1629, although from summer 1626 it was waged on fairly small scale, as the Swedish strategy focused on fighting the Poles in Prussia. It is worth remembering that the Khotyn War indirectly led to great Swedish military successes, improving their strategic situation on

25   The topic was discussed in great detail in: Jan Okoń, 'Wojna chocimską 1621 roku i jej pogłosy w poezji i sztuce – w czterechsetlecie', *Ruch literacki,* volume LXIII, issue 4 (373) (Kraków: Polska Akademia Nauk, Uniwersytet Jagielloński w Krakowie, 2021), pp.515–540.

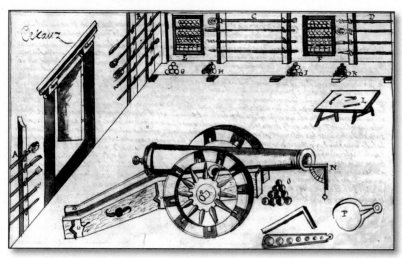

Polish arsenal, known as *cekhauz*, from German word *Zeughaus*. Andrea (Andrzej) dell'Aqua, *Praxis Ręczna Działa na Trzy Xięgi Podzielona*, 1630 (Kórnik Library)

the Baltic and in any future conflict against the Polish-Lithuanian Commonwealth or Muscovy.

In October 1621, despite the fact that the campaign against the Swedes in Livonia was still ongoing, it was decided that practically the whole Polish-Lithuanian army that had taken part in fighting against the Ottomans was to be disbanded. The intention was to keep in service just the small 'quarter army': 16 banners of hussars and cossack cavalry (total 1,800 horses), one banner of Polish infantry (200 portions), and infantry at the garrison at Kamianets-Podilskyi (also 200 portions).[26] Releasing foreign soldiers was not a big problem, after all they had taken huge losses during the campaign and the units were severely depleted. It seems, though, that they were underpaid, as the soldiers received poor quality coin. As a German officer complained in his *News from Wallachia* 'salaries were paid to the Germans in Ruthenian Lemberg [Lviv], on Market Square. For one Silesian *ort*[27] they gave 20 Polish *groszy*, which they did not want to accept anywhere, neither in Greater, nor in Lesser Poland, nor in Mazovia, nor in Prussia, Kashubia and Pomerania.'[28] While Lithuanian troops were paid off without large problems, it was much more difficult when dealing with native Polish troops. The soldiers were angry, as they had received only advance pay, which did not cover the whole period of service. It is estimated that the taxes from Poland agreed on by the *Sejm* in November-December 1620 would provide 3,235,051zl and after adding taxes from Lithuania and the Papal support, the Commonwealth would have a budget of 4,431,500zl. Unfortunately, the country's financial system yet again was not up to the task and by the time of the new *Sejm* in August 1621, only 1,304,734zl had been gathered. Alongside some smaller funds remaining in the treasury, in total there was 1,621,486zl available. Of this, 1,413,737zl was spent on military preparations. While a small part of this was spent on paying delayed wages to troops in Livonia and preparing defences on the border with Silesia in Wielkopolska, the vast majority was to be spent on the Khotyn campaign. 223,996zl was the pay owed to troops taking part in Żółkiewski's expedition in 1620; 45,351zl was for the Zaporozhian Cossacks and 26,648zl was paid to Royal Prince Władysław to cover his preparations to take part in the war. The rest was assigned as pay for troops that were to take part in

---

26   Jan Wimmer, 'Wojsko i skarb Rzeczypospolitej u schyłku XVI i w pierwszej połowie XVII wieku', p.41.
27   Silver coin, worth one quarter *Reichsthaler*.
28   *Zeitung aus der Walachei*, p.21.

the Khotyn campaign: 684,616zl for the first quarter of service and 410,027 for the second quarter. As can be seen, there were already not enough funds available to even cover for the whole of the second quarter, which was clear indication of the future problems. The *Sejm* of 1621 did agreed further taxes but there were massive problems in collecting them, especially from those lands that were affected by troops passing through and later by Tatar raids. Many provincial pre-*Sejm* gatherings, known as *sejmiki*, were reluctant to agree more taxes, seeing them as a large burden on their provinces.[29] It did not give a great hope that there would be enough funds available to answer to the financial demands of the Khotyn veterans.

King Sigismund in his instruction to the army commissioners, issued in Lviv on 23 October 1621, ordered them to focus on paying off and disbanding foreign units (reiters and infantry), Polish-Hungarian infantry and mercenary *lisowczycy* cavalry. Zaporozhian Cossacks should be paid as well, to prevent any unrest from them.[30] As for the national cavalry, priority was to be given to those units whose time of service had already ended, with soldiers from other units advised to wait until early 1622, once more money from taxes could be collected for their pay. The main problem with such an approach was that each unit looked at its own period of service completely differently. As mentioned in Chapter 6 above, the commissioners that accompanied the army decided that a time of service should start from the day when the unit entered the camp, was mustered by the Crown Field Clerk, or announced that it was ready to be mustered. Additionally, following the negotiations of August 1621, between two to four weeks was to be added to the pay, to cover the period of travel to the army camp. King Sigismund III confirmed in his instruction sent to Khotyn this method of calculating the service period, so in the eyes of the army, this was treated as official and should be honoured. Hetman Chodkiewicz and the commissioners on 18 September offered the soldiers an additional quarter of pay (*ćwierć darowana*) that was to be added to their arrears period of pay.

Well armoured and armed hussar, with estoc visible under his leg. It is worth noting the single wing attached to the saddle. *Journael van de Legatie in Jaren 1627 en 1628*, Abraham Booth (Amsterdam: 1632). (National Archive, Gdańsk)

The commissioners arrived in Lviv in January 1622 and here it quickly became clear that their offer did not match the soldiers' expectations. With the funds available, they offered only pay for 2 quarters (one of service and one 'bonus'), also based on the coinage value of 1622. The soldiers demanded pay for 5 quarters, based on the coinage value of 1621. It seems that the army envoys included in their demands the last quarter of 1621, which soldiers had spent near Lviv while waiting for money. The angry and unpaid soldiery

29 Anna Filipczak-Kocur, *Skarb koronny za Zygmunta III Wazy* (Opole: Wyższa Szkoła Pedagogiczna im. Powstańców Śląskich, 1985), pp.128-131.

30 Unless otherwise noted, this sub-chapter is based on the most detailed study of the Confederation of Lviv: Jerzy Pietrzak, 'Konfederacja lwowska w 1622 roku', *Kwartalnik Historyczny*, year 80, issue 4 (Warszawa: Państwowe Wydawnictwo Naukowe, 1973), pp.845–871.

began to make additional demands, focusing on the internal politics of the country. They wanted better judicial and political protection for those fighting in the defence of the country, and at the same time pointing out that deserters should be sentenced to lose all of their estate land, which should be given as a reward to those that stayed to fight at Khotyn. Noble companions also wanted to limit the power of the hetman, especially with regards to the ways that he could sentence soldiers for different offences. They were also unhappy with the idea of the commissioners, who were seen as an attempt at civilian control over the Hetman, they were, according to many soldiers, just a hindrance and did not help during the campaign in any way.

A very important aspect of the demobilisation of the army was the crucial, but ill-advised, step taken by Sigismund III. He was unhappy with Lubomirski's role in signing the peace treaty with the Ottomans. The King was hoping for a decisive campaign and a significant victory over Osman II, so he believed that Lubomirski's decision to negotiate an end to the war was too hasty. As such he decided to dismiss the magnate from his command and ordered him to leave the army. This was to have serious repercussions, as when the soldiers started to mutiny, the popular and well liked Lubomirski, who had shared with them the miseries of the Khotyn campaign, was not available to calm the situation.

Negotiations did not really take place however, since the commissioners felt that they did not have the authority to discuss the wide list of demands issued by the army, especially those regarding internal policies. The soldiery decided to appeal directly to Sigismund III, thus on 8 January 1622 they wrote down all their demands and sent four envoys to the King. These four were all hussar companions: Barczykowski (from the banner of Jan Zasławski), Hołowiński (from the banner of Tomasz Zamoyski), Obuch (from the banner of Stanisław Lubomirski) and Marcin Strzyżewski (from the banner of Mikołaj Sieniawski). Prestige and the elite cavalry played the most important role even in this early stage of the mutiny. The envoys travelled from Lviv to Warsaw, where they arrived on 21 January. They presented the petition from the troops, asking the King for his support and help. They insisted that the army should receive its due and advised that, if the money was not paid, the soldiers would start an official mutiny, known as a confederation (*konfederacja*). If the issue had been just about money – a problem that was after all too frequent in the Commonwealth – it might have led to some negotiations, but the fact that the soldiers demanded political changes caused a great stir among Sigismund's inner circle; men such as Crown Great Secretary Jakub Zadzik, the Bishop of Cracow Marcin Szyszkowski and Vice-treasurer Daniłłowicz. They suggested to the King, that it was the beginning of armed rebellion, where a number of nobles (the backbone of the army) wanted to force the monarch to give in to their demands. Sigismund previously, in 1606–1607, had to deal with such a rebellion (*rokosz Zebrzydowskiego* or *rokosz sandomierski*) and he did not want history to repeat itself. The army envoys were informed, that he would discuss it with senators and by 14 February would provide his answers through another group of commissioners that would travel to Lviv. For the time being the soldiers were to stay in their assigned quarters, were not be a burden to the local population and were to listen to their commanders. Sigismund also advised that Lubomirski and Zamoyski would be creating a new army to defend Ukraine against Tatars, indicating that some of the soldiers might wish to join its ranks.

The new group of commissioners was composed of seven senators, but only one of them – Jakub Sobieski – was part of the commissioners' council during the Khotyn campaign. The six newly assigned to this mission were: Stanisław Lubomirski, Tomasz Zamoyski, Jan Ledóchowski, Stanisław Żórawiński, Stanisław Mniszech and Jan Trzebiński. Wealthy magnates and powerful senators, they were chosen because the King hoped that they could use their influence to pacify the military-political movement. There was also a chance, that they would pay from their own funds to bribe the leaders of the mutiny. Mniszech, Sobieski and Ledóchowski were in Lviv by 1 February and their negotiations seemed to be going in the right direction. Suddenly, on 8 February, despite promises of money, the soldiers decided that they had had enough. In their gathering they officially started a Confederation, choosing their own leaders. These were Marshal Aleksander Kowenicki, an unknown number of colonels and nine envoys – one from each cavalry regiment taking part in the mutiny. On 11 February, in the Franciscan Order church in Lviv, they 'gave an oath on the naked sabres', agreeing with the points central to their movement and focusing on the political changes that were to defend the minor and lesser nobility. They wrote to some of the powerful senators, asking them to take the Confederation under their protection, to help in saving their rights and freedoms. It was predominantly composed of soldiers from hussar banners, with other troops in the minority. Depending on which account you read, there were between 3,000 and 6,000 mutinous soldiers. Initially these were only from regular army units, but they were also in touch with *lisowczycy* and district troops from Wielkopolska, hoping that they would support the movement. Confederation had, at least officially, its own 'articles of conduct' that would be obeyed by its all members. The soldiers were to stay with their units and in their assigned quarters, and not pillage the local population. There was a list of penalties for crimes, from losing expected pay, through being dismissed from the ranks, even to the death penalty for killing, wounding or rape of the local populace.

On 15 February, Royal secretary Stanisław Zadorski brought Sigismund's answer to the soldiers' January demands to Lviv. The King was grateful to the army for their sacrifices but ordered them to disperse and not to demand more money than had been initially offered. They should accept what was offered by the commissioners, which would be paid in Polish coin but based on its value of 1622 not of 1621. The country was in a dire situation, facing Turks, Tatars, Muscovites and Swedes, and the nobility should focus on their duty as the defenders of the Homeland and not try to worsen the internal situation. As for the political demands, the King was elusive, and stated that they could only be changed during *Sejm* and not by him. He confirmed that deserters and those that, despite taking advance pay, did not participate in

Unarmoured soldier of cossack cavalry, armed with sabre and bow, from the scene of the triumph of King Zygmunt III at Smoleńsk in 1612. Tommaso Dolabella and Tomasz Makowski, 1612 (Muzeum Narodowe, Kraków, MNK XV- R-6908)

the Khotyn campaign, would be punished, while loyal soldiers that fought bravely during campaign would be rewarded. Overall, it was a rather generic letter, and did not address the majority of the army's demands, especially in regard to the laws and the judicial system. It is perhaps no surprise then, that it was not warmly welcome by mutinous troops. Things seemed to escalate quickly, spiralling out of control of the Royal Court. The Confederates decided to assign themselves quarters in Red Ruthenia, Cracow Voivodeship, Volhynia and Mazowsze; with the first two regions suffering the worse from marauding soldiers and their camp servants. However, at least initially, the soldiers tried to limit any unruly behaviour, they also avoided those lands and estates that were owned by the King and the Clergy, but as the movement spread and more soldiers became involved, such estates were also affected.

On 16 March, the King gathered the council of senators (*konwokacja*), where he wanted to address what he saw as the anti-royal, and possibly even anti-Catholic, movement of soldiers. There were rumours that the Confederation was inspired by political opponents of Sigismund III, bringing memories of 1606–1607. The King was supported by the clergy, he even asked Papal Nuncio Torres for his intervention. Torres reminded the Polish priests that they should obey Sigismund and convince the soldiers to leave the movement. They were to refuse confession and absolution to soldiers, punishing them for harms done to the Church's lands. Soldiers expected to be heard during the *Sejm*, where they could argue about their issues, but they were to be disappointed. Although many senators were absent in Warsaw, due to a combination of bad weather and various different excuses (as many did not want to take part in the council), those that arrived agreed with the King in delaying the assembly of the *Sejm* to focus on pacifying the Confederation. There were concerns that soldiers might arrive in large numbers in Warsaw to try to put pressure on the *Sejm*, so the pro-royal part wanted to avoid any risks. It was decided that commissioners were to be despatched to Lviv, where on 11 April they would start a new round of negotiations with the mutineers. Sigismund's inner circle was hoping that those senators that the soldiers had previously written to asking for support – such Prince Jerzy Zbaraski, Archbishop of Lviv Andrzej Próchnicki, Tomasz Zamoyski and Jan Tęczyński – would also play a part in calming down the situation and convincing the Confederates to break up their movement.

Unit of Polish infantry from the beginning of the seventeenth century, from the copy of 'Stockholm Roll' showing the Royal entry into Cracow in 1605. Artist unknown. Original painting currently in the collection of the Royal Castle in Warsaw. (Author's collection)

The April negotiations in Lviv were not easy. Many senators did not want to take part in talks with mutineers, giving a variety of excuses. Finally a group of 11 senators, including Stanisław Lubomirski, Tomasz Zamoyski and Jakub Sobieski – was gathered and travelled to Lviv to meet the soldiers. They had with them some funds issued from the national treasury, hoping that they could use these to calm down the situation. The Confederates were more focused on their political demands though, while as for the pay they insisted on pay for three quarters. The commissioners were offering only two quarters however, which almost led to the breaking off of talks. Facing rumours that 4,000 mutineers were planning to ride to Warsaw to force the gathering of *Sejm*, Lubomirski saved the day, appealing to the general gathering of the Confederates on 16 April. His authority, reinforced by the way he had led the troops at Khotyn, calmed down the angry voices and brought both sides back to the negotiating table. The same day the commissioners agreed to offer the soldiers three quarters of pay, they also guaranteed a full pardon to everyone involved in the mutiny. It seems that some bribes were involved as well, with commissioners paying off the main leaders of the Confederates, so that they in turn would convince their fellows. The soldiers were no longer insisting on an assembly of the *Sejm*, although their political demands were still to be presented to the so-called chancellor's book and discussed during the next *Sejm*. The mutineers sent 35 envoys, accompanied by five commissioners, to Warsaw, to confirm the agreement and ensure that the full pardon would be given. Sigismund III met them at an audience on 12 May, and allowed them to present the agreement. Once again the soldiers stated that their movement was not aimed at the King but they were just demanding justice and the money that they were owed. While Sigismund was not happy with the final agreement, especially with full pardon to leaders and treating the Confederation not as mutiny but as a gathering of soldiers defending their rights, he had to confirm it. By many it was seen as proof of the King's weakness and it led to resentment amongst many senators. Once again, as after the Confederation raised after the 'Time of Troubles', the soldiers managed to enforce their own point of view, in a negative way affecting the monarch's power. Nonetheless senators did confirm the assurance (*asekuracja*), where they gave their oath and financial collateral (100,000zl based on their land estates) that the mutineers would not be prosecuted.

Despite all agreements, gathering funds for making the payment for three quarters of service took a long time, frustrating the awaiting soldiers. It was not until the beginning of August that the soldiers received some money, with approx. 500,000zl paid to the Confederates alone. In total, 1,654,083zl was paid to troops taking part in the Confederation of Lviv[31], with more funds spent outside of the national treasury to pay off district troops as well. It was a huge financial burden on the Commonwealth, especially when some lands were badly affected by the war, marching troops through, marauding Confederates and the *lisowczycy*. It is worthwhile highlighting that the inefficient Polish fiscal system meant that money that was supposed to be gathered from taxes in 1621 took years to arrive. As late as in 1633, some districts and clergy were still due to pay 64,545zl of the taxes agreed for the Khotyn war.[32]

---

31 Anna Filipczak-Kocur, *Skarb koronny za Zygmunta III* Wazy, p.132.
32 Jan Wimmer, 'Wojsko i skarb Rzeczypospolitej u schyłku XVI i w pierwszej połowie XVII wieku', p.37.

Proclamation of King Sigismund III, issued to land-holders of royal lands in Lithuania in October 1622. He advises them that there are marauding groups of ex-soldiers taking part in the Confederation of Lviv, that are pillaging Polish land. As there is risk that they may move to Lithuania, the King orders his officials to fight off and destroy such groups (AGAD, Warsaw)

Many soldiers did not want to disband, with large units reaching Silesia and pillaging along the Polish-Silesian border. It was thus not surprising, that when the *Sejm* finally gathered in January 1623, one of its main points was discussing the issues of future confederations. One of the crucial statements from the *Sejm* that sat in Warsaw between January and March 1623 was giving assurance to all troops taking part in the Confederation. All mutinous soldiers 'both elders [leaders] and other companions, will not be troubled in front of our Majesty nor any courts, for raising the confederation, also for any other damages and wrongs caused [by them] during its time.'[33] In other words, in other to pacify the mutiny, they were all offered amnesty, despite the massive problems that they caused. An important lesson was learnt though, as during the same *Sejm* another resolution, entitled, 'About Prevention of the Military Confederation and all Other Sudden Domestic Wantonness' was put in place. It specified which senators would be assigned as a special council to stop a confederation of the troops from gathering, especially in a situation when soldiers were already paid off. It also put emphasis on the way that the military should deal with any 'loose men' that appear during times of war – all kinds of marauders, ex-soldiers and those that just saw the opportunity to loot and pillage. Such men were to be 'punished, scattered and exterminated', with any nobles amongst them to be sentenced to infamy. Such 'loss of good name' was a serious punishment and a noble known as *infamis* lost his status, could not hold official ranks, et cetera. Infamy could be revoked, though, and the status returned, for example for military service. In this case it was stated that 'quarter army' should act against such 'loose men', the same obligation was also placed on all officials holding any Crown lands. In a worst case scenario, the King himself was to gather a levy of nobility and lead it in military campaign to punish outlaws. The *Sejm*'s resolution even stated that anyone that killed mutinied soldiers or 'loose men', including one of their leaders, should not be prosecuted and instead was to be allowed to take over belongings of the deceased. Any soldier that would join a military confederation was to be forbidden from receiving inheritance after their parents and kinsmen, also prevented from taking any country's office.[34] It clearly shows the huge impact that post–1621 events had on the Commonwealth and its internal politics.

For the Ottoman Empire, the main political repercussion of the Khotyn war was a mutiny of the janissaries in May 1622 and the death of Sultan Osman II, (see Chapter 4 above). While there were a few factors that affected the revolt – from the lack of success during the war, through famine and

---

33   *Volumina Legum*, volume III, p.215.
34   *Volumina Legum*, volume III, pp.216–217.

issues caused by bad weather – it was Osman's plans to reorganise the army that brought about his doom. Facing his new idea of marching to Syria, Lebanon, and possibly to Egypt, the *kaipikulu* soldiers clearly had enough. As described by Evliya Çelebi 'this caused a revolt amongst the troops, and the emperor finding no support, either in the serai (palace) or in the barracks of the janissaries, was thrust into a cart by the wrestler Bünyan and strangled within the walls of the Seven Towers'.[35] For a few days rebellious janissaries were in control of Constantinople, looting and killing officials closely linked to Osman II. Only after they received two months' pay and additional gifts, did they return to their barracks. It was estimated that close to 4,000 people were killed in country's capital during the uprising.[36] Sir Thomas Roe, who was present in Constantinople during the events, summarised the demise of the young Sultan with the comment that he was 'the first emperor that every they laid violent hand on; a fatall signe, I think, of their declynation'.[37]

The problems did not end with the deposing of the young monarch, as the country was now thrown into political turmoil. The throne was taken by Mustafa I (1600–1639), who had already previously been Sultan for a short period between November 1617 and February 1618. Sultan Mustafa, who has been called 'the Mad' by historians, decided to take a bloody revenge on those that killed his nephew. 'Khoaja Omar Efendi, the chief of the rebels, the Kizlar-âghâ Soleimân Aghâ, the vezir Dilaver Pasha, the Kâim-makâm Ahmed Pâshâ, the defterdar Baki Pâshâ, the segbân-bâshi Nasûh Aghâ, and the general of the janissaries, Ali Aghâ, were cut to pieces'.[38] The Sultan was not popular amongst his subjects and was, quite frankly, not fit to rule the empire. He was a puppet in the hands of his ambitious mother, Halime Sultan (1576–1623), who held the title of Valide Sultan (the legal mother of the ruling Sultan). To worsen the already strained situation, Abaza Mehmed Pasha (1576–1634), Governor of Erzurum in Anatolia, gathered an army of the disgruntled provincial troops and local volunteers with which he marched towards Constantinople, to avenge the death of Osman II. The instigator of Osman II's death, Grand Vizier Kara Davud Pasha, who took office on 20 May 1622, was deposed, and then executed on 18 January 1623, in order to calm the situation. Facing the rebellious army of Abaza Mehmed Pasha, Halime Sultan was forced to agreed to Mustafa I being dethroned. He received permission to live in the palace in the capital though and died in 1639. Eleven-year-old Murad IV (1612–1640), son of Ahmed I (1590–1617) and Kösem Sultan (1589–1651) became the new Sultan. Halime Sultan lost her power in the court and died in September 1623. Murad IV would see further turmoil during his early reign, such as the Ottoman-Safavid War of 1623–1639, the plague of 1625, revolts in the local population in Anatolia

Ottoman *sipahi* cavalryman, armed with bow, sabre and dagger. *Rålambska dräktboken*, mid-seventeenth century (National Library of Sweden)

35   Evliya Çelebi, *Narrative of Travels in Europe, Asia, and Africa in the Seventeenth Century*, Volume 1. (London: OrientalTranslation Fund, 1834) p.115.

36   *Kronika Pawła Piaseckiego biskupa przemyślskiego*, p.307.

37   *The Negotiations of Sir Thomas Roe, in his Embassy to the Ottoman Porte, from the year 1621 to 1628*, p.42.

38   Evliya Çelebi, *Narrative of Travels in Europe, Asia, and Africa in the Seventeenth Century*, Volume 1, p.115.

(part of the so-called Celali rebellions), and another uprising of janissaries in 1631. Eventually, he did manage to pacify the country, dealing with both the internal and the external struggles. He even made an attempt to start a new war against the Polish-Lithuanian Commonwealth between 1633 and 1634, hoping to take advantage of the Commonwealth's involvement against Muscovy. The Ottoman attacks were stopped by Grand Hetman Stanisław Koniecpolski and there were no further direct conflicts between both countries until 1672.

Conclusion

The war between the Polish-Lithuanian Commonwealth and the Ottoman Empire, waged in 1620 and 1621 is often seen as one of the peripheral conflicts of the Thirty Years' War. While both countries did not officially participate in this latter conflict, their interests and politics were to some extent linked with both Catholic and Protestant sides of the war that engulfed a large part of Europe. The campaign of 1620, with the ill-fated expedition of Crown Grand Hetman Stanisław Żółkiewski, started as a local conflict focused on the struggle for the Moldavian throne. The surprising defeat of the Polish troops, Żółkiewski's death and the destruction of most of his army, left the country open for Tatar raids and provided Sultan Osman II with a good excuse and opportunity to engage in open war. The Commonwealth managed to raise a strong army and, with the invaluable help from Zaporozhian Cossacks, stopped the Turkish invasion in 1621 at Khotyn. Although, another Grand Hetman, this time Lithuanian Jan Karol Chodkiewicz, paid with his life for this success. Khotyn would be forever remembered as the best example of the cooperation between Polish, Lithuanian and Cossack forces during the entire history of the Commonwealth. While the Tatar raids did not stop, at least the Ottoman threat was pushed away for a time. It would not be until 1633, when the Polish-Lithuanian Commonwealth was engaged in the Smoleńsk War against Muscovy, that the Ottomans would try yet another local, and unsuccessful, offensive move, leading to the small-scale 1633–1634 war between the two countries. Not until 1672 would the Commonwealth and the Ottoman Empire wage an open conflict again.

The Khotyn campaign became known as one of the best defensive military operations in the Polish-Lithuanian Commonwealth's history. Contrary to the doctrine that was the most popular at that time in the country, and which always leans towards offensive actions and engaging the enemy in pitched battle, Hetman Chodkiewicz managed to prepare and coordinate a coherent defence, stopping the Ottoman offensive, tying Osman II's forces around Khotyn and prolonging the fight through September, when worsening weather and lack of supplies had to impact the invading army. It is also important to praise the other commanders of the allied army, especially Lubomirski and Konashevych-Sahaidachny, who after Chodkiewicz's death kept the army together until the end of the conflict. While it is easy to ignore the impact that Royal Prince Władysław had on the overall course of the campaign, it is worth remembering that his presence alone was a meaningful symbol that helped the morale of Poles, Lithuanians and Cossacks alike. The

Khotyn campaign is also the high-water mark of the military cooperation between the Commonwealth's regular army and the Zaporozhians. While the latter would still take part as support troops during Smoleńsk War, also helping the 'quarter army' to fight against Tatar raids in the 1620s, mutual relations started to gradually worsen during and after 1634, leading to the uprisings in 1637, 1638 and finally the most important one in 1648. Almost 50 years after the Khotyn campaign, in May 1669, Cossack Hetman Petro Doroshenko would seek to ally himself with Sultan Mehmed IV, demonstrating how complicated the history of the region was throughout the seventeenth century.

Colour Plate Commentaries

Plate A, Polish or Lithuanian Hussar

Well-equipped hussar, fighting dismounted: possibly a Polish companion during the retreat from Moldavia in 1620, or a Lithuanian companion that has lost his horse during the famous charge at Khotyn on 7 September 1621. His armour is a breastplate and backplate and he also has a short leather coat (under the plate, so not visible) with long mail sleeves. The helmet is *szyszak* (*zischägge*), adorned with white feathers. The hussar is well armed, with a long wheellock pistol (often known as *półhak*), sabre and horseman's pick (*nadziak*). He is wearing a shorter version of the red *żupan*, finished at the knee, common amongst the soldiers serving in the cavalry. His tight black trousers are mostly covered by long yellow boots, made from Saffian (Moroccan) leather. The red outer garment, with a yellow lining, worn over the armour, is known as *delia*.

Plate B, Unarmoured cossack or *lisowczyk*

Unarmoured cossack cavalryman or *lisowczyk*, armed with sabre and *bandolet*, the latter was a word used to describe any sort of firearm that cavalrymen could fire while in the saddle. This soldier has decided to fight without using mail but his head is protected by a *misiurka* helmet. He could also be equipped with a pair of pistols, although they would normally be carried in holsters on his horse. Many soldiers serving in such units, especially those of companion status, were using bows instead of firearms – not only as a useful weapon but also as a symbol of their noble status. The striking, golden-yellow outer garment is based on a satin *żupan* attributed to Hetman Stanisław Żółkiewski, which is currently in the collection of the National Museum in Cracow. A well-off companion or mercenary *lisowczyk* who managed to capture enough loot during his campaigns in Bohemia and Transylvania, could afford fairly luxurious items of clothing, especially if they were serving in units of a more important status, such as those under the command of a hetman or colonel. This is also an opportunity to present a reconstruction of a very interesting piece of seventeenth century clothing worn in Poland. Such *żupan* was not just a nice piece of clothing, as it was quilted with wool or wadding allowing it to serve as light armour.

Plate C, German infantryman in Polish service

German infantryman serving in the one of the regiments from Royal Prince Władysław's command, at the end of the campaign in October 1621. His ragged attire and overall rugged look matches the eyewitness descriptions of the miserable fate of such troops. He is armed with a sword and matchlock musket; the match can be seen in the soldier's left hand. His blue breeches are worn out, with some makeshift repairs applied during the campaign. His jacket is not visible but most likely would also have a few additional patches. The soldier has managed to obtain a coat with a hood, to better protect him from harsh autumn weather, and also a pair of brown gloves to better survive cold nights and rainy days in Moldavia. He has a black felt hat that has definitely seen better days. His stockings and shoes are badly battered, which is not surprising, since soldiers like this one had to march from Prussia to Moldavia, often without receiving any replacement clothing. The inspiration for this illustration is taken from Pieter Snayer's painting of the siege of Aire-sur-la-Lys, showing Spanish troops during the winter operation in 1641.

Plate D, Zaporozhian Cossack

Zaporozhian Cossack, taking part in the night sally at Khotyn or defending the camp against one of the Ottoman assaults. He appears to be a veteran of Crimean raids, as he is well armed with both a sabre and an axe for hand-to-hand combat. The powder horn and leather bag at his belt indicates that he is also normally equipped with a firearm, probably a *rusznica* caliver. While early seventeenth century Cossacks are often reconstructed as bare-chested warriors, dressed only in baggy trousers, this is simply a fantasy that has nothing to do with the reality. This Zaporozhian's clothing is based on the surviving iconography and written accounts, to make it as accurate as possible. He is wearing a white garment known as a *siermięga*, made from thick homespun cloth (*samodział*) or kersey (*karazja*), with tight cloth trousers and long, brown leather boots. The red hat is, as was often the case in the Commonwealth, trimmed with fur.

Plate E, Ottoman janissary

Ottoman janissary at the start of the campaign of 1621. He is armed with the typical weapons of the janissary corps: an ornamented *fitilli tüfek* (matchlock musket) and a sabre. At his belt he is carrying a powder horn and a satchel for bullets. A long cord of match can be seen around his left hand. His headgear is the famous ak börk, used normally for ceremonial purposes only – janissaries would wear it during the parade exit from Constantinople and during formal musters in front of the Sultan, Osman II. The soldier is wearing a long green kaftan, blue breeches and red leather shoes; with a blue scarf alongside his thin black belt. While in theory only janissary officers were allowed to wear beards, in practice many rank and file also tended to have them, possibly as a symbol of veteran status.

Plate F, Ottoman *sipahi*

Well equipped Ottoman *sipahi* horseman, either from *kapikulu* cavalry or some wealthier provincial *timariot*. He is protected by mail and a çiçak helmet (the Turkish equivalent of a Polish szyszak), additionally he has vambraces. Next to his sabre and bow, this sipahi is also equipped with light javelin. As per Prince Krzysztof Zbaraski's observations from 1622, such weapons were usually made from rattan (or 'Indian reed') and were ideal for throwing. Sipahi would also use a javelin in the initial stages of combat, before engaging in hand-to-hand melee. His red kaftan is covered by mail but easily visible are baggy red breeches and brown leather shoes. As with the janissary, this soldier is also wearing a beard, a very common fashion among kapikulu cavalry.

Plate G, Ottoman *serdengeçti* volunteer

Ottoman serdengeçti volunteer preparing to attack the Cossack camp in September 1621. While many of such men were recruited from amongst camp servants, others were drawn from amongst the ranks of the retainers of the provincial cavalry and irregular infantry units. If they survived the attacks and were noticed for their bravery, it could lead to social advancement, including being admitted into ranks of *timariot sipahi*. This serdengeçti is well armed, with a sabre, bow and axe; he has also managed to obtain a round *kalkan* shield. Such a combination of weapons is well documented with assault detachments of serdengeçti recruited from among the janissaries. His clothing is a simple green *kaftan* with a yellow lining, blue trousers and brown shoes. He is wearing a simple hat without the ornaments normally used by janissaries on their ceremonial ak börk. Being of lower standing, he is not allowed to wear a beard, so has just a short moustache.

Plate H, Crimean or Nogay Tatar

Crimean or Nogay Tatar, armed with a sabre and bow: the bow case can be seen next to his left leg, while the arrow case is next to his right leg. He is wearing a red hat trimmed with fox fur, a blue woollen *kaftan* coat with sheepskin on the inside – it can be seen on the parts that are tucked under the wrapped scarf to make it easier for this Tatar to ride his horse. He is also wearing tight, red cloth trousers and long, brown leather boots.

Plate I

1. Polish flag from 1620s, possibly of cossack cavalry banner. Dimensions of the original flag: 112x137 cm, with a flagpole of 211 cm. 17th century drawing by Olof Hoffoman of the standard captured by Swedes (Armémuseum, Stockholm)
2. Polish flag from 1620s, from unit of Polish or German infantry. Dimensions of the original flag: 690x400 cm. Very large size indicates that it was possibly ceremonial one. 17th century drawing by Olof Hoffoman of the standard captured by Swedes (Armémuseum, Stockholm)

Plate J

1. Cornet of Lithuanian reiter company of Wilhelm Tyzenhauz, previously owned by company of Johan von der Osten-Sacken. Flag was captured by Swedes in 1626 in Livonia but is interesting example of type of cornet used by Western-style cavalry in the Commonwealth's armies. Dimensions of the original flag: 234x176 cm, with a flagpole of 264 cm. 17th century drawing by Olof Hoffoman of the standard captured by Swedes (Armémuseum, Stockholm)

2. Obverse of the Polish flag with date 1616, possibly associated with unit of hussars. Example of religious motif very common on Polish and Lithuanian flags, Madonna with the Infant Jesus. On the reverse (not visible here) Crucified Christ. Dimensions 121x101 cm, with flagpole of 297 cm. 17th century drawing by Olof Hoffoman of the standard captured by Swedes (Armémuseum, Stockholm)

Plate K

1. Set of large Ottoman flags. From *Icones habitus monumenta Turcarum*, between 1586 and 1650. (Jagiellonian Library, Cracow)

2. Another set of Ottoman flags, this time single-coloured. From *Icones habitus monumenta Turcarum*, between 1586 and 1650. (Jagiellonian Library, Cracow)

Plate L

1. Examples of much smaller and single-coloured Ottoman flags. From *Icones habitus monumenta Turcarum*, between 1586 and 1650. (Jagiellonian Library, Cracow)

2. Ottoman standard-bearer, probably from deli provincial cavalry, with characteristic self-mutilation, lack of armour and pelt of the exotic cat. *Rålambska dräktboken*, mid-17th century (National Library of Sweden)

Additional (front and back cover)

Lithuanian Grand Hetman Jan Karol Chodkiewicz during one of the War Council talks at Khotyn. He is wearing black *żupan* with a yellow *delia* outer garment over it. In his left hand he is carrying a *buława* mace, which was used as the hetman's symbol of office. As with every Polish and Lithuanian noble, he is also equipped with a sabre. He is wearing yellow shoes, made from Saffian (Moroccan) leather.

Ottoman Sultan Osman II during the muster of his army at the beginning of the Khotyn campaign. In a green *żupan*, with a rich red *kaftan* lined with sable worn over it. The *kaftan* has long, false sleeves. Around his waist, the Sultan has a silk sash, known as *kusak*. To highlight his high status, he is wearing blue boots, known as *basmak*. The large ceremonial turban is made from white muslin, reserved for only the Sultan and the Grand Vizier. Because of his young age, the Sultan does not have a moustache or beard.

Appendix I

The Polish army in the Cecora campaign, August–October 1620

Estimates of Hetman Żółkiewski's forces during the campaign of 1620 vary from source to source. For example Paweł Piasecki in his chronicle described the army as 'in total no more than 1,600 hussars or lancers, 1,200 reiters, 4,000 lightly armoured cavalry and 2,000 infantry, [and] next to them large number of the camp servants, as Polish [army] camps tend to be full of those burdensome lot'.[1] Miron Costin, probably partially based on Piasecki's account, described the Polish army as '1,600 hussars all in iron, 4,000 cavalry other than hussars, that they called lancers,[2] 1,200 German reiters, 400 cossack-*lisowczycy*,[3] 2,000 German infantry. These were enlisted men but additionally there were also the magnates' [private] retinues of approximately 2,000 men plus those that came as volunteers [looking] for loot'.[4] Another, more detailed relation, gives the total number of 9,000 men, as follows:[5]

1,500 hussars
1,600 cossack cavalry (regular troops)
1,200 *lisowczycy*
200 reiters
2,000 infantry 'of all types'
800 'Ukrainians' [Ukrainian subjects of Polish magnates] under Stefan Chmielecki
400 'Ukrainians' under Janusz Tyszkiewicz
400 men of Walenty Kalinowski
300 men from Bar
600 Moldavians with Voivode Graziani

---

1   *Kronika Pawła Piaseckiego biskupa przemyślskiego*, p.280.
2   Clearly mistake, as there is no evidence that cossack cavalry that he thinks about used lances or spears.
3   This number seems to be far too low.
4   Miron Costin, *Latopis ziemi mołdawskiej i inne utwory historyczne*, p.131.
5   BK 974, p. 37, *Wołoskie dzieje niektóre z relatiei pewnych osób*.

Bases on those and a number of other sources, the organisation of the Polish Army during the Cecora campaign was researched in great detail by Ryszard Majewski, who in 1970 published a study of the campaign and the battle itself.[6] Majewski attempted to reconstruct Hetman Żółkiewski's force, its composition and strength, but there are major gaps in the first names of a few lesser known officers and in the exact information about the volunteer forces present during the campaign. Where possible, I have added additional information – such as identifications or further materials about the units – to Majewski's original researches. Officers marked * were killed during the battle of Cecora or during the retreat (including those that drowned while escaping). Officers marked ** were taken prisoner.

The initial contingent under Żółkiewski's command, from the muster of 1 September 1620.

The contingent had about 7,000 men and was divided into five regiments (*pułki*)[7]

1. Regiment of Crown Grand Hetman Stanisław Żółkiewski, under command of *rotmistrz* Makowiecki

Formation	Name of *rotmistrz*	Strength	Additional comments
Hussars	Hetman Żółkiewski*	270	Under command of Małyński**
	Jan Daniłłowicz	150	
	Makowiecki	150	
Cossack cavalry	Aleksander Bałłaban**	150	
	Dworycki (Dworzycki)	150	
	Jan Daniłłowicz	300	
	Wolmar Farensbach**	50	
Infantry	Haiduk banner	300	Court unit of King Sigismund III under Captain Almady
	Wolmar Farensbach**	50	German infantry
	Jan Daniłłowicz	150	German infantry

6   Ryszard Majewski, *Cecora rok 1620* (Warszawa: Wydawnictwo Ministerstwa Obrony Narodowej, 1970).
7   Ryszard Majewski, *Cecora rok 1620*, pp.141–145.

2. Regiment of Crown Field Hetman Stanisław Koniecpolski, under command of Stano, lieutenant of his hussar banner

Formation	Rotmistrz	Strength	Additional comments
Hussars	Hetman Koniecpolski**	200	Under command of Stano*
	Marcin Kazanowski	150	
	Mikołaj Potocki**	150	
	Strzyżowski	150	
Reiters	Herman Denhoff*	200	
Cossack cavalry	Jan Odrzywolski	150	Under Ujazdowski**
	Lewikowski**	100	
Infantry	Hetman Koniecpolski**	230	*Wybraniecka* under Damięcki
	Rybiński**	200	*Wybraniecka* infantry

3. Regiment of Mikołaj Struś

Formation	Name of *rotmistrz*	Strength	Additional comments
	Mikołaj Struś**	100	
	Maliński	150	
Cossack cavalry	Mikołaj Struś**	100	
	Łukasz Żółkiewski**	100	
	Kowalski*	100	
Volunteers	Various	Approx. 1,500	Most likely serving as cossack cavalry

4. Regiment of Stefan Korecki:

Formation	Rotmistrz	Strength	Additional comments
Hussars	Samuel Korecki**	150	
	Andrzej Górski	100	
	Wrzeszcz*	150	
Cossack cavalry	Samuel Korecki**	100	
Tatar cavalry	Samuel Korecki**	100	
Infantry	Wiadrowski*	200	Both probably Polish infantry
	Ujazdowski**	100	

5. Regiment of Walenty Kalinowski:

Formation	*Rotmistrz*	Strength	Additional comments
Hussars	Walenty Kalinowski*	150	
	Firlej	150	
Cossack cavalry	Kaliński	100	
	Wachowski	100	
Polish infantry	Walenty Kalinowski*	100	
	Walenty Kalinowski*	100	Composed of Ruthenians

The Army was equipped with 16 small-calibre cannon and a few dozen hook-guns, carried on tabor wagons. Artillery was under the command of Teofil Szemberg, who wrote and published a few detailed accounts of the whole expedition.

On 7 September 1620 the Polish army encamped at Łozowa was reinforced by the following forces:

> Moldavian Voivode Gaspar Graziani, with some of his court officials and 500–600 soldiers (Moldavian cavalry, Serbian mercenary cavalry, 100 infantry). Further units of Moldavians joined near Cecora, so before the start of the battle they were approximately 1,000 strong.
>
> Polish magnate Janusz Tyszkiewicz** with four banners (probably 400 horses in total) of cossack cavalry and two banners (probably 200 men in total) of Polish infantry.[8]

Two days later Stefan Chmielecki arrived with 800 men, they could have been either Zaporozhian Cossacks or cossack cavalry raised from Ukrainian estates of Polish magnates.

On 11 September the Army was joined by further reinforcements:

> *Lisowczycy* regiment under Walenty Rogawski. It had 12 banners, with up to 1,700 horses
> Słowiński banner (cossack cavalry?) of 100 horses
> Another cossack cavalry banner of 150 horses, possibly a private unit of one of Zbaraski's princes

A document entitled 'Register of the prisoners that are in the enemy's hands'[9] mentioned even more officers that were captured by Turks and Tatars, with most of them likely to have been from the private volunteer units:

---

8   'Dyariusz expedycyej cecorskiej Stanisława Żółkiewskiego kancl. i hetm. w. kor. Przeciw Skinderbaszy tureckiemu e. 1620' in: Stanisław Żurkowski, *Żywot Tomasza Zamoyskiego*, p.381.

9   'Rejestr więźniów, którzy są w ręku nieprzyjacielskich', *Pamiętnik Warszawski Czyli Dziennik Nauk i Umiejętności*, volume 14 (Warszawa: Zawadzki i Węcki, 1819), p.110–111.

Rotmistrz rank – Kazanowski, Kaliński, Ferecberg (shot in leg – it would be Farensbach), Lenikowski, Broniowski, Kozicka, Chmielecki (Stefan's brother), Dunikowski, Lanikowski, Bogusławski

Lieutenant rank – Mysłowski, Dębiński

Appendix II

Examples of the Polish-Lithuanian army lists from the Khotyn campaign of 1621

As mentioned in Chapter 5, there are at least 16 different documents depicting Polish and Lithuanian troops during the campaign in 1621. Some of them mention only units at banner level and their strength, others also provide the detailed information about the composition of each regiment. This information is from some of these documents, focusing on regimental structure and strength of units.

Year 1621, first [day] of month September. Komput of the Polish army and [of] Grand Duchy of Lithuania under command of His Grace Jan Karol Chodkiewicz, Voivode of Vilnius, Crown and Lithuanian Grand Hetman

The first of the documents is a very valuable source, as it seems to have been written in the Polish-Lithuanian camp, probably by someone from the close entourage of Stanisław Lubomirski. It mentions the presence of Cossacks and even includes armed camp servants. Additionally, it acknowledges – as in its title – that for the period of campaign Chodkiewicz was temporary Crown Grand Hetman, following the decision of the *Sejm* from 1620. The document survived in the collection of the National Library in Warsaw and this translation is based on the edition published in 2013 by Karol Żojdź and Zbigniew Hundert.[1]

---

1   Karol Żojdź, Zbigniew Hundert (ed.), 'Komput chocimski 1621 z rękopisu Biblioteki Narodowej' in Zbigniew Hundert (ed.), *Studia nad staropolską sztuką wojenną*, volume II (Oświęcim: Wydawnictwo Napoleon V, 2013), pp.245-257.

Regiment of Crown Field Hetman Stanisław Lubomirski:

8 banners of hussars – total 1,250 horses
7 banners of cossack cavalry – 900 horses (including 200 of *lisowczycy*)
2 units of infantry – 1,400 portions
Total: 3,550 horses and portions

Regiment of Maciej Leśniowski, Vice-chamberlain of Bełz

2 banners of hussars – 600 horses
3 banners of cossack cavalry – 400 horses
Total: 1,000 horses

Regiment of Jan Mikołaj Boratyński, *starosta* of Lipnik

4 banners of hussars – 500 horses
3 banners of cossack cavalry – 550 horses
Total: 1,050 horses

Regiment of Mikołaj Zenowicz, castellan of Połock:

3 banners of hussars – 450 horses
4 banners of cossack cavalry – 600 horses
1 banner of reiters – 150 horses
3 banners of Polish infantry – 600 portions
Total: 1,800 horses and portions

Regiment of Lithuanian Grand Hetman Jan Karol Chodkiewicz:

10 banners of hussars – 1,550 horses
5 banners of cossack cavalry – 600 horses
4 banners of Polish infantry – 650 portions (one banner lacks a number of
    portions next to it)
Total: 2,800 horses and portions

Additionally three banners of hussars (total strength 600 horses) were ad hoc attached to this regiment, awaiting the arrival of Tomasz Zamoyski, in whose regiment they were to serve. As he never reached the army, it is likely that they formed part of Chodkiewicz's regiment for the whole campaign.

Regiment of Aleksander Sapieha, *starosta* of Orsza:

7 banners of hussars – 1,000 horses
4 banners of cossack cavalry – 500 horses
1 banner of Polish infantry – 200 portions
2 banners of reiters – 400 horses [this appears to be a mistake by the scribe
    compiling the list as these two units were in fact also banners of Polish
    infantry]
Total: 2,100 horses and portions

Regiment of Piotr Opaliński, castellan of Poznań:

3 banners of hussars – 450 horses
4 banners of cossack cavalry – 400 horses
3 banners of reiters – 350 horses
2 banners of Polish infantry – 400 portions
Total: 1,600 horses and portions

Regiment of Stefan Potocki, *starosta* of Kamieniec:

4 banners of hussars – 500 horses
6 banners of cossack cavalry – 600 horses
3 banners of Polish infantry – 500 portions
Total: 1,600 horses and portions

Regiment of Mikołaj Kossakowski, *starosta* of Wizna

2 banners of hussars – 300 horses
5 banners of cossack cavalry – 600 horses
1 banner of Polish infantry – 400 portions
Total: 1,300 horses and portions

Regiment of Mikołaj Sieniawski (Crown *krajczy*) and Prokop Sieniawski:
(the document does not mentioned how the troops were divided into banners)

600 hussars
500 cossack cavalry
200 Polish infantry
Total: 1,300 horses and portions

Units that arrived later to the camp:

1 banner of hussars – 150 horses
5 banners of cossack cavalry – 500 horses
4 banners of Polish infantry – 750 portions
3 units of German infantry – 1,250 portions
Total: 2,650 horses and portions

Regiment of Royal Prince Władysław Waza:

7 banners of hussars – 1,250 horses
3 banners of reiters – 560 horses
3 banners of Polish infantry – 1,600 portions
5 banners of cossack cavalry – 600 horses
5 units of German infantry – 4,800 portions [two small banners mentioned as part of those five units were in fact of Polish infantry]

Total: 8,810 horses and portions, although the document states 8,800 and there is note that 'there was supposed to be 10,600'.

The *Komput* provides an incorrect total number of troops, stating that 'without Zaporozhian Cossacks [there were] 31,260 [horses and portions]', while in fact it should be 29,550 (or 29,560 if the correct total is used for the regiment of the Royal Prince). The Zaporozhian Cossacks are mentioned as 21,260 [men].

A very interesting addition is on the end of the document, stating that 'servants (*luźna czeladź*) mustered by [Mikoła] Chamiec, senior servant to Hetman [Chodkiewicz], if they were to attack Turkish camp: 26,660 [men]'.

Register of the whole Polish army during the Turkish expedition at Khotyn in 1621

Another interesting list of Polish and Lithuanian troops taking part in the campaign, one probably compiled by Jakub Sobieski. It includes some important comments describing the state of the army at the start of the campaign. The *Register* includes units of volunteers and *lisowczycy*. As with other documents presented in this study, the names of individual commanders (on the banner level) were omitted. The translation is based on the edition by Jan Wimmer.[2]

> hussars – 52 banners – 8,280 horses
> reiters (under the name of *arkabuzerowie*) – 15 banners – 2,701 horses
> cossack cavalry (including volunteers) – 61 banners – 8,200 horses
> regiment of *lisowczycy* cavalry under Stanisław Rusinowski – 1,400 horses
>
> Polish infantry – 36 units – 8,508 portions (incorrect summary in the document, it should be 8,500 portions)
> German infantry – 5 units – 6,016 portions (four regiments and one company, with the latter identified in other sources as a dragoon unit)
> Zaporozhian Cossacks – 'at least 30,000 that were mustered on foot, [the majority of them] with *rusznica* [caliver] as not everyone had a sabre'
> Total summary of Polish [and Lithuanian] troops – 35,105 [the total is incorrect, it should be 35,097]

The author of the register added a lengthy comment, in which he criticised the preparation of the army:

> But [to tell the truth] there were less of those troops on the muster than on the paper and many banners arriving in the camp were very short [of men] and had

---

2   Zdzisław Spieralski, Jan Wimmer (ed.), *Wypisy źródłowe do historii polskiej sztuki wojennej. Zeszyt piąty. Polska sztuka wojenna w latach 1563-1647* (Warszawa: Wydawnictwo Ministerstwa Obrony Narodowej, 1961), pp.134-141. Original document: *Regestr wszystkiego wojska polskiego tureckiej pod Chocimiem ekspedycji w roku 1621*, Biblioteka Czartoryskich, no 111, p.411.

to serve in that way. Few banners of cossack cavalry were disbanded as they were so poor. Infantry died and deserted with each hour. As of Zaporozhian Cossacks, one week after their arrival, many of them dispersed in the area [looking] for food, so Turkish Sultan found much less of [our] army that it should be on this paper. And after fighting for few weeks army was diminished due to hunger [causing] many men and almost all horses [to die], [taking losses] due to desertion, due to so many different illnesses, due to constant death at the hands of Tatars and bandits on pastures and roads, as in [normal] fight, thanks to God's Mercy, not many died and rarely any good [soldier], mostly servants, so when we started negotiations [with Turks] probably only one-third of the army was still [alive], and when we crossed the Turkish bridge [to return to Poland] our army was so ravaged in horses and men [alike] that we all witness here that there we no more than one good regiment [in total].

Order of the regiments of Polish and Lithuanian troops

Another register of the regiments and banners of Polish and Lithuanian troops taking part in the Khotyn campaign in 1621 is entitled *Order of the regiments of Polish and Lithuanian troops in the sudden campaign against Sultan Osman, Turkish Emperor, on the field of Wallachia near Khotyn in Year of Our Lord 1621* and survives today in Sweden.[3] When compared with other musters, this one has slightly different organisation of the regiments, it is also missing the Cossack troops altogether.

Regiment of Crown Field Hetman Stanisław Lubomirski:

7 banners of hussars – total 1,000 horses
7 banners of cossack cavalry – 800 horses
1 banner of *lisowczycy* – 200 horses
2 units of infantry – 1,400 portions
Total: 3,400 horses and portions (the document incorrectly gives 3,900)

Regiment of Maciej Leśniowski, Vice-chamberlain of Bełz

2 banners of hussars – 600 horses
3 banners of cossack cavalry – 400 horses
Total: 1,000 horses

---

3   Riksarkivet, Skoklostersamlingen, E 8603, pp.52–54

Regiment of Jan Mikołaj Boratyński, *starosta* of Lipnik

4 banners of hussars – 450 horses
3 banners of cossack cavalry – 400 horses
Total: 850 horses

Regiment of Mikołaj Zenowicz, castellan of Połock:

3 banners of hussars – 400 horses
4 banners of cossack cavalry – 700 horses
1 banner of reiters – 150 horses
3 banners of Polish infantry – 600 portions
Total: 1,850 horses and portions (the document incorrectly states 1,750)

Regiment of Lithuanian Grand Hetman Jan Karol Chodkiewicz:

9 banners of hussars – 1,550 horses
6 banners of cossack cavalry – 700 horses
1 banner of reiters – 200 horses
4 banners of Polish infantry – 1,050 portions
Total: 3,500 horses and portions

Additionally 3 banners of hussars (total strength 600 horses) were attached to this regiment, awaiting the arrival of Tomasz Zamoyski, in whose regiment they were to serve. As he never reached the army, it is likely that they were part of Chodkiewicz's regiment for the whole campaign.

Regiment of Aleksander Sapieha, *starosta* of Orsza:

4 banners of hussars – 500 horses
4 banners of cossack cavalry – 500 horses
2 banners of reiters – 400 horses
3 banners of Polish infantry – 600 portions
Total: 2,000 horses and portions

Regiment of Piotr Opaliński, castellan of Poznań:

3 banners of hussars – 450 horses
4 banners of cossack cavalry – 400 horses
3 banners of reiters – 350 horses
2 banners of Polish infantry – 400 portions
Total: 1,600 horses and portions

Regiment of Stefan Potocki, *starosta* of Kamieniec:

4 banners of hussars – 400 horses
5 banners of cossack cavalry – 600 horses
1 banner of Polish infantry – 400 portions
Total: 1,400 horses and portions

Regiment of Mikołaj Sieniawski (Crown *krajczy*) and Prokop Sieniawski:

600 hussars
500 cossack cavalry
400 Polish infantry
Total: 1,500 horses and portions

Units that arrived later to the camp:

1 banner of hussars – 150 horses
4 banners of cossack cavalry – 500 horses
5 banners of Polish infantry – 950 portions
2 units of German infantry – 1,050 portions
Total: 2,650 horses and portions

Additional regiment (without the name of its commander or a list of banners):

150 hussars
500 cossack cavalry
950 infantry

[Note: the document omits the regiment of Mikołaj Kossakowski, *starosta* of Wizna which is present in other registers]

Regiment of Royal Prince Władysław Waza:

7 banners of hussars – 1,250 horses
3 banners of reiters – 560 horses
5 banners of cossack cavalry – 600 horses
5 banners of Polish infantry – 600 portions
3 regiments of German infantry – 5,400 portions
Total: 8,410 horses and portions (the document incorrectly states 10,210)

Additional banner of reiters (without the name of its *rotmistrz*), mustered on 1 October

300 horses

Order of the regiments that should be and in which way they should march

The final 'army list' is slightly different, as it does not cover the whole army. It seems to have been compiled before the arrival of Royal Prince Władysław's regiment at Khotyn, with a few other regiments and some other late arrivals missing as well. It is based on the version published in 1908.[4]

Regiment of Crown Field Hetman Stanisław Lubomirski

7 banners of hussars – 1,000 horses

8 banners of cossack cavalry (including one Hungarian unit and one banner of *lisowczycy*) – 1,050 horses

2 units of infantry – 1,400 portions

Maciej Leśniowski, Vice-chamberlain of Bełz

2 banners of hussars – 500 horses

3 banners of cossack cavalry – 450 horses

Jan Mikołaj Boratyński, *starosta* of Lipnik

4 banners of hussars – 450 horses

3 banners of cossack cavalry – 400 horses

Stefan Potocki, *starosta* of Kamieniec

4 banners of hussars – 500 horses

1 banner of reiters – 150 horses

4 banners of cossack cavalry – 600 horses

3 banners of Polish infantry – 600 portions

Lithuanian Grand Hetman Jan Karol Chodkiewicz

9 banners of hussars – 1,450 horses

1 banner of reiters – 200 horses

6 banners of cossack cavalry – 800 horses

4 banners of Polish infantry – 1,050 portions

additional 3 banners of hussars – 600 horses

---

4   *Zherela do istoriï Ukraïny-Rusy,* volume VIII, pp.244-248.

Aleksander Sapieha, *starosta* of Orsza

4 banners of hussars – 500 horses
2 banners of reiters – 400 horses
4 banners of cossack cavalry – 500 horses
3 banners of Polish infantry – 600 portions

Piotr Opaliński, castellan of Poznań

3 banners of hussars – 450 horses
3 banners of reiters – 350 horses
4 banners of cossack cavalry – 400 portions
2 banners of Polish infantry – 400 portions

Stefan Potocki, *starosta* of Kamieniec

4 banners of hussars – 500 horses
7 banners of cossack cavalry – 700 horses
3 banners of Polish infantry – 400 portions

Mikołaj Kossakowski, *starosta* of Wizna

2 banners of hussars – 300 horses
5 banners of cossack cavalry – 600 horses
1 banner of Polish infantry – 400 portions
200 horses of 'Muscovite Don [Cossacks]', with the annotation 'those are supposed
    to march at the end'

Additionally one banner of Stanisław Żurawiński was to be added to one of
the regiments. It seems to be the hussar banner of 200 horses, that in other
documents is included in Stefan Potocki's regiment.

The 'Army List' also has a summary, which incorrectly states that there
were 10 regiments, as only 9 are mentioned. The total numbers of units and
troops are as follow:

44 banners of hussars – 6,900 horses
44 banners of cossack cavalry – 5,500 horses
19 'well equipped' banners of infantry – 3,950 portions
6 'well equipped' banners of reiters – 960 horses
1 banner of Muscovite Don [Cossacks] – 200 horses

With a total of 17,400 horses and portions in 84 banners. [The actual total it
17,510]

Appendix III

Two registers of Zaporozhian troops in 1621

As mentioned in Chapter 5, there is a lot of contradictory information about the strength of the Cossack army at Khotyn in 1621, with notes in different sources showing a wide range in numbers between 20,000 and 45,000 men. There are, however, two more detailed lists, which provide the names and strengths of all regiments, giving more insight into the structure of the Zaporozhian army in 1621 and into units present at the allied camp at Khotyn.

The first, the *Komput of the Zaporozhian Army for the Khotyn War*, is dated 6 July 1621 so had to have been written during the time when the Cossacks were marching to Moldavia.[1] Despite the fact that Konashevych-Sahaidachny was not present with the army, we can find his regiment here, although it is unconfirmed who was in charge of it.

Yakov Nerodych (Jakub Nerodicz Borodawka) – 3,000 men
Bohdan Konsha (Bohdan Konsza) – 1,600 men
Petro Konashevych-Sahaidachny (Piotr Konaszewicz-Sahajdaczny) – 2,200 men
Tikhiv (Tichow) – 2,200 men
Tymish Udovic (Tymosz Udowic) – 4,000 men
MoisePenko (Mojsiej Pieńko) – 2,500 men
FyodorBoloborodek (Fedor Biłoborodki) – 3,200 men
Danylo Dołgan (Daniło Dołgan/Dowgan) – 3,000 men
Adamko Pidigriksyi (Adam Podgórski) – 3,700 men
Sydir Semakovich (Sidor Siemakowicz) – 3,500 men
Vasyl Luchkov (Wasyl Łuczkowicz) – 4,100 men
Datsko Gordienki (Dacko Gordijenko) – 2,900 men
Wojciech Usat (Wojciech Usaty) – 2,800 men
Semyon Chechuga (Semen Czeczuga) – 3,400 men
Gurski – 2,000 men

---

1   Petro Sas, *Khotyn War of 1621*, p.118.

In all there are 15 regiments, totalling 44,100 men, although the clerk composing the original document made a mistake and gave the total as 42,900 men.

The second, entitled *Register of the colonels of the Zaporozhian army for the Turkish expedition in Khotyn in 1621*, is dated to late August 1621, probably after 25 August. It already reflects changes in the leadership of the Cossack army, as Jakow Nerodicz Borodawka is no longer in charge and Petro Konashevych-Sahaidachny took over the command. The *Register* provides the names of 13 colonels and the strengths of their regiments (*pułki*). This is a translation from the version published in 1908.[2]

> Petro Konashevych-Sahaidachny (Piotr Konaszewicz-Sahajdaczny), Hetman of the Zaporozhian army – 3,000 horses
> Ivan Zyskar (Iwan Zyszkarz) – 2,320 horses
> Bohdan Kurosh (Bogdan Kurosz) – 1,600 horses
> TymoshFedorovych (Tymosz Fedorowicz) – 4,000
> Moysykh Pisark (Mojsicz Pisarek) – 2,500
> Fyodor Bilogorodek (Fedor Biłohorodek) – 3,200
> Danylo Dorokoł (Daniło Dorokoł) – 3,000
> Adam Pidhorsky (Adam Podgórski) – 3,700
> Sydor Semakovich (Sidor Siemakowicz) – 3,500
> Vasyl Lukchevich (Wasyl Łuckiewicz) – 4,100
> Yatsek Hordenko (Jacek Hordenko/Gordijenko) – 2,700
> Tsetsiura Semrok (Cieciura Semrok) – 3,200
> Ivan Gardzsia (Iwan Gardziel) – 2,000

Total 38,820 Cossacks, although the document incorrectly mentions 41,520 men. Additionally the *Register* includes information about Cossack artillery: they had 20 bronze and three iron cannon, plus 12 tabor wagons with cannon balls and black powder.

---

2   *Zherela do istoriï Ukraïny-Rusy*, volume VIII, p.250.

Appendix IV

A true certificate of what men Sir Arthur Aston Knight brought to sea with himself and his commanders out of England and Ireland.

This document lists the number of troops recruited and despatched from the British Isles by Arthur Aston Sr. As mentioned in Chapter 5 above, they were raised after the diplomatic mission of Jerzy Ossoliński although most of the men were stopped in the Danish Straits and only a few hundred, under command of Arthur Aston Jr. arrived in Poland. They were too late though to take part in the Khotyn campaign, so were sent to Livonia to fight against the Swedes, where they took part in actions around Mitau (Mitawa). Additional notes and comments were added in brackets to the original text to make some points clearer.[1]

A true certificate of what men Sir Arthur Aston Knight brought to sea with himself and his commanders out of England and Ireland.

In primis himselfe hired two shippes in wch there were shipped from the port of London} 300–60 [360 men]
Item Captaine Arthur Aston [Jr] shipped from the same porte} 300 –
Item Captaine Frauncis Blaby shipped from the same port} 300 –
Item Captaine Allen and Captaine Lasie [Lacey?] from the same port} 200 –
It[em] Captaine Thomas Howard shipt from Newcastle} 200–40 [240]

Out of Ireland
First Captaine Lawrence Maisterson shipt out of Wexford – 200
It[em] Captaine Brian FitzPatricke shipt out of the port of Waterford in two shippes 600–10 [610]

---

1   The National Archives, State Papers Poland, SP/83/4 folio72. I would like to thank Kevin Mulley from The National Archives in Kew for providing me with this document.

These men were all at sea and my two ships with my sonnes shippe passed the Sound the rest were dispersed some into Holland, some returned for England and Captain Brian's company returned for Ireland.

Besides all these I paid money to these four captaines to have brought me 200 men apiece out of Ireland who could not get shipping that year, yet had raysed their men and had them in readinesse viz.

Captaine Christopher Blunt
Captained John Doyne
Captaine Bingley
Captaine Fraunces Williams
Had we by the Embassadours meanes had passage in the Sound I had brought into Poland 3,000 men
[signed] Sir Arthur Aston Sr.

Appendix V

An Account of the War in Poland from 1 to 21 September from *Nieuwe Tijdinghen*

As mentioned above, news about the war with the Ottoman Empire reached many European countries, where both courts and the public were interested in hearing about the campaigns. A very interesting relation was published in Antwerp in issue 171 of *Nieuwe Tijdinghen*, dated 23 November 1621. It was double-length issue with *An Account of the War in Poland from 1 to 21 September*. Below is the full relation translated by Paul Alblaster, and all comments in square brackets are made from him.[1] Additional information, where identification of the certain regions of Poland was possible, has been added in footnotes by myself.

1 September: Having assembled a large force, the Turkish emperor made war on us. After initial skirmishes and raids, 1,200 artillery shots were fired at our army, without harming anyone in it. For our army was so skilfully placed that only one side was exposed to the enemy. The southern flank was protected by a loop of a wide river, the eastern by high mountains, with the strong castle of Choczijn [Khotyn] and high peaks, and the northern by a very deep ditch.

2 September: The Turkish emperor sent some Wallachian noblemen to the lord general, as a cover for spying out opportunities to set fires in our army. Having come to our army and having made their greetings, one was immediately seized and put to the torture on the orders of the illustrious lord general, and confessed the whole scheme. His accomplices being betrayed were also tortured and confirmed his story. All were beheaded together, and in such quietness that neither the Turks nor the Poles were aware of what had happened. On the same day he changed his lodgings and had dry wood brought to the former lodgings, with dry old thatch, old huts and barracks of soldiers, anything that burns easily, and made fires in

---

1   *Nieuwe Tijdinghen*, Antwerp, Erfgoedbiblioth. English translation by Paul Alblaster available on https://www.facebook.com/NieuweTijdinghen (last entry 01/06/2023). Translation used with permission (all rights reserved).

various places. The Turkish emperor seeing the flames burning high, thought that the Wallachian noblemen had successfully carried out his treacherous scheme, and sent his army forwards to the burning lodging without proper order, which presented the illustrious lord general with an opportunity he would not let go to waste. He sent a great troop of Cossacks, and another sort of people who serve the Cossacks, as well as the German infantry, who were in readiness for just this, against enemies who thought that victory and plunder were assured. The fighting was fierce. On our side 4,000 were killed, and on the enemy's 60,000.

3 September: On the advice of two Wallachians who had gone over to the Turks, the Turkish emperor commanded his pashas to take the encampment of the Zaporozhian Cossacks that same day by any means necessary, as he wished to dine there. Several thousand Turks and Tatars were sent, whose first assault ours resisted magnificently. Seeing he had achieved nothing, the enemy sent his second assault with greater force. The fighting was fierce. In a sortie from their encampment, ours captured several cannon from the enemy. Some they cast from their wheels or carriages, others they spiked. And they sent a courier to the illustrious lord general asking speedy succour, as they could not long resist many such assaults.

4 September: This was a Saturday, on which the enemy made a greater assault on the Cossacks. Seeing they would not be able to resist it, the Cossacks left their encampment to join the illustrious lord general's main army. Drawn up in battle order, they made a path through the midst of the Turks and Tatars. The illustrious lord general's main force was about 8 miles from there, along the route they would have to fight through. The illustrious lord general sent 960 Cossacks (those who had served his imperial majesty against the rebels in Bohemia and Austria)[2] to their aid. Harrying the enemy's flanks in their fashion they inflicted no small losses. The German cavalry and infantry followed, bearing themselves in brave and manly fashion. Finally they were joined by teamsters, cooks, boys, and such low hangers on, who pursued the enemy back to their own camp, where they carried off some cannon and set fire to some tents and suchlike. About 100,000 Turks died in that battle. The Turkish emperor escaped, but lost his turban, which the looters found and presented to the illustrious lord general.

5 and 6 September: On Sunday and Monday there was no fighting, with both armies remaining quiet.

7 September: On 7 September, the eve of the Nativity of Our Lady Mary, Queen of Heaven and Earth, the Turks divided their forces in two. One part, with the heavy guns, they set against the Cossacks, firing at them continually, but not killing any of our men. The Cossacks did not fire a single shot against the enemy throughout that day. They were awaiting the opportunity of the night to attack and capture the enemy's guns. Suspecting as much, the enemy moved his guns a few hours before nightfall. At about the same time, the other part of his army advanced to the

---

2   In this case it would be *lisowczycy*, so cossack cavalry, not Zaporozhian Cossacks.

entrance of our encampment, which was guarded by the illustrious lord general, who at once gave leave to engage the enemy. The battle was terrible and perilous, for our men were in amongst the enemy, and the dead bodies heaped one upon another like bridges. There were terrible losses on both sides, as is not uncommon in war. In the fighting Lord Hyguaroski, the king's steward, quit himself well. If any other leading noblemen died in the fight, it is not written.

8 September: The Turks, in an attempt to divide and weaken our army, sent several thousand Tatars to bring fire and sword to Podolia and Ruthenia, raiding as far as Leopoldin [Lviv]. The illustrious lord general would not (contrary to the Turk's expectations and desire) diminish our army, saying it was better for a part of the commonwealth to suffer than for the whole commonwealth to be endangered. So he kept the men together in the army, refusing to allow any to be sent against the Tatars. While this was happening, Lord Chamogsty [Tomasz Zamoyski], Palatine of Kyiovien [Kyiv], led his men behind Nestrum and coming towards our army happened upon a large party of Tatars and killed many of them, taking their booty and liberating their prisoners. We trust that God will grant that the vaunting spirit of those barbarians will be brought low.

9 September: After the Nativity of Our Lady the Turk did his utmost, with renewed assaults on our camp, and it was agreed by common consent to allow our soldiers to take the battle to the enemy. The enemy was attacked with great courage and hope in God. And God granted us good fortune, our men making inroads into the enemy and making blood flow like a river. The Turkish emperor for very fear withdrew from his army to a place 5 miles distant.

10 September: Letters from the army were written to Warsaw saying that almost the whole Turkish army had been defeated in pitched battle, with the Turkish emperor present in person, and that things had gone so badly for him that he had fled to Transylvania. His imperial majesty was informed of this victory, and the illustrious lord general asked his majesty to bring all Polish forces with such speed as was possible to pursue them into enemy territory. We were advised of the same from Cracow.

11 September: News came to Warsaw that the Swede had arrived in Livonia with a fleet of twelve ships. He had laid siege to the principal city of Livonia and fought some battles, with two of his largest ships lost with all the men drowned and the guns sunk. Other ships were scattered by a storm and foundered. In his anger he bombarded the city with fireballs, shooting over 100 fireballs at one gate alone, but those inside remedied it with sacks of wet stuff or flax which took all effect from the fireballs.

12 September: The king of England sent our king of Poland 2,000 men against the Turk, which out of friendship to the king he would himself pay until December.

13 September: The diet [Sejm] at Warsaw concluded and in thanks Matins was sung in the parish church an hour after midnight. 1. It has been decided that soldiers should be raised throughout the whole commonwealth. 2. That contributions for

the war would be collected at Stuyr. 3. That the clergy are exempt from the war. 4. That each citizen owning property worth more than 8,000 florins shall equip and maintain one cavalryman. 5. Those with property worth only 4,000 florins should maintain an infantryman against the Turk. 6. That the four capitals of Poland, Cracow, Vilnius, Leopoldis [Lviv] and Camence [Kamianets-Podilskyi] should be exempt from the common levies of war.

14 September: The Polish ambassador arrived here [in Warsaw] from Holland, having been sent there to procure equipment, armour and gunpowder for the war against the Turk.

15 September: In Lithuania, Samogitia [Žemaitija] and Livonia, men were mustered against the King of Sweden, to relieve the city of Riga. In the diet these same provinces refused to raise men against the Turks, as they had to make provision against the Swedes.

17 September: The men from Greater Poland [*Wielkopolska/Polonia Maior*], Posonia [Poznań] and Calis [Kalisz] marched to war.

18 September: The Cuiaviensers *[ziemia kujawska/Terra Cuyaviensis]*, Bresenser, Inowladonienser[3] and the land of Dubrin[4] sent their aid.

21 September: The Palatine Siradiensers *[ziemia sieradzka/Terra Siradiensis]* and those of the land of Virlunia sent their men against the enemy.

22 September: The illustrious king of Poland Sigismund went to war with great preparedness. His majesty was accompanied by the provinces, Moscovien, Slocen, Toldavien, and it is hoped that he will reach Leopolim [Lviv] before 4 October, which is the Feast of St Francis.

23 September: Five palatines, to with those of Kyovien[5], Braclavien[6], Molchovien, Bressien and Ruthenia, came to meet the king to accompany his majesty.

24 September: The Palatine of Sendomiren [Sandomierz] and his men followed. The Most Reverend Lord Bishop of Cracow has been appointed for the preservation of the frontiers of the kingdom of Poland.

God grant this endeavour success and prosperity to the honour and glory of God and the strengthening of the Catholic Apostolic Roman Faith. Amen.

How will the traitors to Christendom crow now, who so thirst to drink the blood of Christians, and publish such falsities to dampen good courage? That the Poles, who are a wall of our Europe, had been defeated, the king dead, the valiant prince

---

3   Inowrocław.
4   Dobrzyń.
5   Kiev.
6   Bracław.

impaled, is a good German flute, of which many are to be found in Holland. It is said they are shipped from Riga in Livonia.

Appendix VI

Treaty and peace with Turkish Emperor, [signed] 9 October 1621

As already mentioned in Chapter 7, above, after the negotiations that took place during first few days of October 1621, Polish and Ottoman envoys signed a preliminary treaty. The whole content of the treaty, signed by both sides on 9 October 1621, was included in Jan Ostroróg's diary.[1] As it is very interesting, and a fairly long, document, I thought it would be best to include it as a separate appendix, to provide readers with the diplomatic conclusion to the conflict, especially in the context of the reasons behind the start of the war. As was customary in Polish documents of the period, the Sultan is called Emperor (*Cesarz*) while Moldavia is called Wallachia, so I will keep such forms in the translation as well.

Treaty and Peace with the Turkish Emperor

We, Stanisław Żórawiński of Chodorostaw, Castellan of Bełż and *Starosta* of Włodzimierz, [and] Jakub Sobieski, *wojewodzic*[2] of Lublin, Commonwealth's commissioners in the name of His Majesty Sigismund III, King of Poland, Grand Duke of Lithuania, [of] Ruthenia, Prussia, Mazovia, Samogitia, Livonia and hereditary King of Sweden, [of] Goth and Vandals [Venedi] and of all the Commonwealth, and from the army of His Majesty, under command of His Grace Stanisław Lubomirski, Count of Wiśnicz, Vice-Cup bearer and Crown Field Hetman, *Starosta* of Sandomierz, Spis, Biała Cerkiew and Dobczyce; also from all [other] commissioners, our colleagues, designated by the Commonwealth to discuss the peace and send to His Majesty and mighty Sultan Osman Khan, Grand Tsar of Constantinople, Asia, Europe, Persia, Arabs, Cyprus and Egypt, to negotiate the holy peace and to ensure the ancient, and lasting for so many years unbroken friendship between House of Ottomans and our Majesty King

---

1 'Jana hrabi z Ostroroga Dziennik wyprawy chocimskiej', pp.33-36.
2 A Polish title, used to describe son of voivode.

[Sigismund], our merciful lord, we did agreed upon honest and permanent treaty and its condition with His Grace Dilaver Pasha, Grand Vizier of the [Sublime] Porte of his Majesty the Emperor.

To further strengthen and confirm this renewed treaty, Stanisław Suliszewski, secretary of His Royal Highness [and] messenger of the grand envoy, as per the old custom will now travel to His Majesty the Emperor, while from the [Sublime] Porte of His Emperor Majesty [one] Cavus will go with us to the [Polish] camp and from there to his High Majesty the King, to take [our] grand envoy and, as it was in older times, to ensure his safety and guide him to [Sublime] Porte, [and] as soon as possible His Majesty the King will despatch some noble and wise man, to ratify this treaty, with whom will arrive our agent [ambassador] to the [Sublime] Porte, who, as it is custom of the other agents [ambassadors] of the Christian monarch to live and work there. And once [the Polish] grand envoy returns, His Majesty the Emperor will also send to His Majesty the King some noble man, in the same way as he has done it before when signing peace with other Christian monarchs.

The Commonwealth is required to free Dnieper River from Cossacks, so they will cease, by attacking into the sea and the pillaging of the Emperor's country and that with any announcement from the Emperor [about attacks], the Commonwealth will bring them [Cossacks] to justice.

Wallachians[3] and Tatars from Dobruja, Budjak, Bender (Tahinia), Klia, Ochakiv and Crimea to cease raiding and damaging countries, castles, towns, estates, belongings and men of His Royal Majesty and the Commonwealth. Tatar tract from Ochakiv is to be barred by The Emperor; and if despite this treaty Tatars will continue to attack countries of His Royal Highness and the Commonwealth and they will not be brought to justice; then the damages need to be repaid and the Tatar Khan punished. But if in the empty lands [between the countries], before the border is settled, if hunters would look for fish and game and, as it happens sometimes, they would encounter and fight each other, then it will not break the treaty between His Royal Highness and the Emperor. And if [Tatar] Khan was to lead his troops to serve the Emperor somewhere or he was leading them on his own [mission] to the neighbouring countries to the Commonwealth; for him to avoid the lands of His Royal Highness, not to attack, pillage and loot them, otherwise risking breaking of this treaty.

For the better confirmation and agreement of the border between countries of His Royal Highness and His Majesty the Emperor, both sides will nominate men [that are] prudent and with good knowledge of the region, on the time that will be agreed upon by His Royal Highness and His Majesty the Emperor.

The Commonwealth will be delivering annual pay[4] for the Tatar Khan, that will be brought to Iași to the current Wallachian[5] Voivode; once the Voivode has confirmed it, the Khan will send his envoys to Iași to pick up the pay. And if, as in times of the predecessors of His Royal Highness, [the Khan] will be summoned with his army to support His Royal Highness against the enemies of

---

3   In this context it means Moldavians.

4   They were the so-called 'gifts' (*podarunki*) that the Poles were paying on an annual basis to the Tatars to prevent them from raiding.

5   Moldavian.

the Commonwealth; he will not hesitate to arrive, so show his friendship in such way.

One of the main reason why holy friendship between House of Ottomans and [Polish] Royal Highness was broken is this: some Wallachian6 Voivodes are spiteful and greedy; therefore there should be [on the throne there] people watchful and composed, who will ensure that the treaty is obeyed by both sides and will keep, as per old times, their obligations towards his Royal Highness and the Commonwealth.

After signing the treaty, [the fortress of] Khotyn, in such state that we have found it when His Royal Highness's army arrived here, will be returned with all [belongings] to the current Voivode of Wallachia.[7]

Finally, Our Lord, His Royal Highness is a friend to the Emperor's friends and the enemy to his enemies; likewise the Emperor to be a friend to the King's friends and the enemy to his enemies; and the old pacts, agreed by grandfathers of both King and Emperor, and confirmed by many grand envoys and now agreed by us, which will be [further] confirmed by grand envoy who will travel to the [Sublime] Porte, will be renewed and our Lord, His Royal Highness, will obey them; for which we, as long as God Almighty will keep the King in this world, in the name of Jesus Christ, [our] God and Saviour, so swear and promise to obey all conditions of this treaty, if only the Emperor will keep on [his part of the treaty] towards King and Commonwealth. For the eternal memory we sign it here with our own hands, with our own seals.

From the camp at Khotyn, on the ninth day of October, year 1621.

---

6   Moldavian.
7   Moldavia.

Appendix VII

Letters from Patrick Gordon

Patrick Gordon (Gordone) was, between 1610 and 1625, working in the capacity of a factor of James I's court in Gdańsk. He often mediated in issues related to Scottish and English merchants in Poland. Gordon also provided very useful insight into the campaign of 1621, based on the information he received from Poland. It is an interesting example of how news about the war was exaggerated and tweaked, adding to growing rumours and misinformation about fighting sides and the outcome of the battles. In this appendix I have given three of his letters, directly connected with the Khotyn War, based on an edition prepared by Charles H. Talbot in 1962.[1] Additional comments in brackets and footnotes are mine.

First letter, addressed to King James I, dated 18 December 1620, and written from Warsaw, provides information about Żółkiewski's expedition to Moldavia and its fate, also the assassination attempt on Sigismund III made by Michał Piekarski on 15 November 1620.

Varsaviae, 18 Decembris 1620
Patricius Gordon
ad Iacobum I regem Angliae
de morte in bello Stanislai Zólkiewski, de frustrate tentamine Piekarski occidendi Sigismundum regem, de attributione Ducatuum Prussiae et Curlandiae etc.

[f.203r]
Please your sacred Majestie,
Becaus my last lettres sent hence the tuelveth day of October may in these troublous tymes be misscaryed, your Majestie will hereby surmmarlie understand the cheef occurrences here sinee my coming hither. In respect of my joumey throw Prussia, infected with the plague, four weekes were spent before I got audience of the King. Concerning his proposition to joine with your Majestie by way of mediation for settling of the troubles in Germanie, first he alleadged that he had given no commission to Lord Pole to informe Captane Buck therof but

---

[1]   Charles. H. Talbot (ed.), *Elementa ad Fontium Editiones*, vol. 6: *Res Polonicae Iacobo I Angliae regnante conscriptae ex Archivis Publicis Londoniarum* (Rome: Institutum Historicum Polonicum Romae, 1962), pp.208–210 & 245–247.

considering the Weightines of the mater, and your Majesties readines to concurre with him, he thought good to exspect the Emperours resolution. Which although doubtles he hath gotten already, yet he delayeth to give me anie ansuer therof, or of anie other purpose concerning him self, becaus he is minded to send his owne Ambassadour to your Majestie once this winter.

Caspar Gratianus[2], a German, maid by the Turkish Emperour Pruatin of Valachia, surrendred the same to the Polonians: Who mynded to have reteened it by force, in September last lossed allmost ther Whole armie of ten thousand men by the dexteritie of Scander Bassa secounded by a multitud of Tartares. The General, Solkiefski [Żółkiewski], great Chancellour of Poleland was slane. Never one Commander escaped death or captivitie. Many flying were drouned in the River Prut. The Polonians to excuse ther breach of peace, alledge that the Estates of the Low countries, together with the Hungarians, Bohemians and ther Confederates sollicited the Turk to invade thier countrie (yea, it is written hither from Constantinople that your Majesties Oratour there joined with them, as Lord Weiher show me but is thought by wise men incredible) to withdraw the Cosackes[3] from Hungarie and Germanie.

Upon the first day of November, a Polonian gentleman named Pekarski,[4] intending to have murthered the King entring the Church doore strook him with a Polonian hammer behind upon the head, but the furred Cap following the stroak, the yron fastned in the Pikkadill. Nevertheles as the king looked about, the traitour strook him agane with the staffe upon the syd of his head and face that he fell allmost to the ground. In the meantyme the Prince [Władysław], who had stayed a little behind his father, reading a Patent on the church doore, hastned and wounded the villane. Incontinent arose a cry in the Church: The Tartares, the Tartares. Wherof the multitud of people conveened at Parlament, esteeming the king to have bene slane by some barbarous Scythian stratagem, became so stutpefact that manie fled out of the toun, and a terrible tumult arose. Which shortlie Proclamation being maid that the king lived, was stilled.

[f.203v]

Upon the seventeenth day of the same moneth the traitour was carryed upon a moveable scaffold thorow this citie, and in divers streets diverslie tormented. His breastes were nipped with hote tonges, his skin cutted in thwanges, his hand and the hammer in it burned in fyre, his quarters distrructed with four homes and then burned to ashes. The reason of his attempt is alleadged this, becaus being superexpended in the Muscovian warres he was not rewarded as he expected.

The Parlament was ended upon the first day of December. Therin it is concluded that five millions of Polonian florens (each reckned to an half croun English) shal be contributed to mantene warres against the Turkes and Tartares. Everie forrane merchant shall pay for his person four florens.

The Silesian controversie with Poleland and the conditions of the composition therof will appeare of the Silesian Ambassadours harangue and of

---

2   Gaspar Graziani.
3   In this context 'Cosackes' will be *lisowczycy* mercenaries.
4   Michał Piekarski.

the ansuer given therto by the Estates of Poleland. Which herwith I have sent to your Majestie.

Your Maiesties lettre of intercession of the Elector of Brandeburg was delivered to the king here in tyme of Parlament, but your Majesties Lettre to me cam not to mine handes before the Parlament had ended. Neither have I gotten audience since. Whether the King deferreth of purpose (as appeareth) I know not. In the meantyme the investiture of the Electour of Brandeburg in the Dukedome of Prussia is delayed by the King, although the whole Estates have most willinglie condescended therto. Yea the King granted that it shal be done, Onlie he pretendeth now that it is an inconvenient tyme, in respect of his great domestick and forranea does, and of the plague, wherwith that province of Prussia is infected. If these be fained subterfuges, as the Ambassadours of Brandeburg suspect, my nixt letter shall declare, for I expect everie day audience.

The Ambassadour of Mekelburg interceding for the restitution of the Duke of Churland [Courland], and I also in your Majesties name is to get ansuer within few dayes. Since the Parlamentthrie Ambassadours ar come hither at divers tymes (in case one had bene stayed by the way, another might come forward) with one instruction from the Emperour to seek help against his enemies. What an answer they get tyme will try.

From Bohemia here is no certantie, for all is openly reported in favour of the Emperour. Nevertheles manie affirme secreie that in the Late Convention of Estates at Wratislavia in Silesia, Contribution is granted to the King of Bohemia to renew his forces, and to joyne with the armies of Moravia. In Parlament no mention of religion was maid, especiallie by reason of the deaths of the Duke of Westrog [and] Castellan of Cracow[5], and of Prince Janussius Radzevil[6], who died making preparation to 'come to Palrament. His brother Christophorus Radzevil[7] sent to me his lettre to your Majestie most ernestlie requesting for a gratious ansuer with the first oportunitie

[f.204r]
In case these Come not to your Majesties hands I shall send the copie of the same within few weekes.

So praying daylie for your Majesties good heolth long lyfe and prosperous reigne I most humble kisse your Majesties hands.

Your Sacred Majesties
Most humblie and loyale servant
Patrick Gordone

Warsaw the 18 of
December set. vet. 1620

---

5   Prince Janusz Ostrogski (1554–1620).
6   Janusz Radziwiłł (1579–1620), Castellan of Vilnius.
7   Krzysztof II Radziwiłł (1585–1640), Lithuanian Field Hetman.

In dorso: To the King his most Excellent Majestie, my most gratious soveraigne.
Aliamanu: 18 Dec. 1620. Mr. Gordon his Ma-ties Agent in Poland to his Ma-ty. Rec. 16 Feb. 1620

Second letter, addressed to George Calvert,[8] dated 23 September 1621 from Gdańsk, describes the Khotyn campaign until 15 September

Gedani, 23 Septembris 1621
Patricius Gordon
ad Georgium Calvert
nuntiat victoriam Pol'Onorum in bello contra Turoos
de Gustavo Rege Sueciae Riga mobsidente

[f.261r]
Sir, Though I never know if my lettres of occurences come to your honours handes, yet I omit no occasion to write in memorie of my dutie and grateful mynd.

The present estate of Polland is this. The extraordinarie Parliament at Varsaw continued onlie from the 13th of August st. vet. untill the 5th of September, in respect the Turkish Emperour was entred into Valachia [Moldavia] with an huge armie of four hundreth thousand fighting men. No special thing was concluded in it, but that the whole gentrie should with all diligence prepare them selves in propre persone to follow the King to the fieldes against the barbarous infidels Turkes and Tartares.

The General of the Polonians armie Johannes Carolus Chotkievicius [Jan Karol Chodkiewicz] not having above eightie thousand men then conveened near by the River Thyras, divided them into tuo several campes. In the one were about fourtie thousand Cosackes. In the other him self with as manie Polonians.

The Prince Vladislaus [Władysław] accompanied with sixtene thousand men, most part strangers was in the meantyme stayed to passe forthward by reason of the extraordinarie inundations of waters which not onlie hade caryed away all bridges, but also in divers partes had drouned great numbers of people and cattel besydes the damage of corne and hay, wherof great dearth is already ensued. Yet happelie before any conflict he past all dangers and joined with the General.

Upon the 23th day of August, the Turkish Emperour commanded tuo Bassaes[9] with an hundreth thousand men to provid his diner the nixt day in the Gaurs campe (so contemptuoslie he calleth the Christians, Dogges) els if they returned they should loose their heades. These Bassaes assailed the Cosackes thrice in one day, but were always repulsed. Tuodayes they rested, upon the fourt day the General sent some Musketers and Polonian horsemen to assist the Cosaques.[10]

---

8   George Calvert, 1st Baron Baltimore (1580–1632), between 1618 and 1625 Secretary of State.
9   Pashas.
10   It seems that Gordon could not decide which form: Cosackes or Cosques, to use, so he utilised them both in the same letter.

Whereby they were so encouraged, that falling out of their trenches they put the Turkes to flight, took both the Bassaes prisoners, killed about thirtie thousand men, and got tuentie peeces of Ordonance. They onliee skirmished thereafter until September.

[f.261v]

Upon the second of September the Turkes were defate in open battell, above fiftie thousand of them were slane, about sixtie peeces of Ordonance taken, and their stockes and wheeles cut, because they could not be then caryed away. How manie of the Polonians ar killed is uncertane. In the General his Lettre to the King these words ar indefinit: With no notable skaith of your Majesties armie.

Nevertheles the Polonians fearing that the multitud of Tartares who have spoiled a great part of Alba Russia,[11] almost from Chiovia[12] to Lublin, shall joine with the Turkish greatest forces, have entrenched them selves in a strong hold, expecting the Kings approche with the whole nobilitie.

The King began his jomey from Varsaw toward the Campe upon the 15th of September, and past that day eight Germane leagues.

Tuo dayes before the Kings removing, the Electour of Brandeburg obteened feudum Brussiae, the conditions as yet I know not.

Gustavus King of Swedin[13] hath besieged Riga, and hath made five assaultes already. Duke Christophorus Radzevil[14] is appointed with the Lithuanian forces, to put him thence if he take it not before his comming.

The Muscovians have also an armie readie, as appeareth, attending the event of the present Polonian expedition.

The Polonian Ambassadour [Jerzy] Ossoliński got not audience of the King of Denmark. The few soldiours that arrived here under the conduct of Captan Arthur Aston, attend as yet resolution from the King of Polland. The others were not suffered to passe thorow Orsund in Denmark.

Of all further proceedings here your honour shal be advertised by my letter untill my returning to England (if God will) in November, when all warres must cease by reason of the intolerable cold in the fieldes.

So confiding in your honours favour, I duetifullle take my leave.

Your honours most addicted

Patrick Gordone

Danskin the 23th of September, s.v. 1621

In dorso: To the Right honourable Sir Georg Calvert, one of his Majesties principal Secretaries. *Sigillum*

Alia manu: 23 Sept. 1621. Mr. Patrick Gourdon to Mr. Seer. Calvert.

Third letter, addressed to King James I, dated 1 November 1621, with further information of Khotyn campaign post 15 September

---

11   *Ruś Biała* (White Ruthenia) was a term used sometimes to describe the eastern part of what we presently know as Belarus.

12   He possibly means Kiev.

13   King Gustav II Adolf.

14   Hetman Krzysztof II Radziwiłł.

Gedani, 1 Novembris 1621
(styl. vet)
Patricius Gordon
ad Iacobum I regem Angliae
de obsidionearcis (Chocimiensis) in qua obiit Chodkiewicz
de pace cum Turcis, de incursione Suecorum in Rigam et Mitaviam

[f.265r]
Please your sacred Majestie.
Since the 15th of September these ar the occurrences here:

The Polonian armie far inferiour to the Turkish in number contened them selves within strong trenches expecting the Kings approaching with the whole nobilitie. Here they were brought to extreame danger and allmost to desperation. All the soldiours were wearied with continual skirmishes, and defence of their munition, manie were sicke and manie died ex dysenteria, most part of the strangers Musketers were slaine, powder and bullets were nearby spent, necessitie of Vittailles daylie incressed, and to their great discourage their General Palatin of Vilna, Chodkievicius [Chodkiewicz] deceased in the Campe. In this perplexitie there was none hope of relief, for the King could not come foreward as he intended, by reason of the multitud of Tartares burning and spoiling the countrie and touns thorow which he should passe. But before he had mad passage perforce, the Turkish Emperour (of what occasion I know not yet) upon the secound of October offred peace to Prince Vladislaus [Władysław] upon tolerable conditions. Wherof to treate Commissioners were presentlie sent to the Turkish campe, and after six dayes altercation, upon the ninth of October peace was concluded and proclamed. And so Turkes, Tartares, and Polonians retired homewardes. The King was then come to Leopolis [Lviv] on his journie with a strong armie, where being informed of this unexpected peace he subsisted few dayes, and is now returning to Varsaw.

While the Polonians ar thus troubled on the one syd, on the other the toun of Riga is surprised by the King of Swedin, before Duke Christofer Radzevil could convene the forces of Lituania. And not content herewith, he hath also taken the toun and castle of Mitaw,[15] where Duke Friderich of Curland[16] has his cheef residence. Of his further intent, and of the conditions of peace betuene the Polonians, Turkes, and Tartares (whereof I daylie expect certane information) as also of the Electour of Brandeburg his investiture in Prussia, I shall make larger and sure relation at my comming to England, if God will, about Chritmes. So praying for your Majesties good health, Long life and prosperous reigne, I most humblie kisse your Majesties handes.

Your sacred Majesties most humble servant
Danskin the first of Patrick Gordon
November s.v. 1621

---

15 Mitau (Mitawa), currently Jelgava in Latvia. Since 1578 it was capital of Duchy of Courland and Semigallia.
16 Friedrich Kettler (1569-1642), who between 1587 and 1642 was Duke of Courland and Semigallia.

In dorsa: To the Kinghis most Excellent Majestie My most gracious Soveraine.
Alia manu: Mr. Pat. Gourdon to his Mtte. Divers advertissments from Franckfort 1622. *Sigillum*

Bibliography

Archival Sources

Archiwum Główne Akt Dawnych (AGAD) [The Central Archives of Historical Records in Warsaw].
Archiwum Warszawskie Radziwiłłów (AR), II, 813

Archiwum Państwowe w Łodzi [National Archive in Łódź].
Archiwum rodziny Bartoszewiczów; Dokumenty, uniwersały, przywileje

Biblioteca Apostolica Vaticana (BAV)
Barberiniari Latini, vol. 6579
BarberiniariLatini, vol. 6580
BarberiniariLatini, vol. 6660

Biblioteka Książąt Czartoryskich (BCzart.) [Czartoryski Library]
BCzart 111, *Regestr wszystkiego wojska Polskiego tureckiej pod Chocimiem ekspedycji w roku 1621*

Biblioteka Kórnicka PAN (BK) [Kórnik Library]
BK 292, *Panowanie Zygmunta III. Akta od 1613 do 1632 roku*
BK 326, *Acta cancellariatus anni 1616 usque ad 1643 in manuscriptis*
BK 330, *Akta Zygmunta III od roku 1618 do 1621*
BK 333
BK 335, [Jakub Sobieski] *Dyariusz Expedycyi tureckiey pod Chocimiem Roku Pańskiego 1621*
BK 342, *Diarius expeditiey królewicza polskiego Władysława przeciwko Osmanowi II, cesarzowi tureckiemu y chanowi tatarskiemu w osobach swych na woynie będących w Wołoszech pod Chociniem roku 1621*
BK 974, *Wołoskie dzieje niektóre z relatiei pewnych osób*

Biblioteka Uniwersytetu Wrocławskiego (BUWr) [Library of the University of Wrocław]
Oddział Rękopisów, Akc. 1949.439, Steinwehr II F 37 vol. 2

Riksarkivet, Stockholm
Skoklostersamlingen, E 8603

Zakład Narodowy im. Ossolińskich [The Ossolineum, Wrocław]
Unit 4, section 1, manuscript 198, *Miscellanea historyczne z lat 1606–1676*

The National Archives of the UK
State Papers Poland, SP/83/4 folio72

Printed Primary Sources

Birkowski, Fabian, *Ian Karol Chodkiewicz et IanWeyher, Wielmożni, Waleczni, Poboźni, Woiewodowie; Pamięcią pogrzebną wspomnieni* (Kraków: Drukarnia Andrzeja Piotrkowczyka, 1627)

Çelebi, Evliya, *Narrative of Travels in Europe, Asia, and Africa in the Seventeenth Century*, Volume 1. (London: Oriental Translation Fund, 1834)

Copie d'une lettre écrite de Léopol en Pologne, par laquelle se voit l'heureux succcs del'armée contre le Turc (Paris: Clovis Eve, 1621)

Costin, Miron, *Latopis ziemi mołdawskiej i inne utwory historyczne* (Poznań: Wydawnictwo Naukowe, 1998)

'Dwa dyaryusze najazdów tatarskich na Ruś z r. 1618 i 1624', *Kwartalnik Historyczny*, year VI (Lwów: Towarzystwo Historyczne, 1892)

'Dziennik wyjazdu naszego na pospolite ruszenie', in: Hanna Malewska, *Listy staropolskie z epoki Wazów* (Warszawa: Państwowy Instytut Wydawniczy, 1977), pp.216-220

'Dziennik wyprawy wołoskiej w roku 1620', *Pamiętnik Warszawski czyli Dziennik Nauk i Umiejętności*, volume 14, May 1819 (Warszawa: Zawadzki i Węcki, 1819), p.97–111

Eryka Lasoty i Wilhelma Beauplana opisy Ukrainy (Warszawa: Państwowy Instytut Wydawniczy, 1972)

Farczeuoskhi, Sebastiano [name uncertain], *La gran vittoria di Sigismunde III, Re di Polonia, contro i Turchi nel 1621* (Florence: Bartolomeo Sermartelli, 1622)

Fletcher, Giles, *Of the Russe common wealth. Or, Maner of gouernement of the Russe emperour, (commonly called the Emperour of Moskouia) with the manners, and fashions of the people of that countrey* (London: Printed by TD for Thomas Charde, 1591)

Gaugnini, Alessandro, *Kronika Sarmacyey Europeyskiey*(Kraków: Drukarnia Mikołaja Loba, 1611)

Grabowski, Ambroży (ed.) *Starożytności historyczne polskie*, vol I (Kraków: Nakładem i drukiem Józefa Czecha, 1840)

Hurmuzaki, Eudoxiou de (ed.), *Documente privitoare la istoria românilor, supplement 2, volume 2, 1601-1640* (București: Academia Română, 1895)

'Istoriya Khotinksoy voyny Ioannesa Kamenetskogo', *Istoriko-filologicheskiy Zhurnal*, year 1958, volume 2 (Erevan: Akademiya Nauk Armyanskoi SSR, 1958), pp.258-286

'Jakóba Sobieskiego Dziennik wyprawy chocimskiej' in: Żegota Pauli (ed.) *Pamiętniki o wyprawie chocimskiej r. 1621* (Kraków: Nakład i druk Józefa Czecha, 1853), pp.105-184

'Jana hrabi z Ostroroga Dziennik wyprawy chocimskiej' in: Żegota Pauli (ed.) *Pamiętniki o wyprawie chocimskiej r. 1621* (Kraków: Nakład i druk Józefa Czecha, 1853), pp.15-39

Jerzego Ossolińskiego, kanclerza wielkiego koronnego autobiografia (Lwów: Zakład Narodowy im. Ossolińskich, 1876)

Karola Ogiera dziennik podróży do Polski 1635–1636, part I (Gdańsk: Biblioteka Miejska i Towarzystwo Przyjaciół Nauki i Sztuki, 1950)

Kobierzycki, Stanisław, *Historia Władysława, królewicza polskiego i szwedzkiego* (Wrocław: Wydawnictwo Uniwersytetu Wrocławskiego, 2005)

'Kopia listu od pana [Jana] Czaplińskiego do Jerzego Radzimińskiego 1 Octobris z obozu pisanego', in: Hanna Malewska, *Listy staropolskie z epoki Wazów* (Warszawa: Państwowy Instytut Wydawniczy, 1977), pp.206–214

Korrespondencye Jana Karola Chodkiewicza (Warszawa: Drukarnia Jana Jaworskiego, 1875)

Kronika Pawła Piaseckiego biskupa przemyślskiego, (Kraków: Drukarnia Uniwersytetu Jagiellońskiego, 1870)

Kurze Relation was sich in der polnischen Expedition wider den Erbfeindchristlichen Namensvom 1. bis auf 24. September 1621 begeben hat (Augsburg: Andreas Aperger, 1621)

La grande et mémorable défaite de 150.000 Turcs (Paris: Abraham Saugrin, 1621)

Liske, Ksawery, Stanisława Żółkiewskiego hetmana i kanclerza w. kor. klęska i zgon na polach czoczorskich', *Dziennik Literacki*, Year 18, no 16, 20 April 1869 (Lwów: Drukarnia Zakładu Narodowego imienia Ossolińskich, 1869), *Dyariusz wtargnięcia Tatarskiego po Wołoskiej potrzebie w kraju Podolskie in Anno 1620*, p. 56

Liske, Ksawery, 'Stanisława Żółkiewskiego hetmana i kanclerza w. kor. klęska i zgon na Polach Czoczorskich', *Dziennik Literacki*, Year 18, no 15, 13 April 1869 (Lwów: Drukarnia Zakładu Narodowego imienia Ossolińskich, 1869), List P. Szemberka do Ksdza Andrzeja Opalińskiego, biskupa Poznańskiego, w którym opisuje porażkę wojska Polskiego w Wołoszech przez Skinder Baszę a die 18. Septemb. ad 6 Octobris. Anno 1620, pp.239–240

Liske, Ksawery, 'Stanisława Żółkiewskiego hetmana i kanclerza w. kor. klęska i zgon na Polach Czoczorskich', *Dziennik Literacki*, Year 18, no 14, 6 April 1869 (Lwów: Drukarnia Zakładu Narodowego imienia Ossolińskich, 1869), List p. Stanisława Żółkiewskiego K . i H. K. do króla Jego Mci. d. d. z obozu w Łozowej 6. Septembr. 1620, p.224

Listy księcia Jerzego Zbaraskiego, kasztelana krakowskiego, z lat 1621–1631 (Kraków: Nakład Akademii Umiejętności, 1878)

Naima, Mustafa (Naima Efendi), *Dziennik wyprawy chocimskiey*, in: Józef Sękowski, *Collectanea z dziejów tureckich*, volume I (Warszawa: Zawadzki i Wędzki, 1824), pp.145–182.

Naima, Mustafa (Naima Efendi), *Zatargi z Otomanami z powodu Kozaków*, in: Józef Sękowski, *Collectanea z dziejów tureckich*, volume I (Warszawa: Zawadzki i Wędzki, 1824), pp.123–144.

Nevves from Turkie and Poland. Or A true and compendious declaration of the proceedings betweene the great Turke, and his Maiestie of Poland, from the beginning of the warres, vntill the latter end With a relation of their daily millitary actions; shewing plainly how the warre continued and ended, peace was concluded, the troubles appeased, the articles of agreement confirmed, and a full league of amity ratified. Translated out of a Latine copie, written by a gentleman of quality, who was an actor in all the businesse: and now with his consent published (Hage: Edward Allde, 1622)

Newes from Poland Wherein is truly inlarged the occasion, progression, and interception of the Turks formidable threatning of Europe. And particularly, the inuading of the kingdome of Poland. With many seuerall repulses he hath receiued from that braue and military nation: euen to this present moneth of October: as is truly collected out of the originall. Published by authority (London: Imprinted by F K[ingston] for B. D[ownes] and Wiliam Lee, 1621)

Nieuwe Tijdinghen, Antwerp, Erfgoedbiblioth. English translation by Paul Alblaster available on https://www.facebook.com/NieuweTijdinghen (last entry 01/06/2023)

'Opisanie wyprawy chocimskiej' in Józef Tretiak, *Historya wojny chocimskiej 1621 r.* (Lwów: Nakładem Księgarni Seyfartha i Czajkowskiego, 1889), pp.209-218

'Prokopa Zbigniewskiego Dziennik wyprawy chocimskiej' in: Żegota Pauli (ed.) *Pamiętniki o wyprawie chocimskiej r. 1621* (Kraków: Nakład i druk Józefa Czecha, 1853), pp.41-64

Radziwiłł, Albrycht Stanisław, *Rys panowania Zygmunta III* (Opole: Wydawnictwo Uniwersytetu Opolskiego, 2011)

'Rejestr więźniów, którzy są w ręku nieprzyjacielskich', *Pamiętnik Warszawski czyli Dziennik Nauk i Umiejętności*, volume 14 (Warszawa: Zawadzki i Węcki, 1819), p.110–111

Relacya prawdziwa o wejściu wojska Polskiego do Wołoch i o potrzebie jego z pogaństwem w roku 1620…' in *Pisma Stanisława Żółkiewskiego kanclerza koronnego i hetmana* (Lwów: Drukarnia Zakładu Narodowego im. Ossolińskiego, 1861), pp.568–583

'Relacya prawdziwa o expediciey przeciwko Turkom, na którey sam cesarz turecki był Ao 1621, Woyska koronnego y W. X. Litte pod regimentem Pana Karola Chodkiewicza W. X. Litte które pod Chocimiem leżało' in: Józef Tretiak, *Historya*

Wojny Chocimskiej 1621 r. (Lwów: Nakładem Księgarni Seyfartha i Czajkowskiego, 1889), pp.219-229

Rykaczewski, Erazm (ed.), *Relacye nuncyuszów apostolskich i innych osób o Polsce od roku 1548 do 1690,* volume I (Poznań-Berlin: Księgarnia B. Behra, 1864)

Schütz, Ödön (Edmund) (ed), *An Armeno-Kipchak Chronicle of the Polish-Turkish Wars in 1620–1621,* (Budapest: Akadémiai Kiadó, 1968)

Sobieski, Jakub, *Commentariorum Chotinensis bellii libri tres* (Gdańsk: Georgii Forsteri, 1646)

Sobieski, Jakub, *Pamiętnik wojny chocimskiej xiąg troje* (Petersburg: Nakładem Bolesława Maurycego Wolffa, 1854)

Spieralski, Zdzisław; Wimmer, Jan (ed.), *Wypisy źródłowe do historii polskiej sztuki wojennej. Zeszyt piąty. Polska sztuka wojenna w latach 1563–1647* (Warszawa: Wydawnictwo Ministerstwa Obrony Narodowej, 1961)

The House of Vasa and the House of Austria. Correspondence from years 1587–1668. Part I. *The Times of Sigismund III, 1587–1632,* volume I, ed. R. Skowron in collaboration with K. Pawłowski, R. Szmydki, A. Barwicka, M. Conde Pazos, F. Edelmayer, R. González Cuerva, J. Martínez Millán, T. Poznański, M. Rivero (Katowice: Wydawnictwo Uniwersytetu Śląskiego, 2016)

'Stanisława Lubomirskiego Dziennik wyprawy chocimskiej' in: Żegota Pauli (ed.) *Pamiętniki o wyprawie chocimskiej r. 1621* (Kraków: Nakład i druk Józefa Czecha, 1853), pp.65-103

The negotiations of Sir Thomas Roe, in his Embassy to the Ottoman Porte, from the year 1621 to 1628 (London: Samuel Richardson, 1740)

Talbot, Charles, H., (ed.), *Elementa ad Fontium Editiones,, vol. 6: Res Polonicae Iacobo I Angliae regnante conscriptae ex Archivis Publicis Londoniarum* (Rome: Institutum Historicum Polonicum Romae, 1962)

Tytlewski, Maciej, *Narratio De Praeliisgestis inter Polonvm, Et Tvrcam Annis 1620 & 1621* (Naples: Ex Typographia Lazari Scorrigij, 1622)

Tytlewski, Maciej, *Relacion Diaria de las Guerras Tenidas Entre Polacos y Turcosporlos años 1620 y 1621* (Madrid: Per Tomas Junti, Impressor de Rey, 1623)

*Volumina Legum,*volume III (Petersburg: Nakładem i Drukiem Jozafata Okryzki, 1859)

Warzuchtig, Fridrich (Jan Rudomina), *Diariusz prawdziwy expediciey Korony Polskiey, y Wielkiego Xięstwa Litewskiego przeciw Osmanowi Cesarzowi Tureckiemu w roku 1621 pod Chocimiem w Wołoszech Fortunnie odprawioney. Fridrych Warzuchtig Bawarczyk Zoldath ubogi będąc przytomny opisał* (place of publication 1unknown, 1640), Biblioteka Jagiellońska (BJ) 311062.

Wojtasik, Janusz (ed.), 'Uwagi księcia Krzysztofa Zbaraskiego, posła wielkiego do Turcji z 1622 r. – O Państwie Osmańskim i jego siłach zbrojnych', *Studia i Materiały do historii wojskowości,* volume VII, part 1 (Warszawa: Wydawnictwo Ministerstwa Obrony Narodowej, 1961), pp.339–340

Zeitung aus der Walachei (no place of publishing, 1622), copy from the collection of Biblioteka Uniwersytetu Wrocławskiego (BUWr.), 536284

Zherela do istoriï Ukraïny-Rusy, volume VIII (Lviv: Archeographic Commission of the Shevchenko Scientific Society, 1908)

Zimorowic, Józef Bartłomiej, *Historya miasta Lwowa, Królestw Galicyi i Lodomeryi stolicy; z opisaniem dokładnem okolic i potróynego oblężenia* (Lwów: Józef Schnayder, 1835)

Żojdź, Karol; Hundert, Zbigniew (ed.), 'Komput chocimski 1621 z rękopisu Biblioteki Narodowej' in Zbigniew Hundert (ed.), *Studia nad staropolską sztuką wojenną,* volume II (Oświęcim: Wydawnictwo NapoleonV, 2013), pp.245–257

Żurkowski, Stanisław, *Żywot Tomasza Zamoyskiego* (Lwów: Drukarnia Zakładu Narodowego im. Ossolińskich, 1860)

Secondary Printed Sources

Ágoston, Gábor, *Guns for the Sultan. Military Power and the Weapons Industry in the Ottoman Empire* (Cambridge: Cambridge University Press, 2005)

Augusiewicz, Sławomir, 'Werbunki Hansa Georga von Arnima, Georga Friedricha von Kreytzena i Ernsta Georga von Sparra na kampanię chocimską 1621 roku, *Echa Przeszłości*, XXII/2, 2021 (Olsztyn: Wydawnictwo Uniwersytetu Warmińsko-Mazurskiego w Olsztynie, 2021)

Chachaj, Marian, 'O dacie urodzenia i o edukacji hetmana Jana Karola Chodkiewicza', *Studia z dziejów Wielkiego Księstwa Litewskiego (XVI-XVIII wieku)*, Sławomir Górzyński, Mirosław Nagielski (ed.) (Warszawa: Wydawnictwo DiG, 2014), pp.49–58

Czapliński, Władysław, 'Cień Polski nad Sundem 1621–1626', *Kwartalnik Historyczny*, year LXXXVI, volume 2 (Warszawa: Instytut Historii Polskiej Akademii Nauk, 1979)

Filipczak-Kocur, Anna, *Skarb korony za Zygmunta III Wazy* (Opole: Wyższa Szkoła Pedagogiczna im. Powstańców Śląskich, 1985)

Gawron, Przemysław, 'Dyscyplina w szeregach armii polsko-litewskiej na terenie Małopolski i Rusi Czerwonej w czasie przygotowań do wyprawy chocimskiej w 1621 r.', *Czasopismo Prawno-Historyczne*, volume LXXI, 2019, part 2 (Poznań: Instytut Historii Polskiej Akademii Nauk and Wydział Prawa i Administracji Uniwersytetu im. Adama Mickiewicza w Poznaniu, 2019), pp.89–111

Gliwa, Andrzej, 'Dwa najazdy tatarskie na Ruś Czerwoną podczas wojny Rzeczypospolitej z Imperium Osmańskim w 1621 r. Zniszczenia i straty demograficzne na obszarze ziemi przemyskiej', *Rocznik Przemyski*, volume XLVIII, part 1, *Historia wojskowości* (Przemyśl: Wydawnictwo Towarzystwa Przyjaciół Nauk w Przemyślu, 2012), pp.3–58

Goszczyński, Artur, 'Nieszczęścia gorsze od wroga. Głód i niedostatki w armii Rzeczypospolitej podczas kampanii chocimskiej z 1621 r.', *Wschodni Rocznik Humanistyczny*, volume XVIII (2021), number 3 (Lublin: Towarzystwo Nauki i Kultury „Libra", 2021), pp.27–51

Herbst, Stanisław, *Wojna inflancka 1600-1602* (Zabrze: Wydanictwo Inforteditions, 2006)

Kalinowski, Emil, 'Z dziejów elearów polskich – Idzi Kalinowski. Część I: od Moskwy do Chocimia' in Zbigniew Hundert, Karol Żojdź, Jan Jerzy Sowa (ed.), *Studia nad staropolską sztuką wojenną*, volume IV (Oświęcim: Wydawnictwo NapoleonV, 2015)

Kazalak, Kadri; Gündüz, Tufan, 'Osman'inHotinSeferi (1621)', *OTAM: Ankara ÜniversitesiOsmanlıTarihiAraştırmaveUygulamaMerkeziDergisi*, issue 14 (Ankara: Ankara University, 2003), pp.129–144

Kupisz, Dariusz, *Wojska powiatowe samorządów Małopolski i Rusi Czerwonej w latach 1572–1717* (Lublin: Wydawnictwo Uniwersytetu Marii Curie-Skłodowskiej, 2008)

Magnuszewski, Władysław, *Z dziejów elearów polskich* (Warszawa-Poznań: Państwowe Wydawnictwo Naukowe, 1978)

Majewski, Majewski, 'Polski wysiłek obronny przed wojna chocimską 1621 r.', *Studia i materiały do historii wojskowości*, volume VII, part 1 (Warszawa: Wydawnictwo Ministerstwa Obrony Narodowej, 1961), pp.3–39.

Majewski, Ryszard, *Cecora rok 1620* (Warszawa: Wydawnictwo Ministerstwa Obrony Narodowej, 1970)

Majewski, Wiesław, 'Chocim 1621 rok' in *Wojny polsko-tureckie w XVII w.* (Przemyśl: Wydawnictwo Towarzystwa Przyjaciół Nauk w Przemyślu, 2000), pp.9–22

Mugnai, Bruno, *Wars and Soldiers in the Early Reign of Louis XIV. Volume 3 – The Armies of the Ottoman Empire 1645–1718* (Warwick: Helion & Company, 2020)

Murphey, Rhoads, *Ottoman warfare 1500–1700* (London: UCL Press, 2001)

Okoń, Jan, 'Wojna chocimską 1621 roku i jej pogłosy w poezji i sztuce – w czterechsetlecie', *Ruch literacki*, volume LXIII, issue 4 (373) (Kraków: Polska Akademia Nauk, Uniwersytet Jagielloński w Krakowie, 2021), pp.515–540

Paradowski, Michał, *Despite Destruction, Misery and Privations…The Polish army in Prussia during war against Sweden 1626–1629* (Warwick: Helion & Company, 2020)

Pietrzak, Jerzy, 'Konfederacja lwowska w 1622 roku', *Kwartalnik Historyczny,* year 80, issue 4(Warszawa: Państwowe Wydawnictwo Naukowe, 1973), pp.845–871

Pietrzak, Jerzy, *Po Cecorze i podczas wojny chocimskiej. Sejmy z lat 1620–1621* (Wrocław: Wydawnictwo Uniwersytetu Wrocławskiego, 1983)

Podhorodecki, Leszek, *Jan Karol Chodkiewicz 1560–1621* (Warszawa: Wydawnictwo Ministerstwa Obrony Narodowej, 1982)

Podhorodecki, Leszek, *Sławni hetmani Rzeczypospolitej* (Warszawa: Wydawnictwo MADA, 1994)

Podhorodecki, Leszek; Raszba, Noj, *Wojna chocimska 1621 roku* (Kraków: Wydawnictwo Literackie Kraków, 1979)

Sas, Petro, *Khotyn War of 1621* (Kiev: National Academy of Sciences of Ukraine. Institute of History of Ukraine, 2011)

Skowron, Ryszard, Olivares, *Wazowie i Bałtyk. Polska w polityce zagranicznej Hiszpanii w latach 1621-1632* (Kraków: Towarzystwo Wydawnicze „Historia Iagellonica", 2002)

Staręgowski, Bartosz, *Formacje zbrojne samorządu szlacheckiego województw poznańskiego i kaliskiego w okresie panowania Jana Kazimierza (1648–1668)* (Warszawa: Wydawnictwo DiG, 2022)

Szalontay, Tibor, *The art of war during the Ottoman-Habsburg Long War (1593-1606) according to narrative sources* (Toronto: University of Toronto, 2004)

Szejchumierow, Amet-chan A., *Armia Chanatu Krymskiego. Organizacja i taktyka (XV-XVIII w.)* (Zabrze-Tarnowskie Góry: Wydawnictwo Inforteditions, 2021)

Tezcan, Baki, 'Khotin 1621, or how the Poles changed the course of Ottoman history'

Tretiak, Józef, *Historya wojny chocimskiej 1621 r.* (Lwów: Nakładem Księgarni Seyfartha i Czajkowskiego, 1889)

White, Sam, *The Climate of Rebellion in the Early Modern Ottoman Empire* (Cambridge: Cambridge University Press, 2011)

Wimmer, Jan, 'Wojsko i skarb Rzeczypospolitej u schyłku XVI i w pierwszej połowie XVII wieku', *Studia i Materiały do Historii Wojskowości*, volume XIV (Warszawa: Wydawnictwo Ministerstwa Obrony Narodowej, 1968)

Wisner, Henryk, *Lisowczycy* (Warszawa: Dom Wydawniczy Bellona, 2004)

Witkowicz, Andrzej, *Bułat i koncerz. Poprawki do obrazu wielkich bitew polsko-tureckich (1620-1683)*, volume I (Zabrze: Wydawnictwo Inforteditions, 2021)

About the author
Michał Paradowski is a Polish independent researcher who lives in Scotland. While he is interested in all aspects of early modern warfare, his principal field of study is the Polish-Swedish Wars waged between 1621 and 1635. He has published historical articles in Polish, English, Russian and French. His first book was *Studia iMateriały do HistoriiWojen ze Szwecją 1600–1635* (*Studies and Materials Regarding Wars against Sweden 1600–1635*, Oświęcim, Napoleon V, 2013). His first work for Helion was the conference paper 'Aston, Butler and Murray – British Officers in the Service of Polish Vasa Kings 1621–1634', published in *Britain Turned Germany* (Warwick, Helion & Co, 2019). In his spare time, he works as an editor for the Polish publishing house Napoleon V and as an historical consultant for the *By Fire and Sword* miniature game produced by Wargamer Games Studio Ltd. He runs a historical blog at http://kadrinazi.blogspot.co.uk.

About the artist
Sergey Shamenkov graduated from the Academy of Arts in Lviv. He is a sculptor, author and illustrator who specialises in uniformology, military and costume history. His principal area of interest is the study of the Swedish army of Charles XII. When not painting, he is involved in re-enactment, depicting Ukrainian and Swedish units of the seventeenth and eighteenth century

Other titles in the Century of the Soldier series